Gazpacho & Revenge
Best Served Cold

A Cookbook Novel
by
Dennis Quinn and Fritz Knecht

A Cold Gazpacho Press Book
Published 2013

www.coldgazpachopress.com

Library of Congress Cataloging in process.
LCCN 2013921739

ISBN:13: 978-1493713011
ISBN:10: 1493713019

Manufactured in the United States

First Edition: December 2013

What is a Cookbook Novel?

In the words of Fritz Knecht, our author and chef, "A Cookbook Novel provides the reader a story throughout which the characters often interact in the preparation and enjoyment of great meals, be they sandwiches or feasts. Recipes are provided at the end of each chapter to guide the reader in the making of the meals enjoyed by the characters during that chapter."

Gazpacho and Revenge is a Cookbook Novel which contains over 40 recipes, "all made easy," for meals enjoyed by the book's characters as their story of revenge, love, and seeking happiness spans more than 40 years and ranges over three continents.

This Cookbook Novel highlights the truth that the gathering, preparation, and consumption of food are integral, important, and hopefully pleasant parts of the reader's own life story.

DEDICATION

To the men and women who gave their all in Vietnam, We Will Always Honor You! May you now be feasting at the ultimate banquet.

To the men and women who served in Vietnam, Thank You!
Although you may have had to eat C-Rations then, hopefully now you'll be able to enjoy some of the great recipes in this book.

ACKNOWLEDGEMENTS

To our wives, thank you for your constant support through the years and especially during this project. We are OK with the fact that our writing a cookbook provided you a constant source of amusement.

To family, friends, and members of our book and cooking clubs, thank you for your support and your many great ideas on how best to present our recipes and tell our story.

To Blythe, a special thanks for a cover-to-cover review, while recovering from a knee replacement. We recognize we were just two additional pains, this time in your ...neck.
(Readers, when you come across a mistake in grammar or punctuation, it's because we didn't listen to Blythe. When you come across an "aha moment," it's because we did.)

COVER ART

The cover art was created by Lauren Drainville, an incredibly gifted young artist living in New England. Lauren's cover, highlighting a bowl of gazpacho and a Spanish dagger, was selected because she perfectly captured the essence of this work - a cook book and an adventure story.

Table of Contents

1.	Federal Hill – Family Style	1
2.	Plates and Planes	7
3.	Planes and Trains and Memories	21
4.	Confiding and Remembering	28
5.	Recipe for a Soldier - Basic Ingredients	35
6.	Recipe for a Solider - Additional Ingredients	50
7.	Recipe for a Solider - Side Dishes	70
8.	A Place to Seek, Find, and Avenge	96
9.	Flashback - The Jungle and the Beach	136
10.	Flashback - Going Home	193
11.	Flashback - Real, Unreal World	224
12.	Flashback - Peace and War	238
13.	Flashback - End Times	271
14.	A Place of Light, Love, and Revenge	302
15.	Madame Bouvier	326
16.	A Dash of Hope	350

Table of Contents
(cont)

17. Her Dinner   363

18. His Dinner   383

19. Another Train of Thought   404

20. Revenge. Avenge. Justice.   415

21. Judgment Day   438

22. Gazpacho and Revenge   446

    Epilogue   451

    About the Authors   454

Table of Recipes

1. **Appetizers and Soups**
   - Broccoli — 31
   - Eastern Shore Cream of Crab Soup — 319
   - Empanadas — 436
   - Simple Summer Gazpacho — 450
   - Thai Chicken Coconut Soup — 222
   - Vichyssoise — 266
   - Vietnam Spring Rolls — 32
2. **Salads**
   - Avocado and Shrimp — 346
   - Greek Island — 398
   - Kitchen Herb Garden — 360
   - Traditional Caprese — 378
3. **Main Courses**
   - Asian Ginger Chicken — 220
   - Basque Cod with Fresh Vegetables — 413
   - C-Rations — 298
   - Cherry Tomato and Spinach Summer Pasta — 324
   - Chicken Paprika (Paprikas Criske Budapest) — 19
   - China Beach Beer Can Chicken — 190
   - Consensus Pot Roast (Braised Beef/Venison) — 130
   - Julian's Beef Bourguignon — 185
   - Goat Cheese and Herb Quiche — 348
   - Grilled Lamb Chops — 434
   - Hungarian Beef Goulash — 93
   - Mother's Meatloaf — 89
   - Party Lasagna — 183
   - Steak Au Poivre with Mushrooms
     And Sherry Sauce — 268
   - Summer Tomato Pie — 66
   - Three Cheese Pasta
     (Salsiccia Ripiene Conchiglie Con Tre Formaggio) — 234
   - Veal Piccata Bellagio — 379

Table of Recipes
(cont)

	Wiener Schnitzel and Variations	132
	Zia Mary's Family Meatballs	5
4.	**Side Plates**	
	Colcanon (Mashed Potatoes with Cabbage)	25
	Grown-up Grilled Cheese Sandwich	188
	Irish Tea Brack	26
5.	**Desserts**	
	Apple Strudel	134
	Chocolate Ganache	323/403
	French Ice Cream Pie	321
	Great Aunt Lulu's Iron Skillet Apple Pie	91
	Italian Love Cake/Italian Wedding Cake	45
	Pear Tart (Dolche Crostrata Napoli)	381
	Tiramisu	236
	Yvette's Cream Puffs	400
6.	**Breakfast**	
	Cheesy Grits and Variations	47
	Country Gravy and Biscuits	68
	Creamed Chipped Beef on Toast(SOS)	49
	Simple Frittata	358

Tim's Brief Biography

Year	Rank	Pay Grade	Location	Notes
1953			Federal Hill, RI	Tim was born in his parents' home in Providence, RI
1970 (Jun-Oct)	Recruit	E-1	Ft Jackson, SC	Army Basic and Advanced Training
1970 (Nov-Dec)	Private	E-2	Ft Benning, GA	Airborne School
1971 (Jan-Jun)	PFC	E-3	Presidio, CA	Vietnamese Language School
1971-72 (Jun-Jun)	SPC4-SSG	E-4 to E-6	Vietnam	1st Cavalry Div (Airmobile)
1972-73 (Jul-Mar)	SSG	E-6	Vietnam	Military Assistance Command (MACV)
1973-74(Mar-Mar)	2 LT	0-1	Ft. Benning, GA	Officer Candidate School, Ranger School.
1974-75 (Mar-Mar)	1 LT	0-2	Vietnam	Saigon Embassy Support
1975-78	CPT	0-3	Ft Campbell, KY	101st ABN; Company Commander
1978-79	CPT	0-3	Ft. Benning, GA	Infantry Officer Basic Course
1979-81	CPT	0-3	PSU, PA	ROTC Faculty, Penn State
1981-84	MAJ	0-4	Ft. Bragg, NC	82nd ABN; Grenada Conflict
1984-86	MAJ	0-4	Garmisch, GE	US Army Russian Institute
1987-90	LTC	0-5	Heidelberg, GE	US Army Europe Headquarters; Operations Planner
1990-91	LTC	0-5	Iraq	1st Cavalry Div: Operations Planner
1991-94	COL	0-6	Brussels, BE	NATO HQs
1994-2000	COL	0-6	Washington, DC	Pentagon; Army General Staff; Joint Chiefs Staff (JCS)
2000-03	COL	0-6	Washington, DC	White House, National Security Council (NSC)
2004-Present	Civilian		Washington, DC	Consultant to the NSC

CHAPTER 1: FEDERAL HILL - FAMILY STYLE

Day One: Monday, 0400 hours

Tim emerged from a deep sleep wondering, "What's going on?"

His mind responded sluggishly, slowed by the pressure on his eyes and the sound in his ears. The confusion started to clear. The eye pressure came from his own hands rubbing his eyelids open. The sound battering his eardrums came from ... well, who knows where that came from.

His hands slowly pulled away from his eyes. His mind tried to interpret a blurred vision in front of him. His mouth opened in a deep, sucking intake of air. The droning noise continued. His eyes were clearing. A woman in uniform? That damn droning! What the hell was that? His mind pushed through his fog and tried to answer him. It was the droning of an engine. Now he remembered. He was on a plane.

Tim's hands slid from his face, then interlocked, as he pushed his arms out in a long, hound dog stretch that pulled hard on the muscles along his back. Although he had passed the half century mark, he was still a well-muscled man. Well, at least a fairly well-muscled man, he conceded reluctantly. Every day he seemed to ache a little bit more and a little bit longer. At that moment, it was his back that ached.

"Come on, wake up!" his inner voice urged. He was still a little groggy, as his fingers unlocked and his hands fell to his lap. He opened and closed those hands, stretching the fingers to full extension. Looking at his hands, he thought, "People don't appreciate their hands enough, ...or their feet, for that matter. People spend a lot of time focused on their faces, their hair, their waist lines. But it is their feet that get them places and their hands that get things done."

Tim had always taken care of his body, and it had never let him down, ...but now, was it slowing down? "Better get used to it, Tim," he sighed, as his Irish fatalism moved to the forefront of his now defogged mind. "You've got work to do!"

"How long has it been since we last ate?" his eyes asked his watch. The watch said nothing, but showed 0400 hours. Tim wondered why he continued to wear a military watch, which measured the day in 24 hours. Why couldn't he just accept that it was 4 AM, instead of "Zero Four Hundred Hours?" Sometimes he still found himself saying things like, "Meet me for supper at Eighteen Thirty Hours," instead of 6:30 PM. It was over 7 years since he retired from the Army, and about 40 years since he first learned the preciseness military time added to ordering his days. "I guess I still appreciate the precision," he decided. But enough of that. His stomach was giving the orders now. It wanted food.

"Ah, yes, that's when I last ate," he remembered. Angie's kitchen. His Zia Mary DeGuilio's meatballs.

Angie was Tim's kid sister by six years. No longer Angie DePalma; now she was Angela Graffalino. Why his beautiful sister married that dumbass Vinnie Graffalino, Tim would never understand. But hey, that was 30 years ago. They're still married, have five kids, and get along pretty well. Tim reluctantly admitted that the dumbass Vinnie had seemingly negotiated life's gauntlet of romance better than he had; although Tim's gauntlet had been harsher, sadder, and ultimately provided only memories. "Enough of that!"

Although love, or maybe some distortion of it, was the reason Tim was on this plane; it was the memory of Zia Mary DeGuilio's meatballs that was now center in his senses.

In his family, there were many Zia Marys, ...Aunt Marys. This was not unusual in many Catholic families, where the Blessed Mother Mary held a special position. To distinguish one Mary

2

from the other, most likely for the purposes of family gossip, husbands' names or surnames were used. So when husbands' names were used, it was Carlo's Mary did this, or Rocco's Mary did that. When surnames were used, it was Zia Mary Lombardi or, as in this case, Zia Mary DeGuilio.

Zia Mary DeGuilio was Tim's favorite aunt. She was 93 years old but still living on her own. She only relinquished her car keys, quite reluctantly, after her 90th birthday. Over the years, Tim had been to many parties at Zia Mary DeGuilio's house. As far back as he could remember, her meatballs always reigned supreme in the center of her dining room table.

Late yesterday, Tim had been in his sister Angie's kitchen on Federal Hill, Providence Rhode Island's Little Italy. Federal Hill, at its heart, was mostly narrow, treed streets of 3-floor tenement houses, each floor home to a lively Italian family of mostly elderly immigrant Americans and young native-born Americans. The Hill had once been home to the New England branch of La Famiglia – "The Family," "The Mafia". Tim wasn't sure if that was still the case. He had been away in the Army most of his adult life and had lost touch with neighborhood goings-on. However, low-toned stories still persisted. No matter the truth of La Famiglia, Federal Hill was still home, if no longer to him, at least to most of his family. When in Providence, he loved life in Little Italy, although no one called it that anymore, and he loved Zia Mary DeGuilio's meatballs. Whenever he visited, Angie always cooked a pan full just for him. He usually took a week to eat them all.

Zia Mary DeGuilio's meatballs were defined by two characteristics. First, of course, was great taste. That went without saying. Second, was size. Zia Mary's meatballs were the size of baseballs, no kidding ...baseballs. As Zia Mary would say, "Everyone elsa's meat'a balls are like'a golf balls, ...small. But my meat'a balls are like Joe DiMaggio's balls, ...grandissimo!" Tim was sure she meant DeMaggio's *baseballs*.

For decades Zia Mary DeGuilio gave no one her special recipe. However, when she entered her 80's, she was no longer able to stir the meat required to make a batch of such large "meat'a balls." It was then she passed on her special recipe to selected granddaughters and nieces, but never to her grandsons or nephews. "Men are for eating my'a meat'a balls, not'a for cooking them!" she would always say. "Ah, for the old days," sighed Tim.

Angie was always Zia Mary DeGuilio's favorite niece, so of course Angie secretly received a handwritten recipe. Right from the beginning, Angie's meatballs were as good as Zia Mary's. Rumors started that Zia Mary DeGuilio had given Angie the full recipe, while holding back some ingredients from the others.

Unfortunately, last night Tim had not been able to enjoy his dish of Zia Mary's "meat'a balls."

For as Tim was skimming the *Providence Journal* spread across Angie's kitchen table, his meatball-ladened fork dropped heavily onto his plate. His eyes riveted on a picture of an Asian man holding an ornately framed painting. Tim's mind had exploded. "Could it be? Could that really be Truc Nguyen? After all these years, will I finally get a chance to kill that bastard?"

Zia Mary's Family Meatballs

Zia Mary is everyone's favorite aunt, mother, grandmother. Born on Federal Hill in 1920, she married and moved to Central Falls, RI in 1940, where she still lives today. Although 93 years old, she still cooks, but no longer has the strength to make her special meatballs. When invited to family dinners, she is always pleased when her signature meatballs are served. She is even more pleased when someone says, "Great meatballs, but not quite as good as yours, Zia Mary!"

Ingredients: (Four Servings)

1 – 1 1/2 Lbs	Ground Beef (see tip below)
1 – 2	Eggs per pound of meat/sausage
1 – 2 Tbsp	Ground Garlic
To Taste	Salt and Pepper
½ Tsp	Each of basil, marjoram, thyme, rosemary, sage, and oregano
1/8 Cup	Breadcrumbs for each ¼ Lb of meat/sausage
Milk	As necessary to moisten mixture

Directions:
1. Preheat oven to 350F.
2. Crack two eggs into a large bowl and stir vigorously (Zia Mary would remind you that this stirring keeps your arms from getting flabby).
3. Add pepper and garlic to eggs and stir.
4. Add herbs to eggs and stir.
5. Add meat/sausage to seasoned eggs—about 1/4 pound at a time.
6. Add breadcrumbs.
7. Add milk as necessary to bind mixture.

8. Form mixture into meatballs - from baseball sized ones to ping pong ball sized - depending upon preference.
9. Place meatballs on a broiler pan to allow for draining.
10. Bake for 30—40 minutes, turning meatballs every 10 minutes (internal temperature 160F minimum).
11. Place meatballs in your favorite bubbling sauce and simmer for 30 minutes before serving.

Tips:

1. A DePalma family favorite, served with all types of pasta and a hearty vino rosso. Tim likes it best with large penne pasta and a bottle of hearty red.
2. Tim found that mixing two parts beef with one part Italian sausage makes a nice combination.
3. Original recipe called for baseball sized "meat'a balls" but Tim sometimes downsized to a smaller version to suit all tastes.

CHAPTER 2: PLATES AND PLANES

Day One: Monday, 0410 hours, Reminiscing Over the Atlantic

Tim now sat rigid in his airplane seat, his face hard, remembering Truc's image mocking him from the newspaper. He remembered how his hand, which only moments earlier had held a fork full of meatball, had pounded that face, as if the hand was trying to turn the face into raw, bleeding hamburger. Tim's mind raced from Federal Hill to Saigon to Heidelberg, the city captioned below that arrogant, loathsome face. Tim's mind was already in Heidelberg. His hands already around that throat. He just needed to get the rest of him there. Thus, this plane over the Atlantic.

Last night's scene in Angie's kitchen now played out before his mind. He had leapt from the kitchen table, yelled "I gotta go," ran to the guestroom, grabbed his still half full suitcase, threw in his ditty bag of toiletries, rushed through the kitchen, air-kissed Angie's cheek, and left a trail of good-bye words and a sister with a stunned but understanding look. This had happened before, maybe not quite this abruptly, but often just as inexplicably. She knew better than to go after him or question him. He would contact her soon, probably not with information about where he was or what he was doing, just that he was fine and she was not to worry.

His departure from Angie's was followed by a wild ride to the Providence airport and a race to and through the New-York bound flight's closing door. In New York, he had an even longer and faster run to just barely make the final boarding call for JFK's last overnight to Frankfurt. Once on the plane, he collapsed into his first-class seat, followed by a sigh of relief and exhaustion. He asked for a double Jack and Ginger. Drained it. Asked for another. Drained that. Felt the tension seep from his body. Died.

Resurrection was occurring now, five hours later, over the Atlantic, and unknown to Tim, under the interested gaze of a flight attendant. Tim's hardened face softened as he continued to yawn, stretch, and shiver away his sleep. She watched. As he finally came round, he looked this way, then that way, then her way.

She locked on, then approached, "Well, good morning Mr. DePalma. Would you like something to eat? Drink? I didn't have the heart to wake you during the regular food service. So I spread that blanket over you and let you sleep."

"Thanks," Tim mumbled. As he looked at her, his hard face softened. His empty stomach had awakened him, but for the moment, it was his empty heart that was taking control of him. "Hmmm," he hmm'ed to himself. "She must have looked up my name on the flight manifest. Does that indicate she may have some interest? She looks about 40? ... 45? Too young for me? Maybe, ...maybe not."

He guessed from her smile that she had a lot of Irish in her. She was handsome, in that way maturing Irish women often are. The way his mother had been. The way his Brileen would be now, if she had lived. High cheek bones, angular chin, a spray of freckles across the nose, untamed red-gold hair, and of course, those hazel-green eyes. When happy, such eyes would dance for you, laugh with you, side by you. When mad, such eyes would not look at you, but into you, and sometimes through you. When stirred, such eyes would surround you, warm you, make love to you. The Irish at Tim's center always responded to such eyes, ...to such women.

That could not happen now. He was on a mission. The mission demanded focus. The focus was revenge. The revenge must be total.

Tim reluctantly dropped his gaze from her green eyes to her blue uniform. "Hey, thanks for that blanket. And yes, I am a little hungry. What's on the menu?"

The choices were Chicken Paprika, Lasagna, and Baked Cod. Tim ended up in first class because it was the only seat left on the plane. But maybe now the exorbitant cost would be partially offset by edible food. Great food, of course, would be preferable, for great food was a passion of Tim's since boyhood. But on a plane, he knew edible food was the best he could expect.

Tim selected Chicken Paprika, a dish he once had in Budapest, where it seemed Hungarians use paprika like Americans use salt. He knew that none of these airplane meals would taste as good as they sounded. However, he also knew that any one of them would at least fill the void he felt in his gut, just as he knew revenge would soon fill the void he felt in his heart.

As the Chicken Paprika was placed in front of him, Tim was reminded of T3P2. T3P2 was a funny little acronym he and Brileen had formulated so many years ago on a Rhode Island beach, on a blanket, under the stars, looking out across the Atlantic. He was 27 at the time, already ten years in the Army. She was 23, just a year from a college nursing degree.

Brileen was always laughing at Tim's vocabulary of Army acronyms. Sometimes he could talk for minutes, and she would understand nothing. He'd say something like "I grabbed my M-16, PLF'ed off the APC, and ran to the ALO's HUMVEE to jump on the AFNET." Although understanding nothing of what he said, she was a rapt audience of one. Her eyes, a more questioning fan club of two. He loved that way about her. She had loved every way about him.

They had both smiled and laughed their way through that night on the beach, slightly buzzed from a few Narragansett beers, as together they formulated their funny, maybe even silly, she said, new acronym, T3P2. However, this time it was not the Army's acronym, it was *their* acronym. Just his and hers. Sadly, now just his.

T3P2 was shorthand for Tim's Travel Tools: Plates and Planes. Three T's for Tim's Travel Tools, and two P's for Plates and Planes. Together they became T3P2.

As they sat on the blanket that night, gazing at stars and listening to waves, Tim told her of his seemingly life-long desire to see all parts of God's creation: to walk distant lands, to eat different foods, to talk with diverse peoples, to think in new ways. But as a kid, how could you do all that? Over the years, Tim had come to use at least two "tools" for such world travel: *plates and planes.*

The *plates* came first. As a boy, Tim learned that eating dinner with his father's family was much different from eating dinner with his mother's family. Holidays saw him alternating between the red sauces, red wines, and red table cloths of his Italian relatives and the brown meats, golden ales, and lace table cloths of his Irish relatives. Not only did the tables look different, the food tasted different. The Italian plates were full of spicy, zesty, lively colors and tastes. The Irish plates were full of substantial, hardy, filling foods. However, somewhat paradoxically or maybe expectedly, surrounding the differences on the plates were the similarities of family smiles, laughter, and love.

He grew to expect certain tastes, experiences, and feelings while eating a plate of Italian food and certain other tastes, experiences, and feelings while eating a plate of Irish food. It wasn't that one experience was necessarily better than the other, it was just that they were different. He grew to distinguish, appreciate, and love those differences. As his now departed, sainted mother had often said, *"Tim, you're both Gaelic and Garlic; and remember always, you are the best of both."*

At about 11 years old, it dawned on Tim that if he wanted to travel to China, he only had to walk the four blocks to the nearest Chinese restaurant and order its daily special plate. In addition to the plate's different Chinese tastes and aromas, he would hear different accents, see different clothes, appreciate the different décor, and feel the different vibes. His imagination would indeed now sit in another land.

Soon, with the help of a maiden aunt, who shared his passion for different foods and her knowledge of different peoples and places, he was tasting plates of French crepes in Woonsocket, plates of Portuguese grilled cod in Bristol, plates of Polish kielbasa in Pawtucket. Eventually, he was visiting Rhode Island's smaller yet vibrant ethnic neighborhoods of Lithuanians, Ukrainians, Greeks, Lebanese, Syrians. All were opportunities for Tim to taste new plates, practice new accents, hear new histories, experience new cultures. By the time he left home at 17, without ever having placed a foot outside Rhode Island, he felt that, in a certain way, he had already traveled the world. In a certain way, he had. His magic carpet had been plates of exotic foods and their surrounding memories of tastes, accents, complexions, smiles, histories, and most of all, people.

The *Planes* came next. Tim was 18 when he experienced his first plane ride. It wasn't until his sixth flight that he experienced his first landing. It was this story that had first drawn Brileen to his side.

It had happened almost a year before their night on the Rhode Island beach. Tim was a Captain on the Penn State ROTC faculty and was enjoying a night at a local Penn State University hangout, The Rathskeller. He loved The Rathskeller. First, because its name suggested that he was again traveling "by plate," or in this case "by beer stein," to a foreign land, Germany. Second, the very first moment he walked into the place, he felt warmed and welcomed. Of course, that feeling had probably been enhanced by the freezing temperatures he had just left outside the door, and the steamy, rollicking scene he found inside, with students pressed against each other singing and drinking, all toasting their victorious Nittany Lions.

Tim always believed that the right ambiance added to a meal, even if the meal was just a beer and burger. The Rathskeller certainly had ambiance, although you would probably never hear that particular word used by any of its patrons. As patrons walked into the Skeller, as it was often called, it was all dark woods and veneers, ceiling beams, black vinyl and leather. However, all these dark colors were bathed in a yellow glow from the low wattage bulbs, providing a warm, comfortable feeling. To the left was a long, log-timbered bar, with a polished wood top, and backed by shelves supporting scores of different kinds of beer. To the right was a wall of dark-wooded booths with black padded seats and backs. The first booth on the right was the biggest, able to fit eight comfortably. The night Tim first saw Brileen, there were fifteen crowded into and around that booth.

There were already two empty cases of Rolling Rock ponies on the table. "Rock Cases" on the table were a long-standing tradition at The Rathskeller. Students could honestly tell their parents they were working hard on "case studies." There were also empty hamburger plates all way round. Seconds had already been ordered. The Skeller's burgers were the best in town, or at least Tim, and seemingly half the student body, thought so.

This group of fifteen, a mix of graduate and undergraduate students, was playing a game called "The Worsts of the Firsts." The game was played by first picking a category such as first car, or first girl, or first illegal drink, etc. Then each person tried to tell the most entertaining story of his or her "first", ...but it had to be true. The group then voted on who told the "worst" first story. That person had to buy the next round. The loser then picked the next category, and the game started all over again. As Brileen walked in, the most recent loser called out the next category, "Paradoxical Firsts."

Brileen moved easily into the group, for several of them were her good friends. However, she barely heard their hellos. Her eyes and thoughts were lingering on the guy in the far back corner of the booth. His hair was dark brown, really dark, almost black, in an Italian kind of way. Yet, it was not straight. It had a rather unruly, wavy, curly way about it. His eyebrows were also almost black. His lips were full, even a little pouty. "All very Mediterranean and even a little mysterious," she thought. Yet his face was very familiar. She had seen it, in several variations, throughout her life, on most of her male cousins. She smiled as she heard her grandmother saying, "And who are you, laddie? I know you're one of us, cuz you've got the map of Ireland on your face." This man did too. His face was square and flat, with a slight leaning of the jaw to the right, where County Kerry would be. The face was centered by a slightly pug nose. The mouth was wide and seemed ready to widen even more with a forthcoming grin. Ruggedly handsome, with just a little dash of Hollywood, was her subliminal appraisal. She couldn't tell his height, since he was sitting, but she guessed him to be about six feet. That was good, she liked her men tall. Not a requirement, but certainly a benefit for someone trying to court her attentions. Humph, apparently this man hadn't even noticed her.

"Your turn, Tim," the long-haired blonde to his right prodded.

"OK," said Tim. "Here's my paradoxical first. My first airplane ride. I was 18. I had known about the flight date for weeks. I wore the right clothes, knew my seat location, had only one carry-on. I was seated comfortably between two friends when the plane took off. I thought everything was OK. But even though everything went as expected, I was NOT on the plane when it landed. It's a paradox, but it's a fact. In fact, ..." suddenly, his voice and his thoughts drifted for a second. As his eyes were traveling across his listeners, they stopped, for the most fleeting of moments, on the loveliest face he had ever seen, well one of the loveliest. It wasn't the most beautiful face he had ever seen. It was better. It was one of the loveliest. In fact, for Tim, it was one of only two that had ever made his heart involuntarily think lovely over beautiful.

"Tim," the blonde on his right nudged him. "What were you about to say? You seem to have lost your train of thought."

That train started moving again, and Tim's eyes now continued their travels across his listeners, and he said, "In fact, the next four times I flew, the same thing happened. I took off OK, but I never landed."

At first, there was silence from the group. Then the group scoffed, with calls like "No way!" and "You've got to be kidding!" Then one of the players, one who knew Tim better than the rest, piped up, "Oh, I get it. Your first flight in an airplane was also your first parachute jump! Right?"

Tim responded, "Right. You got it."

There was a moment of silence, then a burst of questions. "Wow, you jump out of airplanes?"

"Yup," said Tim.

"How many times have you done that?"

"Thirty-six times," answered Tim.

"Are you crazy?"

"Sometimes I think so," he admitted.

"Why would you do that?"

"Most fun you can have with your pants on," he smiled.

"Why did you have to do it four more times?"

Tim responded with, "The Army's jump school is located at Fort Benning Georgia, and the landing zones are across the state border in Alabama. To qualify for your jump wings, you must complete five jumps in one week, weather permitting."

Then from the back edge of the group, a lovely voice came from the lovely face, "Were you scared?"

Tim was happy to have the chance to linger on that face. He looked into those hazel-green eyes. Her words had been matter-of-fact, but those eyes were dancing. Were they dancing for him?

"Yes, I was scared. I'm still not sure, if on that first jump, I actually jumped, or if the jumpmaster pushed me out the door." 'Did my heart just flutter? Tim thought. Geeeeez, am I scared now? Of talking to this girl? Of this woman?'

In order to keep his face from reddening any further, he started to ramble on a bit more. "But I don't think I was the only one scared. I think everyone was a little scared. I remember my friend John, who was sitting next to me in that plane, saying to me on the way to the drop zone, "Are you scared Tim? I think I'm a little scared. This is my first plane ride, and apparently I'm dumb enough to jump out of this perfectly good airplane. But what's even worse, I'm a black kid from Harlem jumping into Alabama. Now that's scary!"

Tim silently thought for a moment about John. John had lightened a tense moment that day in the plane. He had done so several more times through the next tense year, during their joint tour in Nam. Happily, John was still a good friend.

John's line about jumping into Alabama had caused several laughs and smiles among the group. As the story-telling moved to the next person, Tim's eyes moved back to the lovely face. It gave him the slightest of demure smiles, then turned to her friends.

As the "Worsts of the Firsts" continued around the table, Tim couldn't seem to make eye contact again. However, as the group broke to leave, he felt a touch on his arm. He turned to hear the lovely face say, "Hi. I'm Brileen O'Sullivan. I enjoyed your 'Worst First.' Perhaps, we'll get a chance to share some good firsts sometime." With those daring words and a smile that stretched from Dublin to Galway, she walked out the door with her friends.

Only then did Tim think of such clever responses as, "I hope so," or "Yeah, that would be great." His last response to himself was, "Geeezzz, I'm still such a dork when it comes to women!" For Tim, it was a long, frustrating drive back to his apartment.

For Brileen, it was a short walk with friends back to her dorm; short, both in distance and time, but especially in time. As they walked, one of her friends, who knew Tim, provided Brileen some of the details she wanted to know but was reluctant to ask. Brileen wondered how much she could learn about him before they reached the dorm.

Her friend informed Brileen that Tim was an Army Captain on the Penn State ROTC faculty. She thought his assignment ended in June, or was it next June? His last name was DePalma. He was 26 or 27. No, he wasn't married. Although, he might have some kind of "lost love" thing going on. Didn't date a lot because he didn't have a lot of extra time. In addition to his ROTC duties, he was also taking courses toward a Masters Degree in Political Science or International Relations, or something like that. She had once made a play for him, but it just wasn't happening. Kind of like that blonde who sat herself next to him tonight. He has a nice car though, a Mustang. If Brileen wanted to "accidentally" meet him again, she should hang out at The Rathskeller, the university gym, or the library. If she wanted to make sure she met him again, why not just give him a call? Brileen opted for an "accidental" meeting in the library.

Their "first date," for that's what they would later call it, was a four-hour beer and burger at The Rathskeller, after "accidentally" bumping into each other at the library. Tim, like many smitten men on a first date, let her do most of the talking. He learned many things about her that night. For instance, he learned that her unique name, Brileen, was a joining of the names of her mother's two sisters, Bridget and Kathleen. She told a funny story about a young parish priest who had first refused to baptize her, because *Brileen* was not a real name, not a saint's name. Brileen's mother was not a woman easily bossed or crossed, especially by some unripe boy new to the cloth. She forcefully pointed out, by repeatedly jabbing a finger at his chest, that her daughter Brileen was named not after one saint, but two, and both good Irish saints at that. She then rendered the ultimate threat. If the Holy Trinity Parish would not host her daughter's baptism, she was sure the nearby Polish National Church of the Ascension would. The following day, the pastor of Holy Trinity, old Father Halloran, called her to say that it all had just been an unfortunate misunderstanding. Father Halloran told her that he himself would be honored to pour the water that would "cleanse the infant's soul and cause a host of angels to usher sweet Brileen into the family of the Church." Sitting there listening, Tim could see that the mother's strength and passion had been gifted to the daughter.

Brileen also told him of her life-long dream to be a nurse; a dream that was only a little over a year from becoming reality. She would be a pediatric nurse, specializing in nutrition. As she went on about the importance of good food, the right food, to a child's proper development, he found himself paying rapt attention. Although good food, especially ethnic foods, had always been a keen interest of Tim's, he had never thought much about food's nutritional value. He had only wanted to experience its tastes, aromas, presentations, and what it told him about foreign lands and foreign peoples.

When she explained the importance of a properly balanced diet in developing not only a child's healthy body, but also keen intellectual functions, and an overall happy outlook, her words hit him like a thunderbolt. Tim had always innately understood that man was composed of three parts: body, intellect, and soul or spirit. He also understood that for he himself to be happy, all three parts had to be developed to their full potential, but at the same time be kept in balance. However, although he had always felt these things, he had never actually been able to clearly articulate them, not until that night. Without knowing it, Brileen had opened a new door into the development of Tim's personal philosophy of life. Balance was key, not only in nutrition but in all things.

As the lights flickered for last call, Tim realized the hours had passed as if minutes. He also realized that the young woman sitting across from him was not only beautiful, but she was also strong, passionate, compassionate, and smart. All these things, plus something else he couldn't describe but could feel, made her ...lovely. Rising from the table, he reached for her hand. She gave it to him, along with a smile. As they walked out the door, he leaned toward her and said, "You were very prophetic the last time you walked out this door. We just had our first "good first.""

Almost a year later, they were a couple, creating silly acronyms on a Rhode Island beach called Jerusalem, across the breakwater from a little fishing village called Galilee. Tim had spent many of his childhood summers in a small rented cottage on this same Jerusalem beach. He thought that ironic, for after starting to court Brileen (and he knew that's what he was doing, even if she didn't), he found that she had been born in the Pennsylvania town of Bethlehem and had grown up in the nearby town of Nazareth. That night on the beach, he laughingly told her of the irony he found in the connective biblical aspects of their separate pasts: "You know, like Jerusalem, Galilee, Bethlehem, Nazareth." She looked up at him. Her eyes surrounded him, warmed him. She whispered, "Don't laugh Tim. I believe it's just another sign that our love was made in heaven." Tim froze. Then she smiled, giggled, and said, "Geeez Tim, don't get so nervous. I was only joking." However, as dawn came and they walked off the beach together, they both knew they were walking into a life together.

Now 30 years later, as Tim sat in this airplane on his rendezvous with revenge, his heart sighed for a moment, a long moment. Then his mind brought him back to the last "P" in their silly T3P2 acronym. The P for *Planes*. True, his first five "non-landing" plane rides had only taken him from an airfield in Georgia to a drop zone in Alabama. However, literally hundreds of subsequent planes had carried him to and most had actually landed him in exotic, dangerous, beautiful, ugly, strange, but always interesting places. The youthful desires he had shared with Brileen on that beach so many years ago, the desires to see all parts of God's creation, to walk distant lands, to eat different foods, to talk with diverse peoples, to think in new ways, had all eventually happened. He only wished they had all happened with her.

He looked at the gold wedding band on the little finger of his left hand. On the outside of the nearly half-inch-wide band was engraved an Irish Claddagh. Brileen had selected this ancient Irish symbol for their wedding bands. The band's Claddagh symbol had two gold hands embracing an emerald heart, which was in turn surmounted by an embossed gold crown. The hands represented their friendship, the heart their love, and the crown their loyalty.

This ring on his little finger was Brileen's. "His" ring was now clasped in her hand against her breast for eternity. He took off the ring, the first time in years, and looked at the engraving she had placed inside their bands.

It said, "T3P2&US-4ever."

Paprikas Criske Budapest (Chicken Paprika)

Tim had just sampled his way through the outdoor food market when the guide recommended he continue the experience at Budapest's Great Market Hall just across the bridge from his hotel. This central market (Központi Vásárcsarnok) was dominated by beautiful vegetable stands, flower stands, and the haunting smell of various paprikas from the spice stalls. Tim was taken back to his childhood and the various church dinners where he had his first European Chicken Paprika.

This recipe below is a simple dish to prepare and a great family dish.

Ingredients:(Four Servings)

3 – 4 Tbsp	Butter
1 Onion	Medium size, Sliced
3 – 4 Lbs	Chicken Parts
3 Cloves	Garlic, peeled and minced
4 Tbsp	Hungarian Paprika
1 Cup	Chicken Broth
1 Cup	Sour Cream
1 Bay Leaf	Whole – removed at end
2 Tbsp	Flour
To Taste	Salt/Pepper
1 Bell Pepper	Seeded and chopped (optional)
1 Tomato	Chopped and seeded (or 1 can diced tomatoes)(optional)

Directions:

1. Heat butter in Dutch Oven or large skillet (cast iron)
2. Add cut-up chicken pieces – brown on both sides (about five minutes each) – remove chicken.
3. Add thinly sliced onions; reduce heat; and stir until

19

onions go golden – about 10 minutes.
4. Add paprika, minced garlic, chicken broth, bay leaf, and salt and pepper to taste.
5. Raise heat and bring to a boil, stirring constantly.
6. Return chicken to the pot – reduce to simmer; cover and cook for 20 to 30 minutes – turn once or twice.
7. In a bowl mix sour cream and flour – whisk until smooth.
8. Remove chicken; discard bay leaf and skim off any fat.
9 Bring back to a boil until sauce becomes thick and almost pasty.
10. Add sour cream mixture and return to heat until thick.
11. Taste and add salt, pepper, and additional sour cream as needed
12. Pour sauce over mixture and serve.

Tips:
1. If you like tomatoes and green peppers add them when you return the chicken to pot the first time – if you use undrained diced tomatoes you will have to back off the chicken broth a bit.
2. Very flexible recipe – adjust to your tastes and cooking methods. If something is not quite correct – just blame your Hungarian grandmother or Tim's Hungarian friends.
3. Can be made ahead and reheated just before serving.
4. Serve over noodles, Hungarian nokedli, or rice.

CHAPTER 3: PLANES AND TRAINS AND MEMORIES

Day One: Monday, 1015 hours, in a Train to Heidelberg

Tim was now seated in a private train compartment, staring out the window, closing in on Heidelberg. He needed to focus on what was going to happen there. But he couldn't. Thoughts of Brileen again returned to grip his mind so tightly he could think of nothing else but her. This used to happen often, just after she was taken from him. Over the years, these bouts of despair came more infrequently and with less intensity. However, this one was strong, intense, and he couldn't seem to shake free of it.

Earlier, when he deplaned in Frankfurt and headed for the train station, his movement and the activity around him had again focused his mind on why he was here, what he must do, and how he was going to do it. The train ride from the airport to the main train station in Frankfurt had only taken about 15 minutes. Then, he only had seven minutes to make the connection with the next train to Heidelberg. He had barely hopped from the platform on-to that train when it started moving. German trains ran on time.

Perhaps it was the German countryside, as he watched it slip by his window, that brought Brileen back to sit with him. This part of Germany looked similar to the Pennsylvania countryside where she had grown up, they had met and married, and she had died.

Tim knew, as he sat there alone in this train car with Brileen, that he must now struggle through some sad memories to again make peace with himself. Only then, would Brileen smile on his heart and release his pain. It always happened this way. Would it this time? It had to. It just took time.

Brileen left him in 1983. He had not been there to say good-bye. He could never forgive himself for that.

In the spring of 1982, Brileen graduated from Penn State. That same week, Tim was promoted to the rank of Major and re-assigned from the Penn State ROTC unit to the 82nd Airborne Division at Fort Bragg, North Carolina. After a June wedding, Brileen took her new nursing degree, Tim took his new Major's rank, and they moved to North Carolina for their new life.

"Wedded bliss" was not too cliché a term to describe their first year together. They both loved their work. They both loved each other. They both loved life.

Then on a late October day in 1983, the reality of Army life intruded on their bliss. He called her at work, told her it was an emergency, and asked if she would meet him at home in fifteen minutes. She was not to mention this to anyone. When he ar-rived, he saw in her eyes something he had never seen in them before: fear. He pulled her toward him, wrapped his arms around her, and told her he did not mean to scare her, ...but, he had to leave immediately. His unit would be moving out right away. He couldn't tell her anything more, other than not to worry. He would return to her. He promised.

Her eyes settled on his. They surrounded him. They warmed him. They made love to him. It was the last time he would see those eyes. It was how he would always remember them.

Several hours later, he was on a plane to a Caribbean island called Grenada. One day after that, he was in several battles clearing and securing objectives around an enemy airfield. Two days after that, he was tracking down and rounding up remaining groups of enemy soldiers. For a lifetime after that, he would be mourning the loss of the woman who had been the center of his world.

Late on the fourth day of operations in Grenada, Tim was called to his commander's tent. The lights were low, but his boss's voice was even lower. Tim could not remember the words, only the feelings. Brileen had been in a serious automobile acci-dent. Her parents had been killed. She was in critical condition.

A plane was ready on the runway to fly him back to the States. He protested, but only half-heartedly he would later admit to himself, that he was needed here on the battlefield with his troops. His commander, who was also a friend, moved closer. "Tim," he said, "this operation is all but over. You and your men have done a great job, but believe me, it's over. Get on that plane. Go to Brileen."

In little over 24 hours, he was at her side. But not in a hospital. In a mortuary.

A triple wake was held for Brileen and her parents. Normally, Irish wakes not only mourn the death of the deceased; they also celebrate the life that was lived. However, because of the tragic circumstances, Brileen's youth, and Tim's dark presence, there was no celebrating going on. The funeral home, being a long-established service to the old Irish neighborhood, had the old-style wake rooms set off from the viewing parlor. In one wake room, the women mingled and served cups of coffee and tea, along with small slices of homemade Soda Bread, Irish Tea Brack, Preacher Cake, and that ultimate comfort food, a small bowl of Colcannon. In the other wake room, the men smoked and talked, while here and there bottles of Jameson or Bushmills were furtively tilted into the cups of coffee and tea.

As Tim sipped a double-hard Bushmills coffee, before returning to Brileen's side, he learned that after he had left for Grenada, Brileen had returned back home to Pennsylvania so she would be in the comfort of her family, ...just in case the worst happened.

All these words, that were meant to comfort him, just deepened his grief. It was he who was supposed to be in danger, not her. If the worst happened, it was supposed to happen to him, not to her. He could not forgive himself for not being there to protect her. Even worse, he felt that he was the cause of her being in that car, on that road, at that moment.

For days his grief grew deeper and darker. Tim was a man with a strong sense of discipline and responsibility. He felt he was responsible for her death. He could not shake that sense of responsibility. He was inconsolable. He loathed himself. A darkness had settled over him that would not dissipate.

However, on the day of the funeral, when he returned her to her Pennsylvania hills, Brileen came to comfort him. As he gently placed a rose on her descending coffin, he felt a rush of her love sweep up, over him. In turn, his heart seemed to release its own burst of love, leaving him breathless and unsteady. For a moment, it was as if he was caught up in a swirling dazzle of hazel-green light and warmth. At that moment, sorrowful acceptance had gently replaced mournful grief in his heart and in his soul.

Now, as Tim sat in this German rail car, working through the memories of both sad and wonderful moments, Brileen once again released his grief, swept over and through him, and left.

He knew all this might sound a little crazy to someone else. Hell, it sounded a little crazy to him. So he never mentioned it. He never tried to analyze it. He just knew that, whenever he descended into those states of depression, Brileen always came and relieved his grief. She did so again this time.

However, this time Tim had a problem he did not want. Although a part of his heart was now filled with a warmth from Brileen's love, another part was still filled with a lust for revenge. How could both these feelings exist within him simultaneously? Reluctantly, Tim realized that he must focus on one, at the expense of the other. He could not help himself, his focus was now on revenge. A revenge, oddly enough, which had its origin in another long ago love.

Colcannon (Mashed Potatoes with Cabbage)

Almost any Irish family has this recipe in the file. Tim's Irish grandparents tell the story of preparing this most often at the end of the month, when pennies were stretched to the next month with this filling dish. Over the decades it has morphed into a fall dish when fresh potatoes and cabbage (especially white cabbage) are readily available. Bacon is often added and kale can be substituted for cabbage.

For some unexplained reason it also became a staple at Irish funeral wakes, with guests obliged to take a spoonful to their plate, supposedly to remind them of the homeland. When queried Tim's grandfather would opine, privately, that it was all that the altar guild ladies could produce with continued success.

Ingredients:(Four to Six Servings)

2 -4	Large Russet Potatoes
3 - 6 Cups	Shredded/thinly sliced cabbage
½ - 1 Cup	Milk
2 - 4 Tbsp	Butter, cut into small pieces
Salt/Pepper	To taste

Directions:

1. Peel and dice potatoes; add to a saucepan and cover with salted water; simmer about 15 minutes.
2. In a separate pan, steam cabbage until tender.
3. Drain potatoes and add milk and butter; beat until smooth, adding additional milk as necessary.
4. Fold in cabbage and season with salt and pepper.

Tips:

1. This can be made this with instant potatoes and almost any type of potato from the grocer.
2. A great way to use leftover potatoes and cabbage.

Irish Tea Brack

As a youngster Tim loved to visit Grammy Margaret, especially when she made "Tea Brack" which Tim always referred to as "Tea Cake." Common in Irish families around the holidays, Tim and his siblings always would chew slowly to find the prizes baked in the cake. Tim would hope for the coin which prophesied wealth but had to endure the laughs of his cousins when he came across the button signifying a bachelor status.

Over the years Irish Tea Brack also became a standard for funeral wakes, but served without the baked-in trinkets. The origin of the word probably stems from the "breac," meaning speckled, reflecting the fruits in the mix.

Ingredients: (Six Servings)

1 - 1 ½ Cup	Raisins
2 Cups	Tea (Preferably Black Breakfast or Orange Pekoe)
1 Cup	Brown Sugar
2 Cups	Self-rising Flour
1 - 2	Eggs
½ Tsp	Allspice
¼ Cup	Orange Jam or Jelly

Directions:

1. Place raisins and brown sugar in large bowl, add hot tea to dissolve sugar, cover, and let stand overnight.
2. Preheat oven to 325F.
3. Grease and flour a 9" baking round (Tim prefers a spring-form like pan - it is just easier.)
4. Add egg, flour (a little at a time), jam, and allspice to the mixture - blend well.
5. Pour into the cake pan, smooth, and bake until

toothpick comes out dry (about 80 - 90 minutes).

6. Cool for one hour before removing the cake from the form.

7. If you like it warm - serve after an hour; especially with butter.

8. If you want cleaner, neater slices refrigerate for 4 - 6 hours and serve.

Tips:

1. Depending upon oven and setting, always check after 50 minutes and slide a piece of aluminum foil over the top if it browns too quickly.

2. You can adjust the moistness by increasing/ decreasing the tea amount.

3. Tim's family has experimented with (and liked) other re-hydrated dried fruits, especially when he ran out of raisins.

4. For Irish fans, in addition to the coin and button, the other trinkets commonly used were ring for marriage, pea for poverty, thimble for spinsterhood, and a religious medal for a religious life.

CHAPTER 4 – CONFIDING AND REMEMBERING

Day One: Monday, 1025 hours, in a Train to Heidelberg

As the train to Heidelberg swayed back and forth along the rails, and the telephone poles rippled by his window, Tim's mind emerged from its grief-driven despair. Yes, working through thoughts of those last moments with Brileen had finally freed his mind from its debilitating depression. Now, even as his heart was stilled, his mind was again quickly and intently focusing on Heidelberg and what he must do there.

Tim shook himself alert and grumbled, "Tim, me'boy, you always think better on a full stomach. Let's find something to eat." He got up and headed out to find the dining car. He knew that train food wasn't going to be much better than airplane food, but from previous Army assignments in Germany, he knew that German trains often had decent dining cars; dining cars had menus; menus meant variety; and variety often provided the opportunity for at least a few tasty somethings.

Three minutes of staggered walking on the moving train brought Tim to the dining car. The car was only about a quarter full. Tim took a table by a window; of course, in a train, all tables were by a window. The entire ride from Frankfurt south to Heidelberg was scheduled for 57 minutes. Tim's watch told him he had about 30 minutes left. "Better just look at the appetizers," he thought. Tim opened the menu and recalibrated his mind to read German. When Tim was last stationed here, most menus were in both German and English. This one was only in German. Did that mean anything? Apparently Tim's mind wasn't at all interested in trying to answer Tim's question; rather, it was reading the list of appetizers, trying to appease the rumblings of his hungry stomach.

The first item that caught Tim's interest was broccoli soup. His sainted mother had often served broccoli soup, both hot and cold. It was a way of getting his unsuspecting sister to eat vegetables without her knowing it. Today, the train's broccoli soup was "kalt." "Hmm, today cold soup might just hit the proverbial spot," he said to himself.

Then his eyes stopped abruptly, fixed on the last appetizer listed. "How appropriate," he sighed. He closed the menu, signaled the waiter, and ordered, "I would like to have the Vietnamese Spring Rolls, please."

Within 5 minutes, the two Vietnamese spring rolls arrived, accompanied by two sauces. One was an Asian hoisin sauce, but he wasn't sure about the other. Obviously the rolls had been frozen and popped into a microwave, but they still looked pretty good. How would they taste? With the first bite, he was pleasantly surprised. As he continued, he could distinguish the different flavors and scents. The amount of shrimp was sufficient, without overpowering the tastes of basil, mint, and cilantro. Not bad for frozen food. He closed his eyes a moment, enjoying the scents and flavors. With his eyes closed and his body tired, these scents and flavors started Tim's mind on travels to distant memories, ...memories of Nam.

It was less than 24 hours since Tim had been seated in his sister's kitchen enjoying a plate of Zia Mary's meatballs. Then a rage exploded from within him with almost total uncontrolled ferocity, belying its almost four decades of dormancy. The source of that rage and the focus of its revenge was the man who had murdered Quan.

Tim and Brileen had talked of Quan only once. One evening, about three months before their wedding, Tim confided in Brileen that he had been in love only once before, with a young Vietnamese woman named Quan. She had been his first love, and he had loved her deeply. It had been a love of both full passion and total commitment, developed and forged in a time of danger, death, and war. Tragically, Quan's love for Tim resulted in her murder by the hand of a jealous Vietnamese.

Tim softly and slowly had unburdened himself to Brileen, telling her that he truly, fully loved her, but that Quan remained a part of him and probably always would. While listening to him open his soul to her, Brileen's eyes once again surrounded him, warmed him, held him. When Tim finished, she whispered that she understood, and that she believed his heart was big enough to fully love her, while still holding the memory of Quan. Quan was never mentioned again.

Over the years, Quan receded deeper into his subconscious, only faintly reappearing now and then as an involuntary sigh or a skipped heart beat when a beautiful young Asian woman passed by. He also thought of her and her death when an image of the war appeared in a book, or on TV, or when he heard someone make a reference to Vietnam. Tim always assiduously avoided books or movies about Vietnam. He joined no Nam veterans organizations. He deftly avoided most questions and discussions about the war, ... or his part in it.

It wasn't that Tim wanted to forget the war, because he knew he never could, nor did he want to. Rather, he wanted to hold that experience close, contain it, channel it. The war had changed him. It had hardened him, and it had softened him. It hardened him against those who would force themselves and their beliefs on others. It softened him for those who needed help, comfort, protection.

For him, the war had first been mostly about seeking, finding, and destroying the enemy. But later, it had also been about securing villages, building orphanages, providing hope, protecting people. The road to the battlefields of Vietnam had been short and direct. The road back from those battlefields was long, arduous, and still not completed. Tim's mind was now again traveling those roads.

Broccoli Soup

From Tim's mother's recipe book – a simple and tasty soup good in the summer or winter. If you don't tell the children what it is – a good way to incorporate broccoli into a meal.

Ingredients:(Four to Six Servings)

¾ Lb	Broccoli
1 Cup	Chicken Broth
1 Onion	Medium Size
1 Tsp	Nutmeg
¼ Tsp	Cumin
1 Can	Condensed Mushroom Soup
1 Tbsp	Butter
1 Cup	Sour Cream

Directions:

1. Remove stems and cut broccoli into small pieces.
2. In a saucepan combine broccoli, chicken broth, onion, nutmeg, and cumin.
3. Boil for five minutes – add mixture to blender.
4. Add condensed mushroom soup and softened butter; blend until smooth.
5. Add sour cream; blend until incorporated.
6. Easily refrigerated until use.

Tips:

1. Serve with a dollop of sour cream and a garnish of chives.
2. Can be served hot or cold.
3. Package of frozen broccoli can be substituted for fresh.

Vietnamese Spring Rolls

Arriving aboard a Pan Am charter to Saigon's Tan Son Nhut air-port, Tim and the other recruits remained at Camp Alpha near the airport until matched with the frontline units. A Staff Sergeant returning for his second tour decided to take the first timers into town before they went forward. After giving Tim a quick reference for getting back to base and where not to go, he and the others were let loose on their own. While a large number of the group headed immediately to the seedier sections, Sam and Tim strolled down the main street, found a bar, and had their first Biere Larue, a local Vietnamese beer served in a one liter bottle. After quench-ing their thirst they continued down the street, and smells reminis-cent of Tim's favorite Chinese restaurant back in Providence waft-ed through the air. Some Tim recognized, but others were unique and inviting. Going against every hygienic rule from basic train-ing, he wandered up to a street vender and pointed at one familiar and one new kind of egg roll. After the first was fried in the ever present wok, it was offered and consumed quickly, with a soy-like sauce recognized from the distinctive bottle shape. Tim then waited for the second, smaller, thinner roll, to be fried but unre-pentantly it was picked off the block of ice and passed with a squeeze bottle of brown liquid. Throwing hands up in the interna-tional sign of question, Tim was greeted by a toothless smile by the vendor and motions indicating to bite the end off, squeeze some sauce on it, and enjoy - which he did - finding a new and crisp taste. Feeling no ill effects Tim ordered another and im-plored Sam to try - which he did but after the first bite handed it over with a pained look. Rather than eating or throwing it away, Tim unrolled it to discover the ingredients. Before he left the stand he asked the name of this spring roll and after multiple at-tempts was given a mimeographed strip of paper with "Spring Roll" and "Goi Cuon" in the characteristic purple - obviously Tim was not the first to ask this question.

Ingredients (Spring Roll): (Four Servings)

8 -10 Rice Wrappers	8 - 9 inches in diameter.
Handful	Rice Noodles (vermicelli/pancit noodles)
½ Lb	Large Shrimp(peeled/cooked/deveined/sliced in half)
Basil Leafs	To taste
Other Herbs	As desired
Lettuce Leafs	Use as internal wrappers
Carrot	Peeled and sliced thin
Cucumber	Peeled and sliced thin
Handful	Bean Sprouts

Ingredients (Mamma Sans Dipping Sauce):

4 -5 Tsp	Fish Sauce
¼ - 1/3 Cup	Water
2 Tbsp	Lime Juice (Juice of 1 fresh lime)
2 Tbsb	Honey
1 Tbsp	Crushed Garlic

Directions:

1. In a large saucepan boil rice noodles until cooked; rinse and cool.
2. Fill shallow bowl with warm water and quickly dip each side of wrapper - lay flat on prep surface.
3. Place a leaf of lettuce on the wrapper, add shrimp and the mixture of herbs, bean sprouts, carrot and cucumber strips, and finally the cooled rice noodles.
4. Fold sides of wrapper in and roll tightly.
5. Mix all sauce ingredients until the honey is assimilated.

Tips:

1. Rolling spring rolls is an art – Tim suggests you watch others or find an on-line video.
2. There are many brands of rice paper wrappers - find one with imprinted patterns - they seem to be stronger.
3. Do not overfill - you don't need to use all the filling material.
4. The fish sauce seems to work best but it is routinely served with bottled hoisin sauce mixed with crushed peanuts.

CHAPTER 5: RECIPE FOR A SOLDIER:
-BASIC INGREDIENTS-

Day One: Monday, 1035 hours, in a Train to Heidelberg

As Tim savored his Vietnamese Spring Rolls, his mind left the body that was traveling to Heidelberg and again began its own travels. This time these travels took Tim from Army Boot Camp in South Carolina to the long-ago battlefields of Southeast Asia, for there lived the beginning of his present rage for revenge.

Tim joined the Army the week after he graduated from high school in 1970. He was only 17. It would be two months before he would see his 18th birthday. He was an enlistee, not a draftee, in both fact and temperament.

Vietnam was near the forefront of almost every mind in his graduating class, as it was for most all male graduates across the country. In those days there was no "volunteer" Army. There was just the draft, and the infamous draft lottery.

Like most Americans, Tim watched the evening news, heard the protests, felt the divisiveness. Yet, for him, the path was always clear. Looking back now, he might concede to having been a little naïve, but what 17 year old isn't? However, even knowing what he knew now, given the choice again, he'd enlist again.

Part of his DNA was a core belief that no man was free till all men were free. Even as early as high school, he believed that the United States and its form of government was the best political system that free men had yet developed, and the best hope of all those round the world wanting to be free.

He learned this truth at the dinner tables of two immigrant

cultures. Although his dual families loved the Irish and Italian lands of their forefathers, they both came to America to become Americans.

Communism and the ever present specter of the Soviet Union were real concerns of Americans in 1970, even kids. From First Grade, hiding under his desk during atom bomb drills, to the previous summer watching the American-Soviet space race end with Americans walking on the moon, Tim always felt he was somehow a part of that worldwide struggle between us and them, between freedom and totalitarianism, between good and evil.

Even as a 17 year old, Tim viewed the worldwide US-USSR confrontation not only as a clash of political ideologies, but also as one of prisoners on one side of the Iron Curtain and free men on the other. To Tim, the Iron Curtain manifested itself in several guises. For example, in Europe it was the Berlin Wall and barbed-wire borders. In Vietnam it was the 17th parallel.

Since Tim knew he would soon be in Vietnam, he sought to learn as much as possible about the war and its causes. The 17-year-old Tim came to a simple understanding of what others saw as, and in fact was, a more complex issue. For Tim, the simple facts were that the 1950's Geneva Accords separated Vietnam into communist North Vietnam and non-communist South Vietnam. Those Vietnamese who wanted to be communist could stay in the North or migrate North. Those Vietnamese who did not want to be communist could stay in the South or migrate South. People voted with their feet. Over a million left North Vietnam and went South. Less than 50,000 left South Vietnam to go North. However, as time went on, the communists of the north decided to reunite Vietnam into one Communist state ...by force. That was all Tim needed to know.

Tim seemed to always know that when the time and place came, he would be there to help tear down that barbed wire, destroy that Iron Curtain. For Tim, the time was his 18th year, and the place was Vietnam. ...or so he thought.

Tim's high school graduation party was one of those rare times when both his Irish and Italian families came together. The dining room table was laden with homemade desserts. From his Italian aunts had come a Panettone, a Neapolitan, a Millefoglie, a Tagliatelle, two Ricotta Pies, and Tim's favorite, an Italian Love Cake. From his Irish aunts had come a Baileys Pumpkin Pie, a Baileys Irish Cream Mousse, a Michaelmas Pie, an Apple Amber Pie, a Chocolate Potato Cake, and a dozen Donegal Oatmeal Cream parfaits. The sideboards were filled with Italian wines and Irish whiskeys, while coolers filled with Narragansetts were located on the back porch.

With plastic champagne glasses of Asti Spumante held high, his blended family toasted him and wished him well. Family members, who were a very important part of the recipe that had made him the young man he was, were there to launch him on the adventure that would help make him the man he would become. Tim loved the pies, the drinks, the toasts, the traditions, but most of all, he loved the people who were his family.

Throughout the evening, several of Tim's uncles and cousins took him aside to give him tips and advice on how to survive the Army. Oddly, it didn't seem to matter whether or not they had actually served in the Army. Those who hadn't served still felt free to give him advice anyway. However, he understood that some of these whispered wisdoms had, in fact, been hard-earned and had safely returned the whisperers to their families. He should listen, each told him, for their particular piece of advice would bring him home safely too. He listened, or thought he did.

The next day saw Tim on a Greyhound bus bound for Fort Jackson, South Carolina. Twenty hours later he would be a GI Joe in Army Boot Camp. It was the first time he had ever been outside Rhode Island. He would not return for three years.

Tim thought his road to Vietnam would be short, that he would be in those jungles within a few months. He was wrong. It would be almost a year before he arrived in Vietnam. During that time, the Army would try to eradicate Tim-the-Civilian and create Tim-the-Soldier. Along the way, Tim would learn more about people, about food, about sex, about fate, about the world, but mostly, more about himself.

BASIC TRAINING

The 20-hour bus ride to South Carolina was the first part of that long road to the battlefield. Fort Jackson was basically a school. But a school like none Tim had ever known, or even imagined. The first eight weeks were called BCT (Basic Combat Training, -yes, that is when the acronyms began!). It was a time of rigorous physical training, at least for the out-of-shape guys.

Tim had been his high school's best cross country runner, so his lower body strength was strong and his stamina was high. Even though Tim had been just a bench warmer on his football team, he had worked hard in the weight room, so his upper body strength was also strong. Tim immediately went to work showing his Drill Sergeants that he could run and do pushups with the best of them. Big mistake! Soon teams of Drill Sergeants had his lungs gasping for air and his arms quivering like jello. Only then, too late, did he remember his uncle Jimmy's advice at his graduation party: "Tim, in boot camp, never be first, never be last, never be noticed." During the next several weeks of Drill Sergeant torment, Tim wished he had remembered Jimmy's advice. Then, he tried hard to remember all the other words, of apparently true wisdom, he had heard that night.

During those first eight weeks of rigorous physical training, Tim learned just how much punishment his body could take. Just like in those Timex watch commercials he saw on TV, he learned his body could take quite a licking and keep on ticking. But maybe even more importantly, he learned what mental toughness was all about.

The Drill Sergeants were constantly at him and his fellow recruits day and night, yelling, pushing, prodding, exhorting, stressing, testing, evaluating. These Sergeants had all been to Vietnam. More importantly, they had all made it back. They knew what was required to survive on the battlefield. Central to that survival were physical and mental toughness. However, for the Drill Sergeants the essential goal of boot camp was not just to have their recruits graduate with strong bodies and tested psyches. The goal was to graduate a soldier like Tim, who emerged from eight weeks of Basic Combat Training well on his way to possessing the true warrior essence of complete self-discipline: the total discipline of body, mind, and spirit. Tim was not a complete warrior yet, but they all knew he would be.

ADVANCED TRAINING

The very day Tim graduated from BCT, he moved into the barracks of his new AIT (Advanced Individual Training) unit. After BCT, the Army assigned graduates to their branch AIT units. The Army, as a means for personnel management, organized its soldiers into Branches such as Armor, Engineer, Intelligence, Finance, etc. Most recruits, especially draftees, sought assignment to any branch but Infantry. Tim volunteered for Infantry.

At Fort Jackson AIT, infantry Drill Sergeants took the strong bodies and hopefully strong minds sent to them from BCT and trained them in the skills and tools needed to become effective infantrymen; skills necessary to survive the battlefield. The skills were those of squad-size (7-10 men) combat tactics. The tools were those of destruction and death: M-16 rifles, M-60 machine guns, Claymore mines, LAWs (Light Anti-tank Weapons), M79 grenade launchers, hand grenades, and even the ancient weapon of bronze age warriors ...the knife.

In addition to these U.S. tactics and weapons, the new soldiers were also expected to become knowledgeable about some tactics and weapons used by the enemy VC (Viet Cong) and the NVA (North Vietnam Army). As Tim would find out 12 months later, sometimes it was more important to know how to detect and destroy an enemy mine or mantrap, than it was to emplace one of his own.

During those eight weeks of advanced training, Tim learned a lot about weapons and tactics. However, he wondered, did he learn enough? One night near the end of his eight weeks of training on weapon ranges and jungle-like patrols, Tim asked the Drill Sergeant he admired most, Sergeant Pack, "Are we, am I, really ready for Nam?"

Sergeant Pack looked at him hard and then said, "DePalma, you're as ready as we can make you in four months. But always remember, Vietnam is not like a rifle range. You won't be in trenches picking off the enemy at 300 yards. In the jungle, you'll often meet the enemy by surprise or in ambush. Nobody is static. Everyone is jumping around looking for cover. No time to aim. Everyone just points his weapon towards where he thinks the enemy is. Then everyone lets loose! The winners are the guys who put out the highest amount of fire, in the shortest amount of time, with the greatest amount of accuracy. Your two most important weapons on that battlefield are first, the skills you learn here, and second, your brain. Always use both."

Pack was silent for a moment, then said, "Don't worry DePalma. When the time comes, you'll be ready." In less than a year, Sergeant Pack's training and counsel would save Tim's life, and those of the men with him.

"ETHNIC" PLATES

Although there was little time in BCT and AIT for much else but training, Tim tried to continue his passion for seeking out *"plates"* of different ethnic foods in different ethnic environments. To do this at Fort Jackson, Tim came to think of the Army as a totally different ethnic group. Sometimes he thought the Army to be even a totally different species! As usual, he found this new ethnic group had its own way of preparing and serving food. Army food was certainly a learning experience.

By the end of his first eight weeks of BCT, Tim had lost about 20 pounds. His just-over-six-foot frame then carried only about 145 pounds, instead of its normal 165. However, after his next eight weeks of AIT, Tim had regained 10 of those lost pounds. He credited, or blamed, this "regain" on the AIT battalion's Mess Sergeant, Staff Sergeant Betit, a Frenchman who could cook. As one would expect, Betit's mess hall didn't put out a lot of great exotic foods. But unexpectedly, to Tim's delight, it did serve a lot of great tasting basic meals. During AIT, Tim got to really like two dishes he had never eaten before joining the Army, grits and SOS. When going through the AIT food line, he always tried to talk the cooks into giving him bigger portions of these items, usually by saying something as simple as, "Man, those grits tasted great yesterday. Can you pile on a little extra today?" Even though those words sounded odd coming out of a Yankee's mouth, they usually got him another ladle full. What Army cook doesn't like to hear that his food tastes great!

However, for Tim, it took awhile to acquire a taste for grits. He saw them on his first morning in the Fort Jackson Basic Training mess hall, and absolutely every morning after that. He passed them up on the first day, just based on their looks. After several days, he realized the guys from up north hardly ever took a scoop, while the southern Bubbas, a word he never said out loud, were always begging the line servers for more. After about a week of this, one morning in the food line, Tim stopped in front of the grits pan, offered his plate, and received a ladle full. After reaching his table, the first thing he tasted was his grits.

"Geeez," he said, almost choking, "this stuff tastes like wallpaper paste." He spit the remaining half mouthful back onto his fork.

"You Northern boys eat a lot of wallpaper paste, do ya?" asked Brax Bufford. Everyone laughed, especially the Southerners.

Tim had to smile too, and then answered, "Only if it's a choice between wallpaper paste and this stuff!" Now it was Brax's turn to smile.

Tim liked this big Southerner from Georgia. Tim found it humorous that Brax was short for Braxton, a name he had never heard before. It was the first name of some Confederate general for whom Brax's parents must really have had a liking. It hadn't taken Tim long to recognize that a lot of people south of the Mason-Dixon Line still took "The War" ...and their grits... seriously.

Tim never even thought about taking another bite of grits while in Boot Camp. However, about eight weeks later, after he joined the Advanced Individual Training (AIT) Battalion, things changed. Walking through the breakfast food line during that first week in AIT, Tim noticed that the grits there at least looked a little more appetizing. Ever the adventurer in food, Tim eventually decided to give grits another try. This time, as a few of his friends watched, there was no choking and spitting. Tim had to admit, these grits were pretty good. What was the difference?

From a few places down the table, Brax leaned forward and yelled, "Like those, don't ya Yankeeboy!" He continued, "Don't blame ya. These grits are damn good. They're 'cheesy' grits. Almost as good as my momma makes."

Later that day, the taste of those grits was still on Tim's mind. During a training break, he asked Brax why the grits they had that morning tasted so good, while the ones in the other mess hall were "barfo."

Brax furrowed his brow, squinted his eyes, and then drawled, "Listen here Yankeeboy, there ain't no such things as 'barfo' grits. True, some grits might taste better than others, but all grits are great." Brax then went on to tell Tim about the great and varied kinds of grits his momma made back home. After a few minutes of this, Tim was beginning to think Brax might be going into some kind of food trance; he almost expected him to start drooling at any moment.

Brax talked about all the things you could add to grits to make them great, starting with butter and of course cheese. But there were also pepper, honey, syrup, shrimp, onions, scallions, chopped bacon, lime juice, eggs, etc. The list of add-in ingredients seemed to have no end. Tim eventually interrupted Brax and recapped by saying something like, "... in other words, what makes grits taste good are not the grits but all the other stuff you add to them."

Brax gave him a confused, uncomprehending stare. He shook his head, and with a long, exasperated sigh, said, "Man, you damnyankees are really slow on the uptake. Your mouths talk fast, but your brains do slow."

Brax went on to explain that it's how you cook the grits, not just what you add to them, that makes them great. First, you had to have just the right amount of water, or if you were cooking them "Charleston Style," just the right amount of milk. Too much water, and you'll have soup. Too little water, and you'll have paste. Just the right amount of water, and you'll have Goldilocks' perfect grits porridge. Second, the cook has to know exactly when, how, and how much to stir the grits while they boil. As Brax told it, grits stirring is apparently not just a skill, but more of an art. Finally, Brax acknowledged that next to his momma and a few aunts, Mess Sergeant Betit put out some of the best grits he had ever eaten.

A training sergeant, who had come up behind the two soldiers as they talked about grits, yelled into their ears, "If you two ladies are done exchanging recipes, we'd like to welcome you back to our machine gun range instead of your little cooking range. Get moving!" As they moved to the firing sites, Tim heard the Sergeant say in low tones to Brax, "You know, Bufford, you're right about the Mess Sergeant. He sure makes some great grits."

Tim was learning a lot about grits, about Southerners, and about the Army.

In addition to acquiring a taste for grits, Tim also actually acquired a liking for the Army meal of mysterious magical appeal, SOS: Sh#T On a Shingle, a.k.a., creamed beef on toast. Never having ever seen or heard of this dish before arriving at Boot Camp, Tim tried some his very first day of BCT. Like with the wallpaper-paste-grits, Tim couldn't finish his first bite and never went back for more. The toast actually tasted like a shingle, and the creamed beef actually tasted like sh#t. Talk about truth in advertising!

Again, things changed in the AIT mess hall. Just as the grits had looked and tasted better on Mess Sergeant Betit's food line, so did the SOS. After a few days of eyeing it that first week, Tim took a helping. That was the beginning; Tim became a big fan.

This SOS had creamy smooth white sauce, which Tim believed must have been 50% butter, with slight tastes of onions and garlic. The chipped beef was shredded, not chopped, and had probably been well washed, for there was just a slight taste of salt. The toast was not the usual hard shingle, but rather had a soft, well-buttered consistency. Some days Mess Sergeant Betit would surprise the troops by unexpectedly replacing regular toast with French Toast, and sometimes even adding a fried egg on top of the creamed beef. On those days the troops would ask for more "Sublime On a Shingle."

Eating in the mess hall was a shared Army experience that united soldiers, both in their appreciation for the food and in their right to complain about it. Although it had now been a long time since the retired Army Colonel had eaten in a mess hall, and an equally long time since he had had either grits or SOS, he would never forget the experience.

Young Private Tim DePalma was soon to learn about another shared Army experience that unites American soldiers across the globe and across the generations. He was about to learn the roles that fate and the Army Personnel System play in a soldier's career and his life, ...on both the path of that life and, sometimes, even on its duration.

Italian Love Cake (Italian Wedding Cake)

Mixed heritage always allowed Tim to pick and choose his favorite foods, especially when both sides of the family would come together (weddings, funerals, reunions, etc). A favorite through today is Italian Love Cake, from Zia Mary's daughter, Rose. The family story is that Rose was pushed by Zia Mary to cook and enjoy it, this being the way to a man's heart. ("You are 26 and still don't have a man - you need to start some good'a cooking!"). Rose soon produced this cake without Zia Mary's help or even presence in the kitchen. Zia Mary was impressed and asked for the recipe. Rose, a lot of her mother in her, quickly said that she would first share it with her husband and then share with Zia Mary. Within two years Rose found her love and credits this recipe as a help. Rose never shared the recipe with Zia Mary, but one of her cousins confided in Rose, "Isn't this like the recipe on the side of the cake mix box?"

Ingredients (Six to Eight Servings)

1 Pkg	Chocolate or Marble Cake mix
2 Lbs	Ricotta Cheese
4	Eggs
¾ Cup	Sugar
1 Tsp	Vanilla
1 Pkg	Instant Chocolate Pudding Mix
1 Cup	Milk
1 Container	Whipped Topping, thawed (12 - 16 oz.)

Directions:

1. Pre-heat oven to 350F; mix according to directions on box.
2. Pour into 9 x 13 inch greased baking dish.
3. In a large bowl mix eggs, cheese, sugar, and vanilla.
4. Spread evenly over cake mixture.

5. Bake for 75 minutes or longer depending upon the baking dish, cool.
6. Mix pudding and milk in a large bowl, fold in whipped topping, and spread over cake.
7. Refrigerate for 1 - 2 hours until topping is firm.

Tips:
1. Tim prefers using a glass dish but if you use metal, extend time.
2. Keep in dish, it is best served with a spatula.
3. You can experiment with different cake mixes, but chocolate/fudge/marble provides the best taste and contrast.

Cheesy Grits and Variations

While Tim's fascination with grits started in Georgia, he was able to find it, and many of its cousins, all over the world. The varieties are almost endless, but all begin with the basic cornmeal, a favorite milk product or broth, and a lot of butter, ending with whatever the cook desires to throw into the final mix.

Numerous visits to Italy confirmed that creamy polenta was nothing but cornmeal mixed with broth and served with whatever was bountiful from the garden. In Norway Tim loved the ancient Rommegrot, made with wheat flour and sour cream served sweet with butter, sugar, and cinnamon.

Variations continued but Tim learned that this dish could also be prepared ahead as a casserole and popped into the oven when breakfast was within a half an hour. This served well when other breakfast brunch dishes required attention. To that end two of Tim's favorite recipes are provided.

Ingredients (Basic Cheesy Grits in a Pot)((Four to Six Servings)

2 Cups	Water
2 Cups	Milk
1 – 1½ Tsp	Salt
¼ Tsp	Pepper
1 Cup	Stone Ground Cornmeal/Grits (for the purists from the South)
4 – 6 Tbsp	Butter
4 Oz	Cheddar or other sharp cheese, grated/shredded.

Directions (Basic Cheesy Grits in a Pot):

1. Add water, milk, and salt to a large pot and boil.
2. Add cornmeal in batches, whisking to incorporate.
3. When blended lower heat and simmer for 20 to 25

minutes, whisking every few minutes.

4. When any lumps are gone and mixture is creamy, remove from heat, add half of butter, salt and pepper to taste.
5. Add cheese in small amounts until blended, and top with remaining butter, serve immediately.

Additional ingredients (Baked Cheesy Grits):

| 3 Eggs | Large and Beaten smooth |
| ½ Cup | Additional Cornmeal |

Directions (Baked Cheesy Grits):

1. Prepare as above, adding extra cornmeal and milk as necessary
2. Preheat oven to 350F; grease a casserole dish.
3. Add eggs at end of basic recipe after mix is cooled, blend until smooth, and pour mixture into casserole.
4. Bake for 30 – 40 minutes until well heated and slightly firm. Serve hot in the covered casserole.

Tips:

1. If you want to add additional items to the grits, Tim would recommend chopped spring onions, cooked sausage, and mushrooms.
2. In Italy, chopped fresh vegetables are added while in Norway they either serve the basic recipe with a lot of butter (as a quick warming food after cross-country skiing) or, for a heartier meal, add Parma ham. If this is to be the entree, adjust the salt in the basic recipe.
3. Serve as a main dish or smaller as a side.

Creamed Chipped Beef on Toast (SOS)

Tim fell in love with this during AIT and on his first visit back to Providence asked Zia Mary to make this for him. Zia Mary said she had a great recipe, but when Tim tasted this it just wasn't the same. Zia Mary asked Tim if he liked it - and smiling, Tim said it was great, but wasn't that hamburger in it? Zia Mary said of course, "who would use beef from a jar!" Zia Mary was correct - the US Army actually bought chipped beef in #10 cans, straight from the Midwest!

Later, with Brileen in Pennsylvania, Tim found a small farm butcher who still made the original sliced beef before it became popular and it's modern day equivalent was mass-produced by the large beef producers.

Ingredients:(Four Servings)

4 Tbsp	Butter
4Tbsp	Flour
¾ - 1 Cup	Milk (depending upon thickness desired)
To Taste	Fresh Ground Pepper
½ - 1 Lb	Dried Beef
To Taste	Cayenne Pepper

Directions:

1. Add butter to a large skillet - melt until foamy.
2. Wisk in flour and milk and to make a roux.
3. Continue whisking and add Dried Beef and pepper(s).
4. Serve while hot over toast.

Tips:

1. Tim serves over biscuits with great success.
2. Use a cast iron skillet for this dish

CHAPTER 6: RECIPE FOR A SOLDIER:
- ADDITIONAL INGREDIENTS-

Day One: Monday, 1045 hours, in a train to Heidelberg

ANOTHER CHEF IN THE MIX

As the train to Heidelberg continued to race forward, Tim's mind continued to race backwards. He was smiling as he remembered how he got his first set of orders upon completion of infantry training at Fort Jackson. Tim only had one week left until AIT graduation. Most of the other soldiers had already received their orders to their next duty station. For many, those orders were for Vietnam. Oddly, Tim, who had volunteered for Vietnam, was one of the few still without orders. At morning roll call four days before graduation, Tim was told to report to the Personnel Office at Command Headquarters. Tim reported 10 minutes early for his 10 o'clock appointment. At noon, he was still waiting.

For two hours, Tim sat in a waiting room (appropriately named, he thought) with about a dozen other soldiers waiting to talk to a Specialist Fourth Class personnel clerk named Tony Cicionni, according to the nameplates screwed to his door and sewn on his uniform. Spec 4 Cicionni was about 22-23 years old, 5'8", 150 lbs, with slicked-back black hair, a wry smile, and a cocky gait. Tim had known a lot of Tony Cicionni's. However, Tim had no idea the impact this Tony Cicionni was going to have on his life.

After the dozen soldiers became only two, Tim heard, "DePalma, you're next." come from beyond the half-open door. Tim entered and sat down in front of the green metal desk behind which sat green-uniformed Spec 4 Tony Cicionni. The office's pale green walls were bare. Six four-drawer green metal filing cabinets lined the wall to the right of the desk. A green metal coat rack balanced the room to the left of the desk. The desk top was organized into one small stack of papers in the middle and a green metal in-box on one side and a green metal out-box on the other side. Spec 4 Cicionni seemed to be an efficient cog in the Army's lean, mean, green-metal machine. As Tim was about to learn, efficient Cicionni was, but a cog? Hardly.

The first words spoken were, "Private DePalma, what did your hair look like before the Army got hold of it?"

"Just like yours, but a little longer," Tim lied. Tony smiled.

For the next 15 minutes the two soldiers chatted about civilian life. Well, the Specialist Fourth Class chatted; the Private listened. Tim learned that Tony was from New York City but had spent several summers with relatives in Cranston, Rhode Island, only about five miles from where Tim grew up on Federal Hill. They both had visited some of the same beaches, some of the same block parties, some of the same record shops and ice cream parlors, but apparently didn't know any of the same people. Rhode Island had a lot of Italians.

Finally, Specialist Cicionni said, "In your personnel records, I see that you, unlike me, enlisted in the Army and even volunteered for Vietnam. I'm not going to ask you why, because I don't care. But I do admire your 'coglioni.' So, let's see what I can do for you."

Just then, a light knock slipped through the door, along with a raven-haired, olive-skinned, rose-lipped young beauty. Tim jumped to his feet.

"Sorry to interrupt Tony. Here's lunch. Eat it while it's hot. Love you honey. Bye," she lilted, bent, kissed, twirled, gave Tim a glance and a smile, and flowed back out of the room, all in one movement that lasted seemingly no more than one second.

As Tim sat back down to where he had left his jaw, he eyed the foiled-covered plate sitting on the desk between them. The aroma already had his mouth watering, literally watering.

"That was my wife, Maria," said Tony, "brings me lunch every day. We'll be out of the Army and back in New York in less than three months. She can't wait, and neither can I. Let's see what we have today. Ahhh, pizza!" Tony smiled while removing and crunching up the aluminum foil into a small ball. He eyed Tim with a quizzical look.

Tim was overcome by the scents and aromas, by the colors, by the ingredients. He hadn't eaten since breakfast. "Nice try," said Tim. "But I know better. That's no pizza. That's a great looking, a great smelling, and I'm guessing a great tasting Tomato Pie."

"You're right," responded Tony. "Most people around here don't know the difference when looking at one. But they do once they taste one. Here, take a piece."

Maria's Tomato Pie lived up to Tim's expectations. The pie crust was sweet and firm, protected from getting soggy by the traditional layer of mozzarella slices which in turn were sealed by a layer of tomato slices. Maria had then spread her own special mixture of oregano, onions, olives, sage, and basil over the cheese. All this was topped and further flavored with a lengthy drizzle of real Italian olive oil, and then baked to perfection. Maria was indeed more than a pretty face. She was also a pretty good cook.

As they ate, Tony explained his view of the Army Personnel System and his personal role in it. As he saw the personnel system, the officers were the designers of the system, the senior NCOs (Non-Commissioned Officers) were the supervisors who made the system work, and most of the junior enlisted were the laborers, the worker ants. However, Tony did not think of himself as a laborer. Rather, he thought of himself as an artist within this artless business.

As Tony explained it, great Italian chefs, even just cooks, don't follow recipes, they create them. Add to them. Make them better. Likewise, Tony didn't blindly follow the Army's personnel procedures recipe, he "creatively" improved upon it. Rather than just monotonously fill empty personnel slots with names of newly trained recruits, Tony had assumed the role, probably subconsciously, of an ancient Roman god, meddling in the lives of mere mortals. More consciously, he saw himself as a great chef, changing an ingredient here, adding another spice there, stirring things up a little more than most thought necessary.

Tony read many of the recruits' personnel files in more detail than required and flagged some for his closer attention. He then placed individuals, not just names, into positions, locations, and career paths that he thought best for the Army, the mission, and the individual, all according to his own personal judgment and fancy. In other words, he created a personnel replacement recipe he called, "Faces to Places a la Tony!" Nobody, not the officers, not the NCOs, often not even the individual recruits, ever knew. Nobody but Tony, and now because of the familiarity shared over a tasty tomato pie and summers in Rhode Island, Tim knew also.

As Tim left, he also knew one other thing not mentioned over Maria's Tomato Pie; the name tags of the dozen soldiers who sat with him outside Spec 4 Tony, "The Master Chef," Cicionni's office all ended in a vowel. Obviously, Italians would have the chance to appreciate a creative chef more than others.

The next day after training, Sergeant Pack walked up to Tim and handed him a manila envelope marked "Pvt. DePalma: Orders." "DePalma, here are your orders. Seems you're not going overseas anytime soon, not to Nam, not to Germany, not anywhere. Rather, the Army in its unfathomable wisdom has decided to make you a super soldier. This envelope contains your orders to Airborne School, Ranger School, and then Vietnamese Language School. How the hell did you pull this off?"

Tim smiled and said, "Must just be this Dago soldier's Irish luck, Sergeant," knowing that it was both the Gaelic and the Garlic, and perhaps some great tasting tomato pie that created this little bit of luck.

PARATROOPER

Following graduation from AIT and a 300-mile Greyhound run south from Fort Jackson in South Carolina to Fort Benning in Georgia, Tim signed-in at his new Airborne training company and was placed on light duty, which meant he had nothing to do till training began on the following Monday. This week would be the first downtime for Tim since he left home over four months ago. It would give his body time to rest and give his mind time to think. Tim spent the mornings getting to know the post and the Airborne training areas. In the afternoons, he did light workouts in the gym and on the track. Some of the evenings were for thinking about what he had accomplished, where he was going, and whom he was becoming. Other evenings were spent out on the town with other soldiers, learning about the night life that surrounds a military post.

Each day Tim observed the Airborne training that was ongoing all around him. In one area, Airborne trainees were learning the proper PLF, Parachute Landing Fall: the proper way to hit the ground without breaking your neck following the crazy act of jumping out of an airplane. In another area, trainees were jumping out of 34-foot towers holding tightly to zip lines. Yet another area had 250-foot towers from which soldiers under chutes floated to the ground. Troops on the ground in yet another area were trying to gather their chutes while giant wind machines tried to rip those chutes from them. Everywhere troops were on the ground doing pushups, seemingly trying to push the earth into a deeper orbit, while men in black hats urged them to do this futile task better, faster, and ever more perfectly.

Every day these Airborne trainees were running 3-5 miles and doing umpteen numbers of pushups and pull-ups, apparently because of some real or perceived infraction of PLF form or soldier discipline. The masters of that discipline were the Black Hats, Drill Sergeants who wore a distinctive black baseball type cap immediately recognizable, and feared, by every trainee, whether enlisted or officer. Airborne school was voluntary. Everyone wanted to graduate. No one wanted to be re-cycled or washed out. The Black Hats were the sole arbiters of who graduated and who didn't. No one wanted to cross the Black Hats. Yet, based on the Black Hats' demonstrated unhappiness, every trainee offended them in one way or another.

Tim, standing on the sidelines for this rest week, observed as much of the training as he could. He studied the trainees' actions and the Black Hats' reactions. He believed he could effectively execute all the tasks required and successfully evade the seemingly arbitrary wrath of the Black Hats. In just a few days, he would be proved wrong on both points.

On the Friday afternoon preceding his Monday start of training, Tim just finished a five mile run. His chest was still heaving, but his eyes were fixed steadily on the 250-foot jump tower, as the sun set on the horizon behind it. He was reminded of a similar scene of this very spot in the recent John Wayne movie, "Green Berets." He smiled as he now remembered another piece of advice received at his high school graduation party, this time from his Irish grandfather, Joe Connolly, old JC as he was known by his friends and family.

Old JC had said, "In the Army you're going to have many challenges. Whenever in doubt, ask yourself, what would John Wayne do? Then do it! Not the crazy Hollywood stuff like charging machinegun nests, but the important stuff, like making the right decisions to take care of your men, your mission, and your honor. Do what John Wayne would do, and you'll never let your comrades, or your country, or yourself down."

Just as a memory smile was about to spread across Tim's face, another solitary runner, maybe 5 or 6 years older than Tim, slowed down, stopped, and gasped, "Hi. I've seen you out here running the last few days. You Airborne?"

"Not yet," Tim responded, "I start Monday."

"Me too," the runner panted, " I guess we'll be in the same class. You know anything about the course?"

"Just what I've observed watching them this week."

The runner smiled, "Yeah, me too. Lots of pushups, pull-ups, and running. Hope I'm in good enough shape."

Tim thought for a second and then said more to himself than to the man in front of him, "After watching this training all week, I don't think being in shape is what Airborne is all about. I just finished BCT and AIT, and I believe I can easily do all the physical training I've seen here. I think this is about something else. I think being Airborne is all about overcoming fear, about conquering the unknown. At least for me anyway. I've never flown in a plane, but I'm excited about what it will be like. Of course, I've never jumped out of a plane, and I certainly know I've never wanted to. The uncertainty for me, the challenge for me, is that I'm not sure I will actually jump when the time comes."

The runner smiled, shaking his head slightly in affirmation, and offered his hand, "I know exactly what you mean. My name is John, John Robinson."

Tim shook the offered hand. A lifelong friendship had just begun.

ANOTHER MEASURE

Sunday night, the night before actually starting Airborne School, Tim had a difficult time going to sleep. Several new thoughts were running around in his mind, uncontrolled and mostly unwanted. Nevertheless, they were there, preventing him from needed sleep. The first two annoyed him. The third, left him perplexed.

An issue in the press had begun to penetrate his core personal interests. The issue was the voting age which was 21. He began to fixate, well maybe fixate was too strong a word, but he was thinking a lot lately about the fact that he was old enough to fight for his country, but not old enough to vote for the men who were sending him to his possible death. The more he thought about it, the more ticked off he became. He knew he'd "really" be upset about this, if he had been drafted instead of volunteering. At the moment though, he was just strongly annoyed that this issue was annoying him.

The second issue was somewhat connected to the first. Again, he was old enough to fight for his country, but apparently not old enough to drink legally, which again in almost all states was 21. By his senior year in high school, he and most of his friends had some kind of fake ID and knew where to go locally to have a good time. But he was over a thousand miles away from those places, and seemingly almost an equal number of light years distant from those civilizations. Tim found during his first night off post, to his complete amazement and disbelief, Columbus, Georgia was "dry." A city being "dry" was a concept he had never encountered before, certainly not in a bar-on-every-corner Providence. In Columbus, there were no open bars or pubs, nor were alcoholic drinks sold in restaurants. What was that about? He could kill or be killed for his country, but his country thought he was too young to drink? More importantly, he thought, how could you have a plate of good lasagna without a bottle of good Chianti?

The third issue was also somewhat related to his age. Again, he was old enough to fight and maybe die for his country, but... si-i-i-igh (....Tim had a difficult time discussing this issue even with himself). Yes, there was a real possibility that he might die in some distant jungle, never.....well, ...just say it, Tim! ...never having had sex! "Yes, I'm still a virgin," he kept complaining to himself with great exasperation. He hated using that term to describe himself. Girls who had not had sex could rightfully, and respectfully, call themselves virgins. But guys? Boys who hadn't had sex were just that, boys. Sure, he had dated lots of girls in high school: dances, drive-in-movies, parking on the beach, rapid heartbeats, sweaty hands, heavy petting, heavier breathing, desires to go further, fears about going further, etc. All that stuff. But never...

Tim was only 17 when he graduated from high school. But that was then, and this was now. Now he was 18 and saw himself as a fully trained soldier. He decided that this was one soldier's mission he was going to accomplish, ...and soon.

"Soon" came about two weeks later. That night Tim was attending a party at another soldier's place. It wasn't really his kind of party. For Tim, he thought partying should never be just about booze, broads, and boinking. It had always been mostly about friends and having a good time with them. This was Tim's third party since arriving in Columbus. It was OK, but he didn't feel like he really fit in. Like at the others, he'd probably have a few drinks and then catch a ride back to base with other guys who hadn't coupled up.

"Not having a good time?" asked a soft voice from somewhere behind him. Tim turned to see a glow of red hair, not an Irish sun-glowing red, but more of an English fiery red. The hair was moving in sync with nervously swaying petit shoulders beneath a yellow tee shirt, blue eyes behind granny glasses, and a sweet smile surrounded by total cuteness. Tim was interested, more than interested. Of course at this age, Tim was interested, more than interested, in any girl who would talk to him.

Tim now tried to talk to her, "No. Well, yes. I don't mean that no, I'm not having a good time. I mean no, I am having a good time. Well, sought of. I.."

She interrupted, "Let's start over. My name is Grace."

From there the conversation took a more normal course. As they talked, Tim, as men do, started evaluating Grace. She certainly was cute. She was also nice and seemed fairly intelligent. She must like him, at least a little, for she had approached him. However, as they talked, he came to realize she was old, probably about 10 years older than him. As he looked back on that night in his later years, usually whenever he might be having the occasional sausage and gravy biscuit or heard the song *Amazing Grace*, he realized that she had been probably all of 27 or 28, lonely, and wanting to feel special to someone, if only for a night. In wanting to feel special, she had made him feel special too.

After about an hour of talk, a drink, and a dance, Grace asked Tim if he'd like to leave the party and go home with her for some coffee and pie, kind of a midnight snack. Then she'd drive him back to the Fort later that night.

That night, Tim never made it back to the Fort.

On the ride to her house, Tim was nervous. He didn't know what to expect from a woman. He didn't really know what a woman expected from him. He of course knew what to do, but less about how to do it well, and even less about when best to do it, and absolutely nothing about the afterwards.

As they entered the house, Tim accidentally stepped on a toy. A toy! She has kids?!

Grace apologized for the mess. Her son was at her mother's for the weekend. She hadn't expected to be bringing anyone home. She led him through the living room maze to the hall. To the left was the kitchen. To the right was her bedroom. She turned to him, "I'm not really hungry anymore, are you?"

They stood in the middle of her bedroom. The only light eased through the window from the night sky. The room felt warm, soft. Soon she felt warm, soft. He kissed her. He felt awkward. He moved awkwardly. She felt his awkwardness.

She said softly and gently, "Tim, is this your first time?"

He answered in an even softer voice, "Yes."

For Tim, to this day, that night remains a series of incomplete memories. Memories of physical light-headedness; emotional confusion; whispered words that guided him, led him, taught him; soft skin, sweaty skin, heaving skin; smiling teeth, gleaming teeth, biting teeth; wanton eyes, soulful eyes, closed eyes; soft hair, flowing hair, smothering hair; sighs, moans, gasps; all in a jumble of sexual wonder.

The sun woke him. Grace was gone. She was gone from the bed. Gone from the room. But not gone from his memory. Not gone from his body.

Tim dressed and slowly, hesitantly walked into the kitchen. She was making breakfast. What should he do? What should he say? This was all so new to him.

She looked at him. Smiled. Understood. She went to him, put her hands on his face, looked into his eyes, and gaily whispered through a bright grin, "Tim, last night was great. You were great. Come." She led him to the kitchen table. She pulled biscuits from the oven, covered them with steaming sausage gravy from a frying pan, and placed them in front of him and her.

Tim told her how great the biscuits and gravy were. He said they were the best he ever had. Truth was, he had never had biscuits and gravy before. He wanted to say she was the best. In truth she was, for there had been no other. He wanted to say she was the best he ever would have; simply the best. He didn't know how to say any of that.

On the drive to the Fort to drop him off, they talked about this and that, but not about their night. Tim didn't know what to say about it. He didn't know what she expected him to say about it. He just plain didn't know what he should say about it.

After they arrived, and as Tim was about to get out of the car, Grace leaned over and kissed him. "Tim, whenever you think of your first time, please remember me. I loved every moment. You were wonderful. Always remember, you did it your first time with grace, with amazing grace."

As Tim walked to the barracks, he looked back. Grace waved and flashed a smile that warmed him and swelled his chest. He waved and smiled back. He would never see Grace again. She left him with a smile he would always remember, ...a night he would never forget, ...both from a woman he would forever cherish.

AIRBORNE TRAINING

Airborne training extended over three weeks: Ground Week, when the trainee learned the proper ways to use the chute and hit the ground; Tower Week, when the trainee learned the proper form and procedures for exiting aircraft, as well as the first sense of height; and Jump Week, when trainees became paratroopers by successfully completing five jumps from assault aircraft flying at over 1,000 feet.

During the first formation on the first day of Ground Week, Tim spotted John Robinson. However, he saw that it wasn't just John Robinson, it was Sergeant John Robinson. When Tim asked him about it later, John responded that he hadn't mentioned it because his rank wasn't pertinent to their first meeting, and besides, a trainee's rank meant almost nothing in Airborne School, especially to the Black Hats. True, Tim thought, as he remembered seeing Black Hat NCOs all over the training areas requiring officer trainees, from Lieutenants to Majors, to do pushups and pull-ups just like everyone else.

Tim had no trouble mastering the proper PLF form: make ground contact with the balls of your feet, immediately rolling onto your calf, thigh, butt, and back, with your chin tucked in throughout the whole, continuous roll. This time, unlike when he was in boot camp, during all the running, jumping, yelling and panting, he remembered his Uncle Jimmy's advice: never be first, never be last, never be noticed. When the Black Hats told him to do 20 pushups, he made sure he was straining at 17. When they told him to run a mile, he made sure he was gasping at a half mile. Then they told him to do 10 pull-ups. Well, that was different. He truly gave out at 5. The Black Hats had found his weakness. The pull-up was designed to strengthen a paratrooper's forearms, allowing him to better control his chute, especially in strong winds, by pulling the chute's risers one way or the other. From that first day, the Black Hats had Tim doing more than a total of a hundred pull-ups a day, every day. His pull-ups started in groups of 5. By jump week, he was doing the 100 in groups of 20.

Tower Week presented Tim with new challenges: the 34-foot and the 250-foot towers and his newly discovered fear of heights. The 34-foot tower consisted of four open flights of ascending stairs, with an open walk-around landing at the top of each flight of stairs. As Tim advanced up each flight to each of the ever-higher landings, he began to feel a little more panic at each level. At the top of the fourth set of stairs was a mock airplane door. It was like jumping out of a building's fourth floor window. He was supposed to take his practice chute's static line, hook it to a metal zip line that ran past the mock plane's door opening, then jump out in a perfect jump form. The zip line, simulating the rush of air past a plane, would zip him down and away to a landing pad about 100 yards from the tower. Tim had trouble from the very first jump. Each time he jumped from that door, he panicked, losing control of his form and his concentration. Each time a Black Hat, in response, yelled, "Redo!" While most trainees took two or three jumps to qualify, a few might take 8-10. Tim took 15. But by the time he qualified, Tim no longer feared heights or jumping into them.

By the time he got to the 250-foot towers, he viewed them as an amusement park ride. Tim only required one drop from the 250-foot tower to qualify. This training device pulled the trainee by his chute 250 feet up to the top of an erector-set-like tower. Then the trainee was dropped and allowed to float by open chute to the ground, all the way listening to and following any needed guidance from a Black Hat using a megaphone. For Tim, it was the thrill of a lifetime, at least of his lifetime up to that point. Although a great thrill, Tim was glad that he didn't have to jump from this tower 15 times.

The final week, Jump Week, provided new thrills of a life time, five of them in fact. To earn the coveted Jump Wings and the designation "Paratrooper," Tim had to complete five jumps into a drop zone located in the Alabama portion of Fort Benning. One of these jumps had to be a night jump and one had to be a full-equipment jump, which meant that in addition to his chute, he would also carry at least 50 pounds of equipment.

On their first jump, Tim and Sgt Robinson sat next to each other waiting for the aircraft's "jump light" to go green. At one point John leaned over and said to Tim above the droning of the engines, "Are you scared? I think I'm a little scared. This is my first plane ride, and apparently I'm dumb enough to jump out of this perfectly good airplane. But what's even worse, I'm a black kid from Harlem jumping into Alabama. Now that's really scary!" Tim had to laugh, and then he freely admitted that his stomach was also rebelling at the idea of jumping out of a perfectly good aircraft.

Then Tim thought, was Sergeant Robinson really scared, or was he just being the good Sergeant, trying to help lighten the moment because he could tell Tim was scared? Before Tim could give it anymore thought, the jump light went green. Sergeant Robinson and Private DePalma gave each other the thumbs up. They stood up, hooked up their static lines, shuffled to the door, and jumped. John went out first, flawlessly. Tim never knew if he actually jumped or was pushed out by the jumpmaster. To this day, he could still see every detail of the ground, 1,250 feet below, rushing up to meet him.

Each of the following four jumps was more exhilarating than the previous one. Tim loved the feeling of tumbling through the air, waiting for the comforting tug and upward pull of his opening chute. During each jump, Tim laughed loudly, almost uncontrollably shouting directly into the wind, his adrenalin pumping his exhilaration. He couldn't believe it was him, Tim DePalma, floating in the sky, halfway between the plane and the earth; somewhere between his past and his future.

On graduation day, Tim stood tall and proud. He was anchored to the ground, held there by his new, gleaming, black leather jump boots. His head seemed anchored high in the sky, held there by the new, highly-coveted Airborne Patch which now adorned his military cap. His chest expanded with pride as a colonel pinned on his silver Jump Wings. In a paraphrase of the popular Barry Sadler ballad of the day, "Tim had silver wings upon his chest; he felt like one of America's best!"

RANGER SCHOOL

It was not until three days after graduating from Airborne School that Tim received assignment and travel orders to his next duty station. When he did finally receive his orders, he was not happy. The orders did not assign him to Ranger School as he was expecting. Rather, these orders were sending him to somewhere in California, to some kind of a military post he had never heard of, to something called a Presidio.

Tim had eagerly been looking forward to entering the nine-week Ranger Course, headquartered right there at Fort Benning. Ranger School was physically the toughest, most demanding course the Army had to offer. For Tim, wearing the Ranger Tab told the world what kind of soldier you were, proved what you were already capable of doing, and telegraphed your ability, desire, and promise to do whatever your country asked you to do in the future. It telegraphed that promise to the people you were to defend, to your brothers-in-arms fighting beside you, and to the enemies who would oppose you.

Ticked, Private DePalma immediately headed off to the Fort's personnel office. Once there, he was sent from the Colonel of Personnel Assignments office down to the Sergeant Major's office. From there to the Staff Sergeant's office. From there to the Sergeant's desk. From there to Specialist 4 John Gigliotti's desk. That trip, all of it inside the Headquarters building, took three hours. In those three hours, Tim received a crash course on how the military personnel system worked. He didn't like what he learned. As he waited in office after office, being shunted from person to person, he thought back to Fort Jackson and his talk with Spec 4 Tony Cicionni. Tony had certainly known what he was talking about.

Now Tim was sitting in front of Spec 4 Gigliotti, but he might as well have been again sitting in front of Spec 4 Cicionni. They were identical; they could have been twins. "Geeez," Tim thought, "were all Army personnel specialists Italians?"

Tim told his story. Specialist Four Gigliotti listened.

When Tim was done, Gigliotti said, "That's your problem? Instead of the Army sending you to freezing mountains in northern Georgia and smelly swamps in southern Florida where you're going to march your butt off all day and all night just to wear a little patch on your shoulder, the Army is sending you to sunny California, and in winter yet. Get your head out of your butt and report to the Presidio!" He started handing back Tim's orders.

Tim protested. Gigliotti listened, not believing what he was hearing.

Again, when Tim was done, Gigliotti said, "Let me get this straight. If you can't go to Ranger School, you want me to cancel these orders and write you new ones for Vietnam? You're nuttier than my Aunt Rosie's fruitcake. Let me look at your folder."

After several minutes, he looked up, "So, you're one of Tony's boys. He's got a note in here. Let me read it to you: 'If the Ranger School holds fast to its policy that a soldier must have one tour of demonstrated capabilities before acceptance to Ranger Training, then PVT DePalma should be sent to the six month Vietnamese

Language Course at the Presidio of Monterey, California, instead of to the previously planned eight week introductory course in Texas.' Tony based this assignment on your score from your enlistment Language Aptitude Test."

Tim started to say something.

Gigliotti closed the folder, leaned over the desk toward Tim, and said, "Shut up, Private."

Tim shut up. Then started again, but immediately stopped. He saw the look in Gigliotti's eyes. Nothing good could result from Tim saying another word.

Gigliotti continued, "DePalma, you're new. You've got a lot to learn about the Army. So I'm going to give you a break. Tony gave you a break. By all rights you should be in Nam right now getting your ass shot at. He saw something in your files, maybe in you. If you ever see him in a bar in New York City, remember, you owe him a drink. He likes martinis." Holding up Tim's orders, he continued, "Now, thank your lucky stars for these. Stop being such a dumbass. Here, take these and get out of my face. Now!"

Tim grabbed the orders and quickly headed for the door.

Spec 4 Gigliotti yelled. Tim stopped. "DePalma, remember, when you run out of ammo and grenades over there, see if you can use your six months of language training in California to talk the enemy out of killing you." In a softer, more friendly voice, he added, "And DePalma, seriously, good luck over there."

At that moment in time, neither Tim nor Spec4 Gigliotti could know just how prophetic his words would be.

Summer Tomato Pie

While Spec 4's Cicionni's wife's Tomato Pie was delicious, Tim's family was large and one of his aunts, not Zia Mary, but her sister Angela (Auntie Angie), made a better pie. Angie married and lived 'out west' (that is west of Providence) on a small farm near Scituate, Rhode Island. Every summer Tim would visit and in addition to devouring her famous Iron Skillet Apple Pie, there was the tomato pie that was best when the tomatoes first ripened in late July and August.

Auntie Angi inherited the recipe from her husband's Aunt Lulu, and like with many of her recipes, was able to keep it true to its roots --- yet a little easier. With the advent of the prepared pie shell, the recipe has emerged as a real last minute dish which features the taste of ripe heirloom tomatoes. Angie would never make this with those "store-bought" imitation tomatoes; she always waited until the home-grown ones were ready. Over the years this has become the perfect warm contrast to "Insalata Caprese (see Chapter 17)". With stringy mozzarella cheese and tomatoes, Angie's children really loved it and thought of it as a variation of pizza!

Ingredients:(Four to Six Servings)

1	Prepared Pastry Shell
4 Slices	Mozzarella Cheese
½ Lb	Shredded Mozzarella Cheese
1 - 2	Ripe Homegrown Tomatoes - sliced thin
¼ Cup	Olives, black and/or green, sliced
To Taste	Herbs such as dill and oregano, chopped
To Taste	Garlic Salt/Lemon Pepper
Drizzle	Olive Oil

Directions:

1. Pre-heat oven to 375F.
2. Layout pie shell in lightly greased pie pan (9 - 10

inches).

3. Prick bottom of shell and bake for 10 - 12 minutes.

4. While shell is baking, slice tomatoes and place between paper towels to absorb some liquid.

5. Arrange sliced mozzarella on the bottom of the baked shell, forming a layer of cheese.

6. Arrange sliced tomatoes in a layer atop the cheese, lightly salt and pepper, add chopped herbs and olives.

7. Sprinkle shredded cheese over layer, and repeat with tomatoes, herbs and spices, olives, and more shredded cheese.

8. Drizzle top with olive oil; place an aluminum foil ring over edge of crust to prevent burning.

9. Bake 10 minutes and check that the crust is golden - remove and let stand for 10 minutes.

Tips:

1. Never make this with "cello-pack" tomatoes, they are disappointing; there is nothing like homegrown.

2. You can also add chopped onion, cooked sausage, etc --- making it more and more like deep-dish pizza.

3. Can be served as a main dish or cut smaller as a vegetable side.

4. Looks and smells great on the table.

Country Gravy and Biscuits

Grace introduced Tim to a lot of things, including Country Biscuits and Gravy. Her classic recipe was a tried and true recipe that had been in her family for years. Two prime directives that she would tell folks who unsuccessfully tried to reproduce her dish were "Do not over-stir" the dough mixture and don't be afraid to "Knead the Dough with Vigor," which she did while singing an old family nursery rhyme.

Ingredients:(Four Servings)

2 Cups	All Purpose Flour
3 Tsp	Baking Powder
1/8 to ¼ Cup	Sugar
1 Tsp	Salt
1/3 Cup	Shortening
1 Lb	Ground Sausage
To Taste	Salt/Pepper

Directions:

1. Preheat oven to 400F to 425F.
2. In a mixing bowl, add flour, baking powder, sugar, and salt.
3. With a fork cut in the shortening until pieces are fine.
4. Add milk and stir until entire mixture is moistened; do not over stir.
5. Turn dough out onto a floured countertop; turn the dough over and over, kneading and flattening until dough is ½ inch thick
6. Cut biscuits with an old jelly jar or biscuit form; scrape up scraps, knead a bit, and cut again into shape.

7. On a lightly greased cookie sheet place the biscuit shapes in the center so that the sides are touching. Cook for 12 – 15 minutes or until the biscuits reach that golden color. Take out and keep warm until the gravy is ready.
8. As biscuits cook, in a large skillet, brown ground sausage on high heat. When cooked, turn off heat.
9 Add a sliver of butter and cover sausage with flour.
10. Stir to entirely cover sausage with flour.
11. Add enough milk to completely submerge sausage.
12. Salt and pepper to taste.
13. Turn heat to medium high and stir continuously until gravy thickens and begins to bubble; turn to low to heat and hold until biscuits are ready.
14. Open biscuits and butterfly on plate, cover with gravy and enjoy.

Tips:
1. Don't shortcut the kneading; it imparts a consistent flavor throughout.

CHAPTER 7: RECIPE FOR A SOLDIER:
- SIDE DISHES -

Day One: Monday, 1055 hours, in a Train to Heidelberg

Tim continued on the train to Heidelberg. His train of thought continued to the past, this time back to California.

He saw himself sitting on the bluff overlooking Monterey Bay. It was his last day in Monterey. In two hours he would be hopping a bus bound for San Francisco, then on to Travis Air Force Base in Oakland. There he would leave behind his life in California. There he would board a plane for his new life in Nam. "There" would provide an important time portal in Tim's young life.

His six months at the Presidio of Monterey showed Tim a new side of the Army, a new side of America, a new side of himself. Private DePalma arrived at the Presidio a fully trained, ready-to-fight, Airborne Soldier. He was trained to find, engage, and destroy the enemy, or the enemy's will to fight. That was the soldier's mission; his mission. He felt fully capable of accomplishing that mission.

Six months later, Private First Class DePalma was still all of that. But at the Presidio, the Army added a second mission to the first and again provided him the tools and training to accomplish it. "Tim the Airborne Infantryman" must now also to be "Tim the Soldier-Translator and Quasi-Diplomat." The added mission? -- use his new language skills to help win the hearts and minds of the Vietnamese. To win those hearts and minds, he must first understand them. The Army and the Vietnamese people of Monte-

70

rey would help him do just that.

The Presidio is home to the Pentagon's Defense Language Institute (DLI), which in 1971 provided language training in over 30 languages and dialects. It educated linguists for all the military Services, as well as for a few other government agencies. It was the premier military language school in the world.

Instructors at the school were native speakers recruited from around the globe. Students spent six, one-hour periods every weekday in classrooms of 10-12 students. From day one, classroom instruction emphasized student conversation in the new language. Students spent an additional two hours per day studying language tapes. Language instruction at DLI was as close as a student could get to total language immersion, with the exception of actually living in the country being studied.

A SIDE DISH OF ASIAN KNOWLEDGE

When Tim arrived, the Vietnamese language was the Institute's major effort. There were scores of native Vietnamese instructors and hundreds of military students. The curriculum focus was the teaching and learning of Vietnamese military terminology, manuals, expressions, and conversations. Additionally, the curriculum also spent time building vocabularies in, and an understanding of, Vietnamese culture, history, geography, and cuisine.

Tim and his fellow Vietnamese language students, knowing they would soon be in Nam, had an added incentive to do well. They knew that their future commanders and fellow soldiers would soon depend on them and their language skills. These new linguists would have to be proficient enough to acquire information leading to mission success, as well as for keeping everyone aware and alive. Their efforts to learn were strong, because their incentives to learn were strong.

Tim's effort was strong from the very beginning, but his progress was not. Learning Vietnamese was not an easy task for him. Two problems hindered his progress. First, the Vietnamese speech pattern is a steady rhythm of similar-duration and same-stressed syllables. In English, just the opposite occurs. English sentence rhythm is dominated by stressing different syllables to relay meaning. Second, Vietnamese is a very tonal language in which the same word has different meanings depending what pitch or tone the speaker uses.

The first problem, speech rhythm, was solved by practice. The second problem, tonal ability, was solved after an instructor learned that Tim was fluent in Italian. The instructor told Tim to do his mental translations not from English into Vietnamese but from Italian into Vietnamese, and then from Vietnamese back into Italian. It had something to do with Italian being a more lyrical language than English. Tim didn't care why it worked, he was just happy that it did work. From then on, Tim-the-linguist made rapid progress.

Within two months, Tim was among the best non-Asian students in the Vietnamese program. His growing facility with the language allowed him to delve more deeply into other subjects rather than just language vocabulary and grammar.

Of course, Tim spent most of his time learning as much as possible about Vietnamese military terminology, tactics, and theory. He would spend the time between and after classes asking the instructors for more details. Many of these instructors were former soldiers in the Vietnamese army. They were eager to help him better prepare for what they knew he was about to face.

Tim also learned as much as possible about the geography of Vietnam and how it affected military operations. Geography is always an important factor to a military mind. Although only in the Army for less than a year, Tim's mind was already beginning to grasp military tenets beyond pointing and shooting a rifle. Within a month of arriving at the Presidio, he had posted a large map of Vietnam, in Vietnamese, above his study desk. The map added perspective for the geography he studied in the classroom. Additionally, he posted the locations of as many American, South Vietnamese, and enemy units as he could determine from TV broadcasts and military newspapers.

Tim followed the war on a daily basis. He wondered, where

on that map would he end up? He wondered, in which kind of battles would he fight? He wondered, in those battles how would he act? He wondered, would his unit end up on the nightly news? He wondered, if so, would he and his unit be portrayed as heroes or villains? He wondered, why should he have to carry such a thought into battle?

There were other things besides the language of war to learn at the Presidio. The history and culture of Vietnam permeated almost every class. Additionally, there were lessons outside the classroom. The Vietnamese instructors often invited students to their homes for family dinners. They organized larger dinners and parties at local restaurants, especially for celebrations such as Tet, the Vietnamese New Year. For Tim, these events were examples of his "travel by plates" on steroids.

Vietnamese cuisine is considered extremely healthy. Emphasis is on herbs and vegetables. Little oil is used. The Vietnamese instructor-cooks at Monterey emphasized that holiday tables and the foods on them should reflect the five colors of life: red for fire, black for minerals, green for forests, yellow for earth, and white for water. Some of the instructors would switch those colors around telling Tim, for example, that white was for minerals, black was for water, and green was for grasses and vegetables. However, he soon learned that these different renditions were just examples of how individuals from different parts of Vietnam shared aspects of a general history and culture, in this case the five colors of life, but at the same time interpreted these shared beliefs differently, depending on their region or ethnic group of origin.

Most of the instructors were from Vietnam's southern regions. Thus, the dishes at the Tet celebration which Tim attended reflected "southern style" cooking. The colder climate and mountainous terrain of northern and central Vietnam limited the growing seasons and the kinds of foods grown there. In the South, the warmer climate, the flatlands, the floodplains, and the longer growing seasons lent themselves to the cultivation of more and different crops, grasses, vegetables, spices, meats, and of course fish. The methods of cooking and displaying these foods were also more varied and colorful in the South.

The Tet celebration Tim and his fifty classmates attended at a local restaurant was hosted by five of their language instructors. The banquet room was decorated with streamers, brightly colored paper flowers, and a New Year's bamboo pole. There were the traditional small "good luck" gifts for each student. But the true sign of this Tet celebration went beyond what the eye could see and the hand could touch, it was the bouquet of aromas that permeated the room. The tables were laden with traditional Tet dishes. Four must-have Tet dishes were sausages, stews, meatballs, and spring rolls. Around those four, many more foods were enticingly arrayed. Interspersed among the dishes were small bowls of the ubiquitous Nuoc Mam, a foul smelling, and from Tim's point of view, an equally foul tasting fermented fish paste. There was one large serving plate of Tim's favorite Vietnamese dish to date, Glazed Ginger Chicken. There were also several plates of his favorite dessert, Sticky Rice Cakes. For Tim, that night provided a most memorable Tet party.

Now, several months later, Tim, sitting on the Presidio's bluff overlooking the Bay, looked back happily on that Tet celebration. Those memories of good food and good people brought forth other memories, especially of two smaller dinners, each with its own lesson in Vietnamese culture.

The first of those dinners took place about three months into the course. Tim had come down with the flu and was sneezing, sniffling, and coughing his way through classes. Miss Khiem, his primary pronunciation teacher and his chief source of information on Vietnamese folktales, invited him to come by her house that night. She promised him that she would take care of his flu the Vietnamese way.

That night he arrived at Miss Khiem's still sniffling and hacking. She smiled and led him to the kitchen.

"Sit here, Tim," pointing to one of two small wooden chairs bracketing a small glass-topped table. "We get you started right away on your road to recovery."

She went to the stove, took a sauce pan off a burner, and

poured it's steaming contents into a glass mug.

"Start sipping. This is hot ginger water, ancient Vietnamese cold remedy. It half the secret to getting you well. Other half of secret in other pot on stove."

Tim drew the wafts of heat and aroma from the ginger water into his nasal passages. The ginger stung his swollen membranes, while at almost the same moment the moist heat comforted them. He also noted a tinge of sweetness, but could not tell what it was. He drew in another deep whiff, then took a long sip. This time the liquid ginger stung the swollen areas along the roof of his mouth and down his throat, while at the same time the brew's warmth soothed them. With his first sip, he recognized that mysterious aroma of sweetness as the taste of honey.

"Thanks. Miss Khiem. This tastes great. It also feels great on my throat."

"Good. Drink slowly, but drink all." She again smiled, then turned her attentions to the pot on the stove.

As Tim sipped the ginger water, and it did feel good as it bathed his throat, he looked around Miss Khiem's kitchen and into her living room. From where he sat at the kitchen table, he could not see the bathroom nor her bedroom. It was a small apartment, the kind one would expect a single woman would have; a woman trying to make it alone in a new country.

Over the previous three months, Miss Khiem had shared her story, little bits and pieces here and there, with her students. As reassembled by the students, her story started in Vietnam's poor, rural countryside, not in a major city like with most of the other instructors. Her village had been destroyed and some of her friends and family killed in battles between Viet Cong and American soldiers. The Americans relocated her to Saigon where she worked in one of the hotels that billeted American non-commissioned officers (NCOs). She eventually fell in love with one of the Sergeants. They married and returned to Fort Ord, near Monterey. Tragically, her husband was killed little more than a year later in his second tour of duty in the war zone. Her life once again became collateral damage. She too was another casu-

alty of the war. Drawing strength from the memories of her departed soldier-lover-husband and from her own ordeals, she
stayed in Monterey and started a new life in her new country.
Her story made a strong impression on her students. They, for
the first time, came to understand that it was not only American
soldiers like themselves who risked all in Vietnam. The Vietnamese people, flesh and blood people like Miss Khiem, shared that
risk with them.

"You still with us Tim?"

Tim refocused his eyes. Miss Khiem was now sitting across
from him. Sitting in front of him was a steaming bowl of Pho Ga.

"What's this? It looks like chicken soup?" he said, a little surprised.

"Well, that what it is. We call it Pho Ga. Taste it. You see
Pho Ga has a little more in it than your Campbell's chicken water."

Tim laughed as he took a sip. But she was right. The Pho Ga
burst upon his palate. No doubt there was more than just chicken
and noodles here.

"Wow. This is good. Well, maybe the smell is a little strong,
but the taste is great. It feels good, both in my mouth and in my
stomach."

Khiem smiled. "Yes. The aroma be ...what the English word?
...oh, yes, it what you call 'pungent.' That nice way to say something smell 'awful', right?"

Tim laughed again. "Yes. Let's just call it 'pungent.' What's
in it?"

"Well, in addition to full stewing hen, there also several
pounds of chicken bones and necks. As you know from class discussions, Vietnamese people not waste food. Then there some
ginger, cilantro, basil, limes, Thai chili peppers, and of course
some Nuoc Mam. The Nuoc Mam where pungent aroma come
from. According to peasant folklore, it the Nuoc Mam, along with
the bones and necks, that cure your cold."

Initially, Tim had hated Nuoc Mam, but over the past months
he had come to tolerate it. Basically, Nuoc Mam was the rotted
entrails of fermented dead fish. In his coming year in Vietnam, he

would observe the Vietnamese take the fish, put them in big barrels, and let them rot till the fermented liquid seeped to the bottom of the barrels where it was drained out through a spigot into a bottle. In some regions, he would see villagers just hang the fish along ropes strung between trees, tail up head down. The fish would rot in the sun, sometimes for days. Then the liquefied entrails of the fish would drip from their mouths into bottles. The Vietnamese seemed to use Nuoc Mam in everything. Tim didn't seem to like it in anything. Until now. If Nuoc Mam was going to cure his cold, then he was going to slurp it down.

As Tim ate his Pho Ga, Kheim started talking.

"Tim, you really good in Vietnamese language. You doing very well. Too bad you not stay through full nine months of course, instead of just six months. You learn so much more. Your comprehension and elocution be so much better."

"Yeah," he said. "I would certainly like to stay for the full nine months, but my orders are for just six months. I can't do much about that. So I'm just thankful I have these six months."

Left unsaid was that he wanted no unnecessary attention drawn to his orders. He had no idea what Specialist Tony Cicionni had done to get him to the Presidio. No sense in rocking the proverbial boat. In this case, that proverbial boat was an olive drab behemoth called the Army Personnel System.

Khiem smiled a sad smile. She also knew about the capriciousness of Army orders. They had brought her husband to her, and they had taken her husband from her.

She picked up the conversation again. "I always impressed how you have interest in many things Vietnamese, like folktales and geography. Tonight I want to tell you some other things. In this school you learn much. But some things they not teach you. You learn how South Vietnamese people like government and Americans. That true, especially in cities. Most instructors here come from cities, or before worked for Diem government. What they tell you is right. But they not tell you everything. What they not tell you is also right."

Tim put down his spoon and listened more intently. Something was going on here that was a little different. He didn't know exactly what was going on, but this was starting to feel different from other conversations he had with Miss Khiem or with other instructors. He felt she was talking to him on a different level, on a more personal level, on an unofficial level.

"Tim, you learn Vietnamese language well. You learn Vietnamese military things well. Soon you be in Vietnam and talk language and military things with Vietnamese people. So you must learn Vietnamese people very well too. I tell you things tonight, you not learn in class. So listen, please."

Tim continued to eat his Pho Ga. The Pho Ga continued to sooth his mouth, and throat, and stomach. His mind though was no longer focused on the Pho Ga and its pungent Nuoc Mam. His mind was now totally focused on Miss Khiem and what she was telling him.

"It true that most Vietnamese Army and people in cities support war and like Americans. If they lose war, they will all be destroyed. That important incentive. However, people outside cities different story. If when you get to Vietnam, you soldier in the field, then you must understand difference. People outside cities are villagers, peasants. For centuries they abused by outside invaders of Vietnam. For centuries they also abused by their own rulers of Vietnam. These peasants are farmers and hunters and fishermen. They want only peace. They want peace to hunt the jungles, to farm the lands, to fish the waters."

"In day, villagers nice with government soldiers and Americans. At night they nice with Cong. Sometimes both Cong and government are nice with them. Sometimes both are cruel with them. When you are there, be fair and kind as you can be with peasants, with all Vietnamese. They will be fair and kind with you. But remember, the most important things to them are their families and their land, not Vietnam government and not Americans. They do not always trust Americans. They want to trust Americans, but others have told them the same things you will tell them. Many times those others not there when VC come at night. Many times promises broken. I know you must listen and work

with government. You must also listen and work with peasants.
That is how you will win. That is how you will stay alive."

Tim was riveted to her every word.

When he finished his soup, she opened a bottle of rice wine
and poured them both a glass. As her story flowed, so did the rice
wine. After hours of talk about what her Vietnam was like, he was
tired and, admittedly, a little wasted. She gave him a blanket and
a pillow. He immediately fell asleep on her couch.

As Tim now thought back on that night, he believed it might
well have been the most important lesson he learned while at the
Presidio. That night made him look at every facet of his life in a
new way. This was a good lesson for a young man: judge everything on two levels. First, listen to what authority and the general
consensus tell you is the truth. Then always look for the possibility of an alternative truth. That alternative truth may either con-
tradict or complement the commonly accepted version. Over the
years, he found that an alternative truth almost always existed.
Miss Khiem provided him a lesson that night which served him
well throughout the rest of his life. Additionally, she gave him a
hell of a cure for the common cold, but did nothing for a rice wine
hangover.

The other small dinner that provided Tim yet another lesson
in Vietnamese culture occurred just the week before he was
scheduled to leave. Vien, a friend from his twice-weekly Vietnamese martial arts class, invited Tim to his home for what Vien
promised would be a "home style" meal. Tim didn't know what to
expect, but he hoped for something with little or no Nuoc Mam.
He was pleasantly surprised.

Vien and his wife, Lien, had cooked Tim a meal of meatloaf,
mashed potatoes, and peas. Additionally, within minutes after
entering the small apartment, Tim's eyes followed his nose's lead
and found a just-baked apple pie, still in an iron skillet, cooling on
a wire rack next to the stove.

As Tim enjoyed the Nuoc-Mam-less meal, Vien and Lien
talked about how excited they were to be in America.

"Of course, we still want to maintain our Vietnamese heritage and our family traditions," Vien explained. "But we also want to be real Americans. We want to integrate into American life. We want to speak English well. We want to live among Americans, and someday own our own house and send our kids to American college. We come here for freedom. We come here for what we call the American Dream. We want to eat hamburgers in our backyard and set off fireworks on the Fourth of July."

As Tim listened, he was reminded of similar conversations around the tables of his Irish and Italian families. It was just two generations ago that his family was this family. His grandparents had also come wanting the American Dream. To varying degrees, they all achieved it. May it ever be so. Tim thought of Lady Liberty and how she holds her lamp high for those who want to come for The Dream. He wanted that Dream to forever be a reality for all those risking their lives to come to America; for those willing to work hard to achieve freedom and prosperity for themselves and especially for their children. The feeling Tim had, while listening to Vien and Lien's story, was why he felt proud to wear his country's uniform and to fight against those who would deny liberty and happiness to others. Tim was coming to believe that truly, no man was free until all men were free. However, he also wondered, could the idea and the power that was America really make all men free?

"Well, what do you think, Tim?" asked Lien. "Is my meatloaf a real American meatloaf?"

"Lien, I can honestly say that your meatloaf is as American as any meatloaf I have ever eaten."

Then, as he swallowed the last bite of his meatloaf, he added, "You know Lien, I can't tell just how good an American cook you are until I have a piece of that apple pie you have cooling over by the stove. You have to know there is nothing more American than apple pie."

Lien laughed and went over to get the pie. First, she put dessert plates with vanilla ice cream at each of their places. Then she tried to serve the pie from the iron skillet. It was too heavy for her to maneuver, so Tim jumped up to help. As he held the skillet, she scooped out the pieces of pie. It was a messy affair, but a team affair; and after awhile they were all having a good time together.

When done, Tim told them every apple pie should be as American as that pie cooked by Vien and Lien Tran, soon to be new American citizens in their new country, the old US of A. Tim thought, "Mia nonna e nonni DePalma were probably just like this once, newly happy and hopeful about America!"

A SIDE DISH OF AMERICANA KNOWLEDGE

In addition to learning about Vietnam, Tim also learned new things about America. He loved his home state of Rhode Island. He had never really thought of it as small and confining. However, living in California impressed on him just how big and diverse America was. While training in South Carolina and Georgia, he met people from all parts of the country. Yet, due to the heavy training schedules, he had not been able to venture far outside either of those posts to learn much about the surrounding areas or people. Duty at the Presidio was different. His nights and weekends were free. The culture in California, the vibe, was to ease back, to wander, to explore.

Tim didn't ease back much, as he spent most nights studying his language tapes. However, other nights and most weekends he responded to the California vibe. During those times, he was out experiencing Monterey and its surrounding towns, -their stores, restaurants, movie theaters, and nearby beaches. Some weekends he and his friends ranged as far north as San Francisco or as far south as San Luis Obispo.

The California weather alone was enough to capture Tim's imagination. While his friends were freezing and shoveling their way through the New England winter, he was enjoying high mean temperatures in the mid-60's. Early morning cold and fog around the Bay usually gave way to late morning sunshine and warmth.

Yes, California was very different from Rhode Island. It was very different from the rest of America as well. This not too difficult observation was however astounding to young Tim. His Eureka moment came on an admittedly unusually warm January night, on a beach, while drinking a beer. His Newtonian apple was a warm evening breeze.

Along with that warm evening breeze came a new idea; at least it was a new idea to Tim. The idea was simple: weather had a big impact on how people thought, acted, and lived. He realized that what he had learned about the effect of weather and terrain on the people and culture of Vietnam also applied to America. Just as the harsher terrain and weather of North Vietnam produced a culture, a cuisine, and a people harsher and more ordered than those produced by the warmer weather, open terrain, and rich soil in South Vietnam, something similar must have also occurred in America. This idea came to him when he realized that none of his old friends would be down on Narragansett Beach, spread out on a blanket, sipping a beer that January night.

The more he thought about it, the more this idea grew. The harshness of winters in New England and the toughness of its terrain produced a people and culture geared to the four seasons. In early New England, survival required hard work in one half of the year, in order to live through the cold and harshness of the other half year. To survive there, life had to be ordered, structured, planned. This led to a people willing to follow Puritan ethics, furrow rocky fields, and eventually work in demanding factories. Individual success came over time, through hard work, with an idea of always preparing for the future.

The mildness of the California climate and the fruitful fertility of its rolling terrain produced a different people and culture, ones of easier temperament and outlook. The fear for survival did not lurk behind the turning of a calendar's page. Tomorrow would come when it came, and it would be much like today.

The New England sense of orderliness and steadfastness was born out of its Puritan origins, reinforced by its four-season climate. The California sense of freewheeling spirit and today-over-tomorrow was born out of its gold rush origins and its almost single-season climate.

The comparison of California America with New England America soon led Tim to the realization that there were many different Americas: Cowboy America; Dixie America; Florida America; the Frozen Tundra America of the Dakotas, Montana, Michigan, and Mini-snow-tah; Heartland America; Cajun America; Urban America; and all the other Americas out there.

Tim came to realize that all these Americas were in some way differentiated one from the other by their terrains, climates, cuisines, attire, and sometimes by the very way they thought about things and issues. However, he also believed that, although different in many ways, all these Americas were the same in at least one shared belief: the belief in man's freedom as enshrined in one Declaration of their independence and as protected by one Constitution that "secures the Blessing of Liberty" for them and their posterity. He would then sometimes wonder, "If people stopped believing in that Declaration and in that Constitution, would the American Dream stop too?"

That one night, on that one beach, toasting with that one beer, Tim promised himself one thing: God willing, before he died he would step foot and rest his head in every one of the great fifty American States. As he drained his beer, he toasted to the sky, "Lord, be good to me this coming year, because I only have four down and still forty-six to go."

A SIDE DISH OF SELF-KNOWLEDGE

The more relaxed military atmosphere of the Presidio in particular and the more open cultural climate of the Monterey area in general also allowed and encouraged Tim to find out more about himself.

The Army had taken "Tim-The-Teenager," stripped him down to "Tim-The-Bare-Essentials," then rebuilt him into "Tim-The-Infantry-Soldier." Now it started adding additional ingredients and layers to that basic soldier recipe. The Army added these ingredients through more training, testing, travel, and experience. It would continue to do so as long as it and Tim shared their joint journey together. Although Tim didn't know it at the time, that journey would be a long and exciting one.

The first things Tim and the Army developed together were his abilities as a basic infantry soldier. Now they were going to build upon that core. In doing that, he was becoming aware of a growing new social ability to effectively interact with many different kinds of people. Before the Army, his circle was small, consisting of family, teachers, and a few pals. In the Army, he was thrust into difficult circumstances in disparate places with different people. To survive and prosper he had to make fast friendships, establish strong trusts, learn to help others, and learn to let others help him. Then every time he reached a comfort level, he was relocated and rechallenged. The process of fast friendships, strong trusts, helping and being helped had to be accomplished again. In less than a year Tim accomplished that challenge four times.

The present iteration of that challenge, his tour at the Presidio, was in many ways both easier and harder than the previous three. Although the physical requirements were easier, the intellectual and social challenges were harder. Here he had to learn a new subject, in a new language, taught by foreign instructors, with classmates of differing ranks, all while surrounded by a civilian culture which called him to kick back, sip wine, and enjoy life.

In doing all of this and wanting to do it all effectively, Tim for the first time learned the importance of keeping balance in his life. Tim knew he couldn't study 18 hours a day, nor could he lay on the beaches and drink in the bars every night and weekend. He had to find a balance.

It was at the Presidio that Tim truly came to understand that he, like everyone else, was composed of three intricately interrelated parts: his body, his intellect, and his spirit. All three had to be developed. All had to be developed and kept in balance.

An average of an hour or so of exercise per day kept Tim's body in shape. He knew he must arrive in Vietnam physically fit, immediately ready to accomplish any mission to which assigned. To maintain that level of fitness, he ran three miles a day and lifted weights for another 30 minutes. Two nights a week, he took classes in Viet Vo Dao, a Vietnamese style martial art, at a local Vietnamese dojo. This particular physical activity allowed him to expand the basic hand-to-hand combat skills he learned in boot camp. It also provided him new opportunities to learn different aspects of the Vietnamese language and culture. Additionally, two Saturdays per month, two members from the martial arts club taught him to scuba dive in the beautiful but treacherous waters of Monterey Bay. Scuba diving below the surface waters of the Bay opened up yet another whole new world. Thus, during his six months of study at the Presidio, Tim continued, in new and different ways, to expand his physical abilities and his confidence in them, and in himself. He came to think of his new world as a infinite smorgasbord of many possible dishes, an opportunity to try many and select his favorites.

His intellect, of course, was also being stimulated and broadened by his studies. However, Monterey and the California vibe also had their impact on this part of the Tim triad. In high school, Tim had never been much of a reader. When possible, Cliff Notes were always preferred over the actual book. However, when walking around Monterey or eating in its restaurants, especially around Cannery Row, Tim constantly ran into the literary presence of John Steinbeck. Steinbeck, the winner of both a Nobel and a Pulitzer prize for literature, was Monterey's favorite son. Although he died just a little over two years before Tim arrived, the literary giant's presence was, well literally, everywhere.

Before coming to the Presidio, Tim had no idea who Steinbeck was. He had no idea what a Pulitzer was. Although he had some idea of what a Nobel Prize was, he thought they gave them out for peace, not for books. He came to know about Steinbeck, Pulitzers, and Nobels over a bowl of goulash in a café on Monterey's Cannery Row.

It all happened one night when he was sitting in Kalisa's "La Ida Café," having a late supper. He was reading a local newspaper while eating a bowl of Hungarian Goulash. The goulash was better than expected, as it contained lots of both paprika and garlic. But fate didn't play its fickle role until Tim ate his first piece of the bowl's goulash-soaked bacon.

"Damn, that's good," he said in a voice louder than he had intended.

An old man, probably in his late 70's, sitting at the table next to Tim's, chuckled and commented, "Yeah, it's one of my favorites too. I've been coming here for almost 40 years. They don't cook goulash much, but when they do, it's great."

Then the old man yelled over to a waiter, "Tell Eddie to send out a free bowl of his Hungarian swill for this young kid. For some crazy reason, the kid really likes it." The waiter disappeared into the kitchen.

"You in the Army kid?"

Following Tim's yes, the old man added, "Fort Ord or the Presidio?"

Following Tim's answer, the old man chuckled again and commented, "So you're a talker, not a fighter, huh?"

Tim's face and shoulders went taut, and he was about to say something, when the old man put up his hands, palms out.

"Whoa there, young buck. Didn't mean anything by that. Just that the Army combat units are at Ord, and the Army language students are at the Presidio. But I see pretty quick that you are both a talker and a fighter. You also a lover? Is that why you're here at Ida's?" With that comment, the old man expelled a loud laugh.

Tim responded eloquently with a, "Huh?"

"I mean, is that why you're here at the old "Ida Café"? You read about it in Steinbeck's book, and you wanted to see for yourself if it was still a bordello?" With that question, he laughed yet again, this time even louder.

Just then, the free bowl of Hungarian swill arrived. The old man got up from his table and, uninvited, joined Tim at his table. From that moment a new friendship was born. That friendship would give birth to Tim's new love, a love for literature.

It turned out that the old man, whose name was Ronano Campioni, knew all about "La Ida Café," which was Steinbeck's pseudonym for the real Cannery Row's "Edith's Restaurant."

Edith's was more than just a restaurant. It was also a brothel. Old Ronano claimed that at one time, he was its best customer.

Over the next several hours, long after the café's closing, Tim's table became a raucous affair of Ronano, Eddie the cook, and several other old timers of Cannery Row. They told stories of the old Cannery Row and of its salmon and sardine origins; of its century-long ethnic battles for control among the Chinese, Japanese, Portuguese, and Italian immigrant fishermen; of its booms and busts depending on the nation's need to feed its soldiers canned sardines; of its bordellos; of its prohibition liquor; and of its long hours, low wages, and lost dreams. They all claimed to have been friends of Steinbeck's, to have been the models for characters in his books, to be the last of the old Cannery Row rowdies. Tim believed them.

That night Tim left *Kalisa's* excited. He was excited by what he had heard. He was excited about feeling that he was part of history, if only vicariously through these men and by being in this place. He was excited about getting his hands on a copy of Steinbeck's "Cannery Row."

During his remaining time in Monterey, Tim returned many times to *Kalisa's*. After his new friends learned that he would soon be in Vietnam, he could not pay for a dinner. He was accepted as one of them. He asked them questions about things in Steinbeck's books concerning the Monterey Peninsula, its culture, its people. They provided him answers. They provided him context. They provided him perspective. They provided him insight.

Literary context, perspective, and insight were all new to the young Tim. He internalized them without really knowing what they were. He immediately began developing these new skills as he devoured Steinbeck's books about Monterey and the surrounding areas. Books including Cannery Row, Tortilla Flat, Sweet Thursday, and eventually on slow nights in Nam, East of Eden. Some of the subject matter was difficult to plow through, but his friends at *Kalisa's* were like work horses helping him furrow this new soil. *Kalisa's* became like a college classroom to him. Cannery Row and Monterey became a constant literary field trip. The rowdies, as he came to call them, became his professors emeritus.

In addition to his body and his intellect, his spirit also struggled for Tim's attention and time. For Tim, his spirit was more difficult to understand and thus develop. Was his spirit his soul? He certainly had let the care of his soul wane over the past year, especially if he used the teachings of his former grade-school nuns, his former high-school Christian Brothers, and his former parish priests as a guide. Yet, their lessons did guide his present choices in many areas, if only subconsciously. Or were those choices perhaps made under the forceful mental image of his mother's stern look whenever he was faced with California's new-life temptations? California's pot, free love, hippies, and new-age religions were not things she would likely approve.

Yet, was his spirit more than just his soul? Was it how he felt about himself? How he felt about his country? Was it a hodgepodge of how he felt about everything? Was it just feelings? He soon came to the conclusion that he really didn't know what his "spirit" was, only that he had one. However, he felt it had something to do with exploring new places, meeting new people, learning new things. Then, it was about choosing between and among all these new experiences as to what was acceptable to internalize and become part of his hard to describe "spirit."

Tim was learning a basic truth: Life was all about choices. The corollary to that truth was: Life is a long struggle in learning how to make good choices.

Yes, it had been quite an exciting six months. Then, with reluctance and a deep sigh, Private DePalma realized that time for reminiscing on the Presidio's bluff overlooking the Bay had come to an end. Tim stood and faced east. His thoughts soared above the town of Monterey, over the Santa Lucia Mountains, higher over the Rockies, down across the plains, and on to New York City. He yelled as loud as he could and with full emotion and sincerity, "Thank you Tony Cicionni, wherever you are, you marvelous master chef of soldiers' lives!"

Tim then turned away from Monterey and towards Nam. He took the first step on the rest of his journey.

Mother's Meatloaf

The night with Vien and Lien caused Tim to remember a staple from his mother, her wonderful meatloaf. This hearty favorite is best served with simple potatoes and a green vegetable. Tim's Mom never made this recipe exactly the same --- but all loved it when it was served hot and even more cold, between two pieces of white bread slathered with mayo or ketchup. The meat would vary based upon what was left in the freezer – ground beef, sausage, and ground veal can be used. Tim's favorite is equal amounts of all. When Tim's nephews were growing up Tim re-named it "Meatloaf Surprise" by adding a whole dill pickle in the center! It is also a great way to get children involved with the "mixing," especially with their hands!

Ingredients:(Four to Six Servings)

1 – 1 ½ Lbs	Ground beef, sausage, and ground veal (1/2 lb each)
1 Cup	Milk
1 Tbsp	Worcestershire Sauce/Steak Sauce
1	Onion – sliced and diced
1 Tbsp	Chopped herbs/dried Herbs du Provence
½ Tsp	Ground Mustard
To Taste	Salt/Pepper
1 Tsp	Minced Garlic
1	Egg
3 Pieces	Bread / muffins / stale croissants, etc; cut/torn into small pieces

Directions:

1. Heat oven to 350F.
2. Mix all ingredients in a large bowl.

3. Place mixture in a loaf pan.
4. Bake uncovered 60 to 75 minutes or until beef/sausage/veal is cooked (160F on a meat thermometer)
5. Drain excess fat from meat loaf.
6. Let stand a few minutes.
7. Cut in loaf pan and serve.
8. For leftovers, allow to cool, remove from pan, and serve as a sandwich meat, reheat with gravy, etc

Tips:
1. Depending upon tastes you can add peppers, celery, etc. or whatever is in the veggie drawer.
2. This is a very forgiving recipe – if you have too little/ too much meat – make in a smaller pan/use an additional pan.
3. See the Herb Garden page (Chapter 12) regarding herbs, their use, and a great patio herb garden for some thoughts and background regarding why these recipes use herbs so much.

Great Aunt Lulu's Iron Skillet Apple Pie

Family visits were a big thing in the early 1960's and visiting Scituate was an all day trip. Fall trips were the best, not only for the foliage but knowing that Great Aunt Lulu would bake a pie with apples from her orchard accompanied with a scoop of homemade ice cream. Not only was it in a cast iron skillet but it was cooked on/in a coal-fired stove and the aroma from the right side of the oven highlighted the meal. Brought forward to today this is still one of the best desserts. Tim's recipe uses the same basic preparation but rather uses a prepared pie crust and whatever baking apples are available. Tim likes to prepare this just ahead of the meal and have it cooling on a rack when guests arrive (yes --- he does love the comments that follow).

Ingredients:(Six to Eight Servings)

3 – 4 Lbs	Baking Apples (Granny Smith, Braebum, Gala, Fuji, Honeycrisp, etc)
1 – 2 Tsps	Ground Cinnamon
¾ Cup	Granulated Sugar
½ Cup	Butter
1 Cup	Light Brown Sugar
1 Pkg	Refrigerated Pie Crusts
1 Egg White	Wash for top
2 Tbsp	Granulated Sugar

Directions:

1. Preheat oven to 350F.
2. Peel apples, cut into wedges, and toss with cinnamon and granulated sugar.
3. On the stove melt butter in a large cast iron skillet (10 inch best), add brown sugar, and cook until the sugar dissolves and the caramel is smooth.

4. Remove from heat and place one of the prepared piecrusts over the mixture in the skillet.
5. Place the apples on top and arrange to make the top as smooth as possible.
6. Place the second piecrust atop, crimp the edges, brush the egg white, and sprinkle with the remaining granulated sugar.
7. Cut slits in the top (Tim usually makes slits to correspond with the number of pieces he plans).
8. Bake at 350F for 60 to 75 minutes – until golden brown and bubbling.
9. Cool on a wire rack for at least 30 minutes before serving.

Tips:
1. Serve from the skillet – this does not serve neatly. If you want a nice, even, non-runny pie slice – look in the frozen section of the supermarket.
2. Serve with a scoop of French Vanilla ice cream.
3. Makes easily in a 10 inch pie plate - reduce the butter and light brown sugar and cook to 60 minutes.
4. Put a cookie sheet under it in the oven in case it bubbles over. If it browns too quickly you can cover the top and/or the edges with aluminum foil.
5. Cover and store remainder for up to a day or two.
6. Don't attempt with a Teflon or lightweight skillet --- needs an iron skillet.

Hungarian Beef Goulash

*Tim's mother went to housekeeping with her favorite cookbook –
The Boston Cooking-School Cook Book of 1937. When Tim married
Brileen her favorite cookbook was a battered 1961 edition of The
French Chef Cookbook by Julia Child. Over the years recipes have
morphed and times have changed, but it wasn't until Tim started
cooking in earnest that he began to realize how different, yet similar, some of the recipes really were. So with the advent of the
crock pot and the desire to produce fine meals in as easy a form as
possible, Tim developed his own Hungarian Beef Goulash, combining the simple paprika flavor of the original goulash with the more
complicated, yet enduring taste and style of classic Boeuf Bourguignon.*

*As you will see in the tip section this has many variations --- but
by using the crock pot and some last minute additions this can truly be a painless process. And yes, in keeping with an old tradition,
you deglaze the pan with about four ounces of red wine, saving
the rest of the glass "for the cook."*

Ingredients:(Six Servings)

2 – 3 Lbs	Chuck Eye Roast or Steak - cut into one to two inch cubes (don't be fussy, go with the natural divisions of the meat)
1 Large	Onion, chopped fine
3 Strips	Bacon – cut into one inch lengths
3 Tbsp	Flour
2 Tsp	Crushed Garlic
3 Tbsp	Butter
3 Tbsp	Paprika (Hungarian)
1 Cup	Red Wine
4 Cups	Beef Broth/Bullion
To Taste	Salt and Pepper
1 Small Can	Whole New Potatoes
1 Small Jar	Pearl Onions

Directions:
1. Toss cubed chuck eye in flour to coat.
2. Pan-fry cut bacon stripes until fat is released; remove bacon pieces to crock pot.
3. Add chopped onions and garlic and fry until soft and translucent; remove to crock pot.
4. Add butter and sear beef in bacon/butter until all sides are brown; remove to crock pot.
5. Deglaze pan with red wine – reducing by half; drain liquid through sieve into crock pot.
6. Add beef stock to cover meat in pot, adding liquid as necessary.
7. Bring to a boil, add paprika, then reduce heat and simmer for three to four hours.
8. One hour prior to serving add pearl onions and small whole or cut potatoes.
9. Thicken/thin sauce as desired; serve with egg noodles, wild rice, or plain.

Tips:
1. Reserve liquid from the pearl onions and potatoes – use in the beef stock. Tim prefers the instant bouillon granules for preparing the stock (saves room in the cupboard and refrigerator).
2. To avoid having to thicken in the end, Tim sometimes uses a small can of beef gravy.
3. For a less starchy product – omit the potatoes and add one cup of sliced mushrooms. This also would allow you to serve mashed potatoes as a side for those who love those carbohydrates.

4. This recipe can easily be converted to a beef stew by adding more vegetables as desired.

5. Complete the meal with a simple green salad, hot French bread or garlic toast, and the rest of the bottle of red wine you used in the sauce.

CHAPTER 8: - A PLACE TO SEEK, FIND, AND AVENGE

Day One: Monday, 1110 hours, in Heidelberg

Tim stepped off the train onto the platform. He faced the sign which read "Heidelberg." A kind of Deja Vu moment was being lived. Tim had been on this platform, in this train station, facing this sign before. It was back in the summer of 1985. Brileen had been gone a little over a year. It was his first real reassignment since she had left him. Well, she never really left him. She was there that day with him on this very platform. Back then, he thought a new assignment in Europe would help him cope. It had. A little.

But that was then, and this is now. With a shiver, Tim shook the feeling from his mind and with suitcase in hand, he didn't believe in rollers, strode east from the *bahnhof* (train station) up Heidelberg's *Hauptstrasse* (Main Street) toward the *Altstadt* (Old Town). His body needed the exercise the mile walk would provide. His mind needed the time and fresh air to think. Once in Old Town, he would work to become lost among its many tourists; among its narrow, winding, ancient streets; among its old, nondescript hotels; in one of its many tiny dark rooms. In that tiny dark room he would plan his large dark deed.

The impetuousness of his flight to Heidelberg was very unlike Tim. Throughout his long military career, he had always been composed and calculating under pressure, professionally methodical and focused in approaching and executing his assignments. But that had been business, this was personal, very personal. The raw emotion he felt when seeing Truc's picture was like nothing he had ever experienced. It overwhelmed the normal counsel of his reason and judgment. Across the years, taking counsel from his usually sound reason and judgment had kept him alive. He knew he must again submit to them, but for the moment an awakened, seething hatred still kept them at bay.

Seemingly, all of a sudden, Tim found himself in a foreign country, intent on killing an old enemy, and coming to realize that he intended to do it slowly and cruelly. Somewhat insanely, he now realized, he was here with no preparation, with no cover story, with no plan. Tim knew that a goal without a plan was failure waiting to happen. Here failure could mean death, his death, or probably even worse, as far as he was concerned, his imprisonment. However, as he could feel himself getting closer to his target, he could also feel his instincts and training coming to bear. He knew he must now think of this city as a battlefield. He must now develop a battle plan. He must find a way, as warriors are trained to do, to close with and destroy the enemy. He must first locate Truc. Then close on him. Then destroy him. Then withdraw without a trace. Tim didn't think the locate, close, and destroy phases would be too difficult. But he had to ask himself, had his hastiness in getting to this latest battlefield made the last phase, withdrawal without a trace, impossible?

Although most of Tim's combat experience came from conventional battlefields, he had participated in two clandestine missions in enemy countries. Both had entailed an extraction of a high-level military defector. Both were successful. Both times he was able to withdraw without a trace. In many ways this mission, and he now had to think of it like a military mission, should be easier. Germany was an open society. Westerners, especially, could move about without suspicion. If only he had covered his tracks into the country, it would be easier to leave no tracks as he exited the country. However, Tim knew that "if onlys" were a waste of time. He had left tracks. So now he must incorporate them into his plan. He must make these mistakes work for him, not against him. But how?

Although still deep in thought as he approached the old part of the city, Heidelberg's charm and beauty began to force their way into his consciousness. "Too bad you have to hide; too bad you can't enjoy this city again," he thought. As Tim shifted the weight of his suitcase from his right hand to his left, his thoughts shifted from one side of his brain to the other. Then he smiled. "That's it," his mind blurted out, "as the old saying goes, sometimes the best place to hide is in plain sight." With each, now brisk, step up the cobblestoned Hauptstrasse, he was already fleshing out his new plan.

Tim had flown here first class and under his own name. Those mistakes were two problems for any assassin. He had flown first class because that was the only seat available; however first class made it easier for the flight attendants to remember him. Second, he had used his own name because there had been no time to obtain a false passport. Those tracks had already been laid and could be easily followed by an investigator, if it came to that. He now recognized the stupidity of those actions. However, the professional within him was now working to correct them. A plan, folding these mistakes into its story line, was quickly coming together.

In this new plan he would become Tim DePalma, American tourist on a first class European vacation. First stop Heidelberg. Then Rome. Then Dublin. He was an American tourist revisiting the city of a former military assignment, as well as the cities of his Italian and Irish ancestors. The cover story was taking shape. If done correctly, the death of some old Vietnamese art dealer, while Tim was passing through Heidelberg, would in no way be connected to him. However, if something should go wrong, and Tim, now the rather ostentatious American tourist, somehow became associated with such an unhappy event, would anyone think it more than a coincidence?

Tim now ditched the idea of hiding out in a dark room in a nondescript hotel on an ancient back street. He smiled as he spied his new destination, one of Heidelberg's most celebrated establishments, *Hotel Zum Ritter St Georg*.

Hotel Zum Ritter St. Georg, known to most Americans as The

Hotel Ritter or just The Ritter, was over 400 years old. It had a long and storied past, surviving many natural and man-made disasters from the French sacking and burning of Heidelberg in the late 1600's to the Allied occupation following World War II. The front of the building was visually stunning, causing many tourists to disrupt traffic as they stood in the cobblestone street having their pictures taken against the backdrop of the hotel. The sandstone facade rose five stories with various flutes, columns, carved cornerstones, intricate window treatments, and flapping flags causing one's eyes to hop, skip, and jump their way to the top floor where just one grand apartment window stood watch above the rest. Tim had always wanted to stay in that top room. Today might be the day.

Tim walked beneath the hotel's namesake sign of St. George slaying the dragon and then passed through the ornate wooden doors into the small lobby. On the left was a registration desk and to the right a restaurant. The hotel looked like a museum. Carved wood paneling, wood ceiling beams, colorful stained lead glass windows, standing suits of armor, and other antiques spread across the room surrounded him, contributing to his feeling that he had just walked into the past, into old Europe.

The room on the hotel's top floor was available. A somewhat rickety lift took Tim to the fourth floor. A dark, narrow staircase, irritating to negotiate with a suitcase, took him the rest of the way. The room was a little dank, so he opened the window. The room had no air conditioning, but there was a fan. He turned it on and pointed it toward the window. Then he stood at the window, in front of the fan, defeating its purpose. The window provided both a limited and limitless view of the city. Immediately across the street, blocking a straight view, was the Church of the Holy Ghost and its huge bell tower. Looking to his left over the tops of other buildings Tim could see the distant Neckar River. Below was the busy Hauptstrasse with its many shops and restaurants flowing to the left. The city's main market place and trails up to its majestic castle flowed to the right. He was in the center of this charming old town. Or more correctly stated that day, he was in the center of this challenging new battlefield. He fell into the center of his bed, exhausted, and instantly asleep.

Hours later Tim stirred. His hands went to his head. "What was that noise? Bells!" His eyes opened. "Bells? Geez, that's right. I'm in Heidelberg." He sat up, reached forward, and slammed the window shut. The bells were quieted but not stilled.

Tim looked at his watch. It read 1600. Was that 4 PM Providence time or 4 PM Heidelberg time? Then he remembered. He had changed his watch to European time while on the train. He looked out the window, bending his head around the Church tower, toward the river. The sun was getting low on the horizon. Probably around three or four hours of daylight left. He had only slept about two hours, but they had been a sound two hours, before the tower bells rang him back to consciousness.

The needs of his body were pulling Tim in two different directions, and his mind in yet a third. His stomach was arguing for food, his muscles for exercise, and his mind for a plan. Tim decided on a way to satisfy all three. He pulled on his running clothes and started down the stairs. After reaching the lobby, he stopped in the restaurant for a brief moment to reserve a table for 7 PM, and then he was out the door and jogging toward the town's old bridge, the *Alte Brucke*.

In the middle of the bridge, Tim broke one of running's sacred rules. He stopped to admire the scenery. The Neckar River flowed below the bridge, from east to west through Heidelberg. The Heidelberg Bridge, the Alte Brucke, was arguably one of the most beautiful in Europe. On the bridge's southern or town side, the bridge ended by passing through a one-lane-wide, stone archway with a drop gate. The archway was shouldered on either side by 3-story high, circular towers, giving the impression of leaving or entering a castle over a guarded moat bridge. On the opposite side, the northern side, the bridge anchored itself into the stone-fortified banks of low hills. The bridge itself was a long, gentle arch formed and supported by nine smaller archways of large, red sandstone blocks, under which flowed the river's traffic, ranging from three-story-high sightseeing boats and barges to small racing skulls and row boats.

Standing in the middle of the bridge, Tim could look east and see the Neckar River winding its way toward him through the bordering hills. Looking west, he could see several racing skulls being pulled into the sun's glare as the river flowed toward the flatter lands of the Neckar Valley and eventually into the Rhine. South was that arched, towered gateway symbolically protecting entry into the heart of the old city. On a hillside behind and above the city, rose its majestic castle, now providing protection only to the city's fabled past. To his north were the running paths Tim sought today. He sighed and again started pumping his legs.

After crossing the bridge and then running east for about a mile, paralleling the river, Tim turned back toward the Alte Bruche and dinner in the Ritter's dining room. After about a half mile, he unexpectedly came upon Heidelberg's famed "Philosophers' Walk." He slowed his pace and, although certainly not a philosopher, soon was at a slow walk. Finding a bench, he flopped down. He tried to remember the story of "Philosophers Walk," but only bits and pieces came to mind. Apparently, his mind wanted him concentrating on other things; on more important, more immediate things ...like battle plans.

Heidelberg had been a university town almost since its founding, and "Philosopher's Walk" had been used for centuries by Heidelberg's philosophers, professors, and students. Heidelberg's professors were known to emulate Socrates, on nice days freeing their students for wandering walks and wondering discussions along this path paralleling the Neckar, hoping the students' ideas would flow as fast and as far as the river's waters.

As Tim sat on the bench along "Philosophers Walk," he too began philosophizing in a simple kind of way. He began questioning himself. Sometimes such questioning led to better decisions; other times it led to debilitating indecisiveness. Today where would these questions lead? "Am I really going to kill Truc? What would Quan think? She really wouldn't want that, or would she? Hadn't that war ended a long time ago? What good would Truc's death serve now? Can't I just leave it alone? What does Brileen think about all this?" Those thoughts, questions, answers became all jumbled as they tumbled through his mind. Was he wavering?

Then a force, dark and foreboding, welled up from somewhere deep inside him, forcing those questioning thoughts from his mind, replacing them with compulsions of chilling coldness, compulsions of unthinking hate, compulsions for revenge. With a renewed firmness of will, he started running again toward the Old City and toward an act of revenge over which he seemed to have no control. Although he knew compulsions often led to disaster, he seemed unable to temper his, much less control them.

MONDAY EVENING

Tim showered, shaved, and by 7 PM was sitting at a linened and crystalled corner table in the Ritter's dining room. Tim loved this room with its rich brown wood-paneled walls; its stained glass windows; its trophied deer, pheasants, and hares; its standing suits of armor; its paintings preserving a time lost to the past. The lighting made the room seem warm and friendly. It was good that he had made a reservation, for all the tables were full. The background din of talk and laughter gave the room a feel of conviviality. At the moment, he needed some of that.

Tim used his rusty, broken German to ask questions about the menu. The waiter used his almost perfect English to guide Tim through the many choices. They both seemed to enjoy the linguistic back and forth. Tim ordered a dinner much like one he remembered having here years ago. He thought the meal would be much like the ones medieval knights must have eaten after a successful hunt in the prince's woods surrounding the old Heidelberg Castle. The Ritter restaurant was a perfect setting for such a meal, in that the word "*Ritter*" was German for "Knight."

Lost in his thoughts of old Heidelberg and his earlier tour here, Tim was surprised when his dinner began appearing on the table. Placed before him was a plate of roast deer and an escalope of venison with juniper-sour-crème sauce. There were two small side dishes; one of glazed vegetables and one of hazelnut "spatzle," a German noodle delight. An inner voice reminded him, save room for dessert which would be a Grand Marnier Parfait with ragout of oranges, black current sauce, and whipped cream.

As Tim reached to take a sip of wine to start the meal, the gold band on the small finger of his left hand glinted in the candlelight. He thought again, as he often did, of Brileen and the ring's inscription, T3P2-&US-4EVER. If only she were here to share these plates with him. He knew her love, their love, would overcome his present darkness. As he brought the wine to his lips, the darkness slightly lessened. His face remained impassive, but his heart sighed. As he returned the glass to the table, the green emerald heart held in the hands of Brileen's claddagh sparkled. That was just too much. His face broke, because his heart broke. He lifted the napkin to wipe his lips, and then furtively his eyes.

After dinner, Tim needed a walk. He needed to settle his food. He had eaten too much and felt just a little uncomfortable; but damn, that dinner was great. He also needed a little air to clear his mind of those thoughts of Brileen. In more than one way, they were a little unsettling. They seemed to again soften his resolve. Finally, he also needed to begin surveiling the shops, stores, and bustle of the Hauptstrasse. According to his plan, they were going to become part of his alibi, if unfortunately he would require one. He needed to walk through or look into some of the stores and restaurants and determine how they could be useful to his cover story.

After more than an hour of walking the Hauptstrasse and its side streets, he found himself again standing on the Alte Bruche looking at the Neckar flow below him. He had his plan.

As the river flowed, so did the plan's details. Tomorrow, Tuesday, he would inconspicuously hop a train to Mannheim, 10 miles to the south. There he would buy the items needed to construct a disguise. The disguise would not be world-class like those used to support Pentagon or CIA operations, but he believed his hasty efforts would still be effective. Even if he somehow became associated with Truc's death, it was highly unlikely that investigators would think to look for a Mannheim connection. Tim would just have to be sure, as best he could, that no parts of the disguise could be traced back to Mannheim, or to him.

Tomorrow night, Tim would meet with an old Army buddy who had retired in Heidelberg. It would seem normal that Tim would visit old friends while here, strengthening his cover story of being merely a tourist.

Then the following day, Wednesday, Tim, in disguise, would begin staking out Truc's art gallery, hoping to spot and tail Truc, determining where he lived and some patterns of his daily life. Tim had allotted three days (Wednesday, Thursday, and Friday) to determine when, where, and how he would terminate Truc. Tim always winced at that word "terminate." Government euphemisms almost always seemed ridiculous to him. Tim planned to "terminate" Truc on either Thursday or Friday, but he might do it earlier if a really opportune moment presented itself.

Finally, rather than immediately leaving Heidelberg after the "termination," as any prudent assassin would do, Tim, in order to give more credence to his cover as a tourist, would spend one additional day in Heidelberg and then fly to Rome.

One important item was still unresolved. The weapon. Tim would prefer to have a gun. Guns provided an easy way to control a victim, as well as to kill him. Guns also provided a means of needed protection for the assassin should the intended victim have a gun of his own. A gun was also useful if a target could not be separated from a group, meaning the whole group would need to be controlled or eliminated.

However, Heidelberg was not Chicago. A gun would not be easy to obtain here, especially for a foreigner. Tim might be able to impose upon one or two old friends to obtain a gun for him, but that raised all kinds of problems. The friend would be one more person who would know, or at least guess, about his motives. The more people involved in the plan, the less secure the plan. Obtaining a gun might take several days or longer. Tim wanted this over as soon as possible. A gun really needed to be tested, in order to have confidence that it would work effectively when needed. Undetected testing of a gun in the Heidelberg countryside might prove impossible. Tim decided. There would be no gun.

A knife or his hand would probably be the weapon. Perhaps a situation would present itself wherein Truc's death could be staged as an accident. Tim doubted that, as he had already decided that he wanted time with Truc before he actually killed him. He was loathed to admit it even to himself, but he wanted Truc to feel excruciating, unrelenting pain, administered over as long a period as possible. He wanted Truc to beg for mercy, knowing that he would not give him any.

Tim also planned for the post termination cleanup. With forensics being what it is today, Tim had to ensure he left no trail behind. Fingerprints were the least of his concerns; they could be handled by latex gloves. DNA was the issue. Tim could not let Truc grapple with him in any way that would leave some of Tim's skin under Truc's fingernails or Tim's blood or saliva anywhere on Truc's body or clothes. Even falling hairs must be controlled, possibly with a hairnet, if the final scenario allowed.

After Tim returned to his room atop The Ritter, he undressed and sat on the bed. From a hidden slot in his suitcase, "Doesn't everyone have one of these?" he smiled to himself, Tim withdrew the newspaper picture of Truc. Earlier, Tim had cut out just the picture with its caption and disposed of the rest of the Providence Journal pages, making it more difficult to track the picture to its source. Tim stared at Truc. His eyes moved to the caption below the picture, "Rare Spanish Surrealist Painting Sold at Auction in Heidelberg: Owner of Heidelberg art gallery smiles as painting fetched higher price than expected." Tim's eyes went back to Truc's smiling image. They narrowed and darkened. "Soon we will meet again. Believe me, you will not be smiling then."

Tim slipped the picture back into its hiding place. He felt confident that he had a good, flexible battle plan which had an excellent chance of success. Stretched out on his bed, he reviewed the plan once again. His mind finally agreed with Tim and allowed him to find, somewhat paradoxically, the sleep of the righteous.

TUESDAY MORNING

Day Two: Tuesday, 0700 hours, in Heidelberg

The Holy Ghost's bells allowed Tim a good 8 hours sleep before they rang him to consciousness. His outstretched arm's third attempt successfully slammed the window shut against what Tim had come to think of as the "holy howling."

After a quick run and welcomed shower, Tim began his day with two calls on his mobile phone. The first was to his office in the Pentagon. After retiring from the Army, Tim had accepted a job as a private contractor working as a liaison officer between the Pentagon and the President's National Security Council (NSC) in Washington, D.C. In fact, it was the same job he had held as an Army Colonel before retiring. Washington worked in funny ways. His call connected with an answering machine, so he left a message that he was changing his three week vacation itinerary from the previously scheduled trips to Providence and Bar Harbor, Maine to new itinerary of trips to Heidelberg, Rome, and Dublin. That ought to get the office talking, not that anyone really cared what he did on his vacations. Being a retired colonel, or even an active duty colonel, in D.C. was often more like being a little cog than being a big wheel. Tim always laughed when he heard that phrase, realizing how true it really was.

His second call was to Geno Betito, an old Army friend who had retired in Heidelberg rather than take an unwanted assignment to the States. Geno was ecstatic to hear from Tim and agreed to meet him at The Golden Fleece that night at 2000 hours (8 PM).

Before exiting the room, Tim tossed his phone in his luggage bag. He did not want the phone's locating chip tracking today's trip to Mannheim.

Skipping the breakfast buffet at The Ritter, Tim opted for a more traditional, and less expensive, breakfast on the Hauptstrasse. Tim bypassed the Starbucks he had noticed the night before. Yes, a Starbucks, two in fact, now existed on Heidelberg's Hauptstrasse. That certainly was a change from his ear-lier tour here. Tim selected a small German café for breakfast.

As Tim watched his right hand raise a piece of salami from his plate, his eyes momentarily shifted to the watch on his left wrist, 0930 hours; a nice leisurely time for a tourist to be having break-fast. His cover story was taking form. Even though on a tight schedule, Tim couldn't help but take time to enjoy a traditional German breakfast of different varieties of *Brötchen* (bread rolls), marmalade or jam, chocolate spread, cheeses, hams, salami, and honey.

Another 50 yards down the Hauptstrasse, Tim right-turned in-to a clothing store. He bought a tan hat that was really a size too big for him with a floppy all-round brim. As he told the clerk in his broken Germen, it would protect him from *"die Sonne."* That of course was true. However, it was also true that such a hat could be pulled down lower over his forehead, its lower position and wide brim somewhat thwarting the ever-present surveillance cameras. Tim had chronicled several around the city. This wasn't New York or London where there were cameras on every corner and often in between. Yet, cameras were present, and they had to be considered in planning his actions.

After another 50 yards or so, Tim went into a bank and worked a draft against his American Express Card for the sum of 3,000 Euros, not too large a sum for a tourist planning a two week trip across Europe, yet large enough to cover the costs of his plan. Tim broke the cash into six 500 Euro packs, placing each in sepa-rate pockets in his pants, shirt, and jacket. He hoped that by do-ing this he would first, limit any losses to pickpockets who target-ed tourists and second, not draw the unwanted attention from any sales clerk that a large roll of bills might cause.

At 1200 hours, he was at the bahnhof. Looking out from un-der the brim of his oversized hat, Tim bought a roundtrip ticket to Worms, the oldest town in Germany and a tourist destination several stops beyond Mannheim. A destination Tim had no inten-tion of making today. After getting off in Manheim, he would call the Worms' tourist office from a public phone and inquire about the Worms Cathedral and museum. He would ensure the cathedral and museum were open to visitors and then ask about excavations, renovations, etc. that were currently underway. If the need should arise later in an interrogation room, he would try to bluff that he had actually gone to Worms.

TUESDAY EVENING

At 1700 hours, Tim stepped out of the Heidelberg Bahnhof and headed up the Hauptstrasse to Old Town. His trip to Mannheim had been a success. He had acquired almost everything he went for. He was no longer wearing his American tourist clothes. He was now dressed in used work clothes, cap, and boots. He was carrying a used canvas satchel which contained a sweatshirt, sweatpants, a used pair of Adidas, a hooded sweatshirt, a German switchblade, a jewel-handled Toledo dagger, a casual German business outfit, a lightweight duffle bag, and a few other items. These items would be necessary to push to the background the identity of Tim DePalma, American tourist, and pull to the foreground the fabricated identity of John Stiglatti, wildly successful Bronx restaurant owner and amateur art collector of Spanish surrealist paintings.

Tim decided that he would use three personas in executing his plan. First, of course, was Tim DePalma, an American tourist on a sentimental visit to the city of a former military assignment. Second was John Stiglatti, a wealthy owner of several restaurants in the Bronx. Stiglatti was also a collector of Spanish surrealist paintings, the kind Truc had reportedly sold. While in Mannheim, Tim had spent almost an hour reviewing articles about the painting and the artist mentioned in the newspaper about Truc, certainly not enough time, but the most he could afford. The third persona was Giuseppe Gero, an out-of-work Italian laborer, who would be the go-between identity between DePalma and Stiglatti.

Tim decided that both his new personas would be Italians because of his facility with the Italian language. Tim first thought he would make the go-between a German laborer, but then realized he probably couldn't pull it off if he found himself in a complicated social interaction. However, if Giuseppe, a poor Italian laborer, could not understand or speak the needed German for a particular situation, he could start shuffling his feet and bobbing his head and revert to Italian. Most likely, the German with whom he would be talking would not speak much or any Italian, and then Giuseppe could just dumb his way through the situation. Hopefully, any Germans involved would not remember anything the least remotely American about this poor Italian worker.

Giuseppe's go-between role was important. It was designed to prevent any tracking of Stiglatti's actions back to Tim, or Tim's actions to Stiglatti. Whenever Tim wanted to become Stiglatti, he would first pass through the persona of Giuseppe Gero. Whenever Stiglatti wanted to return to being Tim, he also would have to first pass back through the role of Giuseppe.

As Tim, or rather Giuseppe, the slightly bedraggled Italian laborer, approached the heart of Old Town, he took a left and after three blocks found himself in the poorer areas along the river. Giuseppe soon found what he was looking for, a sign saying *"Zimmer Frei* (Room for Rent)" in the window of a small, shabby hotel. All afternoon he had practiced the German needed for the following conversation he knew would occur:

--Giuseppe: Room please.
--Clerk: For how long?
--Giuseppe: One week.
--Clerk: That will be 200 Euros. Paid now. Passport or identification?
--Giuseppe: It's in my car up in the town parkplatz. I'll get it later. Here's the 200.
--Clerk: Get it soon (knowing he was never going to see any identification from this immigrant). Here's the key. Room #5, in the back. Bath at end of the hall. No noise or trouble or you're out.
--Giuseppe: No trouble.

As Giuseppe closed the door to his room, Tim reemerged. The room was worse than Tim expected, but it would serve the purpose. There was a bed, a small dresser, a mirror, and a closet. No window. The overhead bulb was the only source of light, night or day. One major plus for the room was that it was located off the back hall and thus would not be under direct observation from the front desk.

As Tim stood in the middle of the room, he looked at his watch, but his wrist was bare. He forgot that he had put the watch in the satchel. It wouldn't look right for a down-on-his-luck Italian laborer to be sporting an American watch, even if was only a Timex. He took off Giuseppe's work clothes, hung them on a hook on the back of the closet door, and threw the work boots in the corner of the closet. Giuseppe would not be wearing these clothes for the next several days.

Tim quickly put on the old sweatshirt, sweatpants, Adidas, and then the hoodie. These were old clothes purchased at a second hand store in Mannheim. He then removed Stiglatti's casual business clothes from the satchel and hung the pants, shirt, and jacket, one atop the other, on the one hanger in the closet. These were new clothes purchased at a department store. He placed Stiglatti's shoes under the bed.

He stuffed what remained of his 3,000 Euros in the pockets of his hoodie. He then took from the satchel his wallet, watch, and Brileen's wedding band. He looked at the ring for a moment and then put them all in his hoodie pocket, zipping the pocket tight.

Before placing the satchel with its remaining items in the bottom draw of the dresser, Tim pulled the zipper back to the 10th tooth. If the zipper wasn't at the 10th tooth when he returned, he would know that someone had gone through his bag. As he closed the drawer, he placed a small piece of pencil lead between the drawer's facing and the dresser and then gently pressed the drawer closed. If someone opened this drawer, the small piece of lead would drop undetected on to the darkly soiled rug.

He walked to the closet and put a light pencil mark on the clothes rod. He then curled the four fingers of his right hand around the pole to the left of the mark and, with his left hand, pushed the hanger of clothes up against his fingers. If the hanger was more or less than four fingers distant from the pencil mark when he returned, he would know someone had moved the hanger and probably gone through the pockets of Stiglatti's clothes.

Tim then placed his right fist on the floor next to the bed and placed one of Stiglatti's shoes to the right of his fist and one shoe to the left. Again, if the shoes were moved while he was gone, he would know. Finally, he pulled back the blanket and bed sheets, mussed them a bit, and beat on the pillow, hoping to leave the impression that he slept here.

Tim stepped back, surveyed the room, and smiled. The traps he set to detect an unwelcome visitor were part of what they now called "Old Time" tradecraft, or more pejoratively, "Old Timer's" tradecraft. Today's high-tech tradecraft to do the same job would simply entail placing on the dresser a small travel clock with an almost undetectable, motion-activated camera hidden in its face and a digital recorder or transmitter hidden behind the face. With a wry smile he said to himself, "Old Timer's tradecraft will do just fine."

Giuseppe then pulled the hoodie over his head, locked the door, passed by the empty desk, and was soon walking through the streets toward the river and then east along its banks for about 100 yards. At that point, Tim, in the concealment of a stand of bushes and trees, returned his watch to his wrist and Brileen's ring to his finger. He then began jogging along the river, eventually circling back toward The Ritter. Before entering the Ritter, he took off his hoodie and carried it scrunched up in his hand, unrecognizable.

At 2000 hours (8 PM) Tim was sitting with his old friend, Geno Betito, in The Golden Fleece, a small restaurant located about a block from The Ritter. The two old Army buddies had previously served together in Heidelberg. Geno had retired from the Army, remained in Heidelberg, and was now the Army's civilian chief of Intelligence Operations. Would Geno see through Tim's story and wonder why he was really there?

At the moment, Geno was only focused on the meal in front of him, *Wiener Schnitzel* with *Pommes Frites.* As far as he was concerned that was why he and Tim were in Heidelberg, at least for tonight. Geno thought himself quite the cook and prided himself on serving a really tasty wiener schnitzel. When at restaurants he would often order theirs just so he could compare. That's what he was doing now. Truth was, Geno actually was a great cook and he actually did serve up a tasty wiener schnitzel.

Tim asked, "Well, what do you think, my friend, is this fair, good, or great?"

Geno was already halfway through his dinner. He looked up and mused, "Hmm, the veal is juicy, must be freshly cut. The pommes frites are not at all greasy, so the potato flavor comes through quite well. However, the sauce or gravy is the secret to a really great schnitzel. What do you think –good or bad?"

Tim thought to himself, "A typical intelligence guy. They never answer the question asked; they just turn it back on you." Then in a more vocal response he said, "Well, I like this mushroom gravy, mainly because it has a lot of onions. And even though it has a lot of onions, I can still taste the sour cream and even a hint of white wine. Bottom line, I think this is a pretty good wiener schnitzel, especially when served with this German beer." Then he leaned in and added, "Of course, Geno, I don't think it's anywhere near as good as yours!"

Geno laughed, "I see you're still full of that old Irish BS. But this is one time I agree with you."

The old friends talked into the night catching up on old times. They capped off the evening with a couple of shots of Stolichnaya Cherry Vodka, Geno's favorite. When they broke at midnight, Tim was certain the evening would further bolster his cover story, again, if he should need one. However, Tim was confident that he, Giuseppe, and Stiglatti would prevent that from happening.

WEDNESDAY MORNING

Day Three: Wednesday, 0530 hours, in Heidelberg

At 0530 hours (5:30 AM), Tim was exiting The Ritter, passing under the sign of St. George, and ready to begin his jogging pace. He glanced up at the sign and wondered where, how, and especially when, he would be slaying his own dragon. He would start stalking that dragon today.

As Tim turned at the river's edge and started jogging west, he subtly removed his watch and Brileen's ring, placed them in the hoodie's pocket, and then zipped it tight. After another 1,000 yards or so, Tim slowed to a walk. After another 100 yards of slowly strolling along the river, Giuseppe pulled the hood up over his head.

Five minutes later, Giuseppe turned away from the river and into the old waterfront part of town. As he closed in on his hotel, his walk became a little more like a tired shuffle. He rubbed his eyes and several times tugged at his crotch. If anyone was watching, he wanted to give the impression that he was just returning from a night spent at one of the local houses or with one of the local girls, having spent the night adding some pleasure to his otherwise pleasureless life.

At 0600 hours (6 AM), Giuseppe entered his room, flipped on the overhead light, and slowly scanned from left to right. All looked in order. Giuseppe turned the room over to Tim. Tim knelt down and pulled open the dresser's bottom draw. The hidden piece of pencil lead dropped to the floor, indicating that no one had opened the drawer while Giuseppe was gone. Tim pulled the satchel from the drawer. One, two, three, four, five, six, seven, eight, nine, ten. The zipper was still open to the tenth tooth, tending to confirm that no one had opened the drawer or looked in the satchel. He made a fist on the floor between Stiglatti's shoes. Perfect fit. Finally, Tim checked the hanger in the closet. A perfect four finger distance from his mark. He was pleasantly surprised. He had really expected the hotel manager or the clerk to come in and go through Giuseppe's things while he was out.

Tim now focused on bringing Stiglatti to life. Although he knew everything that was in the satchel, Tim went through it again, touching each item, --powder; plastic tubing already cut to fit; a bag of cotton balls; horn-rimmed reading glasses; dark brown makeup; a fake diamond ear stud; six hand towels; a Toledo steel jeweled dagger, "Why the hell did I buy that," he asked himself; a switchblade; a large-faced gold watch; a large ring with a ruby-colored glass stone; a large ring with a dark blue glass stone; and a lightweight duffle bag. He then folded and added Stiglatti's clothes from the hanger into the satchel. Finally, he forced in the pair of shoes. A tight fit, but with a little bit of pressure the zipper did its job. Tim went over the day's plan one last time, then turned the satchel over to Giuseppe.

Giuseppe grabbed the satchel, pulled up his hoodie, and left the hotel. The day before, Tim had selected a morning breakfast restaurant on a side street one block off the Hauptstrasse. It was a middling restaurant where no one would take too much notice of a laborer like Giuseppe walking in, or too much notice of a guy like Stiglatti walking out.

After entering the restaurant, Giuseppe walked directly down the hall to the WC, the restroom. If the room was in use, he would return to the dining area and order coffee and a roll. He was in luck. The WC was empty. Giuseppe turned on the light, closed the door, and locked it. He pulled on the door twice to make sure it was locked. Giuseppe turned the bathroom over to Tim, and silently said, "You have five minutes, maestro."

Tim quickly took off Giuseppe's clothes and placed them on top of the commode. He opened the satchel, took out Stiglatti's clothes and quickly dressed. The clothes were purposely a size too large for Tim. He placed three of the hand towels under the shirt around his stomach. He placed another under the back of his pants over the top of his rump. He took the remaining two towels and put one into each of the upper sleeves of the suit jacket and put the jacket on. The result: Stiglatti looked 15 pounds heavier than Tim. He'd been in the room just over two minutes.

Tim took the can of white powder, shook a little into his palms and mixed it into his hair, which immediately went from a little salt and pepper look to a lot of salt. He took the fake ear stud and held the fake diamond part to the outside of his earlobe, while he affixed the magnet part onto the backside of his earlobe. Voila! A sexy-looking ear stud. He placed the ruby colored ring on his right hand and the sapphire colored ring on his left. He then slid the stretch band of the garish gold watch over the faux sapphire and onto his left wrist. He slipped the switchblade into his right pants pocket. Total time in the bathroom: four minutes.

Tim then took a dab of the dark brown makeup and rubbed it into the fleshy bag under each eye. They immediately looked darker, older, and more tired. Next, he grabbed the cotton balls and shoved two each into the space between the last inch or so of his upper and lower gums and the inside of his cheeks. His face immediately looked fatter. He was at five minutes.

Carefully, he placed a nonprescription, purely cosmetic, blue contact lens in each eye. "Too much like Paul Newman?" He laughed when he asked himself that. "Stop the nonsense," he told himself. "You've passed your five minutes." Quickly, he rubbed a little petroleum jelly over the one-inch-long plastic tubes and inserted one into each nostril just deep enough not to be noticed by someone with whom he might be talking. He wiped away the excess jelly. His nose now looked fatter, flatter, and accentuated by flared nostrils. Finally, he slipped on the black rimmed glasses. Seven minutes total. Two minutes over his target time, but not bad for a guy who didn't do this for a living.

Tim took another 30 seconds to take a close look at his creation. He was happy with what he saw. "John Stiglatti, you are a handsome fellow, in an ugly, brutish kind of way. Too bad you're also going to have such an irksome personality. Your chances of getting laid while here are nil!"

Tim then took out the lightweight, tan, rayon duffle bag from the satchel and shook it out to its full size. He put the satchel, all the unused articles, and Giuseppe's clothing into the duffle bag.

He handed the duffle bag to Stiglatti saying, "John, now it's all up to you." John took the duffle bag, left the bathroom, and walked out of the restaurant. A tired, thin, Italian laborer carrying a satchel had walked into the restaurant. Eight minutes later, an aggressive, stocky, American businessman carrying a duffle bag walked out. No one seemed to notice either one of them.

Now a minor but crucial part of the plan must be carried out. Stiglatti had to stash the duffle bag in a safe place. The bag had to be stashed for two reasons. First, today Stiglatti planned to locate and tail Truc from his place of work to his home. It would be hard to stay unnoticed lugging a duffle bag around. Second, and more importantly, the duffle bag was a great threat to Tim. The bag contained items connecting Tim, Giuseppe, and Stiglatti. Harmless at the moment, but possibly catastrophic if any one of those three were connected to Truc's death.

As soon as Stiglatti stepped onto the Hauptstrasse, he saw a taxi. This was unexpected, as the Hauptstrasse was mainly a pedestrian walkway. However, taxis sometimes used it anyway to bring guests to the street's various hotels. Stiglatti literally jumped at the opportunity and into the taxi's backseat. He was off to the bahnhof. Once there, he walked directly to the travelers' lockers. He stashed the bag in locker # 3. He smiled as he thought of the three personnas now locked inside locker #3. He then went outside and, again, literally jumped on the bus which was just leaving and would take him back to Old Town.

Stiglatti had been in the bahnhoff less than two minutes. No doubt he had been recorded on camera. Tim was willing to take the chance in order to stash the duffle bag in a safe place. A lot would have to go wrong with his plan before the German *politzei* would be breaking into that locker.

THE TARGET

Back in Old Town, Stiglatti walked around the city, getting a feel for the early morning pace. It would probably be a long day of surveillance. Heidelberg was a tourist city, over three million per year. So he should blend in nicely. However, spending a possible 8-10 hours walking around a 2- or 3-block area might raise someone's suspicions. He would have to be extremely careful, especially at this hour with most of the tourist crowd apparently still in bed.

Stiglatti made his first pass on the target, *Die Kunstgallerie Heidelberg*, Truc's art gallery, at 0800 hours. He maintained the same slow pace he used while passing the previous storefronts. However, here his observations and concentration intensified. There was no sign of life in the gallery. The night lights throughout the two rooms viewable from the front windows were still on. Gold lettering painted on the front door announced that the gallery was scheduled to open at 0900. He moved on to the next store's windows with seemingly the same degree of interest, just in case someone was watching.

After a few more minutes of tourist-style strolling, Stiglatti crossed the street and entered *Kunter's Konditori*, a great smelling German bakery with several tables placed along its front windows. He ordered a strudel and coffee and then set up camp at a table by a window. Stiglatti had a clear view of Truc's gallery located about 30 yards to his left on the other side of the narrow street. He took a sip of the coffee and then a bite of the strudel.

"Wow," Tim thought to himself, "this might be the best piece of pastry I've ever had." The dough was cooked to a soft, sweet consistency, light but not so flaky that it disintegrated into a snowfall of crumbs. The apple filling was still warm, neither sweet nor tart, giving a full apple flavor and aroma. Tim involuntarily began comparing this strudel to the sfogliatelle, a flakey clam shaped pastry, he used to get at the Scialo Brothers Bakery near his old house on Federal Hill. As a kid, whenever Tim would go to Scialo's to pick up an order for his mother, the owner would always slip him a free sfogliatelle. "....hmmmm, now which was better, this strudel or my childhood sfogliatelles?"

"Tim! What the hell are you doing?" he caught himself yelling in a harsh whisper. Tim had let a piece of strudel, admittedly a piece of great strudel, break his cover, if only internally. "Stiglatti, this is your fault. Take control of the situation!" Tim said as he withdrew into himself.

Stiglatti took back control of the situation, as he licked some apple filling off his finger and set his gaze back on the art gallery's front door. At 0845 hours his body tensed and leaned forward. A man had just stopped in front of the gallery and was inserting a key into the door. This man was not Truc.

The man opening the door and going inside was about 6'2", around 220 pounds, in his mid-50's, and had graying blond hair. He wore a nicely tailored light brown suit. The man disappeared into the store's darkness. The overhead lights did not come on. Stiglatti thought on what he had just observed. This guy looked like the world's stereotypical German, -a tall, blond, rugged, Teutonic knight. Was he a coworker of Truc's? An employee? A co-owner? Was this guy's presence going to complicate the plan?

Stiglatti mulled all this over. After a few minutes, an attractive young woman walking down the street caught his eye. She seemed to be heading for the konditori, but then stopped, turned back, and walked over to the gallery. She tried the door and, when finding it locked, reached into her purse and pulled out a ring of keys. She opened the door and entered. She too was swallowed by the darkness. However, within about a minute, the store's overhead lights came on. After several more minutes the woman returned to the front door and unlocked it. Stiglatti looked at his watch. It was 0900.

He remained at his post for another 15 minutes. One apparent tourist entered the gallery, looked around for about 10 minutes, and then left, empty-handed. Stiglatti had been in the konditori for almost an hour. It was time to relocate. In military terms, it was time to find a new observation post. He paid for his coffee and three strudels; yes, he had eaten three strudels.

Upon exiting the konditori, he turned right, away from both the Hauptstrasse and the art gallery, and casually strolled to the corner, where he crossed the street and began to casually stroll back toward the gallery. When in front of the gallery he slowed and focused on the interior. The young woman was standing on the far side of the room shuffling papers in a reception area. There was no sign of the older man. There was no sign of anyone else in the gallery. There was no sign of Truc.

Stiglatti continued to stroll down the street. When he came to the Hauptstrasse, he crossed to the other side, then turned and looked back down the street from which he had just come. He could no longer see the full front of the gallery, but he would be able to see anyone who might go in or out.

He loitered in this general area for the next hour. No one entered or exited the gallery. He entertained himself by allowing one eye to watch a street performer, dressed like a musketeer, who stood upon a box like a statue until someone dropped a coin into a basket in front of him. The performer then drew his sword; performed a few expert fencing moves; comically juggled the sword; then juggled the sword with a dagger; then the sword, dagger, a sheath, and a scabbard; and finally ended with a flourishing move that cleanly dropped the dagger into its sheath, the sword into its scabbard, and both the sheath and the scabbard back onto his belt, at which time he reverted to being a human statue. Stiglatti wondered if Tim would be able to use his knife or dagger so expertly when the time came.

It was again time to change observation posts before someone noticed this American loitering in the area. Stiglatti crossed back over the Hauptstrasse and strolled in the general direction of the gallery, but this time on the opposite side of the street. After just 20 yards he turned into a bookstore, moved to the stacks near the front windows, and peered out. He had a clear view of the gallery which was across the street and this time about 20 yards to his right. Over the next hour and a half, he moved around the store, seemingly reading a little from one book and a little from another. Mostly he remained among the stacks near the front windows, keeping close watch on the gallery. During that time, eight persons, mostly tourists he figured, entered the gallery and subsequently left, only one with a purchase.

WEDNESDAY AFTERNOON

As the day wore on, more tourists filled the streets. This was both good and bad. On the one hand, more people on the streets made it easier for him to blend into the background. On the other hand, more people on the streets made it more difficult for him to keep a clear view of his target. Like a lot of stakeouts, this one was becoming boring. Worse, however, was the realization that if this stakeout lasted several days, he would probably have to devise more disguises, if he was to avoid suspicion.

It was time to move again. Stiglatti bought two books that he had been carrying around the store for the last hour and left. This time he strolled back up the block to the Hauptstrasse and entered the Starbucks on the corner. Tim again thought about how things had changed since he was last in Heidelberg. Of the two new Starbucks, this one was the bigger and nicer. As Stiglatti entered he walked into a split foyer bordered by white banisters on both sides. A set of stairs descended to the right into a large sitting room that in turn connected to another equally large room containing the sales counter and coffee urns.

To the left of the entrance foyer was a small set of stairs that ascended into a cozy room, windowed on two sides. One set of windows fronted the Hauptstrasse, while the other overlooked the side street where Truc's gallery was located.

Stiglatti immediately moved up the stairs to his left and to the empty table by the window overlooking the side street. Although he would like to go to the bar and order coffee and a sandwich, he couldn't take the chance that someone else would grab this table.

As Stiglatti settled into his new observation post, a smallish man exited the gallery. "What the hell?" Stiglatti's whole body became alert. His mind focused, as he leaned closer to the window. He had not seen this man enter the gallery. The man was about Truc's height. His gait suggested a man about Truc's age.

Stiglatti's heart began to beat faster. His body began to get up, while his mind raced over plans for trailing Truc. As the little man turned into the street, he lifted his head a bit. Stiglatti got a good look at his face. It was not Truc. Damn!

Tension drained from Stiglatti. His muscles relaxed. His body eased back into the chair. But his mind was still focused on the smallish man as he slowly walked away. How had he missed this man entering the gallery? He must have entered the gallery sometime while Stiglatti was either in the bookstore or while he was moving from the bookstore to this table in Starbucks. If he missed this guy going into the gallery, what else might he have missed while walking around the book store, or while buying strudels for that matter? The possibility that Truc may have entered the gallery unnoticed while he was moving from one observation post to another bothered him.

Several hours later Stiglatti was still at his post in Starbucks. He had left it for only two short periods, once to get a coffee and sandwich from the other room and once to use the WC. Both times he left his books on the table and asked the person sitting at the next table to watch his spot. Both absences totaled only 10-15 minutes. Had he planned better, while at the konditori he would have bought some rolls or extra strudels, yeah it probably would have been more strudels, and saved them for lunch. Short of wearing a pilot's pee bag on his leg, he still would have had to leave the window for a potty break.

Traffic in and out of the gallery had been light. Around noon, the good looking blonde who had opened the place earlier went to the konditori and brought back two bags, ostensibly containing her lunch and probably lunch for the older guy as well. Did the bags also contain lunch for Truc? Had Truc slipped into the gallery while Stiglatti was getting his sandwich or using the WC? Could Truc have entered the gallery through a back door?

Stiglatti felt he was doing a good job of surveiling the gallery. But Tim was becoming uneasy. Tim the planner was now taking over the operation. Although it was still John Stiglatti sitting at the table and watching the gallery, it was Tim reevaluating the situation and planning the next move. Tim did not like how this operation was unfolding. He had expected to see Truc by now, perhaps even follow him home for lunch, learn where he lived, find out what kind of car he drove, or even determine what kind of physical condition he was in. Tim had allocated three days to tail Truc, learn his patterns, select the spot, and then do the deed. However, he hadn't allocated three or four days to sit in Starbucks and drink coffee or in a konditori and eat strudels. Tim needed to alter his plan, go on the offensive. He gave Stiglatti new orders, then Tim again receded into the subconscious.

Stiglatti went over the new plan. He was satisfied that the plan was flexible enough to cover several scenarios that might develop. He mentally gamed each scenario, planning what he would say or how he would act. He was ready. As he left, he dropped his books on a shelf of Starbucks's little lending library, doubtful that he would ever be back to read them. He walked around the corner and toward the Die Kunstgallerie Heidelberg. As he entered the gallery, the young blonde came out from behind the reception desk and asked if she could help him.

"Guten Targer, Ich eine touristica. Nixt sprechen German," replied Stiglatti, managing in just a few words to change his sex, mix Spanish with German, and convey his total helplessness in a foreign country, all while burning that image of John Stiglatti in this girl's mind should later events lead police investigators to her.

"Good day. No, your German is fine. How may I help you?" she said. Stiglatti used the direct approach. "I understand you sell Spanish surrealism paintings. Do you have any I could look at?"

"Yes, we have a few. Please follow me. My name is Helga. Yours?"

"John, but honey, you can call me Stig," he answered.

Stiglatti followed her, perhaps a little too closely for Helga's comfort, into a back room containing many paintings on easels and more on the surrounding walls. As Helga talked about the paintings, Stiglatti appeared to be studying her more than the paintings, but was really memorizing the layout and trying to locate cameras. There were the two front rooms, this room, and a fourth exhibition room off to the right. Off to the left there were two smaller rooms with closed doors, probably office or storage areas. He saw no sign of the older man or, more importantly,

Truc.

He interrupted Helga, "Honey, these are all nice paintings, but really, I'm looking for something special, something by Pablo Detero. I read where you sold one of his paintings just last week. Perhaps I could talk with the owner of the gallery?"

Helga seemed slightly disturbed by Stiglatti's reference to Detero's works, or maybe by his request to talk to the owner rather than with her, or maybe it was just because "Stig" had called her "Honey" and was mostly leering at her rather than looking at the paintings.

"Yes, of course. Just a moment. I'll get Mister Buckner for you." With that, she turned, walked to one of the closed doors, knocked, and then went in, closing the door behind her.

Stiglatti closed his fingers around the switchblade in his right pocket. He assumed that he was being observed over closed-circuit TV used to monitor the customers as they walked amongst the expensive paintings. Was Truc looking at him now? Would he notice something about the build, or the movements, or the mannerisms of this American tourist that would trigger memories from long ago, in a place far away? If Truc came out to meet him face to face, would the flatter nose, the flared nostrils, the blue eyes be enough to fool Tim's old enemy?

The door to the office opened. Stiglatti braced himself. It was Helga, not Truc, who emerged. In her almost perfect English and with her absolutely perfect smile, she informed him that Mr. Buckner would be out in just a moment.

Stiglatti remained alert, ready for all eventualities. At least he hoped that was the case. After a minute, the tall German walked out of the office and toward Stiglatti with an outstretched hand.

"Good day. I'm Peter Buckner. I'm the owner of this art gallery. Helga said you wanted to speak with me."

Stiglatti was ready for this scenario where the tall German claimed to own the gallery. He started to play the role as he planned.

"Hi. I'm John Stiglatti, from the Bronx in New York. Please, call me Stig."

"OK, Stig. Call me Pete. Now what can I do for you?"

Stig and Pete then began talking about Stig's interest in early 20th century Spanish surrealist paintings. Stig weaved into the conversation how he had been interested in such paintings since his youth when he saw his first Dali, and how his five restaurants in the Bronx now provided him with the means to build a modest collection of such paintings. He even claimed to have a Dali in his collection.

Pete showed Stig the only three Spanish surrealist paintings in the gallery. When Stig showed little interest in purchasing any of these, Pete stated that he knew several art brokers who specialized in Spanish surrealism, and that he could find and coordinate the purchase of any painting Stig desired. This provided Stig the opening he wanted.

"You know Pete, the real reason I came to your gallery is that I thought you or your partner had access to rare Spanish surrealist paintings, especially Deteros."

Pete seemed taken aback for moment, and then said, "But Mr. Stiglatti, I have no partner. This is my gallery. It is true that I auctioned a Detero a week or so ago, but I don't have a large clientele that is interested in Spanish surrealism. That doesn't mean I can't get such paintings for you, because I can. Maybe even another Detero."

Now it was Stig's turn to be taken aback. What did Buckner mean, he had no partner? What about Truc?

"I'm sorry Mr. Buckner. I must have been mistaken, but you see, I have this picture of your partner and the Detero. I ..." as he talked Stiglatti pulled the newspaper picture of Truc from his jacket pocket and showed it to Buckner.

"May I take a closer look," Buckner interrupted as he reached for and took the picture from Stiglatti's hand. He frowned, then smiled, then frowned again. "I'm surprised this picture appeared in a Bronx newspaper. This auction was just last week. But see, this is a bad translation below the picture. This man is the owner of the painting, not the owner of this gallery. Well, he no longer owns this painting either. He sold it at the auction, and for a very large sum, - 100,000 euros."

Stiglatti was thrown off a bit by what he had just heard. Tim, hiding behind Stiglatti's blue contacts, was stunned. Tim had planned on locating, closing on, and killing Truc right here in Heidelberg. He hadn't thought of something as simple as a poor translation from German to English throwing his plan into chaos. Why had he let himself be so easily misled? He knew why. He had let his emotions take control. He should have asked himself why a man who had disappeared so long ago, and no doubt wanted to remain hidden, would open an art gallery in one of Europe's busiest tourist towns.

How was Tim going to recover? How was he going to find Truc now? This man in front of him, Herr Buckner, was his only chance, his only link to Truc. He must be careful to solicit leads to Truc's whereabouts without scaring Buckner into silence.

Tim, talking through Stiglatti, found his voice. "Oh, sorry Pete. I just assumed the information in the paper was correct. I should have called to check the facts before jumping on a plane and coming here. I was just so excited by the Detero. I too would have paid a hundred grand for it. Do you think this guy, what's his name, might have another Detero for sale?"

Herr Buckner, apparently now "Pete" again to "Stig", saw the possibility of another big commission coming his way. He thought carefully for a moment on what he was going to say. He didn't want to scare this rich American away. He also didn't want to deflate the American's hopes by telling him the whole truth. Even if he could not get another Detero from the mysterious Asian, he might be able to get Stig another equally valuable painting, and himself another equally large commission.

Choosing his words carefully, Pete started, "The Detero was an extremely difficult sale. The Detero's owner was a very difficult person to work with, as was the buyer. As in many sales of these types, I did not, and do not, know the names of either man."

Tim's heart sank at this news. Stiglatti just stared at Buckner; the intensity of his stare clearly demanding more information.

Pete continued, "I'll give you what I believe you Americans call a 'recap.' Several months ago a picture of the Detero painting, along with a description and with a base asking price of 40,000 euros, appeared in my mail from an art dealer in Paris. I put the picture of the Detero in my auction brochure, which was then sent to major art dealers and collectors throughout the world, almost two thousand. During the auction, which was held in our Castle's ballroom, the Detero received moderate-to-high bidding. The price seemed to stall at 75,000 euros. Just as we were about to gavel it out at that price, one of our international audio-video monitors received a bid of 100,000 euros. There were no further bids, and the Detero sold for 100,000 euros."

"Then something irregular happened. The bidder said he would only buy the picture if the seller would meet him here in Heidelberg within 48 hours. The buyer wanted to hear firsthand the known history of the painting: who owned it, where had it been stored, why was it being sold, etc. The seller, this Asian fellow here in the picture, balked at this demand. He offered to send his art broker with all the required information. The buyer responded that no middleman would do; that he wanted to look into the eyes of the seller and hear from his lips the story of the painting. The seller, working through his Paris broker, continued to balk. Finally an agreement was reached.

The seller, his translator, his body guard, and his art broker came to Heidelberg and met with the buyer who was Chinese, who also had a translator and a body guard. They met in a sitting room off the Castle's ballroom. I was the only other attendee. There the painting's story was told. A few other questions relating to the painting were asked and answered. The painting and 100,000 euros in cash were exchanged. Then both groups left."

Stig interrupted, "Do you recall either the buyer's or seller's name. I'd like to contact them about buying this or another Detero."

Pete shook his head from side to side, "No Stig. I'm sorry, but in many sales like this one, the names often remain anonymous to us all. However, one way or another, the government's tax agents may find out or they might just turn their heads another way,---is that the right expression? I just report that a sale occurred and the amount of my fee."

Stig interrupted again, "How about the others? Any names for the translators, the bodyguards?" As these words were being spoken, Tim thought to himself, "Whoa there Timmy me'boy! You're getting too excited. You're forgetting to maintain Stiglatti's mannerisms and voice patterns. Be careful. Get back in the role."

Stig, now more like himself, continued, "How about the Paris art broker, shouldn't you have a name there?"

Pete thought a moment. "Names associated with this kind of sale are usually held confidential. This sale was a particularly touchy one concerning confidentiality."

"Why so?" asked Stig.

"Well, I don't usually talk about any of my private sales," responded Pete. "But this seller was a particularly unpleasant man. He was difficult to deal with. On, I think you say, on a personal level, he was not very likeable. First, he wouldn't come. Then when he did come, he hardly spoke with me. He wouldn't give me his name. Usually, I get at least a false name. The buyer was not much better. Then something unusual happened. Following the completion of the sale in the private sitting room, as we all walked out into the Castle's ballroom, there were a number of photographers who started taking pictures. The seller was startled and visibly upset. He tried to move aside. However, the Chinese gentleman put his arm around him and smiled for the photographers. After a couple of seconds, the buyer broke away from the Chinese man's grasp and quickly, and unhappily, walked away."

Pete continued, "The next day I got a call from the seller's Paris broker who, as I think you say, acted me the riot. The seller complained about having to come to Heidelberg, meet with the buyer, and especially have his picture taken. He was extremely upset, especially with the photographers. The seller reportedly stated that he would never deal with me again. But much worse, the broker also said the same thing. I tried to smooth things with the broker, I hope successfully. So in this case, I think I must protect the confidentiality of the broker. My reputation is my business."

Stig persisted. "Pete, I'm a businessman like you. I know how important personal business relationships are. I will not involve you in any way. When I approach this Paris broker, your name need never be mentioned. Look, I really want one of these paintings for my collection. What d'ya say?"

"I would like to help you Stig, but really, that whole sale was tense and didn't end well. I don't want to make it any worse."

Tim was about to reach out with Stiglatti's hand and wrap it around the German's throat and choke the information out of him. He resisted. For the moment anyway.

As the tension eased in Stiglatti's arm, he leaned in close and whispered, "Look Pete, I like you. In this short time I think we've made a connection. We're both good businessmen, so here's the deal. I'm going to buy more paintings, and I'm going to do my best to buy a Detero, even if I have to go to China to do it. The only link I have to a Detero is this Paris broker. See this sapphire ring? My mother gave it to me with her dying breath. I promise right now, with my hand on my dear mother's ring, I will buy my next three paintings through you, if you give me that broker's name. What d'ya you say?"

Pete hesitated, thought, then also leaned in and sighed, "I wouldn't normally do this Stig, but I like you. You have to promise to keep my name out of any dealings with the seller or his broker." After receiving Stig's nod of assurance, Pete said, "Wait here. I'll be right back." He then returned to his office.

Stiglatti started to stroll among the paintings, appearing to study them closely just in case Herr Buckner was watching him over the ceiling cameras.

As Pete returned, Stig strolled back to the counter.

Pete handed Stig a card and said, "Stig, I trust you to be a, how do you say, a man of your words. About everything. Good luck. Auf wiedersehen."

Stig looked at the card and answered, "You can trust me, Pete. I look forward to you helping me build my art collection." Lifting the card and looking straight into Pete's eyes, he said, "Again my friend, thanks. This really means a lot to me. Auf wiedersehen, or should I say, Au revoir." With that, he turned and left the gallery.

Outside, Tim looked at the card one more time before he put it in his pocket. On the back was written a Paris telephone number. On the front was printed:

Madame Bouvier
Paris Galerie d'Art et Centre Restauration
10 Rue DeBilleyne
Paris

Consensus Pot Roast (Braised Beef/Venison)

Tim's fondness for venison successfully crossed the Atlantic - but not the ability to recreate the dish. When he returned from Europe he routinely tried to find the deep flavor of the venison he enjoyed – but never was able to. Not only was venison not featured in the commissary or local supermarket, but on the occasions when he found it at a specialty butcher he could never settle upon a simple recipe. One day in Rhode Island he stopped at a rural butcher shop in search of venison; no, they didn't have any, the health regulations for processing venison had made it just too problematic to process and sell. After a brief discussion on recipes the butcher suggested that Tim try his wife's recipe for pot roast as it worked for venison as well as any meat that was cooked moist. Tim purchased a small chuck roast from the butcher, and, along with the traditional root vegetables, tried the dish that night - it has been in the quiver even since.

Ingredients:(Four to Five Servings)

3 – 4 Lbs	Beef Chuck Roast or Beef Seven Bone Roast or Venison Roast
1	Large Onion, thinly sliced
1 lb	Small Carrots
8 Medium	Red Thin-skinned Potatoes – halved
1 – 2 Pkgs	Dried Onion Soup Mix
2 - 3 Cans	Condensed Cream of Mushroom Soup
½ - ¾ lb	Shitake or Wild Mushrooms
½ Cup	Red Wine (optional)
To Taste	Mixed Fresh Herbs
To Taste	Salt/Pepper

Directions:

1. Preheat oven to 350F.
2. Line a baking pan with sufficient aluminum foil to al-

low you to fold over the covered pot roast and en-close meat in a tent, sealing in the flavors.

3. Spray the foil-lined pan with oil; season roast lightly with herbs, salt and pepper.

4. Place the roast in the center of the pan, surround with carrots, cut potatoes, and top with mushrooms. Distribute thinly sliced onions over the meat and vegetables and sprinkle onion soup mix over all.

5. Pour condensed mushroom soup atop meat – it will spread out during cooking.

6. If desired, add ½ cup red wine; drink rest.

7. Seal foil tent, pop in the oven, and cook for three hours.

Tips:

1. Figure about one pound of uncooked meat per person; cooking will release the fat from the meat and reduce volume – don't be fussy with trimming.

2. Adding the wine creates a nice gravy/sauce – but not necessary.

3. Easy dish to prepare ahead, refrigerate, and just pop in the oven three hours ahead. If dinner is delayed – just turn the heat to 200F. When you remove remember to let the steam escape. Serve with a green salad.

4. Hearty meal; pairs nicely with Cabernet Sauvignon or Pinot Noir.

Wiener Schnitzel and Variations

As a Major and Lieutenant Colonel Tim spent a lot of time in Germany. During both tours Tim was frequently invited into the homes of German Officers. Tim loved the hospitality but all too often he would find himself paired with a cousin of the hostess or a local schoolteacher. As an eligible bachelor at the Headquarters, he suffered bravely. The pairing around the table became a little wary but the pairing on the table was often simple and superb; good home cooking - his favorite being Wiener Schnitzel and its many variations. Years later this remains a favorite.

Cutlet Ingredients:(Four Servings)

4 Veal Cutlets	Approximately ½ inch thick before pounding
1/3 Cup	Flour
1 Egg	For coating
1 Cup	Italian Seasoned Breadcrumbs
¼ Cup	Butter
3 good glugs	Olive Oil
Salt/Pepper	To Taste

Mushroom Sauce Ingredients:

4 - 6 Large	Mushrooms
1 Large	Onion
½ Cup	White Wine
1 Cup	Sour Cream
Salt/Pepper	To taste
Pinch	Favorite Herbs

Veal Directions:

1. Trim and clean cutlets; pound until double the size, about ¼th to 1/8th inch thick.

2. Spread both flour and breadcrumbs on separate plates; whip egg in a wide bowl.
3. Heat butter and olive oil in large pan, do not burn (the olive oil helps in this).
4. Dredge pounded cutlets in flour, dip and coat in egg, and finally in breadcrumbs.
5. Fry cutlets in oil – about 2 – 3 minutes per side – salt and pepper to taste.
6. Place cutlets on paper towels to drain; if necessary keep cutlets warm in a 200F oven.

Sauce Directions:
1. Slice mushrooms and onions, sauté in olive oil until golden brown.
2. Add white wine to skillet, reduce heat to low, and stir in sour cream.
3. Taste and add herbs and salt and pepper as necessary.
4. Serve over plated cutlets.

Tips:
1. Pound veal in a plastic gallon freezer bag – keeps it neat!
2. Can be served without sauce, with another favorite sauce, or a halved lemon.
3. When in a rush use both canned soup or sauces and add mushrooms and onions!

Apple Strudel

As Tim strolled the market streets of Europe on the weekends his nose would almost always encounter the familiar smell of apple pie, but this was neither Rhode Island nor Pennsylvania, nor apple pie. Apple strudel, with its flaky dough and dumpy roll shape, soon became a weekend vice, especially when served with whipped cream. In later years Tim's attempts to produce an acceptable strudel were usually short circuited by the stretching of the European strudel dough. Enter American puff pastry in a box and suddenly the creation became a reality. Practice makes perfect for this recipe but even if it is lopsided and has holes in it – it is all great with vanilla ice cream.

Ingredients:(Six to Eight Servings)

1 Sheet	Puff Pastry (usually ½ of the box)
2 - 3 Apples	Granny Smith, Golden Pippen, Golden Delicious, etc
½ Cup	Sugar
¼ Cup	Chopped Walnuts
½ Cup	Raisins
2 Tsp	Cinnamon Powder
1 Tbsp	Dried Bread Crumbs
2 Tbsp	Melted Butter
2 Tbsp	Cold Butter, chopped
1 Tbsp	Lemon Juice

Directions:

1. Preheat oven to 375F with rack in center.
2. Peel, core, and dice apples. Add sugar, cinnamon, walnut, lemon juice, and cold butter – toss and set aside.

3. Lay out a kitchen towel, lightly dust with flour, and place one sheet of puff pastry atop. With dusted rolling pin roll out to about 1/8th inch thick (12 x 18 inches). With a brush, moisten 1 inch along the sides. Brush center of dough with melted butter.
4. Sprinkle bread crumbs over center of dough.
5. Add apple mixture to one end of the dough, about 2 inches from edges.
6. Gripping the towel, turn over the filled part of the dough onto itself, pat as necessary, and roll the towel again and again until your log is complete.
7. Press the ends together and tuck under. Using the towel to assist, transfer to a buttered, rimmed baking pan.
8. Brush melted butter on top, sprinkle with a little sugar, and make three small cuts.
9. Bake for 30 to 40 minutes until the pastry is puffed and golden brown. Cut in portions and serve.

Tips:
1. You can roll the dough without the towel; likewise you can line the pan with parchment/wax paper.
2. Follow instructions on the box for the puff pastry; don't let the dough warm, it becomes more difficult the longer you work it.
3. If it starts to fall apart, smile and get more ice cream.

CHAPTER 9: FLASHBACK – THE JUNGLE AND THE BEACH

Day Four: Thursday, 0950 hours, in the Train, Heidelberg to Paris

Tim leaned back into his large, comfortable recliner. The footrest popped out to support his feet and lower legs. His muscles relaxed. His body settled. It was hard to believe he was on a train.

He looked out the window into the far distance. There, the houses, trees, and cars moved slowly across his vision. He dropped his eyes to closer versions of these same things. They whizzed past as unrecognizable blurs. Tim was on a bullet train to Paris.

Yesterday, after leaving Herr Buckner's gallery, Tim checked plane and train schedules from Heidelberg to Paris. To his surprise, a train was not only the cheaper but also the quicker and easier way to go. This morning, he took a train from Heidelberg at 0915 and then switched to a bullet train in Mannheim. The 300 miles from Mannheim to Paris would be covered in three hours, an average of 100 miles per hour. In some spots the train would be traveling over 150/mph. Tim was impressed. He thought Field Marshall Rommel would have been really impressed.

Tim was not only impressed with the train's speed but also with its comfort and overall relaxed atmosphere. He had a first class ticket and was receiving a first class experience. His railcar offered several seating arrangements, from a single recliner to double side-by-side seats to four seats around a table. He immediately took a solo seat with a pull down table next to a window.

He did not want to share this ride, and especially this time, with anyone. It was his intention to share this time exclusively with his plans for Paris. However, as he would soon realize, this time would not be spent on vengeful plans for the future, but rather on unfulfilled plans from the past.

As he recessed deeper into his recliner, his stomach began to complain about his apparent distain for its needs. This morning he had slept through his alarm. Well, that was not exactly true. The alarm had awakened him, but he had stayed in bed, drowsily reviewing the many ways to "terminate" Truc. It was only after his mind cleared, and he remembered that his trail to Truc had grown dim, that he bolted upright and checked his clock. He was late; behind schedule; no time to eat.

"Why didn't those damn church bells awaken me?" he thought. "They tortured me the previous two nights. Why not last night? Why not this morning?"

From deep within him an answer was offered, "Perhaps God is not with you on this one, Tim." He stopped, cold running through the bumps on his skin. He shook that thought from his mind; shivered that feeling from his body.

Although now settled in his railcar, Tim realized he couldn't focus on his Paris plans if his stomach was going to continue to harass him. He gave in, got up, and headed for the dining car.

The dining car was quite a surprise. Tim thought its design to be modernistic, ...no, futuristic. It had a "wow factor" about it. The colors were lively. He liked the bright chartreuse formed-plastic composite that encapsulated the top half of the car.

"Chartreuse?" he thought, "Why do I even know that word?"

Instead of large block windows along both sides of the car, the walls were lined with rectangular windows, three feet long and one foot high, inset horizontally into the chartreuse plastic, in columns of three, one above the other. The lower half of the car's walls and the floors were carpeted in blended greens, blues, and grays. The standup eating counters were styled in curves rather than straight lines, and the tops were bright brushed steel or aluminum. The sit-down tables were a black glass, each with a computer screen inset or attached. The total effect was a very up-to-date, lively, fun place to meet and have something to drink or eat with friends. Unfortunately, Tim was not there to meet and eat with friends. He was there merely to shut up his stomach, so his mind could get some work done.

The kitchen had a rather extensive menu, mostly sandwiches and salads, but also a few more substantial meals. He chose a lasagna plate and a small bottle of Bordeaux. For a moment he thought about eating in the dining car, but then decided to return to his own seat, eat quickly, and get to work.

Back in his recliner, he opened the Bordeaux, took a sip, let it sit on his lips and the tip of his tongue for a moment, then rolled it back along the tongue and across his palate. "Nice," he said to himself. He then took a forkful of what had to be microwaved lasagna. "Good. For train food," he thought, "but certainly not what Uncle Carmine would serve in his Federal Hill restaurant." Tim imagined what Carmine would say if he knew Tim was eating his lasagna accompanied by a French Bordeaux, instead of an Italian Chianti.

Tim then smiled as he thought of his mother's many attempts at making lasagna. Her Italian sisters-in-law would pay her such compliments as "Not so bad," or "Your lasagna's getting better, Mary." After awhile, she just wouldn't make it anymore. His father didn't seem to mind.

Then thoughts of Brileen slipped into these memories. Brileen was one Irish colleen who could cook up a mean dish of lasagna. Even Tim's dad would ask her to make it almost every time he visited. Tim wasn't sure how his mother felt about that.

Sometimes Brileen would even make lasagna for her parents. No doubt, old Dan O'Sullivan told his friends that his Dago son-in-law was corrupting his daughter, making her cook that Dago food. Tim always believed, at least hoped, that Dan would then probably admit the Dago food tasted pretty good. Old Dan liked to use the word "Dago," even though his son-in-law was half Irish. In those days, his father-in-law used it out of habit, not malice, and Tim knew, with a lot of affection.

Brileen's secret to great lasagna was a recipe which reportedly came from a great Italian cook, Sue Paterno, wife of the great Penn State coach, Joe Paterno. Of course, almost everyone in Nittany Lion Country claimed they had Sue Paterno's recipe, and that she had given it to them personally. Where the recipe actually came from didn't matter; Brileen could really make it work.

After now being reminded of Brileen's great tasting lasagna, Tim pushed away the remainder of his microwaved version.

"Oh, how I loved that woman. Oh, how I miss her," chanted his soul.

"No! Stop it!" Tim screamed in silence.

He could not think of her now. He could not let himself again descend into despair. He had to think of something else, and do it quickly. As he brutishly massaged his temples, he asked himself, "What's the opposite of love? Hate! Truc!"

His mind now focused on Truc, the reason he was on this train, on this quest.

"No," he thought, "this was not a quest; that would be too positive a word for what I'm doing. Hunt? Yes, that's more like it. I'm on a hunt. Truc is malevolent prey that has to be found, cornered, and slaughtered. Then the world will be a better place. I will be a better man; well, at least a happier man."

He thought for a minute and then asked his reflection in the window, "Will you, Tim? Really? Will you?"

Tim then pictured Truc as he had last seen him. Truc as a South Vietnamese Army Major, about 25 years old, decent looking in a cruel kind of way, more politician than soldier, disliked Americans, hated Tim, and of course loved Quan.

"But how could a man who loved a woman, kill that woman?" a question Tim had asked himself a thousand times.

The answer was always "Vietnam." For most American soldiers, Vietnam was about killing or being killed. For most Vietnamese soldiers, it was also mostly about killing or being killed. For most Vietnamese people, it was about trying to avoid being killed, while still building a life for themselves and their families. Vietnam of the war decade was primarily a killing field.

Tim could still remember his first day in Nam. After landing at Tan Son Nhut Airbase in Saigon, Tim got on a bus for the short ride to Camp Alpha, the major processing center for troops entering or departing Vietnam. The bus looked like an old school bus, but painted a light Air Force blue. However, the bus's defining characteristic was not its color, it was its windows. Wire grating and iron bars covered its windows. This grating was meant to prevent the VC (Viet Cong) from tossing grenades into the bus.

These windows were Tim's first lesson on the paradox that was Vietnam. The Army told him that he was there to protect the people. The bus told him that while there he had to be protected from the people. Of course he knew that was too simple a phrasing for the complicated reality that was Vietnam, but that was his first feeling on his first day. He did not like that feeling.

The Camp Alpha in-processing procedures were typical Army. The personnel specialist took his orders and threw them into the trash can, with those of everyone else who had just arrived from the States. "We're going to send you where we need you. For you DePalma, that will be the 25th Infantry Division in Tay Ninh Province northwest of Saigon. You'll be here three days till new orders are completed. Next."

"But I'm Airborne," Tim protested. "I'm supposed to go to the 1st Cav."

"You're going to the 25th, Private. Move on. Next."

"Geeeezzz," Tim mumbled to himself as he headed to the line for jungle fatigues and boots. "No matter where you go, this damn Army seems to be run by Spec 4 personnel clerks."

Tim had been looking forward to joining the 1st Cavalry Division (Airmobile). The 1st Cav was basically a new kind of army division developed especially for Vietnam, with a new jungle warfighting concept built around the capabilities of the division's helicopters. This new division of airmobile units was capable of carrying out air assault missions over thousands of square miles. The air assault concept overcame the "tyranny of terrain," allowing US troops to move almost anywhere, at almost any time, taking almost any equipment, with almost complete surprise.

That first night in Vietnam, as Tim stretched out on his bunk, his mind reviewed the events of that very eventful day. His body however tried to drift off to much needed sleep. He had just finished reading his Saint Joseph's Soldier's Prayer. Two days before he left for boot camp, his postman, Jim Nolan, had knocked on his door and given him a gift. He had given Tim a prayer card and told him that every soldier who said that prayer to Saint Joseph and carried that card came home safely from war. For the first time, on that first night in Nam, Tim said that prayer. He said it almost every night for the next four years. Unbeknownst to him then, that's how long his Vietnam sojourn would last. Not one year, but almost four years. Its repercussions, however, would last a lifetime.

As Tim drifted toward sleep, his mind wondered back to his prayer card. Did prayers work? Would prayers keep him alive? Or would it be Sergeant Pack's training that kept him alive? Would anything keep him alive?

He was young in his religion. Like with most soldiers, war would test his religion. War would form his religion. He would emerge from this war with a new understanding of life's purpose, life's meaning, life's worth. He would emerge with a new understanding of religion's meaning, its power, its diversity, its shortcomings. His beliefs would in some ways be confused, but still strong, burnished and hardened in a hellfire called Nam.

Did he believe in prayer? Did he believe in the prayer card? He often asked himself those questions. Things had happened to him on the battlefield that were hard to explain. Some would say those things were just plain luck. He always wondered. Did he believe? Well, he carried that card for over 30 years. Then he gave it to a nephew, as the young Lieutenant shipped out for Iraq. His nephew, his sister Angie's son, had come home safely.

Tim, his first day in Nam coming to a close, finally found sleep.

That sleep was short lived.

THE NIGHT DEMONS

Shouts pierced his sleep. "What are you doing in bed, Private? Get out of the damn bunk, Private! There's a war on, Private!"

Tim bolted awake. His head still thick with sleep. His thoughts confused. Where am I? Who's shouting at me? What's going on?

More shouts. "I said get out of that damn bunk, Private! You've got a war to fight, and I'm taking you there to fight it. Get moving."

Tim stumbled from his bunk. His eyes were still caked half closed. The voice bellowed from an area somewhere above a flak jacket and beneath a helmet. He saw an M-16. Was it pointed at him? He rubbed his eyes again. The barracks was dark. Blackout curtains. He could hardly see a thing.

"Yes, Sergeant. Yes, sir. I'm up. Where are we going?" Tim mumbled, stammered, and stumbled.

"Hey, quiet over there." shouted a voice from another bunk. "Shut up you A-holes. We're trying to get some sleep here," contributed another voice from deep within the darkness. Another few "Yeahs" and "Quiets" and "What the hell's" drifted from other parts of the barracks.

The bellowing, gun-toting, flak-jacketed demon in front of Tim grabbed him, told him to pick up his things, and practically dragged him from the barracks while yelling in his ear, "What are you doing sleeping in there with those worthless 'legs.' You're supposed to be a paratrooper."

Out in the moonlight, Tim could now see the face from which all the yelling came. He smiled. He pulled his arm away from the flak-jacketed demon and laughingly shouted, "Jesus, John, you scared the crap out of me. What are you doing here?"

The flak-jacketed demon of the night was John Robinson, Tim's jump buddy from Fort Benning. Tim was surprised and happy to see him. However, over the next hellish year, Tim would be visited by many more demons from many demonic nights to come. John would be the only welcomed one.

Staff Sergeant John Robinson laughed and said, "What I'm doing here is saving your butt from life as a leg."

As he said "leg," he turned his head to the right and spit at the ground, a universal action all paratroopers did when they said "leg," referring to a regular infantry grunt.

"I'm here to take you to the 1st Cav, a real fighting unit."

Tim stammered, "But John, Sergeant Robinson I mean. Oh, wow, wait a minute. Is that a new rocker on your sleeve? Wow, another stripe. You got promoted to "Staff Sergeant?" Congratulations!"

"Thanks Tim. But looky here on your sleeve! Your first stripe! Congratulations to you, 'Private First Class' DePalma."

"Thanks. But you know all I had to do to get that stripe was to continue to fall in for revelry every morning. But 'Staff Sergeant,' now that's really something."

"OK. So were both brilliant soldiers," said John looking around. "But we need to stop patting each other on the back and get out of here before we both get demoted. Get in my jeep. I'm taking you to the 1st Cav, home of the best air-assault paratroopers in the world!"

Tim began, "But John, I've just been reassigned to the 25th Infantry Division. I have orders. I have to …"

"Never mind that. Get in the damn jeep and hurry up about it. Remember this, there's the Army way of doing things in the States; then there's the Army way of doing things in a war zone. I've just personally reassigned you to the 1st Cav. Now let's get you there before anyone around here realizes you're gone. The personnel guys can straighten it all out later."

That didn't sound too kosher to Tim, but he went with "Staff Sergeant" Robinson anyway. Whom was he going to trust, a Spec 4 who threw his orders in a file 13, or John Robinson, the man who helped get him through Airborne School?

That first night Tim got his first lesson in surviving Vietnam, if only in a small way: do whatever you have to do to get the mission done, while at the same time still getting yourself and your buddies home. Staff Sergeant Robinson just showed him how to take action and get a mission done and was now taking him to a new home, the 1st Cavalry Division

In later years, when Tim looked back on Vietnam, he categorized his time there into three parts. First, were his War-fighting Years, June 1971 - March 1973. Second, was his Unreal-Real-World Year, April 1973 - March 1974. Third, was his Peace-Fighting Year, April 1974 - April 1975. Quan would be a part of all three.

In June 1971, Private First Class Tim DePalma entered the jungle a fresh-faced, teenaged, American soldier; well-trained but untested. In April 1975, four years later, First Lieutenant Tim DePalma would emerge from that jungle a proven warrior and diplomat; ...but as a man, he would be just a man, a man with a broken heart.

THE WAR-FIGHTING YEARS:

Part 1: 1971 - 1972

As Staff Sergeant Robinson helped Tim move his gear into the 1st Cav's barracks, he noticed Tim had a book titled "East of Eden" by John Steinbeck. "What are you reading this for. This is crap."

Tim, wide-eyed and a little offended, briefly tried to explain how he had become interested in Steinbeck while studying at Monterey.

Robinson cut him short. "Steinbeck is crap. If you want to read about social ills, read some James Baldwin."

James Baldwin? Tim wanted to ask, "Who the hell is James Baldwin?" but John had already turned away and was rummaging around for something in his jeep.

Robinson pulled out a book from under the driver's seat and tossed it to Tim. "Better yet, take this. Not that you'll have much time to read around here, but if you find some, read that. You might learn something from history that you can use today, in this crazy world you're now living in. It's a book about Bedford Forrest, a racist bastard but the greatest cavalry officer who ever lived. Even though he lived a hundred years ago, you might still find something useful there. I did."

Staff Sergeant Robinson had no idea what he had just given Tim. What he had given him was a lifetime of enjoyment in reading, studying, and applying military history. Just as reading "Cannery Row," while living near Cannery Row, had engendered in Tim a lifelong passion for socially significant novels; now, reading about the exploits of a great Civil War cavalry officer, while being in a cavalry unit, would engender in Tim a new lifelong passion for military history.

Tim's first weeks with the 1st Cavalry Division were spent going through its Combat Training Center. The Center's intent was to ensure that no 1st Cav soldier would go into the jungle until he was properly trained and psychologically ready. The training was hard and realistic. It impressed upon every trooper that not only did his life depend on being properly trained and prepared, but also the lives of all those around him. This was strong and sobering incentive to fully apply yourself and learn everything and anything that might keep you and your buddies alive.

Tim soon tested the Training Center's effectiveness, as his unit immediately deployed to the boonies where it went about the business of hunting the Viet Cong and North Vietnamese Army. What he learned at the Combat Training Center kept him alive for the first three months. What he learned in those first three months kept him alive for the next three years.

The 1st Cav's mission was to interdict and disrupt sanctuary-based enemy supply lines from Cambodia. Those supply lines brought weapons, ammo, and fresh troops to enemy supply depots located in provinces around Saigon. What the Army meant by "disrupt enemy supply lines" was kill every enemy soldier possible and blow up everything else. For a teenage soldier, that was a very sobering mission.

Although a lot of the information on enemy activities was obtained through aerial and satellite reconnaissance, a lot was also obtained by soldiers on ground patrols and from talking with villagers. Tim's role in executing this "interdiction" mission was twofold: first, as a rifleman on search and destroy patrols and then second, as an interpreter seeking information from villagers and coordinating with South Vietnamese military units. From the start he was right in the middle of it all. He excelled in these roles, learning along the way a lot about the jungle, the enemy, the friendlies, and himself.

On his first patrol, Tim was scared out of his mind. He constantly expected either a VC to pop up from a covered hole and kill him, or a North Vietnamese sniper to send a silent bullet to do him in. However, his first patrol saw no action, nor did the second one, nor the third. Somewhat paradoxically, Tim was becoming bored, thinking or at least hoping that ants, mosquitoes, leeches, and snakes might be all he really had to worry about.

Of course he was soon proved wrong. His first combat was in the dark of night. His 30-man patrol had set an ambush along a suspected enemy supply trail. Tim, along with the rest of his platoon, had lain in wait, not moving, or at least trying not to move, for over an hour. Then his greasepaint-encircled eyes grew wide as he watched the dark shadows of enemy troops silently move left to right along a trail not 20 yards in front of him. They were now almost completely in the ambush kill zone. His hands began to sweat as his finger moved to his trigger. His heart pounded so loudly he was sure the enemy must be able to hear it. Tim DePalma, an average American kid, from an average American home, in an average American city, with an average American education, and believing in an average American religion was about to kill another human being. And all those American institutions had sanctioned it.

Upon the patrol leader's command, two claymore mines detonated, each spewing about 700 steel mini-balls into the enemy. Almost simultaneously, every trooper in the ambush line opened fire. Tim opened fire. The enemy soldiers opened fire. Everyone's 20-round magazines were replaced, and replaced again, and then replaced again. Sergeant Pack's words from Fort Jackson jumped into Tim's head, *"Then everyone lets loose! The winners are the guys who put out the highest amount of fire, in the shortest amount of time, with the greatest amount of accuracy."*

For the next few moments, all went quiet, except for his pounding heart. Then a yell from Tim's left, "Damn it. I'm hit. Medic!" In response, bangs, muzzle flashes, and whizzing bullets erupted from the darkness in front of him. Then return fire from his left; then from his right; and then, as if on its own, from his rifle too. Then again, silence.

After what seemed like hours but was only minutes, his patrol let loose another "mad minute" of weapons fire into what was left of the enemy and then quickly and quietly withdrew to its predetermined rally point about 200 meters behind the ambush site. After everyone had reformed there, the patrol silently moved out on a three mile march to a predetermined LZ (Landing Zone) where choppers would pick up the patrol in the morning and move it, not back to base camp, but to another ambush site.

Tim was in a daze from his first trigger pull, through the entire chopper ride, to the securing of the new LZ. "Did I kill anyone?" he kept asking himself over and over. "I must have. How could I not have? Why didn't we look at the killed? Why didn't we try to get some intelligence information from the bodies? Were they combat troops or just support troops carrying supplies?"

The questions kept flowing. No answers followed. He would learn later that such intelligence gathering actions were decided by the patrol leader at the time of the action. Often such intelligence collection was too dangerous in night ambushes. Some of the enemy might still be alive, playing possum in the darkness, ready to shoot any GI's coming to collect documents, to identify equipment, or to count bodies. There might be more enemy on the trail or in the area. The enemy might be quickly responding to the noise of the firefight and moving more troops to the ambush site. It was best for his patrol to slip away into the darkness of the night.

Now Tim fully understood the meaning of the mission to "interdict" enemy supply lines. Over the coming year he would become intimately familiar with both the act and the art of "interdiction," with its killing of the enemy, with its blowing of bridges, with its destroying of depots, but mostly, with its killing of the enemy. That's what his patrol had done that first night, what he had done. They and he had done it well.

For almost the entire next year Tim was in the boonies on search and destroy missions. He conducted ambushes, was himself ambushed, was part of platoon-size surprise engagements, as well as company-size and larger battles. With each mission he became more sure of his tasks and his abilities. However, as the combat continued, he became concerned. Concerned because for him, the killing was becoming easier. Although it never became easy, it did become easier.

There was something else at work. Tim had a sixth sense about the battlefield, an innate ability to anticipate and compensate as the battle unfolded. From the first shot, time and motion around him seemed to slow, while his decisions and actions seemed to accelerate. It was as if he was the only person moving at normal speed in a slow motion movie. When the threat ceased, so did the slow motion movie. He couldn't explain it, and he never talked about it. While in battle, it was just part of him and what he was.

Tim found the enemy crafty and tough. For that he grew to respect them in a fighting man's sort of way. However, he also found them cruel. The VC were especially brutal in the ways they controlled villagers. For that Tim grew to despise them, in both a fighting man's and a human kind of way. Any villager caught co-operating with Americans would often be put to death, a merci-less death administered in front of the entire village, as a warning to others. When learning of such actions, Tim became internally enraged and determined to avenge such deaths. He carried that determination and resolve into the jungle on every mission.

As the months upon months of fighting continued, Tim became confirmed in his belief that for almost everyone involved, Vietnam was about killing or avoiding being killed. However, he understood instinctively that knowing when and how to kill was only part of what it meant to be a soldier, and not the most important part. He believed he was there, that the US Army was there, to stop the killing and secure a people's freedom. Did he have to kill in order to stop the killing? Street demonstrators back home would chant "No!" Tim's experiences in Nam would shout "Yes!" Tim thought the history of mankind tended to agree with him.

R&R: REST and RECUPERATION - SAIGON

After almost eight months of what seemed like constant field operations, Tim was enjoying three days of down time at the Brigade's base camp. He was sitting in his tent and had just finished his daily stripping and cleaning of his M-16. He was reaching for his still unfinished, but almost finished, book on Forrest, the Civil War cavalry officer, when Sergeant First Class Robinson walked in.

"Let's get moving there Sergeant DePalma. We're going to be on an R&R chopper in 20 minutes."

Robinson had been promoted to Sergeant First Class (E-7) after a recent move up to 1st Cav Headquarters, a rank and pay grade belonging to the enlisted leader of a 30-man platoon. Tim, who had remained down in the fighting units, had received a battlefield promotion to Sergeant (E-5), leader of a fireteam of four air-assault paratroopers. Promotions came quickly in Nam, unfortunately that was due to positions quickly opening up, as casualty rates quickly went up. The two friends had not seen each other in over a month.

"Well, I'll be," said Tim, looking up from his cot. "Look what happens when you visit Headquarters. You get to see all the big mucky-mucks, even the Army's newest Sergeant First Class. I won't call you a platoon sergeant, because up here you're not pushing a platoon, you're just pushing paper."

"Watch yourself there Sergeant," John responded, with a smile, "or you'll find yourself back in the boonies instead of going on R&R."

"R&R?" questioned Tim. "But I don't have any R&R orders."

John tossed some papers on Tim's cot. "Here you go. Seven

days at China Beach. I heard you were here in camp, and I needed someone to carry my bags. So get moving! We haven't got all day! Damn, you're slow. It's amazing you're still alive."

Tim ignored the gibes and looked at the orders. "Hey, you said we were going to China Beach, but these orders say Saigon."

"Yeah, well, that's true, but we can discuss it later," the new Sergeant First Class threw over his shoulder as he headed out. "You better move it. You got 10 minutes till liftoff. I'll meet you at the chopper pad. If you're not there, I'm leaving without you."

Ten minutes later found Tim's butt in the chopper. Five hours after that found it sitting in a chair in The Guillaume Tell, the best French restaurant in Saigon. Tim couldn't believe where he was, what he was looking at, how he was feeling.

In front of him was a white tablecloth. On that white tablecloth were china dishes. Those china dishes were flanked by gleaming silverware. The gleaming silverware pointed to crystal glasses. Those crystal glasses were filled with wine. It was all almost too much.

For the past eight months, Tim had eaten mostly canned C-Rations, and those mostly cold. A great meal was an infrequent hot one transported in heat-retaining, army-green mermite containers choppered out to the boonies by some good-hearted Mess Sergeant.

When meeting with villagers, he would eat what they ate, mostly rice, noodles, and soups, served in wooden or clay bowls. At times, because Tim was Tim, he also ate what was skeptically referred to as "exotic" Vietnamese fare, such as rat-on-a-stick, snake and snake heart, monkey brain, silkworm larvae, and duck egg embryos. Tim drew the line at dog, a Vietnamese delicacy. He just couldn't, wouldn't do dog.

But now, here in Saigon, a French restaurant! A real French restaurant! Tim was at a loss for words. He ordered what John ordered, not knowing what it was, but knowing it sounded French. Then he stared at all the beautiful women in the room, Asian, American, European. Where did they all come from? Who were these people? He decided that there really were two Vietnams, one city and one rural."

"I didn't know there were French restaurants like this in Nam," he said with some awe in his voice.

"I thought you were some kind of super history buff, DePalma. Didn't you tell me that you once researched the causes of this damn war? Well then, you should know the French were one of the big reasons we got into this mess. Vietnam was a French colony for a couple hundred years. After WWII, the local Commies here started one of their revolutions and eventually defeated the French troops at someplace called Dien Bien Phu. America now sees the world as a zero-sum game between us and the Commies, that means that if the Commies win something somewhere, then we think we must be losing something. Therefore, we couldn't let them win Vietnam. So now, as the French say, 'Voila!' Here you and I sit amongst the remnants of French culinary influence in Vietnam, trying to keep this bottle of fine burgundy wine from falling into the hands of the Commie hoards."

"Continuing in that vein," John added, "let's make a toast." He lifted his wine glass, "To a night in civilization!" Tim clinked and drank deeply.

After a moment, John again lifted his glass. "Toast! To the French! They might not know how to fight, but they sure know how to cook!" Tim, looking around a little sheepishly for any Frenchmen, clinked and drank.

The wine classes were refilled.

After another few minutes, John once again lifted his newly refilled glass. "Toast! This time to my new set of orders! I leave Nam on my Freedom Bird one month from today!" Tim clinked, but this time only sipped. He was getting the idea that this might be a long night of toasting.

"Toast!" said John yet again. "To my second set of orders! Two months from today, I will be a wimpy civilian again!" Tim clinked, and sipped, and thought this would be a good time to stop the toasts, before he became toast.

"What?" he exclaimed. "I didn't know you were getting out

of the Army. I thought you were a lifer. You're going back to the real world, ...AND... you're going to be a civilian! That's great!"

"I'll drink to that," said John, picking up his glass in what now seemed to be a continuous motion, this time spilling a little wine as he did so. "Let's drink to the United States Army. I loved being a part of you, but I'm going to love departing from you." Tim clinked, and sipped, and thought John might already be getting a little slack lipped.

John finally removed his hand from his wine glass, eased back into his chair, and sighed, "Well Tim, what do you think about this place? Nice, huh? Just remember, while you and I are slogging around in the boonies dodging bullets, these REMFs are living like this every night."

"REMFs?" queried Tim, accenting the word with a raised eyebrow.

"Ahhh, finally a Vietnamese word my favorite Vietnamese linguist doesn't know. Well, it's really not a Vietnamese word; it's a Vietnam word. Another one of the Army's great acronyms. This time very apropos, as the French would say. It means Rear Echelon Mother Fuckers. REMFs! They are the guys who get all the medals but don't do any of the fighting. Word is that it takes seven of them back here in Saigon, to support just one of us out there in the boonies. So that means lots of REMFs. Saigon is full of them. Beware!"

Just as John again reached for his glass, probably to make another toast, this time most likely to all the REMFs surrounding their table, the dinner arrived. A good thing, thought Tim.

John had ordered Beef Bourguignon, and Tim had mimicked him.

"Well, what do you think?" asked John, as he picked up his knife and fork. "Looks great, huh? Ah, the aroma! It's going to taste even better."

Tim looked up from his plate to John, then back down to his plate, then again back to John. "Well, to tell you the truth, it looks just like Irish beef stew, only it's on a plate instead of in a bowl."

John almost spit out his mouthful onto the table. "Geeez, I

thought you Guineas were suppose to know a lot about food. You got to know there's more to great food than pasta. You should experience a little more French cuisine." He put a little extra Harlem flare on the word "cuisine."

Coming from a culture where guys give as good as they get, Tim reflexively responded, "Yeah, I know. It's like you guys are supposed to be big on great soul food. But you got to know there's more to good desserts than watermelon."

John chuckled, "Again, as the French would say, 'touché.' You're right. I'll try to remember that when I end up in civilian life shining some goombah's pointy black shoes. But seriously, Tim, look at this plate, take in that aroma. This isn't stew. This is succulent beef, cut from the finest parts of Bessie, and then basted and cooked in the finest of French wines and French sauces."

That comment got Tim talking about his old hobby of eating different ethnic foods and appreciating their differences. He explained to John how his hobby came about almost a decade ago when, as a kid, he first ventured from his Italian neighborhood to the closest Chinese restaurant.

Their table conversation revealed that John also knew a lot about food and cooking. He and his brother had learned to cook from an early age. Both his mother and father were educators. Many nights in his high school years, John and his brother would cook the evening meals before their parents returned home.

As John finished the last bite of his Beef Bourguignon, he asked, "Well? What do you think now? Still think it's just Irish stew, only on a plate instead of in a bowl?" He again coughed out a laugh at that description of one of the world's great dishes.

Tim had to admit, it was some of the best tasting "stew" he had ever eaten.

John went on to say that the main ingredient that set it apart for him was the cup or two of burgundy wine that went into making the basting juices. He added that the word, Bourguignon, was the French word for Burgundy, the region in France in which both burgundy wine and this recipe originated.

John then lifted up their second bottle of burgundy and, seeing that there was still a bit left, poured till the bottle went dry, providing them each a half glass of the rich red liquid. "One more toast. To Columbia University! A place full of smart people who were dumb enough to let me join them. I got my letter of acceptance this morning. Cheers!"

Tim was excited for his friend. No wonder John wanted to go on R&R to celebrate; stateside orders, separation orders, and a college acceptance letter. What a night! They waved for coffee and talked for another hour about John's plans for the future. Tim was surprised to find out those plans ambitiously called for a post-grad degree from Harvard Business School, followed by a career on Wall Street.

Listening to John got Tim thinking about his own future. He knew he had only four months, if his luck held out, till his tour in Nam was over. He would then get to ride his own Freedom Bird back to the "Real World." After that, what? He was genuinely surprised to find out that he had no ideas about, and no plans for, his own future.

R&R: CHINA BEACH

The next morning, two Army Sergeants, each with an M-16 slung over his left shoulder and a small duffle bag dangling from his left hand, slowly walked across the already sizzling tarmac at Tan Son Nhut Airfield. The shorter, black Sergeant looked toward a row of Air Force cargo planes, checking out their unit insignias and tail numbers. He seemed to focus on one plane and then headed toward it.

"I still don't understand why we just don't stay here in Saigon for the week," grumbled Tim. "That's what our orders authorize. And besides, there are some nice looking women here."

"That's because you haven't seen China Beach yet. Look wonder warrior, you've spent too much time in the boonies. You don't see any round-eyed women in Cav country. That doesn't mean there aren't any here in our own Disney Adventureland known as Nam. Believe me, women in uniform in Vietnam are an untold story. Nurses, doctors, donut dollies, air traffic controllers, all kinds of them. They're all here showing real courage. What gets me, unlike most of us, they're here as volunteers. They want to be here, with us, where the action is. I have to admit, that kind of turns me on. And when these women are ready to play, they go to China Beach. A woman in uniform is a sexy thing. But a woman in a bathing suit on China Beach? Lots of women in lots of bathing suits on China Beach? Well, you'll soon see."

"Can I help you?" asked an Air Force Captain as the two Army Sergeants approached his plane.

"Well, yes sir, I hope so. We need a hop to Da Nang. Do you know if this or any other aircraft is heading there today, Captain?" Sergeant First Class Robinson's most professional military tone and manner were accompanied by his and Tim's best salutes.

"Yeah, Sarge," responded the Captain, in usual Air Force informality and with a half salute of his own. "This bird is heading that way in about 15 minutes. Sorry though, we don't have any room for passengers. If I were you, I'd head over to the terminal and get yourselves on the space-available waiting list. I'm sure there'll be another plane going to Da Nang in a day or two"

Just as the Captain was turning back toward his aircraft, Sergeant Robinson said under his breath but still loud enough to be heard, "Damn. That sucks. Wojonski wanted to see me today. Come on Tim, let's head over to the terminal."

The Air Force Captain turned back to Sergeant Robinson. "Hold on there, Sarge. Did you say Wojonski wants to see you? You got a set of Wojonski orders?"

"Yes, Sir. Right here." John produced some highly wrinkled, worn, and soiled papers from his fatigues pocket.

The Captain looked at them, holding them between his thumb and forefinger in a manner indicating that he really didn't want to be touching them. "OK, Sarge. You and your buddy jump in. We'll be taking off in a matter of minutes."

They secured their weapons and strapped themselves into two small cargo seats, which the crew had just cleared off. Tim looked at John with amazed and questioning eyes. John just smiled and chuckled. Over the building noise of the engines, he yelled, "I'll tell you about it later. Big night last night. I need some sleep."

With that he crossed his arms, lowered his head, closed his eyes, and was gone. Tim soon joined him. Soldiers always need sleep and seemingly are always able to grab some at a moment's notice. A little help from a lot of burgundy didn't hurt.

After an almost two-hour hibernation-like nap, the two Sergeants woke with a jolt as the wheels of the huge C-130 cargo plane smacked down on the Da Nang runway. After a few minutes the plane came to a stop, the Sergeants deplaned, thanked the loadmaster and the pilots for the ride, then quickly headed for the shade of the terminal area. There they found a cyclo (pronounced: see-clo), a man-pedaled rickshaw, to take them to the Army part of port operations.

Tim could not take his eyes off the skies over the airfield. They were filled with planes of all sizes and types; both American and South Vietnamese military aircraft, as well as civilian commercial aircraft. He had never seen so many planes. At the height of the Vietnam War, Da Nang was the busiest Airport in the world, averaging about 2,500 takeoffs and landings per day.

Da Nang itself was the third largest city in South Vietnam, located on the country's eastern coast along the South China Sea, about 400 miles northeast of Saigon and only 85 miles south of the North Vietnam border. Its major asset was a well sheltered and easily accessible port. The U.S. had been using and improving that natural harbor since the mid-1960's, primarily to support military operations in the central highlands. Its 20-mile coastline of powder-sand beaches and azure water, which soon became known as China Beach, made it a major R&R destination for the troops conducting those highland operations.

The cyclo ride to the Army's 1st Logistics Command Headquarters took about 15 minutes; this was a big base. On the way, Tim asked if he could take a look at the "Wojonski Orders."

"Sure," said John, again pulling the mangled, soiled set of orders from one of his fatigue pockets and handing them to Tim.

After a moment of bumpy reading, the rickshaw not being the smoothest ride Tim had ever had, he said, "What the heck are these? They're not like any orders I've ever seen. They just authorize you to come to Da Nang, and they're signed by some Major outside our command, so they probably aren't even valid. There are no dates, no duration, no purpose."

John smiled. "Well, all that's true. But as you saw, they work. Look, if some officer really gets all up tight and I think he's going to ask me what's up, I will quickly fill in all that stuff. That's never happened. This way, with all the blocks left blank, I, or anyone else, can keep using these orders over and over again."

Tim then pointed to the orders. "And what's with this hand scribbled note stapled to the top, that says, 'To whom it may concern, I want to see this warrior. Wojonski.'"

"Geeez, Tim. What are you, an admin clerk? Didn't you see what happened when that pilot read that note? He didn't care whether or not I had orders. All he knew was that Wojonski wanted to see me. That's all he needed to know. He gave us a ride."

Tim thought for a moment, then asked, "Who or what is a Wojonski?"

John smiled, "Major Platon Wojonski, US Army Transportation Corps. That's what a Wojonski is."

Tim squinted with thought, "Why does an Air Force Captain, like that C-130 pilot, give a damn about what an Army Major wants? I don't get it."

"Good question," said John. "Wojonski has been in Nam probably longer than any other soldier. He is the Army's body of knowledge on Vietnam, who is still in Vietnam. He arrived in 1965, helped set up Cam Rahn Bay in the south, and then was in the initial Army logistics outfit here in Da Nang. He knows more about how to order, get, move, and replace supplies in Vietnam, from toilet paper to tanks, than any other REMF in the world. By the way, never call him that. He doesn't like it, and you don't want to piss this guy off."

"Now, back to the subject." continued John. "The Pentagon

has this crazy policy of bringing people to Nam for a year, then replacing them with someone new, who will take six months to learn what the guy he replaced already knew. Then after that first six months, the new guy becomes an old guy and is looking not do anything that will get himself killed before it's his turn to go back to the real world, and be replaced by another new guy. So instead of one long ten-year experience in fighting this war, we have a series of ten one-year experiences. No wonder progress is so slow."

John went on, "You and I know this is no longer a local Viet Cong guerrilla war. It hasn't been since Tet 1968, when we killed about 90% of the VC. This is an invasion of one country, South Vietnam, by another country, North Vietnam. We should be fighting this war like we fought WWII, when Germany invaded France and then was getting ready to invade England. No one went home till we won the bloody thing. I believe, in the long run, such a policy would save lives here, and we would have won the damn thing by now."

"Now on the other hand, Wojonski has his own crazy policy. He's been here seven years straight, and says he's not going home till he wins this war. Of course, he lived in Cleveland, so who would want to go back there anyway, with their rivers on fire and all. He knows how logistics are supposed to work. More importantly, he knows how they actually work. From what I hear, he even runs his own units of off-the-book trucks, boats, and choppers. That way, if the normal supply chains breakdown for whatever reasons, to include incompetence and callousness, Wojonski can get what's needed, to where it's needed, by when it's needed. Remember several months back, when we ran out of 40mm rifle grenades, and we couldn't get them anywhere? Then I disappeared for a day, and the next day three truck loads of grenades appeared? That was Wojonski. And from 400 miles away! Everyone who knows him trusts him to get things done, if they're smart; from generals down to sergeants."

"Well, just what things are we here in Da Nang to get done now?" asked Tim.

In retort, John smiled and said, "The only thing I want some-one to do while I'm here, is do me! Hey, here we are. This is Major Wojonski's office."

Tim and John unassed the rickshaw and went into the long, one story, wooden building which housed the 1st Logistics Command. Within five minutes they were back out front in the hot sun. Major Wojonski wasn't there. Seemed the Major was having lunch in his BOQ (Bachelor Officers Quarters) room.

"Now what?" asked Tim.

"No sweat," answered John. "I know where he lives." He waved down another cyclo. Within 5 minutes they were about to knock on a BOQ door that had no name on it.

"Tim, now remember, none of your ethnic bullcrap. No verbal jousting about Frogs, MicKs, Dagos, or whatever other slurs you guys continually hurl around in your hometown. Especially don't use the term Polack. I know you Whities up there do it as some kind of perverted sense of humor, but Wojonski doesn't have a sense of humor."

"But John, you just..."

"Yeah, yeah, I know. I just called you, Whitey. I was just making my point, ...and having some fun. Don't do as I do, do as I say. Here goes."

John knocked on the door.

"Who's there?" the words gruffly exploding through the door.

"Sergeant First Class John Robinson. Here to repay you for three truckloads of 40mm toilet paper, Sir!" John responded, just as loudly and just as gruffly.

The door swung open, revealing a big man, in his early-30's, with a wide smile and an outstretched hand. "John, great to see you. I've been expecting you. Come in. Come in."

The two Sergeants entered. Introductions were made, then John presented payment for the three truckloads of grenades. Payment was the delivering of three packets of pipe tobacco that Major Wojonski had ordered from a tobacco shop in Saigon. The shop had been supplying Wojonski with his own special blend for over five years. John and Major Wojonski then settled into a catch-up conversation.

Tim smiled, mostly to himself, as he assessed Wojonski. If Tim had been asked to describe the Major before he met him, he would have described Wojonski pretty much to a T. "A typical Polack," thought Tim, "Probably pure blooded. From one of the two traditional lineages; this time the nobleman, not the peasant. Tall, about 6'3", broad shouldered, high cheekbones, flat face, blue eyes, and thinning sandy blond hair, all typical Slavic features to which the major had added a mustache."

Just as Tim had met a lot of Tony Cicionnis in Providence, he had also met a lot of Platon Wojonskis around Providence's Olneyville section, locally known as Polish Hill or Beer Hill.

"And John doesn't think there's anything to this ethnic stereotyping?" Tim laughed to himself.

He turned away from the two friends, who were deep in conversation, and took the opportunity to take in the room and its contents. The Major's room certainly was not stereotypical. From the outside, the barracks and the door into his room looked as expected. However, once inside, there was a world of difference. Nothing was as expected.

Tim had seldom been in an officer's or a senior sergeant's barracks room. On those few occasions when he had, they were always stark, 10-foot by 10-foot rooms enclosed by plywood walls with the minimum furnishings of a bed, a small field table, a single chair, and a small window. This room, however, was more than a little different.

Major Wojonski, by taking out the plywood walls that had separated four rooms, had created one large room, 10-feet wide and 40-feet long. Tim figured the Major must be able to get away with this because of his long time in-country and by the fact that he was a Major. On one end of the room, where John and Wojonski were talking, was a bed, a card table and four chairs, a 6-inch-screen TV on the card table, a small refrigerator, a window air conditioner, and a built-in counter and sink. The counter was almost totally cluttered over by three hotplates, a toaster, a coffeepot, a breadbox, a griddle, and two large ashtrays holding four pipes.

Both of the room's 40-foot-long side walls were covered from ceiling to floor with plastic-overlaid maps. The maps in turn were covered with grease-pencil drawings of supply routes, depots, and landing zones. Tim strolled the length of the room trying to decipher the information on the maps. It was like walking through a general's command center.

Tim then reached the far end wall, which was lined with three field tables topped with six field phones, scattered notebooks, all kinds of manuals, and a half assembled, or maybe half disassembled, .45-caliber pistol. Tim had the urge to immediately assemble the pistol. After eight months of combat, he felt uneasy around a weapon that was not immediately ready for use. He restrained himself.

Tim then focused on the really unexpected. Covering almost every inch of the end wall, above the field tables, was a varied assortment of pictures and paintings. He stood there open-mouthed, trying to comprehend. He thought them an odd collection. There was a traditional portrait painting of John F. Kennedy as 35th president; an impressionistic painting of Martin Luther King with the Lincoln Memorial as background; a black and white print of Saint Thomas Aquinas; a black and white poster of General Patton, with an overprint of his words: "Politicians are the lowest form of life on earth. Liberal Democrats are the lowest form of politicians;" and a Warhol-like, split-canvas painting of a smaller Karl Marx portrait juxtaposed against a larger portrait of a man Tim did not recognize. Next to that split-portrait painting was a tri-portrait painting of North Vietnam leader, Ho Chi Minh, and North Vietnam military leader, General Giap, along with another Asian face which Tim, again, did not recognize. Tim's gaze halted for a moment on the next painting, an intriguing portrait of a woman surrounded by red and white roses, with a gauzy looking French Arch of Triumph in the background. Finally, there were several paintings of white seagulls soaring in dark blue skies over turbulent blue seas. Tim noted that all the paintings had an almost indiscernible ? in the lower right corner.

"Like'em?" a gravel voice jolted Tim from his silent appraisal.

"Yes, sir. I don't mean to offend, but I never expected to see anything like this in somebody's bedroom in Nam."

"Well, as you can see," said Major Wojonski, swinging his right arm across the map room behind him and his left arm across the field phones in front of him, "this is more than just somebody's bedroom."

"Oh, yes Sir," said Tim. "I think I understand that. I guess I just didn't expect all these paintings. And they seem such an odd lot."

"How so?" said the gravelly voice, now seemingly less gritty.

"Well, Sir, they're all so different, both in content and style. Where did you get them."

"I painted them. Surprised?"

Tim began to say something, but Major Wojonski, not really wanting an answer, continued, "You're right that each is quite different from the others. However, when taken together, they represent a whole. They represent my philosophy of life."

Tim turned to face him straight on. "Sir? Your philosophy of life? I don't understand. I thought they were just a lot of paintings and pictures you liked."

"They are that, but more. I painted each to say more than a thousand words about a facet of my personal philosophy. Sometime, somewhere in each man's life, he should come to understand the philosophy he has created to guide him through his life. These paintings help me graphically explain my philosophy, mostly to myself."

"How so, Sir?" asked Tim, intently focusing on the Major's words. A personal philosophy of life was something Tim had never thought about.

"Look, Tim. Ah, is it OK if I call you Tim?"

Tim nodded. No one had ever asked him that. In the Army, everyone, at least all those of higher rank, just called him whatever they wanted to call him. John was right, this Major Wojonski was a different breed of cat.

"Well Tim, every man, at least by his late 20's, hopefully earlier, should be asking himself why he does the things he does, what he believes, why he believes it, and where he is going. Somewhere along the way, a man has to stop doing things because other people want him to do those things, and from then on only do the things he really wants to do. From that moment, a man has developed a philosophy of life, and he uses that philosophy as an overarching framework of principles to guide his individual actions. For the rest of his life, he is constantly either reinforcing that philosophical framework, ...or renovating it with new and better ideas. He then uses that philosophical framework, consciously or subconsciously, to guide him through his choices. Life is primarily a series of choices. Or it should be. However, a lot of people just let things happen to them, rather than choose what happens to them."

Tim was mesmerized. He had never heard anyone talk this way. He slowly and lowly exhaled the words, "Tell me more."

"Well, my philosophy has many facets, but over the years I have realized that the major ones are my political beliefs, my social beliefs, my economic beliefs, my professional beliefs, and my religious beliefs. They all interact with each other to form an integrated whole. For example, my painting of JFK. I tried to express my admiration for him as a politician who did something no one else had done; he was a Catholic politician who overcame long-time religious and political prejudices to become president. He inspired me as a younger man to believe I too could become anything I wanted to become. Additionally, I come from a family of hard-working stiffs who believe in the Democratic Party and its attempts to improve the lot of the working people. I wanted all this to come through in my painting. Of course, as you can see from my Patton poster, maybe I'm not so enamored with the Democrats at the moment. They just don't understand this war. There's something going on in American politics today, some kind of sea change is happening. I can't quite put my finger on it. But I don't think I like it."

"Now, this picture of Martin Luther King provides insight into my social conscience. I worked hard on this one. In it I tried to portray the complexity of my thoughts on needed social changes. Again, I admire King for doing something that no other American had successfully done. He made a whole nation recognize the injustice it had done to a whole race. The genius of King was that he did this not through violence, but through peace. He knew from decades of experience that the people would demand the government answer violence with violence. However, he believed in his heart that the majority of people would answer peaceful demonstrations with peaceful justice. I know in my own heart, that had I been born a black man, I probably would have sided with the Black Panthers, not MLK. But the Panthers had the wrong answer. Dr. King had the right answer."

"This next painting containing the smaller portrait of Karl Marx, the father of Communism, overshadowed by the larger portrait of Adam Smith, the father of Capitalism, provides insight into my economic and social philosophies. I think Capitalism is the best economic system ever formulated. It has provided more material comfort and social mobility to more common people than any other economic system known to man. Yet, I believe it has to be tempered by some of the social concerns proffered by Marx. That proper balance, that yin and yang, between Marx and Smith is extremely important and must be maintained. Otherwise you end up with raw Capitalism's sweatshop exploitation of a minority, or with Communism's tyrannical suppression of the majority. The secret, the challenge of course, is finding that right balance. I think America has that proper balance, that yin and yang, just about right. The trick is keeping it in balance in the future. How do you like the Warhol effect of the painting? Kind of like looking at a film negative. It's symbolic of looking through the surface of a picture into the soul of the picture's subjects."

Tim had never heard language and ideas expressed like this before. Many of the words and references he didn't even understand. Forgetting military rank distinctions and proper ways to address an officer, Tim blurted out, "Where did you learn this stuff? How did you come up with these ideas? I mean, I don't understand half the words you're using, but I think I understand what you mean."

Major Wojonski reached for a pipe in his fatigues' right pantleg side pocket. He seemed to be carefully choosing the words he was about to speak.

"Tim, I was lucky enough to have working-class parents who had hard but decent jobs, making little but adequate money, and who were willing to work their butts off to help send me and my sisters to college. I went to a Jesuit University where the staff and curriculum educated both my mind and my soul. After that, I went to a state university and picked up a Master's Degree in Business. I believe education is the key to success, especially for minorities, the working class, and the socially oppressed. I also believe education, both formal and informal, should be a life-long endeavor for everyone. My time here in Nam proves that. I've learned things here that none of the great universities could ever teach me." He paused a moment, looked directly at Tim, thoughtfully hesitated, and then continued, "I believe you have too."

It seemed like a million thoughts were tumbling in Tim's mind, trying to break out into questions, but all his mouth could produce was, "You mean you have a college diploma and a Master's Degree, and you still got drafted?"

Wojonski looked a little surprised, but then understood. "No, Tim. I didn't get drafted. I volunteered. Like JFK said, I don't constantly ask what my country can do for me. I understood my country was in a fight, and I asked what I could do for my country. So here I am. Hey, I'm hungry, and you guys probably are too. Let's eat."

"Sir, could you first explain these other two paintings?" asked Tim, pointing to the tri-portrait with Ho Chi Minh and the painting of the woman.

"Sure. I'd be glad to," grinned Wojonski, as he turned back to his wall of painted philosophy. "I don't get to give many tours of my art gallery. First, let me say something about this print of Saint Thomas Aquinas. I've tried several times to transform that picture into an impressionistic painting symbolizing my religious beliefs, but have always failed. Thomas was a great mind, a philosopher and theologian. He lived in Italy and Paris in the 13th Century, the dawn of science in Medieval Europe. His genius was combining Aristotelian logic and the developing scientific methods of his day into a better way to understand and formulate the teachings of faith. He applied real intellectual rigor to man's study of both God and nature. He believed man's intellect should be unfettered and on a continuous quest to understand his world and his God, Who in Thomas' words is "The Uncaused Cause." I myself, like many others, are on that same complex quest. I just haven't been able to capture all that I feel about his teachings and transfer it to a portrait of Thomas. Yet!"

"Now, these three,..." said Wojonski, moving on to the tri-portrait Tim asked about and pointing to its first image.

Tim wanted to stop him there. He wanted to ask more questions about the Major's thoughts on religion. He too had experienced many complex and confusing thoughts about God and religion since being in Nam-Hell. But he didn't stop Wojonski. He didn't ask. The moment passed. Yet, his need had not.

"Hopefully you will recognize my rendition of Ho Chi Minh," Wojonski humbly stated. "Is he a national patriot or just another Communist dictator and war monger? I know what I think. However, history, not I, will make the final judgment. Like in so many other cases, it will probably depend on whether he wins or loses. This next chap is none other than the murderous bastard, General Giap. This guy sends his soldiers down here by the hundreds of thousands to be slaughtered in a war he knows he cannot win on the battlefield but realizes he might win in our television sets and newspapers. I hate the way this son-of-a-bitch wastes his soldiers' lives. Finally, this third image in the painting is my interpretation of Sun Tzu, a Chinese general, a strategist and philosopher. He lived more than 2,000 years ago. He wrote the book, *The Art of War*. If you haven't read it, do. It's a must-read for every soldier, no matter his rank. Sun Tzu's philosophy of war can be distilled down to four phrases, which have guided me since the first day I set foot in Nam: *'Know yourself; know your enemy. A hundred battles; a hundred victories!'* Think about it. You'll come to understand that all of martial history is contained in those four simple phrases. I fear that Ho Chi Minh and General Giap understand what Sun Tzu meant much better than do our leaders."

"Now, you also asked about this beautiful lady," Wojonski sighed. "Honoring beautiful women is also an important part of my personal philosophy. I do it every chance I get, usually at the Officer's Club. This particular beauty is Madame Curie, the famous physicist and chemist, known worldwide for her research on radiation. Her beautiful face could not hide her even more beautiful mind. She was the first woman to win a Nobel Prize. The only woman to win two Nobel Prizes. I have the Arch of Triumph as a hazy background because most people think she is French, because of her married name. However, these red and white roses that surround her, Poland's national colors, symbolize that she is really Polish, born in Warsaw as Maria Sklodowska. I hate it that everyone thinks she was a Frog, when in truth she was a Polack."

Tim, with a big smile widening on his face and his arms spreading wide apart, turned to John, as if to say, "See! I'm not the only one who uses those names and understands how they are meant!"

John, who had silently moved up behind Tim and the Major, ignored Tim's gloating face, and asked Wojonski, "And these several paintings of seagulls, what do they symbolize?"

"Them?" mused Wojonski, "They are all 'Jonathans.' You know, the #1 bestselling book, *Jonathan Livingston Seagull*, about the mythical gull. I tried to capture Jonathan's quest to be all he could be. I tried to portray his drive for perfection and his search for adventure. We should all be Jonathans. Or..., these paintings can mean whatever their buyers want them to mean. You want to buy one? No? Well then, let's eat!"

"Just one more question, Sir," said Tim. "The symbol "?" here, the question mark in the lower right corner of all your paintings, what does it mean?"

Major Wojonski smiled, "You have a sharp eye, Sergeant. Instead of a signature on my paintings, I put a 'question mark.' A signature suggests something final. A question mark indicates that there is still more to know, that nothing is ever really finished. Man's ability to question is what continues to move us forward. OK, let's eat. I'm really hungry."

As they walked to the kitchen end of the room, Wojonski said, "I was just about to eat when you arrived. I'm whipping up my favorite lunch; what I call a Grownup Grilled Cheese Sandwich. I guess when it comes to feeding myself, I'm still a kid at heart, so that's the grilled cheese part. Then I add a few extra ingredients that push it into grownup style."

As he talked, Wojonski turned on two hot plates and the griddle. Within minutes he had onions sautéing on one hot plate and coffee perking on the other. He slathered some butter on the griddle, then pulled a loaf of bread from the refrigerator.

"Here's the secret," he exclaimed. "Hawaiian sweet bread, or sometimes Portuguese sweet bread. Hawaiian is easier to get of course, especially since I run the port operations around here. Oops, better not say that too loudly. My colonels, generals, and admirals are under the impression that they run things."

Wojonski then placed six pieces of Hawaiian sweet bread on the griddle, placed some kind of dark cheese on each piece, then poured the sautéed onions on top of the cheese. Taking the six pieces of the now cheesed-and-onioned Hawaiian bread, he made three sandwiches, flipped them on the griddle several times, then slid them onto paper plates. He placed the plates, along with a cup of coffee for each of them, on the card table. Within seconds, Tim was enjoying the best grilled cheese sandwich he had ever tasted, and it seemed so easy to make.

The lunch conversation jumped from subject to subject, with Wojonski finally informing them that he would get them rooms at a hotel close to the beach; they could secure their weapons in his unit's weapons room; and they were invited to his weekly "Beer-Butt" chicken roast the next evening on China Beach, telling them to be there before sunset. He guaranteed there would be a good assortment of nurses, doctors, and donut dollies to meet. Tim shifted in his seat, looking a little uncomfortable.

"Something wrong?" asked Major Wojonski.

"I guess not," said Tim. "But I was thinking, well, perhaps I oughtn't, ..well, maybe a party with officers and all isn't a place for a Sergeant, E-5."

Wojonski smiled. "No fear there, young Sergeant. China Beach is not a place where rank matters. In fact, with bathing suits and shorts, no one has any place to pin their rank, especially the nurses. On the beach, it's what you say and how you act that matters. Believe me, warriors from the boonies, like you and John, have the places of honor around the bonfires. Well, maybe not John anymore, now that he's moved up to division headquarters."

Major Wojonski then got up, indicating that lunch was over, and he needed to get back to his daytime headquarters. John and Tim jumped up to help clear the plates and rinse the cups.

As Tim stood up, his eyes swept across the ceiling. He stopped, surprised. On the ceiling right above the Major's bunk was painted a 3-foot red square trimmed in black. It contained a quote in black block letters: "THE TASK OF DESTRUCTION IS INFINITELY EASIER THAN THAT OF CREATION. –Antaeus, Borden Deal"

Tim silently remarked to himself, "This must be the last thing Major Wojonski thinks about before he goes to sleep at night; and the first thing he thinks about after he wakes up in the morning. It must be hard being both a warrior and a philosopher in this place called Nam."

ON CHINA BEACH

It was just a little more than 24 hours since Tim had lunched with Major Wojonski. Since then, he had been exploring what Da Nang had to offer.

Now he walked along the beach, wearing a white T-shirt and red swim trunks. Powder-like white sand slipped through his flip-flops. His camouflaged boonies hat, the only thing that reminded him he was still in a war zone, protected his eyes from the glare of the lowering sun. He should have felt great, but he didn't. He felt wrong. He felt uncomfortable. He felt naked.

At first he couldn't understand any of those feelings, but especially his feeling of nakedness. But once he gave it some thought, he realized he felt naked, because he was naked. He was without his constant companion. He was without his M-16.

Since his first day in the Cav, over eight months ago, Tim had been wedded to that weapon. Where he went, it went. Usually it was attached to his hand or to his shoulder. Seldom was it more than a few feet away. On a daily basis, he carefully tended to its needs: deftly stripping it, spreading it across his bunk or poncho, massaging away the day's wear from each of its parts, meticulously applying oils here and there, redressing it, running his hand over its stock, admiring its form, appreciating its faithfulness. It had always been there by his side, ready to protect him, defend him, save him, obey him. It had never failed him. Truly, he felt, and was, naked without it.

His feeling of nakedness, he now understood. The cause for his feeling of discomfort however was harder to define. The first two days of R&R had gone well. It was just today, in the city and on the beach, that the discomfort started. It was not a discomfort of body; it was more a discomfort of mind. No, Tim decided; it wasn't really that either. It was more like an uneasiness, an uneasiness somewhere deep down inside him. Suddenly, without realizing it, he stopped dead in his tracks.

He stood there, not moving. Then he turned, slowly, in a complete circle, his arms outstretched, his eyes on the distant horizon. He could see for miles in any direction. From miles away, anyone could see him. "Oh my God!"

"No wonder I feel uneasy," he yelled to a seagull flying overhead. He was feeling uneasy because he was not in the jungle. His past eight months had been spent almost entirely in the jungle, where he seldom could see 100 yards, never mind miles. His body, his mind, all his senses had become attuned to the jungle; attuned to keeping him alive in the jungle. At the start of his tour, he had viewed the jungle as a constant threat. Now, he often viewed it as cover, concealment, protection. In the beginning, the jungle had been his enemy. Over time, if not his friend, the jungle had at least become a close acquaintance.

Now as he continued to walk the beach, he understood his feelings of nakedness, -no M-16, and his feelings of discomfort, -no jungle. But what about his feeling of "wrong." How was "wrong" something that he should...

"A penny?" boomed a voice.

Tim shook his head, to clear it. Focused his eyes. It was John.

"A penny for your thoughts?" repeated John. "You seem deep in thought, when in fact, you should be deep into one of those lovely young honeys over there frolicking in the surf. No doubt all that 'frolicking' is making them cool, but I'm telling you, it's making me hot!"

Tim smiled. He hadn't seen John since supper the previous night. By the look of him, John had been doing some "frolicking" of his own. A lot of it in fact. He looked like he could use a nap, a really long nap.

"What's wrong, Bro?" asked the sleep-deprived Sergeant First Class. "You look a little down."

"Bro?" laughed Tim. "You spend the night with the brothers? Hmmm, more likely with the sisters, by the look of you."

John's eyes rolled down his body to his sandals and then rolled back up, giving himself the once over. He then looked at Tim, "Damn! I got to find me a place on these trunks to sew some rank. I ain't getting no respect today."

"Probably none last night neither," quipped Tim.

The two friends started walking down the beach.

"I don't know, John. I just feel kind of funky today. Nothing physical. I guess I'm just in a bad mood."

"Feeling uneasy?" asked John. "Feeling like there's something wrong? Feeling like there's something wrong with you being here? Feeling like you shouldn't be here, when your fire team's back there?"

"Yeah," Tim slowly nodded, gradually realizing that John was describing how he was feeling better than he could describe it himself. "That's exactly how I feel."

"Gut guilt," said John matter-of-factly. "Nothing to worry

about. Take four beers, three whiskies, and two girls, then see me in the morning. You'll be cured."

Tim laughed, but then, more seriously, "Gut guilt? What's gut guilt?"

"Don't worry about it, Tim. We all suffer from it at one time or another. It often happens on the first R&R. At least it happens if you are any kind of a real soldier. You know in your mind that you need some R&R; everybody does. However, your gut tells you that you should be back with your unit, with your men. You're thinking or feeling, what if there's an attack, and you're not there to lead them, to support them, to fight alongside them? Thoughts go through your mind like, why are you lying on the beach, while they are lying in ambush? Why are you carefully avoiding stepping on beer cans, while they are carefully avoiding stepping on landmines? Why are you, hopefully, lying in a dry bed with a warm woman, while they may be lying in a monsoon puddle with a cold snake? And worst of all, way down deep inside, you fear going back and finding that one of your men has been killed. You'll have to ask yourself, if you had been there would he still be alive? That's gut guilt. It's nonsense; yet, it's real. Recognize it and deal with it for what it is. It's a sign that you are a good friend, a good soldier, a good leader. Then forget about it. They're there. You're here. That's all there is to it. God, the fates, Lady Luck, or whomever or whatever else you believe is in charge is dealing the cards. We just play the hand we are dealt."

Tim was about to pursue this gut guilt thing further, when John pointed down the beach, "Hey, I think that might be Major Wojonski's chicken roast. Down there, about a mile. See it?"

Yes, Tim saw it. But from that distance what he saw was just a clump of people in front of what looked like an unlit bonfire stack.

The friends started walking a little faster. They closed the distance in about 15 minutes, discussing their day's activities along the way.

Tim's major event of the day was a three hour lunch and beer fest with a Marine Force Reconnaissance squad in a beachside bar. The Marines included him in their group when they noticed that he didn't know the words to *The Animal's* hit song, *"We Gotta Get Out of This Place,"* understandably a song that constantly blasted from almost every GI bar in Vietnam. They made it a point of teaching him the words by sitting the Vietnamese singer on his lap till Tim knew every note and syllable. Tim now knew the song, but sang it with a Vietnamese accent.

"John, I'm telling you. Of all the bars I could have stopped in, fate sent me there. It turned out to be the place where all the 'Special Ops' types hang out when in town. There were Army Special Forces guys, Navy SEALs, Marine Force Recon, even Air Force Pararescue guys who call themselves PJ's. I'm not sure what PJ stands for, but I didn't even know the Air Force had a tough bunch like that. In many ways, the bar reminded me of an ice cream parlor back home where I always stopped after school. All the guys from the different ethnic neighborhoods were there waiting for buses. There was name calling, betting on Saturday football games, warning other guys off our girls, all that stuff. It was a fun, lively place. This was too."

"No fights?" asked John incredulously.

"No. Surprising, huh? That's what I was expecting too. Maybe we've seen too many movies? When I went in, I didn't know who was who, or what was what. Nobody was in uniform of course. Only after hearing them talk and after drinking a few beers did I realize who they were and what was going on. This was really the first time I've ever even talked with guys from the other Services, never mind partied with them, with the best and toughest of them. I think I was accepted because I was airborne. I had a great time."

"So, you didn't find them any different from us?" John prodded.

"Well, no. They were calling each other jarheads, swabbies, grunts, etc. But they were all talking about going home, or hunting the enemy, or which bar girls they wanted to marry, or different fighting techniques. By the way, I've got to check out something called Akido. Sounds like a wow martial arts"

"So," continued John, "when the uniforms are off, everyone is basically the same, right?"

"Well, yeah! Of course." said Tim, seemingly missing John's point. "I particularly liked the Marine Recon guys. They were a hoot. They had a million stories about one of their training officers back stateside. Some Captain they called Recondo Reilly. A big 6'4" redheaded Irishman who apparently was in a constant state of irritation with them. I guess while they were in school, they did nothing but bitch and moan about this guy, about the tough training he put them through. He constantly demanded total commitment in learning and total perfection in execution. Now, however, they all admit they'd kiss his ass, if they ever meet him again. Every one of them said he and his training were the reasons they were still alive. But man, did they have some great stories about the guy. The stories reminded me a little of Sergeant Pack, my training NCO at Fort Jackson."

Tim then grabbed the top of his T-shirt and pulled down its left front side and turned towards his friend, "Hey John, look at this. What d'ya think? Like it? It's a gift from the Green Berets at the bar."

"Geeez, Tim! You had Airborne wings tattooed on your chest!" exclaimed John, with some exasperation. "Apparently, I can't leave you alone for five minutes. You..."

Just then a high-pitched voice belonging to an attractive toothy smile and a bobbing ponytail, yelled to them, "Hey, you guys want to join our chicken roast?"

"We might," John yelled back, with his own toothy smile. "Is this where Major Wojonski roasts chickens that have big old fat beer butts?"

The toothy smile laughed and bobbed a yes.

"Well, great. We were coming here anyway. Glad to meet you. I'm John and this is Tim."

The crowd moved to greet them. Tim counted seven girls and two guys. Pretty good odds, he thought. No wonder Miss Toothy Smile was out hawking guys who were walking by. She needed to even the numbers.

As everyone was introducing themselves, Tim noticed five grills positioned in a straight line parallel to the beach and already hot. He had never seen anything quite like this. On top of each grill, sitting straight up with its little wings spread open, was a full roaster chicken with an apparently full can of beer stuck up its butt. All five of them were just sitting there, each on its own aluminum Budweiser throne, sweating and getting cooked, like five fat goombah wiseguys in a sauna. Tim just had to laugh at the thought.

"What's so funny, Tim," said a southern drawl, as it eased up next to him.

"The chickens," he answered. "All lined up like five fat goombahs sweating in a sauna."

"Hah. I never quite thought of them that way before. Now that I have, I'm not sure I'll ever be able to eat another one," said the tiny southern brunette, in a tiny black bikini. "Maybe I'll be able to wash that image out of my mind with a beer. Want one?"

As she walked over to a cooler, Tim noted, in addition to how nicely she walked, that there must be eight to ten coolers mixed in with the dozen or so beach chairs. This was going to be a good party. Also among those chairs was a large, high-backed wooden one with large arm rests, looking almost like a throne. Two lines of words painted across the top of the throne said, "For THE shortest among us!"

When the little southern drawl came back, it handed Tim a beer and said, "By the way, I'm Ruby."

"Well, hi Ruby," he responded, looking at her, then at the beach throne. "Hey, you appear to be the shortest, I mean the most petite, person here. Is that your chair?"

She laughed, "No, big guy. It's not that kind of 'short.' It's the other kind of 'short.' You know. It's for the shortest of short-timers amongst people here at the party. It's for the person with the fewest number of days left till she or he jumps on the big bird home. It's Plat's idea. Whoever is going back to the real world during the coming week gets to sit on the throne."

"Cool idea. Who's Plat?"

"Plat. Platon Wojonski. Major Wojonski, the guy who throws these parties every week. You know him, right?"

"Yes. Yes, of course," recovered Tim. "However, I just met him yesterday. I don't usually run around calling Majors by their first names. I didn't know people called him Plat."

Ruby now knew that Tim was somewhere lower on the rank structure than a Major. But she had already figured that out anyway, just by his apparent age. She thought him nice looking, maybe a little young, and then there was something else. Something a little more subtle about him intrigued her. She would have to find out just what that something was before the night was over.

She continued, "Well Tim, how short are you?" she said with a little twinkle in her eye, in her smile, and in the way she said it.

Tim, for a moment, wasn't sure what she had just asked him. "Stop the nonsense," he thought to himself. He gulped some Bud and said to Ruby, "I got about four months left."

"Then what?" she asked, lightly brushing her arm across the side of his thigh as she reached for a chair. "Let's sit."

"Then what?" he repeated her question, oblivious to what else was going on. "Well, I'm not sure."

He took another gulp, using the time to quickly think about her question and his answer. This was the third time this subject, his future, had come up in just three days. First, at dinner with John and his talk about future plans for college and a career. Then with Major Wojonski and his philosophy about people, even seagulls, taking charge of their future. And now here, just sitting on a beach with a pretty girl, the question arose again. He might just have to start giving some thought to his future.

"I wasn't sure either," chirped Ruby, breaking the growing silence. "So I extended. I'm putting in another six months here. I guess the real truth is that I'm a trauma nurse through and through. That's all I ever wanted to be. I feel I'm needed here more than anyplace back in the real world. I've decided to stay as long as I'm needed. I guess Plat is my hero. He's extended something like a dozen times. Did you know he's been here over seven years?"

Before Tim could answer, he spotted Major Wojonski walking across the beach toward the group. Wojonski's appearance distracted Tim for a moment. The Major was out of uniform, now casually dressed, wearing a Cleveland Browns football jersey with #32 on it, camo fatigues pants, and camo flip-flops. But what really had Tim focused was the western style six-shooter and holster strapped to the Major's right thigh. Did he really think he was Patton?

Wojonski made the rounds; he seemed to know almost everyone present. After a few minutes, he got to Tim and Ruby.

"Hi, do you mind if I sit myself down here for a while? It's been a rough day! Tim, would you please hand me a beer?"

Tim grabbed a cold one from the cooler and stretched the beer over to Wojonski. After a long day of drinking and maybe feeling a little more relaxed and familiar around the officers than he should, Tim jokingly shouted, "Hey there, General Patton, what's with the six-shooter? You expecting some Indians to attack this campfire tonight, Pardner?"

Ruby giggled. A few others, close by, stared.

Major Wojonski went still. His body tightened, his face hardened, his eyes narrowed, their slits blazing forth ice-blue shafts of fierceness. The air between Wojonski and Tim went still. Their breaths went still. The ocean's waves went still. The sun's decent was stilled.

Tim was petrified in place. He was scared sober.

For a long moment Wojonski was cold hard granite. Then the ice-blue fierceness of the offended warrior receded, and the sky-blue openness of the philosopher emerged. The face softened. The body relaxed. "Hmmm. I guess that's a fair question, my young friend. Let me drain this beer, then I'll answer it."

Then, Tim also began to relax, but more slowly. His heart began to beat again, but more quickly. His mouth was dry, needing to be wetted. His armpits were wet, needing to be dried. Relief slowly radiated through his body. He had never seen a look like that before, and he never wanted to see one like that again. Not directed at him anyway.

Wojonski drained the can, crushed it with one hand, scored two points as it passed into the trash can, then asked Tim for another. Tim passed one to him, this time remaining silent.

"Here's the story on the six-shooter," started Wojonski. "I'm fighting three major wars here, as well as a hundred other minor skirmishes, all at the same time. Adding to my problems is the fact that these wars are being fought against the backdrop of Nixon's Vietnamization Program. So, while I'm fighting these wars, I also have to incrementally turn them over to the South Vietnamese government."

"My first war is managing supplies passing through this port. Da Nang port has more than 5,000 sailors and 11,000 Vietnamese and civilian contractors moving 320,000 tons of cargo per month through almost four million square feet of storage space. It is a monumental task. Things get damaged, are misrouted, go missing; all thanks to both black marketeers and human screw-ups. I'm the only guy with long-term memory of how this port best operates. Thus, I'm usually the go-to-guy for problems. I'm the port's troubleshooter."

"My second war is ensuring those supplies get from my port to the guys that need them, guys like you, warriors on the front lines, or whatever we're calling the battle lines in this war. To do that, I use my long-term experience in and knowledge of the highlands to help plan convoys and convoy protection. Tim, you've seen the convoy maps on my BOQ walls. I've personally been over every foot of those roads and trails, most more than once. When necessary I can quickly produce trucks, boats, and choppers to personally deliver emergency supplies most anywhere in the highlands."

"However, my third war is perhaps my most difficult and discouraging fight. That's the drug war. It's the most discouraging because like Pogo said, 'I have found the enemy, and he is us!' In this fight, I'm actually at war with American sailors, soldiers, marines, airmen, and contractors. They are the enemy, moving drugs from the jungle through my port to the States. They are also the vermin providing drugs to our combat troops, thereby lessening their discipline, their combat effectiveness, and their chances of getting home in one piece. I just don't understand how Americans can do this. All this just for money. I will not stand for it. Whenever and wherever I catch these guys, depending on their role in this war, Americans or not, there's always the chance they may not make it to the brig. I make sure they know that. After all these years I think I know every trick in the proverbial book, yet I still get surprised by the creativity and ingenuity of these bastards. Like the other two, this war drains my energy. Unlike the other two, this war also drains my spirit."

"Now, why this six-shooter? About three years back, some drug vermin left this gun and holster on the main wharf with an attached note addressed to me. The note said something like *'Captain Wojo, Pack up and take the next plane home, or pack this on and go home in a box. Either way, your cowboy days of running this port are over.'* To ensure I understood who was making the threat, this gun was covered in cocaine. I strapped it on that very moment and walked the wharfs ten hours a day for the next several weeks. It was my statement back to them that the sheriff was still in charge of the town. Over the years, several attempts have been made on my life. Whenever I feel a little uneasy and don't know why, I listen to that feeling as though it is a sixth sense. Then I strap this on as warning to those who warned me. Today I felt a little uneasy."

"Anyway, that was a long answer to your short question. Here's a short answer. No, I don't expect any Indians tonight. But John Wayne, or even General Patton, would be ready, just in case."

Before Tim could say anything, Wojonski was on his feet and addressing the crowd, "OK, everybody listen up. Who's going home this week?"

Everyone looked around but nobody spoke up.

"OK then," he continued. "None of our regulars are going home this week, and none of our guests either. That's good. I need good people to stay here with me as long as possible. However, we do have someone who's going home soon. He is a double digit midget, whose short timer's calendar shows 29 days left. We may not see him again before he leaves, so let's give him a good sendoff tonight. John, come on up here. This throne is yours for the night."

John tried to protest, but Wojonski wasn't having any of it. Finally, John got up and dragged his feet to the throne and sat down. Everyone clapped and cheered. Wojonski sat down next to him. He pulled a pint of rum from one of his side pantleg pockets. He and John passed it back and forth, discussing who-knows-what. Perhaps the Major was trying to sell John one of those seagull paintings.

Someone yelled to a tall blonde in a camo bathing suit who was brushing a sauce over all the chickens, "Lisbeth, how much longer?"

Lisbeth looked at her watch, then at the sun, then at her chickens. She yelled back, "Ten minutes to a China Beach Sunset. Twenty minutes to my China Beach chickens."

Ruby leaned over to Tim and whispered, "That's Lisbeth. She's a Norwegian doctor. She's also Plat's main squeeze."

Tim gave this Lisbeth a long onceover. He then said to himself, "I can certainly appreciate that aspect of Wojonski's personal philosophy of life."

After a few minutes, Major Wojonski stood up and started walking to the sea. "Anyone want to join me at the water's edge?"

Everyone got up and followed. Tim grabbed a beer for Ruby and one for himself, and they too quickly closed the 50 yards to the water's edge.

Tim stood there witnessing a sunset that spread red, yellow, and orange fire across the sky from horizon to horizon, as a magnificently stunning sun shimmered its way to touching and passing behind the edge of the earth. He had never seen anything so gloriously majestic as this sunset on China Beach.

Wojonski, twisting left and then right, so all could hear him, said, "OK, here we stand at the nexus of God's creation. Each of us is part of that creation, especially now, as we stand here with one foot on land, one foot in the sea, our head in the sky, and our soul in this war. Who wants to give tonight's salute to the sun?" After a moment's silence, "What, no takers?"

Then one of the guys to Tim's left piped up, "You do it Plat. Since we have a couple of out-of-towners here tonight, they might enjoy hearing your somewhat unique rendition." Everyone murmured in agreement.

"OK, OK. The sun's about to set, so I don't have time to argue with you all. Here goes."

Ruby leaned over to Tim and whispered, "You're gonna love this. Plat certainly has a, let's say, 'different' way of thinking about some things. A China Beach Sunset is one of those things."

Major Wojonski started, "Tonight, people on sunset beaches all over the world will cheer and clap for perfect sunsets. They will thank their God or Mother Nature for giving them another day and another sunset."

"That's not what a China Beach Sunset is all about. On China Beach, we don't thank God FOR sunsets. On China Beach, God thanks us WITH sunsets. With this truly magnificent sunset tonight, and every night, God is thanking us for what we did today, and what we do every day."

"What we do every day, in the face of everything we see and know, is keep the faith. Every day, these doctors try to save lives of young men on death's door, thousands of miles from their families, homes, and churches. Every day, these nurses comfort and care for the mangled, tortured bodies of those who, just a few days earlier, were strong, vibrant young men. Every day, these Red Cross women get on choppers and fly treats and smiles to young men hungry for both in faraway jungles and mountains. Every day, young men, like these with us tonight, go out into the jungles and hunt death, maybe their own."

"While we do all this, in every way, on every day, we somehow still maintain our faith in God. For our miracle of keeping the faith, no matter what we see every day, He must thank us. For our miracle of still hoping for a better tomorrow, no matter all the evil we see every day, She must thank us. With this China Beach Sunset tonight, and every night, God does thank us!"

As Platon's final word traveled out over the sea towards the sun and its Creator, the sun's final fire descended behind the earth's edge, sending out a bright green flash as a final goodbye.

Tim slowly turned away from the sun's waning glow. He had faith that tomorrow would bring a new sunrise, a new sunset, and a new day. Too bad it wouldn't bring a new world.

However, Tim should have had even more faith. For he was about to find a new world. That new world would be found in the heart of a woman.

Party Lasagna

Early in his career, when a Captain, Tim was assigned as a ROTC instructor at Penn State University. While there he met his future wife, a nursing student named Brileen O'Sullivan. Little did he know at the time, not only did this Irish colleen bring with her a dowry of love but also a great lasagna recipe. His Italian heart was happy with her Irish love, and his Italian palate was happy with her hearty lasagna, as long as it was served with a glass of Chianti.

Ingredients:(Eight Servings)

1 Lb	Italian sausage and/or ground beef
1 Onion	Medium size – chopped
1 Tbsp	Garlic
4 Tbsp	Chopped basil, parsley, oregano, or chives
1 Packet	Artificial Sweetener
1 Can	Diced Tomatoes
1 Can	Tomato Paste
Box	Lasagna Noodles
1 Lb	Ricotta Cheese
1 Egg	Beaten
½ Cup	Grated Parmesan Cheese
2 Slices	Prosciutto
1 Cup	Grated mozzarella Cheese

Directions:

1. In a large skillet saute sausage/meat, prosciutto, onions, and garlic until cooked – drain.

2. Add tomatoes, diced tomatoes, and paste, crushing the tomatoes. Add sweetener and half of the herbs – retaining one half for the cheese mixture.

3. Heat to boiling then simmer for 30 to 60 minutes –

reducing the mixture until it thickens.

4. Prepare lasagna noodles according to directions on the package – drain and set aside.

5. In a bowl mix the egg, ricotta, mozzarella, parmesan, and remaining herbs.

6. In an ungreased (9 X 13) baking dish spread one half of the   tomato-meat sauce on the bottom, top with noodles, spread half the cheese mixture, top with noodles. Repeat, ending with cheese. Cover with foil.

7. Bake covered at 350F to 375F for 30 minutes – remove foil and bake for another 10 minutes.

8. Remove and let stand at least 10 minutes before cutting.

Tips:

1. Can be made ahead and frozen. Also great reheated – the flavors really blend.

2. After bringing mixture to a boil and reducing, Brileen sometimes added up to a ½ cup of wine and some olive oil to the sauce –done to taste. This is also the time to add salt, pepper, and additional herbs.

3. The original recipe had a chopped chicken breast included in the sauce, but Brileen, although liking chicken, favored using Italian sausage. Likewise you can substitute crepes for the lasagna noodles – these can be made ahead and eliminate the hassle with the noodles.

4. You can add additional layers by using only one third of the mixtures at a time. Also add some extra mozzarella at the top.

Julian's Crock Pot Beef Bourguignon

While Tim's first exposure to Beef Bourguignon was in downtown Saigon, it was not until later in Washington, D.C. when he met Julian Fastard that he truly appreciated the time and energy to prepare this fantastic dish. Julian was a sous chef at a small restaurant in Georgetown. Tim met Julian when assigned to the Joint Staff and routinely escorting foreign military officers visiting the E Ring of the Pentagon. One night Tim was discreetly making a telephone call when Julian, on a break from the kitchen, lit up a Winston and started to talk about the menu. Julian ultimately opened a small restaurant in a suburb of DC. Tim acquired his rather fussy recipe for Beef Bourguignon but found that he could replicate a worthy replacement in the crock-pot without the drama so associated with the dish --- bon appetit!

Ingredients:(Four to Six Servings)

2 Tbsp	Olive Oil
2 Lbs	Stewing Beef, cut into cubes
3 Strips	Bacon
2 Large	Carrots, diced
4 Medium	Potatoes, diced
1 Large	Onion, sliced
1 – 2 Cups	Beef Bullion
1 Cup	Burgundy or Pinot Noir
½ Tsp	Thyme
2 Tbsp	Chopped Parsley
1	Bay Leaf
Salt/Pepper	To Taste
Minced Garlic	To Taste

For the Sauce:

½ Lb	Sliced Mushrooms
1 Tbsp	Olive
1 Can	Brown Beef Gravy
Salt/Pepper	To Taste
Handful	Pearl Onions

Directions:

1. In a large skillet sauté bacon and remove; brown meat in bacon fat.
2. Add beef to the crock pot, followed by bacon and next nine ingredients, ensuring enough liquid to cover the beef and vegetables.
3. Select high setting on crock pot and bring to boil.
4. Lower to simmer and cook for a total of two to three hours.
5. When ready to serve, brown mushrooms in oil for four minutes (preferably in a large frying pan). Add pearl onions and canned gravy --- heat until onions are soft and gravy is hot. (If necessary add some stock from the crock pot.)
6. Remove beef and vegetables from crock pot --- add to large frying pan. Reserve liquid from crock pot and add to frying pan until desired consistency is achieved --- salt and pepper to taste.

Tips:

1. Tim prefers to use a large cast iron frying pan for browning the beef, the mushrooms, and the final combination.

2. You can make ahead and just reheat – if you do so use a casserole instead of the frying pan for the final step.
3. Simple meal with the red wine you used for the stock and a loaf of French bread.

Grown-up Grilled Cheese Sandwich

Everyone has a favorite way of making this comfort food and since Da Nang Tim experimented with various cheeses, breads, and additions. But it was his Zia Mary who made the not too subtle suggestion that he stop going away from the reservation and try the Portuguese sweet bread that she used all those years in Central Falls, Rhode Island.

As usual, she was right, but Tim settled on Jahlsberg cheese (nutty flavor) as the feature instead of some "yellow cheese" that she recommended and added sautéed onions to complete a rather mellow and satisfying dish. Many variations to this are possible and the tips section suggests a few.

Ingredients:(Two Large Sandwiches)

2 Tbsp	Sweet Butter
1 - 2	Small -sized Yellow Onions, thinly sliced
4 Slices	Sweet Portuguese/Hawaiian bread
½ Lb	Jahlsberg Cheese, shredded
To Taste	Herbs and Spices
As Needed	Additional butter to spread on bread.

Directions:

1. Thinly slice/julienne onions.
2. Heat a large skillet with sweet butter.
3. Add onions to skillet and cook until translucent – about 5 - 10 minutes; transfer to bowl for later use.
4. Butter bread on the outside and lightly on the inside.
5. Sprinkle cheese evenly on the bread.
6. Top with sautéed onions; cover with the top piece.
7. Fry in the large skillet, allowing to brown but not burn; flip and do the same on the other side.
8. Plate and serve immediately.

Tips:

1. You can substitute almost any hard and shredded or sliced cheese, but Tim recommends against soft cheeses.
2. Depending upon the type of onion you are using, Tim usually adds a packet of artificial sweetener - it helps with non-sweet onions and aides in caramelizing.
3. In lieu of the sweetener you can sometimes add thin strips of roasted red pepper, thus adding sweetness and a dash of color.
4. Experiment with fresh herbs when available such as chives and dill. Occasionally spice up with jalapeno slices.
5. Pair with a white or sparkling wine or a Bud.

China Beach Beer-Can Chicken

The origin of Beer Can Chicken or Drunken Chicken probably goes back centuries to the Napoleonic era when canning was first used for troops on the move. Tim's first exposure to it was at Major Wojonski's beach party in Da Nang, a beach later made famous by the TV series – "China Beach." It was prepared en masse by the Doughnut Dollies (Red Cross Volunteers) for units coming off the line. Cold beer, roast chicken, lovely women –what more is there?

Chicken Ingredients:(Four Servings)

3 – 5 Lb	Whole Young Chicken
1 Can	Beer (12 or 16 Oz)
2 – 3 Tbsp	Seasoned Chicken Rub (see next section)
1 – 2 Tsp	Oil (vegetable or olive)

Rub Ingredients:

1/8th Cup	Smoked paprika
1 Tbsp	Dark Brown Sugar
1 Tbsp	Salt
1 Tbsp	Pepper
1 Tbsp	Each of Ground Cumin, Celery Salt, Dry Mustard, Garlic Powder, and Onion Powder per your taste

Directions:

1. Preheat the grill.
2. Clean and rinse chicken – discard excess fat and remove packets of giblets from cavity.
3. Rub the chicken with oil.
4. Rub both inside and outside of chicken with your favorite rub.

5. Open beer can with pull top and add an additional few holes with a church key.

6. Pour off/drink about one third of the beer.

7. Place chicken atop the beer can – transfer to an aluminum pie pan (discardable); spread wings/legs to balance chicken.

8. Place pan and chicken in center of grill; the pan prevents the fat from dripping into the grill.

9. Depending upon the grill, you may elect to transfer to the cool side.

10. Chicken cooks in about 1 to 2 hours depending upon size and heat of your fire --- 180 degrees internal with a meat thermometer.

11. Remove chicken from can with barbecue tongs or fork – let the pan and fat cool before discarding.

12. Allow chicken to cool for five minutes before carving.

13. Easily serves four.

Tips

1. The first five ingredients for the rub are the core. Lisbeth added all the others depending upon tastes, etc. Commercial rubs can also be used; especially if you got them as Christmas gifts.

2. Lisbeth usually paired this with a simple potato recipe she used when grilling out – cut potatoes into bite size pieces (leave the skins on?) – microwave in water about six minutes – drain and lay onto aluminum foil tent– season with salt, pepper, herbs, and drizzle with olive oil – seal tent and heat on side of grill for about 20 – 30 minutes.

3. Gas or charcoal, woodchips, Bud or Heineken - are all your call – it's pretty much a no fail recipe.

CHAPTER 10: FLASHBACK – GOING HOME

Day Four: Thursday, 1030 hours, in the Train, Heidelberg to Paris

"Herr, gehen sie nach hause?"

"What!" Tim thought. In his mind he was still on China Beach in Nam. "Who's speaking German here?"

"Herr, gehen sie nach hause?" the little voice repeated, a little more forcefully.

Tim looked away from the window of blurs and toward a little boy, about 5 years old, looking up at him, expectantly waiting for an answer.

Just then a young woman, apparently the little boy's mother, came along, smiled at Tim while shaking her head, then shooed the boy along. Tim again was left alone with his memories.

Herr, gehen sie nach hause? Mister, are you going home? Tim wondered why the blond-haired, blue-eyed little boy wanted to know. Then an image formed in his mind from long ago. It was an image of a black-haired, chocolate-eyed little boy asking him the same question, "Sergeant Tim, are you going home?" Tim didn't know the answer then, and he didn't know the answer now. Mostly for the same reason. Neither then nor now did Tim really know where home was.

Tim turned back toward his window of blurs, his present portal to the past, to Nam. He again saw himself standing in the glow of that magnificent sunset on China Beach, hearing Wojonski's words, and wishing for a new world. When he returned from that R&R to his 1st Cav base camp, he found that new world.

He could still remember the first feelings he had while walking from the chopper pad to his hooch. Inexplicably, he was actually glad to be back with his unit, with his men, with his mission. However, by the time he reached his bunk, he could sense a new vibe throughout the camp.

"Hey, Sarge, have you heard the news? We're going home! Yeah, man, we're all going home!" were the first words from his hooch mate.

"What?! When?!" asked Tim, sitting down on his cot, wanting to hear the whole story.

The word was official, Tim's unit would be leaving Nam in just three months. The war wasn't over for everybody, but it was going to be over for them. As part of Nixon's drawdown and Vietnamization policies to end the war, most of the 1st Cav's units already had returned stateside a year earlier, leaving only the 3rd Brigade, Tim's unit, still in-country, still in the fight! Now it was their turn to depart. The 1st Cav was the first combat division to fully deploy to Nam, and now would be the last to leave. As happy as Tim was for everybody else, he kind of shrugged his shoulders. He was going home in three months anyway.

"Whoa, there Pardner," Tim told himself. "Maybe there is also a silver lining in all this for you. If the unit is moving back to the States in three months, it's going to have to start standing down now. That should mean fewer interdiction missions and combat patrols. Reduced combat patrols translates to reduced chances to get your butt shot off." All of a sudden, Tim too was joining in the celebration.

As Tim was still joking around, his duffle bag still unpacked, Sergeant Major Shaffer strode into the hooch. "DePalma, about time you got back. Hope you got your fill of booze, babes, and booty, because you got nothing but work ahead of you. Lots of changes going on means lots of work to do, and little time to do it. The colonel wants to see you. Right now! Move out!"

Tim loved the Sergeant Major, the highest ranking enlisted man in the battalion. You always knew where you stood with the guy. He was a no-nonsense warrior. He always knew what he wanted done and when he wanted it done by. He left it up to you to figure out how best to do it. If you did it right, you were golden. If you did it wrong, you were crap. If you did it better and faster than he could have done it, then you got a lot more tasks to do.

Within 10 minutes of getting out of his chopper and with his bag still unpacked on his cot, Tim was standing in front of Lieutenant Colonel Clarke, his battalion commander. "We're glad you're back Sergeant DePalma. Hope you enjoyed your R&R. You needed a break, but your break's over. We've got lots to do in the next 90 days. You've heard the news, right?"

"Yes, Sir. I'm told we're heading home."

"Right. Sit down, I want to talk to you."

The colonel then explained that the 1st Cav would now be turning over its remaining combat missions to the Vietnamese at a fairly fast pace. To better facilitate that, the Cav was forming a new liaison team of two officers and five sergeants. That team was now attached to the Vietnamization Support Office, MACV (Military Advisory Group Vietnam) located in Saigon. Tim was now part of that team.

"Sergeant DePalma, we put you on that team because you're one of our best. You have two bronze stars for valor, and a silver star is pending. We need people like you with proven combat sense and Vietnamese language skills to make this final transition phase actually work. You'll meet your new 1st Cav teammates tonight up at Brigade Headquarters. Tomorrow, you'll meet the rest of your MACV team in Saigon. If you ever need my help in this mission, you call me directly. I mean that; no matter what the reason, you call me. I hope your bag is already packed because your chopper leaves in an hour. Sergeant Major Shaffer has seen to it that all your admin paperwork is getting done. Any questions?"

"No' Sir," Tim stood and saluted. Of course he had a hundred questions running around in his brain. He hoped the Sergeant Major would be able to answer them all in just an hour's time.

Tim executed an 'about face' and was smartly moving out,

when the colonel asked, "By the way Tim, I meant to ask you. Do you know that new Staff Sergeant DePalma we have now?"

Tim thought for a quick moment, "No, Sir. Can't say that I do. But I'll check him out. Could be a distant relative."

Lieutenant Colonel Clarke smiled and walked over to Tim with an outstretched hand. "Oh, I don't think he'll be too hard to find. Just check the first mirror you come to." With that, he shook Tim's hand and presented him with a set of orders and a new set of Staff Sergeant stripes.

Tim was stunned. He stared at the new chevrons. "Thank you, Sir. I had no idea."

"Congratulations, 'Staff Sergeant' DePalma! I was going to present these new stripes in a promotion ceremony this week, but we have been overtaken by events. No one deserves these more than you. Make sure you sew them on before you get on that chopper. Wear them with pride, Staff Sergeant!"

'Yes, Sir! Thank you, Sir!" Then the Army's newest Staff Sergeant strode out of that tent into the 1st Cav's newest mission, and into the newest phase of his own evolving journey.

THE WAR-FIGHTING YEARS:

Part 2: 1972-1973

THE ORPHANAGE

Tim had now been working as part of the MACV liaison team for two weeks. The two officers, Major Clare and Captain Keating, spent most of their time working issues in either the American or Vietnamese Headquarters in Saigon. Staff Sergeant DePalma and most of the other sergeants were in constant coordination with Vietnamese military and civilian leaders in towns and villages throughout the Cav's area of operations.

Tim was presently on a rather peculiar task, delivering a truck load of food supplies to an orphanage. According to Major Clare, one of the MACV generals and the French priest who ran the orphanage had been big drinking buddies, and the general more or less sponsored the place. About six months back, the VC killed the priest, infuriating the general and resulting in a week-long operation searching for the Charlies who did it. They were found and dealt with. Now, one of the priest's assistants runs the place. The general continues to provide needed supplies. No one asks any questions. After telling him all this, Major Clare then assigned this twice-a-month supply mission to Tim. Today was Tim's first trip to the orphanage.

These liaison missions were not supposed to be dangerous, but there were no guarantees. At least when he was out in the 1st Cav's combat patrol areas, Tim always had at least four or five guys around him, all armed like walking weapon stores. Now, as a liaison officer, he usually traveled alone, supposedly only on secure roads, but anything could happen. In the beginning, Tim often felt these one-man road trips to be inherently more dangerous than his former combat missions. As a precaution, Tim still carried his M-16, wore a .45 caliber automatic pistol on his web belt, and always had an M-3 submachine gun, the kind everyone referred to as a grease gun, hidden somewhere in any vehicle he was using.

That day the only trouble Tim expected was bad weather. The monsoon rainy season was just beginning, and it looked like a downpour was due any minute. As he approached a turn, Tim could see the orphanage about a mile up the road. It stood alone atop a hill.

As he drove up the winding road, he looked in the rearview mirror only to find the rain chasing him. He was going to beat the rain, but not by much.

The orphanage was enclosed in a large, square compound, about 250 yards on a side, surrounded by cinderblock walls about 4 feet high. Within the walls were a single 2-story building and four, low 1-story buildings of various sizes. "Hmmm. Looks like an old French fort," thought Tim. "Perhaps at one time it was."

The road passed through open gates and circled in front of the large 2-story structure which Tim assumed was the main administration building where he should report.

As he passed through the gates, Tim involuntarily slowed the truck. His eyes were no longer on the road. They were on a young woman; a woman clothed in the traditional Vietnamese *ao dai* dress; a woman who stood alone in the middle of the courtyard; a woman whose hand was raised in the air, but not to him; yet, a woman who was, in some quiet way, calling him to her.

As the road wound round the woman, so did Tim. As Tim wound round her, so did the wind. As the wind wound round her, so did the rain. She, at the center of it all, seemed not to notice.

Her voice rose with her hand to guide the children running from the playground, trying to avoid the coming storm. Her eyes stayed only on the children, as the wind howled and the rain approached.

Tim's eyes stayed only on her. The wind encircled her, whipping her long black hair from the back of her shoulders, round her neck, and then continually slapping it against her front, from chin to breasts. The white silk skirts of her *ao dai* tunic whipped about her, while the black silk of the *ao dai's* slacks were pressed against her. She stood resolute against the assault, her head unbowed, her eyes and mind watching only the children.

The rain first came as a dampening mist. It matted her hair around the contours of her face, presenting it as if a painted Madonna, a Madonna whose almond eyes could calm and comfort the world. As the rain increased, the *ao dai's* white silk tunic began to cling to her, revealing the delicateness of her body, but also the strength of her will.

Only after she watched the last child scamper to cover did she move to shield herself. As she moved toward the main building, her eyes quickly, yet gently, passed over Tim. She said nothing and disappeared inside.

Tim sat there, still awed by some lingering sense of her. No woman had ever made him feel the way he now felt. While she stood there, against the forces that swirled around her; he had wanted to go to her, stand beside her, protect her. She hadn't needed him. He was going to go to her anyway.

He went inside, both inside the house and inside himself, in search of her.

Immediately beyond the doors was a large hall. Tim stopped, then in a loud voice and in Vietnamese, "Anyone here?" No answer. He moved to the open door to his right and looked into what was apparently a combination office and sitting room. It was empty. He turned to check the room to his left, when out of nowhere a small, elderly woman stood before him, with a rather disapproving look on her face. She asked in Vietnamese, "May I help you?"

When Tim responded in Vietnamese, her face brightened a little. When he followed up with more traditional Vietnamese introductory comments and a few additional compliments meant only for her, she smiled broadly. She led him back into the waiting room and told him she would find the headmaster. The elderly woman also promised tea and teacakes. She smiled at Tim, bowed slightly, and disappeared as silently as she had come.

Tim wondered if the tea cakes would be like the ones he enjoyed so much in Monterey. He also wondered, instead of the headmaster and teacakes, could the kindly old lady please find him that beautiful young woman.

After several minutes, Tim's new, motherly admirer returned with the tea and cakes and said the headmaster would be with him in a moment. Tim's profuse thanks were again answered with a smile, a bow, and a silent withdrawal.

Then she entered. Tim leapt to his feet. She now wore a soft yellow *ao dai* tunic over flowing white silk pants. Her hair was still damp, now with a silken sheen. Her face had been freshened by the rain, like a flower after a sun shower. Her almond eyes settled on him, even as the rest of her made a gentle bow. A small, soft voice announced, in English, "Hello, I am Phan Thi Quan, headmaster of this school. Please call me Quan. Thank you for the graciousness of your gifts."

Tim wanted to say, "You are the loveliest woman I have ever seen." What he actually said was, "You are most welcome. It is our honor to provide them. I am Staff Sergeant Tim DePalma, and it is a pleasure to meet you."

Tim, the young warrior, and Quan, the young headmaster, talked for more than an hour about the orphanage, the needs of the children, how important the American supplies were to her mission, and a little about the continuing threat from those who had killed Father Lefevbre.

What was more important was that which was not said, at least in Tim's mind. As he drove back to Saigon, he relived their conversation again and again. Her every movement, her every word, her every look was played over and over in his mind. Throughout their conversation, she had remained reserved, poised, gracious. Yet, although she appeared to be a few years older than him, maybe three or four, he felt that something personal had passed between them. Had he imagined it? Was this just wishful thinking?

Tim had not been close with many women. All had been American. He had come to understand that when an American woman likes you, she usually has a way of letting you know. However, he knew that Vietnamese customs were different. That Vietnamese women were different. That their expectations were different.

He asked himself, "Are Vietnamese women really that different? If so, then how so? How will I learn these differences? What will I do once I learn?"

He had learned the jungle; had come to understand the jungle; was comfortable in the jungle. He had learned war; had come to understand war; was, if not comfortable, at least accustomed to war. Could learning women; understanding women; loving women be harder?

For the next several days, all he could think of was Quan. He could not wait two weeks to see her again. He wouldn't wait. He didn't wait.

Four days after his first delivery, he was back at the orphanage explaining to Quan how it would be more efficient if he provided supplies on a weekly basis, rather than every other week. He added that he would also stop by between those weekly deliveries to ensure he completely understood what supplies were needed in the next delivery. During his visits, he began helping with some of the more obvious maintenance needs, even once bringing buddies to help with a larger project. The orphanage consisted of seven buildings, including storage sheds and a garage, several small vegetable gardens, and a little more than a hundred children. There was much to be done. Tim became a regular fixture around the orphanage.

The children took to him immediately. He played dodge ball with the younger kids and tried to teach baseball to the older ones. Practicing their English on him was a constant source of amusement for everyone.

Quan seemed pleased with this new arrangement, at least on a professional basis. Tim was more interested, however, about her feelings on a personal level. Quan never revealed them, at least not that Tim could tell.

After a month of Tim's increased presence and attention, Quan asked him to lunch with her. She added that instead of eating in the school's dining hall with the children, they would eat in the dining room of the main house, alone. She would prepare the meal.

"Will you come," she asked. "Of course," he answered.

The next day when Tim arrived, Quan met him at the door. She wore a rose colored *ao dai*. The high-collared tunic, with the long skirt slats in front and back, was a rose-petal red, while the pants were a light pink silk. Her hair was upswirled into a low bun at the nape of her neck, the swirled hair held in place by interwoven pale pink orchids. She wore no makeup; she needed none. As she led Tim to the dining room, he thought her the most beautiful, the most elegant, the most graceful woman he had ever seen. All of him, responded to her simultaneously: his mind, his heart, his manliness. His heart involuntarily quickened. His breath involuntarily deepened. As she turned to find him looking at her, his face involuntarily blushed.

"Tim, would you please sit here, while I bring our meals," she was pointing to an old green, wooden chair at a worn, scarred, round green dining table.

Tim sat. As she walked into the kitchen, he thought to himself, "Apparently, today we are speaking English." Some days they would speak Vietnamese so Tim could practice. Other days they would speak English so Quan could practice. She spoke both English and French fluently. She liked to practice her English on Tim. He had no idea how or with whom she practiced her French.

She gracefully reentered the room, a plate in each hand. She placed before him a dish of glazed ginger chicken.

"This is my favorite Vietnamese dish, " He exclaimed.

"Yes, I know. You mentioned it when you told me about your language training in Ca-e-fone--ya." He smiled at the sweet way she pronounced California.

Quan had positioned herself at the round table at a 90 degree angle to Tim. Tim would have been happier, if she had sat right next to him. However, he thought it meaningful that she had not sat 180 degrees directly across the table, the furthest distance from him. He wondered, "Was there any meaning in where she sat?"

At that moment, Thu, the elderly woman whom Tim had met on his first delivery and who cared for Quan and the main house, brought in a tray with two chilled coconuts. The tops had been cut away, and the remaining coconut bowls were garnished with an orchid. A short straw was placed in the coconut's cool milk. Thu placed the first coconut in front of Tim, as the honored guest. She then placed the other in front of Quan. Her eyes went back to Tim, then to Quan, then she smiled, let escape a little chuckle, then silently departed.

Tim thought, but didn't say, "Damn, I wish my old jungle mates knew how to move so silently!"

The aroma of the ginger chicken awakened another hunger in Tim, this time a hunger for food. The ginger was sharp, but was somewhat softened by the sweetness of the glaze. This ginger glazed chicken was better than any he had eaten in Monterey, and he told her so. She was pleased. He also enjoyed the cool coconut milk, especially its presentation in the coconut shell. She said that Ba Thu would also be pleased.

During their lunch, the young soldier and the young headmaster talked of many things. Tim wanted to know more about the priest's death. Quan was reluctant to talk about it, beyond that he was killed in an ambush by local VC as he returned one evening from Saigon. The VC had long harassed him about teaching Catholicism, English, and Western literature at the school. She gently evaded Tim's further attempts to learn more about VC activity in the villages and rural areas around the orphanage.

At one point she gently commented on her preference not to use the word, orphanage, but rather the word, school. An orphanage was for children without a parent, without a family. Her children had a mother, and they were all a family. Tim only then realized that he had never heard her use the word, orphanage. The subtleness of her ways moved him.

Tim, in turmoil within but calm without, placed his hand over hers.

Her eyes settled on his. "Tim, we cannot be like that," she softly demurred. She did not withdraw her hand.

Tim, his hand remaining on hers did not ask "why?" because he did not want to hear the reasons he already knew. Rather, he found the courage, courage he did not know he had, to say, "Quan, I love you."

Her face colored to match her rose-petal *ao dai*. Her hand became warm, but it did not withdraw. She whispered, "But Tim, it cannot be."

However, it would be. Not now, but soon.

TRUC

Although Tim was accomplishing all his duties related to turning over 1st Cav responsibilities to local Vietnamese forces, Major Clare, his team leader, was aware of the large amount of time Tim was spending at the orphanage, and why. The Major decided to accompany Tim on his next delivery, check out the situation, and determine if he should pull young Staff Sergeant DePalma off the orphanage mission.

As Tim drove the truck up the hill towards the school's gates, he was in the midst of explaining to Major Clare why he should not use the term "orphanage," because...

"What the hell is this all about," exclaimed the Major as they passed through the gates and saw two Vietnamese jeeps up the road parked in front of the main building. The first jeep contained only a driver. The second jeep had a driver and three soldiers with rifles, all pointed at the truck coming through the gates.

"Tim, stop. Stop now! Our friends might be a little trigger happy. I'll get out and let them know who we are." Major Clare stepped down from the truck's cab. He smiled and waved at the soldiers. He gave the universal "OK" sign with his thumb and forefinger, then jumped back into the truck. The soldiers smiled, pointed their weapons toward the sky, but did not take their fingers off the triggers. Tim hated when they did that.

Just as Tim pulled the truck up to the front of the house and next to the jeeps, Quan and a Vietnamese officer walked out the door and stood on the porch, apparently saying their goodbyes. The officer descended the stairs, walked passed his jeep, and headed for Tim's truck.

"Oh crap," blurted Major Clare, "Major Truc! What's he doing here? This guy is a colossal pain in the ass. He considers himself to be a South Vietnamese nationalist. He does not like foreigners. He didn't like the French when they were here. He doesn't like us now that we are here. He's very difficult to deal with."

Clare got out of the truck and shook hands with the Vietnamese Major. After a nod and a smile, the Vietnamese pointed a finger at Major Clare, as if to say, "Wait just a moment," and then walked over to Tim who was now standing in front of his truck, watching Quan more than he was paying attention to the officers, saying "Hello" to her with his eyes.

"Sergeant, move truck over to storage building over there. Help my men take supplies from it. In future you not deliver supplies to orphanage. You leave supplies at my headquarters in Saigon. Save you much time." Tim started to climb back into his truck.

"Hold on there, Staff Sergeant DePalma," said Major Clare, slowly and firmly. Tim stopped in mid-climb, as he watched Major Clare walk up to the Vietnamese Major and stand no further than a foot from him in a classic face-off posture. "Major Truc, I appreciate your concern for my time. However, this little supply mission is no concern of yours. It's been nice to see you again. Safe trip back to Saigon. It should be, since you felt the need to bring a jeep full of bodyguards with you." With that, Clare turned away from Major Truc and started toward the building. "Staff Sergeant DePalma, leave your truck right where it is and come introduce me to the school's headmistress."

The Vietnamese Major's face was a cauldron of hate, as his eyes followed Major Clare up the stairs. They were no less hot when they burnt into Tim, as he tried to catch up with Major Clare. The Vietnamese officer signaled to his driver to start the jeep, and he then jumped in. He headed out of the compound, never unclenching his jaw or his fists.

Their meeting with Quan went well. She explained to Major Clare the school's extreme need for the supplies the general provided. She thanked him for both the supplies and for the time his team and other Americans spent in preparing and delivering the supplies. Then she informed him of the positive impact Staff Sergeant DePalma's presence and help had on the children, as well as on the leaders and people of all the surrounding villages. He was a wonderful emissary from the American military.

On the way back, Major Clare commented on how deftly he had just been handled. The headmistress was both charming and impressive. For a young woman in her 20's, she was certainly capable beyond her years.

Hearing Major Clare use the term headmistress several times, Tim, for the first time, wondered why Quan called herself a headmaster, rather than a headmistress. He would have to think about that.

Then Major Clare turned to Tim and said things that directly pertained to the scene with the Vietnamese Major, but which Tim would remember and adhere to for the rest of his life.

"Tim, remember this. You don't work for anyone else but me. It's my orders you follow. It's my missions you execute. If someone tells you to do something else, your first inclination should be 'F-you.' Always ask yourself, 'Does it fit in with what Major Clare has me doing.' I don't care if a general asks you to do something. If it interferes with your mission, tell him so. He may chew you out, or he may not. It doesn't matter. In his heart, he'll be saying, 'Good for you soldier. You know who you are and what you are about.' The only time you vary from what I order you to do is when you really think I am clearly screwing up and what I have you doing is going to have some seriously bad consequences. If that happens, you better be right. Do you understand what I'm saying? You are a staff Sergeant now. Remember who you are and what those stripes stand for. You are a leader. You know your mission. You believe in your mission. You know how to accomplish your mission. Do you understand what I'm telling you?"

"Yes, Sir. I understand."

"Good. Knowing who you are and what you are about is the key to success in the Army, in any walk of life. Now, it's late. The work day is over. Let's stop someplace for a cold beer."

"Sir, now that's an order I know I understand. One I know I want to follow. One I know how to accomplish. And I believe, one that will have only good consequences." Tim and Major Clare spent the next several hours sharing some beers, as well as thoughts about the Army, the war, and going home.

GOING HOME

As Tim drove up the now familiar road to the school, he hoped Quan would be there. She had not been there the past two deliveries, since the scene with Major Truc.

Tim had less than a month left in-country. He was definitely a short timer. His freedom bird was almost waiting on the runway, but where was the joy? Yes, he wanted to see his family again.

Yes, he wanted to start his new civilian life. But still, where was his eagerness, the expected excitement?

Just then, his heart did a flip. There, walking up the steps to the main building, was Quan. Upon hearing his truck, she stopped in mid-climb, turned, smiled, and waved. God, he thought her beautiful.

Moments later they were in her office talking. She did not mention where she had been the past two weeks, only that she had missed seeing him. He did not care where she had been. He was just happy that wherever it was, it had caused her to miss him.

Then they talked about Truc. He had been to the school twice in the past two weeks. He offered to provide all the supplies the school needed, emphasizing that she did not need to depend on the Americans. She could depend on him. Vietnamese should depend on Vietnamese. Besides, as he reminded her several times, the Americans would soon be gone. Then, she would have to depend on him. Quan deflected Truc's offers, saying the school would wait till a change was necessary.

"Why is this Major so interested in this school?" asked Tim.

Quan hesitated for a moment. "He is not interested in the school," she whispered, slightly lowering her head. "He is interested in me."

Tim's head jerked back slightly. It had never occurred to him that the Major's interest in the school was really all about his personal interest in Quan. "How naive I am," he admitted to himself. He felt jealousy rising within him.

Quan must have seen Tim's thoughts in his eyes. She reached out and gently put her hand on his, "Tim, do not worry. I have known Truc all my life. He will do nothing to hurt this school or me. Our families have always been close. Truc's father is a doctor, as is mine. They both work in Saigon's lead hospital, and they are both traditionalists. Many years ago they agreed on an arranged marriage between Truc and me after I turned 18. I refused. Truc has always liked me. I like him as a friend, most times. But I do not have feelings for him." Her last comment ended in a tone half finished, as if she wanted to add, "...not like the feelings I have for you."

Tim heard what she said, and understood. However, most of his attention was not focused on her words, but on her hand; on her hand touching his. She had never done that before. She had never reached out and physically touched him. In doing so now, she touched more than his hand. She touched his heart.

Quan was then called to deal with a situation in a classroom. Tim wandered out into the play yard to watch the kids. One of his favorites, a little 5 year-old boy with black hair and chocolate eyes, ran up to him and wrapped himself around Tim's leg, hugging it hard. Then the child looked up and asked, "Sergeant Tim, are you going home?"

That night Tim could not sleep. Two images kept him awake. They continually flashed through his mind, one after the other, as if on a spooled film. First, was a small pair of chocolate brown eyes asking him, first in English and then in Vietnamese, "Sergeant Tim, are you going home?" Second, was a small, soft, hand floating gently on his. This image was not accompanied by words or sound. It was accompanied only by feelings; feelings of warmth, of comfort, of love.

Tim knew what he had to do.

THE GIFT

It had been a week since Tim had last been to the school. He had been unable to make his usual mid-week visit. With only little over a week left to the 1st Cav's final departure date, much work still needed to be done, and he had been much needed elsewhere.

As he drove through the gates, he saw Quan walking between the two classroom buildings, on her way to the dining hall, her powder blue *ao dai* dress flowing in sync with her steps. Hearing the truck's engine, she stopped and waved. She remained there, waiting for him.

As he walked from his truck to her, she smiled and said, "I am glad to see you. I was hoping you would come today, and come in time to have lunch with the children."

As the children became aware of Tim's presence in the dining room, they began to clap. Soon they were all standing and clapping.

Quan led him to the front of the dining room. Tim soon learned that the children wanted to present him with a goodbye gift, and perhaps even more, they wanted a piece of a very large cake that said "Farewell SSG Tim, We Love You." The gift was a small picture of the school with a large white border where all the children had signed their names. Tim was moved.

When they asked him to speak, he spoke in English, as Quan asked him to always do with the children, and he kept it short. "Thank you all. This picture will always be very special to me. Also this cake is very special to me, because I also love all of you." His eyes, traveling across the young faces, finally stopped and lingered for a brief moment on Quan. "But before we all get some cake, I have one other thing to say." After a pause, with the kids waiting, either for his words or for the cake, he announced, "I have extended. I will not be going back to my home in America. . I am staying longer here in my home with you."

There was silence. The students were not sure what they had just heard. Tim then repeated his words in Vietnamese. They all clapped and smiled, and started to cheer. The little girl in front of him asked, "Do we still get cake?"

"Yes, we all get cake," he said with a very wide grin. "Dig in!" And they did.

Quan, at first, did not fully comprehend what Tim had just said. At first she didn't understand the word, "extended." Slowly, it unfolded before her like a flower. He would be staying. He would be staying for the children. But she knew, mostly, he would be staying for her.

She said nothing to Tim while they were celebrating in the dining hall. She said nothing to him as they walked from the dining room to her office. Once in her office, she closed the door, turned her back to it, leaned back against it. She looked directly at Tim, in a way she had never allowed herself to do before.

Tim stood there, his hands remaining at his sides. He turned them slightly upwards and declared, not only from his lips but also from his heart, "You must know, I did this for you."

She stood there, leaning back against the door, not moving, her eyes on his. Then slowly, she flowed forward toward him, led by her heart, with the rest of her body following. Tim did not move, he waited for her to come to him. She came, slowly, fluidly. She stretched up on her toes, leaned against him with her body, reached for him with her hands, sliding them up behind his neck. She softly pulled him down to her, to her lips, to her love.

SONGBIRD

It was now two weeks since Tim had extended in Nam. Since then he had been officially reassigned to MACV Headquarters in Saigon, where he remained on the Vietnamization Team. He was also still running the weekly supply mission to Quan's school.

His relationship with Quan had grown deeper. However, she would not allow her personal life to compromise her school or her family. Although she would allow herself to close her office door and steal a few moments with Tim, it was just not possible for him to spend evenings or nights at the school. As the headmaster, that is where she had to spend most all her evenings and nights.

This particular afternoon, at Quan's request, Tim found himself sitting with her in the courtyard of a Saigon restaurant called Songbird, situated along one of the main boulevards running through downtown Saigon. It was apparently a popular place. The trees were full of small wooden cages with singing birds, while the patio was full of small metal tables with paying customers. The waiter just left with their order.

"Tim, I am so happy you could come. I wanted to be with you outside the school. Was this restaurant easy for you to find."

"Very easy," answered Tim. Tim was pleased by the casualness and informality of the place. He hoped they could be more at ease here, more themselves. But she seemed nervous, tense.

He had never seen her quite this way.

"Tim, I want to tell you about my family. My father is doctor here in Saigon. My mother tends our home. I have two brothers and a sister. One brother is lawyer in Can Tho, and other is Captain in Army. My sister owns dress shop, right down street from here. I have talked with my family about you, your help for the school, and a little about my feelings for you. Except for my sister, none of them are happy about us, about our growing relationship."

"Quan, I am sorry about that. I can pretty well guess what their objections are. I'm a soldier, too brutal. I'm an American. They think someday I will leave you. Our cultures are too different to find common happiness. I know hearing all this must be hard for you. But I want to give us a try; see if we can make us work. Quan, I truly love you."

"I know that, but I also understand my family's concerns. I must respect their wishes for me. You both bring your wishes to me out of love."

Just then the waiter served their lunch. Quan had ordered them both Thai Chicken Coconut Soup and a glass of cold sugar cane juice. After a few tastes of the soup, Tim was a fan. "This is really good. What's in it besides chicken and coconut milk?"

Quan laughed, "Tim, so now you are becoming a cook? Now you must know all ingredients. See these? They are fresh ginger slices. And this, which looks like grass? Well, it is grass; it lemon grass. And these? Actual pressed leaves from lemon tree. All these ingredients make very light, refreshing soup for hot Saigon day. Do you know this drink in front of you?"

Tim smiled, "Oh yes. I know that drink; sugar cane juice. I almost lived on that stuff in Cav country. Whenever I visited villages, I would always either be given some, or I would buy some."

As Tim talked, he was still thinking about how nervous Quan was. Even her English was not as smooth as usual. She had never talked about her family before or its concerns about their relationship. "Oh, damn," a new thought just raced through his mind. "Did she ask me to come here to tell me she could not see me anymore?"

"Quan are you OK? Are you feeling ill? You seem nervous, uneasy."

She looked at him, silently. After a moment, "I am fine, Tim. Let us enjoy our soup." They talked some more about the food, the songbirds, the beautiful day.

As they finished their meal, Quan put down her spoon and took a deep breath. "Tim, remember I told you that my sister owns dress shop on this street?" Before he could answer, she continued. "If she were there today, I would introduce you to her. But she is not there, she is in Bangkok for two days."

Tim nodded, having no idea where this conversation was going. Quan shifted in her chair and wiped a little perspiration from her brow.

"My sister also has a small apartment on that side street over there on the other side of the boulevard. Building number 88, apartment number 20."

She passed Tim a piece of paper which contained two numbers, 88 and 20. She leaned close to him, "In 15 minutes, come to me. I will be there for you." She smiled at him, sweetly with her lips but deeply with her eyes, and left.

In 14 minutes and 59 seconds, Tim was in building #88 standing in front of apartment #20. He was sweaty and nervous. "Geeez, why am I like this? I don't do this on the battlefield," he sighed to himself. "I have wanted to be with Quan since the moment I first saw her; in the courtyard in the storm; head, unbowed; spirit, strong; loveliness, undeniable. Now, she is on the other side of this door waiting for me." He knocked.

She stood behind the door as she opened it, not wanting to be seen by anyone in the hall. With the door closed, she turned and stood before him, seeming very small and very vulnerable. She wore a white, silk robe that reached to her knees and was tied at the waist in a bow. Behind her the bed was prepared, candles were lit, subtle flower scents were in the air.

Tim went to her. He spoke no words. He cupped her face in his hands. He slowly and softly kissed her forehead, her eyelids, her cheeks, and finally her lips. She held his kiss, softly but strongly. Enclosing his arms around her, she felt willowy, delicate. As he strengthened his hold on her, she seemed to flow into him. The silk was smooth to his touch as his hands moved down her. He pressed her against him, then slowly eased back, his hands traveling the silk from her back, up her front, across her breasts, and then back down to her waist. He gently pulled at the silk bow, as if opening a special gift. The bow fell away and the robe parted. His hands spread the robe and assisted its flow to the floor. She was there before him, as he had always wanted her to be.

He bent to pick her up, to carry her to the bed, but she stopped him with but a finger lightly placed upon his chest. That finger was joined by others, which then traveled him, loosening buttons and sliding away clothes. Their bodies came together. She felt his strength. He felt her softness.

She took his hand and led him to the bed. She gracefully lowered herself into it, slowly drawing him down into it with her. They drifted off into a dream they both had imagined many times.

SIX MONTHS TO WHAT

Over the next six months of his extension, the couple spent as much time together as possible. Unfortunately, it never seemed enough. As his time with her, with his mission, was coming to a close, Tim extended for another six months. He could not leave. He just could not.

Tim maintained his weekly supply runs to the school. However, the continually growing Vietnamization Program demanded ever growing portions of his time, sometimes requiring that he travel to different parts of the country for several days at a time. For Quan of course, the school was always a 24 hour-a-day job, seven days a week. However, she would always be free to welcome him, to be with him, when he made his supply deliveries.

Their moments of intimacy were few, too few as far as Tim was concerned. Quan was still cautious not to chance bringing dishonor on her school or her family. They usually met at her sister's apartment, two or three times a month. Twice they met in distant cities, traveling separately, but once there, they remained together. Although Tim preferred a totally open relationship, he understood Quan's concerns and respected her wishes.

Christmas proved to be a test of their relationship. Tim asked Quan to accompany him to his unit's Christmas dinner at a well-known Saigon restaurant. She thought about it for several days, but in the end, she told him that she just could not go. She feared it would bring dishonor on her family and her school. She felt that some people would judge such an act as choosing Christian beliefs over her Buddhist beliefs; as accepting American culture over Vietnamese culture; as placing an American soldier's wishes over her soldier brother's wishes; and worst of all, placing her illicit lover's desires over those of her loving family. With tears in her eyes and real sorrow in her heart, she asked him to understand. It was just too much. Tim was disappointed, truly disappointed, but he understood, truly understood.

As a compromise, they had a Christmas dinner, just as a couple, at The Guillaume Tell. He understood the degree of courage it took for her to be with him that night. He fully understood her discomfort at being in this public place. However, after the first few moments she began to smile. She enjoyed the lighted candles, the china dishes, the gleaming silver, the sparkling crystal, but most of all, the smiling Tim. He hoped she understood how proud he was to have her there by his side, where everyone could see her. Where everyone could wonder why such a beautiful woman would be there with him.

As the meal ended, Quan leaned over to him and whispered, "I understand that it is a tradition to give gifts at Christmas. I have a gift for you." She slid a small box across the table to him.

He made the customary "you shouldn't haves," but they were truly meant, for he knew she did not have much money, and any gift would be a real sacrifice. He gently pulled at the small silk bow, a wonderful memory flowed into his mind. He was now again opening another gift from this lovely woman. He took the gift, a golden figurine, out of the box and placed it on the table between them.

"Do you like it? Do you know what it is?" she said, her voice a melody of happiness.

"Oh yes. I like it. Yes, I know what it is, and I think I know what it means. It is a golden songbird. It forever silently sings in celebration of our first time together."

She smiled at him and whispered, "Let us leave. My sister is again away."

THE ONE THORN

Their limited life together was not too difficult for Tim, except for the intermittent run-ins with Major Truc. Tim came to feel about Truc as Major Clare had felt, Truc was a colossal pain in the butt. Truc had tried his best several times to have MACV transfer the school supply mission to his office as part of the Vietnamization process. The American general, friend to the murdered priest, thwarted Truc's every attempt.

The general even once called Tim to his office. Tim clearly remembered the general's final order that day, "Staff Sergeant DePalma, under no circumstances are those supplies to Father Lefevbre's orphanage ever to be disrupted. If you have any problems, you see me personally. And never, ever take any crap from that weasely, little Vietnamese Major. Clear?!"

Oh, it was clear. The general's order couldn't have been any clearer, and it couldn't have made Tim any happier. Only Quan's restraint kept Tim from kicking the Major's butt all the way back down the hill whenever he showed up at the school.

Quan had always defended Major Truc, as one would defend a friend. She explained to Tim that Truc was at heart a good man. He just had several blind spots. One was that he did not want the Vietnamese people to forget their Vietnamese traditions, but he felt that was happening all around him. The second was his disdain for foreigners. He did not believe the French, nor now the Americans, had Vietnam's best interests at heart.

Although Tim understood Quan's need to defend a family

friend, he did not see any good qualities in Major Truc, either as a soldier or a man. He thought Quan's friendship misplaced. He came to dislike Truc immensely. He sometimes wondered, "Am I right, or am I just jealous?" In the end it didn't matter, he just didn't like Truc.

There was one time when Tim even wanted to kill Truc, and almost did, and looking back, should have. Tim was driving back to Saigon after delivering supplies to the school. The empty passenger side of his truck was raked by gunfire, forcing him to swerve off the road into some bushes. His M-16 slid to the passenger side and jammed itself between the seat and the door. Tim grabbed the hidden submachine gun from beneath his dashboard, exited from the driver's side, and circled back the 50 yards to the ambush site. He did not find anyone in the area, but he did find 14 empty 7.62 cartridge shells, probably from an AK-47, the VC's weapon of choice. Tim had been in enough ambushes to know this one was not meant to kill him, only warn him. If they had wanted to kill him, they would have attacked the driver's side of the vehicle, and there would have been more of them.

The question now was, "Who were 'they?' Who was trying to warn him off? The VC or Truc."

The next day American Staff Sergeant DePalma strode into Vietnamese Army Hqs, right to Major Truc's desk, leaned in close so only he and Truc could hear, and said, "Next time you better kill me, because I will kill you. I might still kill you anyway, just because I would enjoy it!" His eyes bored into Truc. Tim could smell Truc's fear. American Staff Sergeant DePalma then turned around and walked away.

Although it seemed right at the time, Tim would come to regret his threat. Forever after, he would always wonder, "Was my threat still in Truc's head when he killed Quan? Did my rage somehow contribute to his rage, and ultimately to her death?"

TUNNEL LIGHT

The MACV Vietnamization teams were all packed into the

general's conference room. No one knew why the meeting was called, but they had been waiting now for over half an hour. Rumors of course were rampant. The sergeants and the junior officers milled about complaining to each other that they didn't have time for this. The work day was almost over, and they still had much work to do. It was seventeen hundred hours (1700; 5 PM), 27 January, 1973.

Someone yelled, "Atten-hut!" and the assembled teams came to attention as the general walked into the room. "Please, all who can be seated, do so." Of course everyone knew that meant just the colonels. The rest lined the conference room walls, two and three deep.

"Gentlemen, I will make this brief. There will be no time for questions." He then paused, for dramatic effect no doubt, and then announced, "Gentlemen, the war is over. A peace treaty is being signed in Paris at this very moment. All U.S. combat and headquarters troops will be out of Vietnam in 60 days. Now, in this time of triumph, let us take a moment of silence in memory of our fellow warriors who sacrificed all to make this happen." After the moment of silent prayer, the general's aide brought it to an end with another "Atten-hut!!!" and the general exited the room.

The room burst into bedlam; everyone was talking and laughing, happy that the war was over and they were going home. A colonel then took control and brought the room back to order. He told everyone to go back to their rooms and hotels tonight and celebrate. However, they better be back on duty by 0600 the next morning and in condition to work, for there would be much work to do in the next 60 days.

As Tim stretched out on his bunk in his darkened room, peace did not bring him joy. Yes, he was happy that no more Americans would die. However, he knew that many more Vietnamese would die. And he was not stupid about politics and history. He knew that no matter how people would try to spin it, Vietnam was now officially the first war that America had lost.

However, none of that mattered to him at that moment, to him alone in the darkness. At that moment, the only thing that mattered was Quan. What would she think? What would she do? What would they do?

After hours searching for answers to those questions, he knew what he had to do. He got up to go and do it.

It was dark as his truck rumbled through the gates, and he pulled up to the front of the building. He was surprised that he had gotten there so quickly. His mind had been on other things as he drove. He knocked hard and impatiently.

Thu answered his call. She hugged him, shook her head sadly, and pointed to the stairs.

Just then Quan appeared at the head of the staircase, but Tim was already half way up, and in the next moment they embraced.

"You've heard?" he asked.

"Yes, of course. The whole world has heard. I am very happy. Your war is over."

He stepped back. She had a smile on her face, but her eyes told another story, a story of sadness. She knew what the news meant for him, for them. He would be leaving.

As he had done once before, he cupped her face in his hands. He gently kissed her forehead, her eyelids, her cheeks, her lips. They both lingered in that kiss. Then he looked into her eyes, "Quan, I love you. Will you marry me?"

THE ANSWER

His proposal surprised her. She had not expected it. An hour earlier, it had surprised him. He had not expected it either. Events had forced him to decide. Now they would force her to decide.

"Tim, I love you. But marriage? It is all so sudden. I want to say yes. My heart already says yes. But I must think on it. Can you wait for my answer? Please?"

That night Tim did not leave. For the first time he entered her room, was among her things, was taken to her bed. They were all her. He did not want to leave them. He did not want to leave her. He would not. He did not. At least not that night.

The coming days quickly passed into weeks. Much had to be done. He tried to spend as much time with Quan as possible. It was never enough.

At first, after their night together, she said, "yes." But later she changed her mind. She was under pressures from her family, from Tim, from the children, from herself, from time. She went back and forth between "yes" and "no." Her heart was a constant yes, but her mind was not.

Tim made his last delivery of supplies with just one week left until his scheduled departure. When he arrived, she took him by the hand and led him to her room. They made love for hours. Finally, they lay next to each other, bodies touching, holding hands.

"You will not be coming with me, will you," Tim whispered.

"My heart will be going with you, but no, I will not."

FREEDOM BIRD

Tim was among a column of soldiers marching five abreast through the gates of Tan Son Nhut Airbase. In his mind he was walking through the gates of her school. Three 747 Freedom Birds were on the tarmac to take him home. Quan was at the school, her home. A North Vietnamese officer was standing on a wooden box, going through the motions of counting Americans as they marched out. Quan would no longer be standing on the stairs of the school, waiting to bring him in. Tim felt humiliated as he walked by the North Vietnamese. He felt saddened that he would no longer walk with her. She had chosen to stay. He had no choice but to leave. The Freedom Bird would soon fly away. The songbird would not.

Asian Ginger Chicken

While Tim first sampled this in Monterey, the best he ever tasted was with Quan in a schoolhouse dining room outside of Saigon. Tim has loved this recipe ever since and had many variation of it over the years. Tim discovered that it is almost impossible to replicate that exact taste without the unique spices and preparation methods (e.g. a wok over hearty flame). The below recipe is an easy way to prepare a whole chicken and retain the Asian flavor. The majority of the prep is done the day before and when you serve it all that is necessary is to pop it in the oven.

Ingredients:(Four to Five Servings)

1 Chicken	3 – 4 pounds, cut-up and served in pieces
¾ Cup	Honey
½ Cup	Soy Sauce
2 Tbsp	Fish Sauce (see Tips)
¼ Cup	Minced Garlic
¼ Cup	Peeled and grated ginger root

Directions:

1. Cook the honey, soy sauce, fish sauce, minced garlic, and grated ginger root in a saucepan until honey is dissolved and mixes with other ingredients.

2. Cut up chicken and place in an oven-tempered baking pan, skin side down. Pour sauce over and cover with aluminum foil, allow to marinate overnight.

3. Preheat oven to 375F degrees and cook for 30 minutes. Remove from oven and turn pieces. Brush a little honey on the exposed skin sides and return to oven, uncovered, and cook for an additional 25 minutes. Finally, broil for an additional five minutes to add color to the skin (if required).

Tips:

1. When chopping up the chicken discard the backs and cut off wing tips. An alternative is to buy a whole cut up chicken which usually contains the most favored pieces.
2. If there is not enough sauce to marinate, you can add rice wine or white wine to fill the void and complement the dish.
3. This recipe can be made with only quarters, thighs, or breasts of chicken, depending upon your taste.
4. If you do not use fish sauce, increase the soy sauce to ¾ cup.

Thai Chicken Coconut Soup
(Tom Ka Gai)

Tim first sampled this popular Asian soup with Quan in Saigon in 1972 and later in Thailand. The blending of coconut and chicken is unique and took time to replicate once he returned from Vietnam. Tim's love of mushrooms added substance to the soup and a proven shortcut allowed it to obtain a thicker consistency.

Ingredients:(Four Servings)

1 Can	Coconut Milk (14 Oz)
2 Cups	Chicken Broth
1 Inch	Fresh, peeled Ginger, sliced thin
1 Lb	Chicken Breast
1 Cup	Sliced Mushrooms
1 Tbsp	Lemon Peel (dried)
1 Tbsp	Lime Juice
1 Tbsp	Fish Sauce
1 Tsp	Sugar
½ - 1 Tsp	Chili Paste
Bunch	Cilantro Leaves (small bunch)
Bunch	Fresh Basil Leaves (small bunch)
1 Can	Condensed Potato Soup

Directions:

1. Boil chicken breast(s) ahead, cool, and shred by hand into small pieces; set aside.

2. In saucepan, combine coconut milk, chicken broth, ginger, lemon peel, and ½ the cilantro (chopped); bring to a boil.

3. Add chicken, lime juice, fish sauce, chili paste, and sugar; reduce heat and simmer until flavors are

blended (5 minutes). If soup is too thin, add can of potato soup and simmer for an additional 5 minutes.

4. Serve in bowls and garnish with basil leaves and cilantro leaves.

Tips:

1. Original Thai/Viet recipes call for lemon grass and kaffir lime tree leaves. Unless you have a nearby outlet for SE Asian food, you can substitute lemon peel/cilantro mixture and lime juice for these.

2. Condensed potato soup is a good thickener and carries little taste.

3. Tim uses chili paste rather than grinding dried chili peppers.

4. Ginger slices may be overpowering and can easily be removed before adding condensed soup.

5. Mushrooms may be omitted but add substance to the dish; Tim prefers to use reconstituted Shitake mushrooms.

Chapter 11: FLASHBACK: THE UNREAL-REAL WORLD

Day Four: Thursday, 1100 hours, in the Train, Heidelberg to Paris

As Tim's bullet train sped through the border of air between Germany and France, his mind's eye was looking out the window but not out the window of a modern train. His mind's eye was still in Nam looking out the window of a long-ago aircraft as it climbed up over the Vietnam coastline and winged its way into the skies over the Pacific. As Tim's Freedom Bird lifted up and headed toward the "Real World," the troops broke into loud cheering and clapping. The stewardesses, obviously the most beautiful Pan Am could provide, were handing out hot face towels, new magazines, and gleaming smiles. Soon, they were taking drink orders. Soon after that, they were fending off marriage proposals. There was not a face that wasn't smiling or a heart that wasn't happy. Even Tim's.

As the troops calmed down, Tim leaned back into his seat. He thought of his family, his home, his friends. He really was looking forward to seeing them all. Yet...

THE UNREAL-REAL WORLD

It was almost 48 hours, almost enough time to fully decompress, before he landed in Providence and was immediately enveloped in the welcoming hugs of his family. They were all at the airport to greet him. It was a wonderful ride home. Yes, after three years, Tim was finally home.

It was fun to again see his home, his neighborhood, his

friends. As he walked the old streets his first week back, he remembered things as they used to be. They had not changed. He had. He would soon come to realize this "Real World" was no longer real for him.

Everyone was a little strange with him. As if talking with him was a little uncomfortable for them. No one came right out and asked him how Nam "was." He guessed they all imagined they already knew from seeing it every night on TV. Even his own father never asked.

In truth, Tim never really wanted to talk about it, and wouldn't have, if they had asked. But they never asked. No one ever asked. Vietnam was something everyone wanted to forget. Tim could not forget. He could never forget. He would never allow himself to forget. He quickly, maybe too quickly, came to accept that this real world was no longer his real world. His real world was now half a world away.

He felt a little like he had felt on China Beach that first R&R, …something was just wrong. Where was the jungle? Where was the heat? Where was the adventure? Where was the danger? Where was his M-16? And of course, the ultimate "where" question: where was his heart?

He knew where it was, it was in Vietnam. It was behind 4-foot high walls, in a school, with a woman. He didn't want it to be there. He wanted it to be here. Yes, he wanted his heart to be with the woman, but with the woman here.

Quan had rejected him. He understood why, but she had a choice. He did not. He must forget her. He would forget her. He would try to forget her. He couldn't forget her.

ITALIAN WINE – IRISH BEER

On Tim's first Saturday night back, Uncle Carmine closed his Federal Hill restaurant to the public and hosted a dinner in Tim's honor, with decorations, an open bar, and a Frank Sinatra impersonator at the piano. All those who had been at Tim's "Going-Away" party three years earlier, to wish him farewell, were now at his "Welcome Back" party to hail him home.

It was a night of good cheer and family. Everyone came by and expressed their happiness over his return. The men slapped his back. The women rubbed his sleeves and kissed his cheeks.

The evening's meal was one of Tim's favorites. The appetizer was jumbo shrimp cocktail. The main course was the restaurant's signature dish, Three Cheese Pasta, or as Tim used to call it as a child, Pasta Cheese Boats. Tim had a special name for this dish because Carmine always made him a special version of it. Whereas the menu item touted Carmine's award-winning white sauce, little Tim preferred his uncle's non-award-winning red marinara sauce. Carmine would always acquiesce and, with great fanfare, serve Tim a special oval plate containing three large pasta shells, one trailing the other, each stuffed with the chef's secret combination of cheeses and sausage, but all surrounded by marinara sauce. What young Tim always saw were three ship-like pasta boats, loaded with cheeses, floating toward him on a red marinara sea. Thus his name, Pasta Cheese Boats.

In Tim's honor, the evening's welcome-home dessert was his absolute favorite, Tiramisu. No one made Tiramisu better than Uncle Carmine. His tiramisu always won the annual award as the "Top of The Hill Dessert" by the Providence food critics.

As a nod to the Irish side of the family, Carmine had placed a brown bottle of beer next to each crystal glass of wine. Under each bottle of beer, as a coaster, was a small Irish lace doily. Tim smiled, Carmine had a rather direct sense of ethnic humor.

After the shrimp cocktail appetizers were served, Tim's big Irish grandfather, JC Connolly, stood up, grabbed his bottle of beer, and almost bellowed so all could hear, "Everyone grab your bottle and raise it in a toast to our returning hero." He then recited an old Irish soldier's toast. He ended with, "Now to Tim! All drink till the bottom becomes the top!"

With that, he proceeded to drain his bottle till the bottom was straight up. Most of the women took only a sip. All the bottles in the hands of Tim's Irish uncles and cousins went bottoms to the ceiling. As his Italian uncles, cousins, and friends were lowering their bottles after a chug, they spotted what JC was doing. Not wanting to be bested, their bottles reluctantly went back to their lips, and the bottoms became tops. JC put his bottle back on the table with a hollow thump, smiled, knowing the DePalmas weren't fans of beer, and clapped for Tim. Everyone clapped with him.

After a few minutes, Tim's other grandfather, Ernie DePalma, stood, holding high his crystal glass of Valpolicella. "A toast to our returning warrior. From Caesar to DePalma, great Roman warriors all! And great lovers too! To Tim!" With that, his grandfather sipped his wine, with great appreciation, as did everyone else. Then he held his glass of wine up to the light of the chandeliers, blew it a kiss, smiled, and sat down. The Italian tables roared their approval. The Irish tables also clapped, showing their enthusiasm for this night of family fellowship.

Then Tim saw his Uncle Sean motioning to one of the waiters to bring more bottles of beer. Tim decided to get up, thank everyone for coming, and hopefully put a stop to what he feared would be a coming battle of toasts.

Uncle Carmine, however, had seen this family act play out before and was ready for it. He signaled across the room to Frank Sinatra, who immediately stopped playing the piano and picked up a trumpet. Pseudo-Frank began to play the Army's official marching song, "When the Army Goes Rolling Along." As the trumpet played the rollicking tune, the door from the kitchen opened and waiters, led by Carmine, came marching in, military style, carrying trays of the main entrée, Three Cheese Pasta. As they placed the white-sauced pasta dish of blended cheeses and sausage in front of the guests, the trumpet-playing Sinatra marched behind Carmine up to the head table where Tim sat. With a flair fit for a movie scene, Carmine swirled a plate down in front of Tim, an oval plate containing three pasta boats full of cheeses traveling across a red marinara sea. Written in red pasta sauce across the top of the plate was, "Welcome Home, Tim."

Tim stood and embraced Carmine, whispering in his ear, "Thanks, Uncle Carmine, for a wonderful welcome home." Everyone rose, clapped, and then settled back down to enjoy the wonderful meal before them. While sipping his wine, Tim looked up to see his Zia Mary DeGuilio at a nearby table looking at him. She smiled, winked, and blew him a kiss. She then pointed to her plate. Tim laughed. She was the only other person in the room feasting on pasta cheese boats in a red marinara sea.

The tiramisu arrived about 20 minutes later, but without a trumpet entrance song. Too bad, it deserved one. Tim had forgotten how really good Carmine's tiramisu tasted. It was soft, yet just a little crispy. The sweetness of the whipped cream was both softened and enhanced by the mocha-flavored cake layers. His taste buds, as always, leaped in response to Uncle Carmine's choice of the divinely inspired Galliano Restretto as the coffee liqueur to blend together all the flavors of the other ingredients. As his mother often said, "Uncle Carmine's tiramisu is like a taste of heaven."

As Tim was enjoying his tiramisu, he looked up and thought, "Oh no. What now?" His grandfather, JC, was again standing up and, this time, raising a glass of wine for a forthcoming toast.

"May I have your attention, please. I have one more toast to make tonight. Tim, I know that instead of receiving this toast, you will want to stand with me in giving it." Tim stood, glass in hand, uneasy not knowing what might follow.

JC continued, "Everyone please join me in a toast to our host, Carmine. Carmine, you sure know how to throw a swell coming-home party. No soldier has had a better one. And you damn sure know how to cook a great meal. I don't know if I've ever had a better one. Everyone, cheers for Carmine!"

Everyone joined in the cheers and seconded the sentiments. It was certainly a great party, and certainly it was great food. However, Zia Mary DeGuillio was later overheard to say that Frank Sinatra left a little to be desired.

As Tim viewed the goings on, he considered himself lucky to have such a great family, to be both Gaelic and Garlic, ...and of course, American.

As the party wound down and people began to leave, there were more slaps on the back and kisses on the cheeks. Among the last to stop by the head table and express his happiness over Tim's return was one of his favorite uncles, Brian Connolly.

"Tim, I have two tickets to the Red Sox-Yankee's game tomorrow night. Right behind home plate. You want to go?"

WHAT WAS HER NAME?

Tim had always enjoyed his time with Uncle Brian. The ride to Fenway was no different. Brian was 42 years old, a lawyer, and still a bachelor. Every Irish family had one; no, not a lawyer, ...a bachelor. Every time Tim saw him, Brian was with a different woman, each one a beauty.

Brian turned off the Cadillac's radio, "Well, how was it?"

"How was what?" Tim squirmed out an answer.

"You know what. Nam."

"It was what it was. I don't want to talk about it."

"OK, Tim. But I'm here if you want to. When I came back from Korea, I felt the same way I know you feel right now. Some day you will want to talk about it. Don't keep it bottled up forever."

Tim was silent. Then, "Thanks Uncle Brian."

"Tim, from now on, just call me Brian. You've earned the right to be treated as a man, as an equal."

After a few minutes of silence, Brian then asked, "What was her name?"

Tim, startled, mumbled, "Whose name?"

"Come on, Tim. I'm a lawyer. My business is reading people. Tell me about her."

"Let me ask you a question first, counselor," Tim said, evading Brian's question for the moment. "You've had a lot of experience with women, how do you know when you are really in love with a woman, and when she is really in love with you?"

"I'm not sure I'm the right person to ask. Perhaps you should ask your dad. He is a man who has been with the same woman for 25 years. Me, I'm a man who has been with 25 women, each for less than a year. He knows more about real love than I do."

"For what it's worth," Brian continued. "Here's my way of judging when I want to be with a woman. Some women you just have to glance at, and they ignite a fire in your loins. Those women I want to meet and be with right away. Then there is another kind of woman whom you meet, talk with, exchange ideas with, spend some time with, and then all of a sudden come to realize that you are having a really great experience with this woman and want to continue. Then there is yet another kind of woman, a woman who tugs, not necessarily at either your loins or your mind, but at your heart. You don't know why, but she just makes you feel that you want to be with her. I have met all those kinds of women. But none of them have I really loved."

Brian's eyes glazed for a moment, as if thinking about someone, or a lot of someones. Then he picked up where he had left off, "However, I still believe there is a woman out there for me. To me, that woman is not just hot, smart, or endearing. She may be all of those, or just some of those, or maybe none of those. Yet, in some special way she will draw me to her and make me feel that I never want to leave her side. That is the feeling I never get, but always want. Some of her I may be able to explain, but the very 'her-ness' of her, that which holds me, will probably be unexplainable. This woman, who is in my heart, I always think of as 'lovely'; the one woman I could love completely. Hopefully, she will love me, wretch that I am, completely in return. Unfortunately, I have not met that woman, ...yet." After a momentary pause, Brian looked at Tim and added, "Have you?"

Tim didn't answer. He just remembered.

After his own more than momentary pause, Tim said, "Quan. Her name is Quan. And yes, she is truly lovely."

FENWAY FULL

As usual Fenway was full. Tim had never had seats like these before: right behind the plate, ten rows up. He was having a fantastic time. Then it happened.

First, there was a tingling of his skin. Then his chest welled-up. His jaw tightened. His eyes moistened. He was no longer seeing 33,000 cheering fans in Fenway. He was looking at the crowd but thinking of and seeing all those who would never attend another baseball game. Their number would fill Fenway almost twice over. The name, Fenway, drove home the hurt. The park was built on back-Bay fens, acres of water-logged marshes, not too unlike the rice patties where the spirits of those he was seeing still wandered.

Tim didn't know what was happening. He had never ex- perienced this feeling before. Although he would experience it many times in the future, this first time would be the most vivid, the most intense, the hardest. He battered himself with silent questions: "Why am I here enjoying this game, and they are not? Why am I here enjoying this life, and they are not? Why am I here, and they are not? Why was I spared?"

Overtime he would come to understand that what he was experiencing was "survivor's guilt." But that understand- ing was still somewhere down the road; not that understand- ing it ever helped much when the feeling came. That night in the fens, he did not understand. He just felt it, lived it, bore it. Then it was gone. It would return, often, but not then.

Yes, he was in an unreal, real world.

OFFICER CANDIDATE SCHOOL (OCS)
and RANGER SCHOOL

When Tim's month leave at home was up, he boarded a Greyhound bus and again headed south to Fort Benning, Georgia, this time for the six month Officer Candidate School, followed by the two month Ranger School. When Tim had extended in Nam, now some 10 months ago, his 1st Cav battalion commander, Lieutenant Colonel Clarke, approved his request on one condition. He wanted Tim to fill out and submit the paperwork for OCS and Ranger School. Lieutenant Colonel Clarke saw in Tim's Nam extension, in Tim, more than a young man in love. He saw a young warrior. He believed both Tim and the Army would benefit from Tim's remaining in uniform. He said that Tim would not incur a four-year commitment until he signed-in at OCS. Submitting the paperwork and getting accepted just kept his options open. After his month back in the unreal, real word, Tim executed that option.

OCS and Ranger School were not hard for Tim. After two years in Nam, he more than excelled at infantry tactics and weapons, both in the classroom and in field exercises. In most cases, he knew more than the instructors. Still, he strived to learn all they had to teach.

In addition to small unit infantry warfare, Tim learned about the larger Army, about the other combat branches, about all the support branches. Following a class on Army personnel assignment policies, he decided to make it his mission to personally manage his next assignment as best he could. He decided his next assignment would be back in Nam. He just had to convince the Army to decide the same thing.

His research revealed that the Army still had personnel assigned to the Defense Attaché Office (DAO) in Saigon. Unfortunately, that same research also revealed that 2nd Lieutenants, which Tim would soon become upon OCS graduation, didn't get assigned to DAOs. Right from the beginning of this personal mission, Major Clare's words rang loud and clear in his memory: "Staff Sergeant DePalma, know who you are and what you are about. Then get your mission done."

Tim knew who he was and what he was about. He was a soldier with a set of demonstrated skills useful to any mission in Vietnam. What he was about, was about getting himself back to Vietnam to use those skills. Of course he also knew, not as a soldier, but as a man, that all this was about something else as well, ...Quan.

Tim spent almost every free minute while at OCS, and there weren't many, writing to every military person he knew, and some he didn't know, seeking advice on how to get back to Nam. With just one month left at the school, two important letters arrived in the same week. The first ended with: "Come see me during your break between OCS and Ranger School." The letter was signed, "Lawrence Clarke, Colonel Infantry, Chief of Officer Assignments Branch, Pentagon." The second letter was really just a note. Its words were brief but potent: "Tim, good to hear from you. It's all going to work out. Come see me as soon as you get back in country. Bring tobacco from Saigon. ---Plat PS: it's no longer MAJ Wojonski; now it's Mr."

Vietnam warriors were now a closed brotherhood. Tim had earned his place in that Band of Brothers.

> ---Shakespeare, Henry V, Battle of Agincourt:
> "...From this day to the ending of the world,
> But we in it will be remembered.
> We few, we happy few, we Band of Brothers.
> For he today that sheds his blood with me,
> Shall be my Brother..."

Three Cheese Pasta
(Salsiccia Ripiene Conchiglie Con Tre Formaggio)

Although a big favorite at Uncle Carmine's restaurant, Tim first learned to prepare this himself while on holiday at a small cooking school on the outskirts of Rome in 1991. At the time, he was on his own "Rome Adventure." A classic in Italian cooking, it can be easily changed to accommodate tastes and availability of ingredients.

Ingredients:(Four Servings)

3 Tbsp	Butter/Extra Virgin olive Oil
1 Lb	Italian Sausage
1 Pkg	Jumbo Pasta Shells
1 ½ Lbs	Ricotta Cheese
1 Lb	Shredded Mozzarella Cheese
1 Cup	Grated Parmesan Cheese
1 Tbsp	Italian Seasoning
To Taste	Fresh Herbs
1 – 1 ½ Cups	Whipping Cream
To Taste	Salt and Pepper

Directions:

1. Melt butter and/or Olive Oil in large frying pan; remove sausage from casing and sauté until done. Remove sausage from pan and set aside.

2. Add 1 cup cream, all the ricotta and parmesan cheese, ¾ cup of mozzarella cheese, Italian seasoning, and herbs.

3. Blend until desired consistency, adding cream as necessary; remove from heat.

4. Cook shells according to package direction but take out when short of allotted time; drain in a colander

and arrange on a dishtowel to dry, cool, and regain some rigidity. Shells should be cool and *al dente* --- not overcooked.

5. Mix a little bit of the sauce with the sausage and stuff shells with mixture.
6. Put stuffed shells in a tempered baking dish; touching, but not overcrowded.
7. Cover with remaining sauce and sprinkle remaining mozzarella on top.
8. Bake in a 350F – 400F oven for approximately 30 minutes.
9. Sprinkle fresh herbs on top and serve.

Tips:
1. Many different cheeses can be used, but always include ricotta.
2. In a pinch you can use a prepared white or red pasta sauce, but add some fresh herbs to make it your own.
3. Depending upon size and servings you may have to increase the volume of the sauce.
4. Recipe is very flexible and cheese sauce can be used with any pasta.

Tiramisu

A traditional Italian dessert in Tim's family that has many forms and differences. On one summer vacation Tim had this almost every evening at different restaurants to hone his tastes. This recipe can be varied to accommodate almost all pleasures – the below works for most occasions and won't keep you in the kitchen too long. Freezes well and tastes better the second day.

Ingredients:(Six to Eight Servings)

2/3 Cup	Powdered Sugar
8 Oz	Mascarpone
½ Cup	Sugar
¼ Cup	Water
3 Eggs	Egg Whites Only
½ Cup	Hot Water
1 Tbsp	Sugar
1 Tbsp	Instant Coffee (Espresso/Dark Roast if available)
2 Tbsp	Coffee Flavored Liquor
20 Plus	Ladyfingers
1 ½ Cup	Whipped Topping
½ Tsp	Unsweetened Cocoa Powder

Directions:

1. Combine powdered sugar and mascarpone; beat at high speed; fold in 1 cup whipped topping.

2. In a double boiler, combine sugar, water, and egg whites – beat over simmering water until stiff peaks form.

3. Stir ¼ of egg white mixture into mascarpone mixture; fold in remaining egg white mixture.

4. In a separate bowl combine ½ cup hot water, 1 tbsp

sugar, 1 tbsp instant coffee, and 2 tbsp liqueur.

5. Divide and layout lady fingers; paint with coffee liqueur mixture.

6. In an 8 inch square baking dish, cover the bottom with ladyfingers.

7. Spread half of cheese and cream mixture over these.

8. Repeat procedure layering remaining ladyfingers over mixture and then add cheese and cream mixture.

9. Over top of this add remaining whipped topping and sprinkle with powdered cocoa.

10. Cover gently and chill for at least three hours to firm (or overnight)

Tips:

1. Reduced fat cream cheese can be used instead of mascarpone.

2. Stiff homemade whipped cream can be substituted for the plastic container whipped topping.

3. For more formal service prepare in a spring-form pan. Line the bottom and then apply ladyfingers to sides – they will adhere if they are moist. They will also release – so be quick with the first layer. If this is done freeze and takeout about three hours before serving and remove the spring-form sleeve when thawed. You may need to slide a knife along the sides to ensure it doesn't stick. If necessary, fill in holes with whipped filling when serving.

4. If coffee liquor mixture remains you can drizzle more over ladyfinger layers.

5. Best cut when chilled.

Chapter 12: FLASHBACK: PEACE - WAR

Day Four: Thursday, 1130 hours, in the Train, Heidelberg to Paris

The bullet train continued to hurtle Tim toward his awaiting fate in Paris. Yet his memories held him to his past fate in Vietnam. Were either his future in Paris or his past in Vietnam really examples of fate? He remembered Wojonski's words from so long ago: "Life is primarily a series of choices."

Didn't Tim still have a choice about what would happen in Paris? Hadn't he had some choice over what had happened in Vietnam? Or was choice not a factor? Even now, wasn't it overpowering compulsion, not he, that seemed to be driving him on to Paris, on to "terminating" Truc? Had it been choice or compulsion that had driven him back to Vietnam?

During that year away from Nam, Tim was never really away from Nam. Every OCS class or field exercise either reminded him of his past tour in Nam or prepared him for his coming tour in Nam. Every minute of his Ranger Training did the same, but in extremis.

During that year away from Quan, Tim was never really away from Quan. For the first several months, he wallowed in the self-delusion that Quan had rejected him. She had a choice, and it was not him. He had decided to forget her. To remove her from his memories. To banish her from his heart. Both his memories and his heart laughed at him.

Beneath his hurt, he really knew that she had not rejected him. He knew she loved him, really loved him. In that realization, he came to better understand that she also loved her culture, her country, and mostly her family. Yes, she was a woman who loved a man. But she was also a daughter who loved her parents, in a culture where filial loyalty and obedience to one's parents was the very essence of a daughter's soul. Yes, of course she had a choice; just like she had a choice to breathe.

After two months back in his unreal, real world, Tim wrote Quan a letter. In it he reaffirmed his love for her, telling her that he would always love her and that he now fully understood why she had not come back with him. It was a month before a return letter landed on his bunk. In it she restated her love for him. However, in more and softer words, she told him once again what she had told him at her school when he first professed his love for her: "But Tim, it cannot be."

He sent her another letter, and another after that, but no return letter ever landed on his bunk. It was then that he decided that somehow, someway, sometime he would return to Vietnam, return to her.

His return to Vietnam would be a year and eight days after he had left in humiliation and sadness. Humiliation, partly because he was part of an army that had never lost a battle but somehow had lost a war. But also because he had to march to his Freedom Bird under the gloating eye of that North Vietnamese Colonel. What kind of craven American diplomat had allowed that humiliation to happen to an American soldier? He had left in sadness, because he had to leave the woman he loved. In that instance, it was he who had allowed that sadness to happen?

His year in the unreal, real world finally came to an end. Upon graduating from Officer Candidate School, Staff Sergeant DePalma was commissioned 2nd Lieutenant DePalma. Upon graduating from Ranger School, 2nd Lieutenant DePalma was awarded the coveted Ranger Tab for his left shoulder and given his coveted assignment orders in his right hand. Those orders read: "2nd Lieutenant Timothy DePalma is assigned to the Defense Attache Office (DAO), Saigon, Republic of Vietnam. Reporting date: 1 April 1974."

"How ironic," 2nd Lieutenant DePalma thought to himself. "A

reporting date of 1 April. Am I a fool to go back to Nam?"

BACK IN NAM

Tim sat in the rooftop bar at the Rex Hotel in the center of downtown Saigon. He had been back in-country for three days. He had not yet made an attempt to see Quan

The Rex was a 5-floor complex that covered almost a city block and consisted of about 100 guest rooms, a movie theater, a dance hall, and a restaurant. Tim now called one of its guest rooms home. The Rooftop Bar covered more than half the hotel's rooftop, and the bar itself was half-covered by its own roof for use as shelter in times of hot sun or heavy rain. Potted plants and shrubbery were decoratively placed throughout the bar and at night, colored lights and lanterns provided a festive atmosphere. An almost 4-foot-high stucco wall surrounded the entire rooftop, allowing patrons to safely look down at the city's activities on the busy streets below, ...or safely look out at the war's activities on the distant horizons. Admittedly, the patrons were happy to be on that rooftop downing shots, rather than on those horizons being downed by shots.

The Rex Hotel had once been the epicenter of information on the war. For most of the war, the military command had held its daily briefings for journalists every night on the hotel's first floor. The journalists irreverently named this daily briefing "The Five O'Clock Follies." Many journalists had little confidence that the Command was telling them the truth about the war. Others were simply unhappy that the truth did not support their own anti-war prejudices. In the final analysis, most journalists didn't believe that the military commanders wanted to give them the true picture of the war, and most military commanders didn't believe the journalists wanted to report the true picture of the war. However, almost everyone believed the best place to attempt to find the truth was at the Rex's Rooftop Bar.

Now, a year after the Follies had ended and most of the journalists had left, Tim was sitting in that Rooftop Bar, at about high noon, looking for truth: truth about the war, truth about Quan, truth about himself.

"Lieutenant, can I buy you a drink?"

Tim looked up to see a rather disheveled looking guy with longish gray hair, probably in his mid-50's, his exact age hidden behind a haze of most likely either scotch or bourbon.

"No thanks," said Tim, his eyes squinting as he looked up towards the sun. "A little early for me. I just came up to take a look at the Rex's famous rooftop. I have to admit, I'm a little underwhelmed."

The disheveled, overweight boozer laughed, looked around, and with a shrug and a sigh said, "Yeah, but this old bar had its day, and it certainly had its nights. Kind of like me, I guess. Hey, if you don't want a drink, how about I buy you lunch."

"Why?" from Tim.

"Well, two reasons. First, I can't remember the last time I saw a US Army 2nd Lieutenant around Saigon, and I don't think I ever saw one here on the top of the Rex. Second, if I sit and talk with you, I can put the lunch on my expense account. Can't get more honest than that. From me, you will always get the truth, at least my version of it."

Tim laughed. "Hmm, I've been looking for the truth. OK, have a seat. I'm Tim DePalma."

"Thanks. I'm Jakub Goblesck, freelance journalist. I still write daily releases on Vietnam for the main news services. Don't panic. I'm not going to write about you, or even quote you. But on the other hand, feel free to use me as a source for anything you want to know about Vietnam."

"Really? Anything? Like what?" said Tim, smiling to himself, not mentioning that he had already spent two years on the streets and in the jungles below the Rex's Rooftop Bar.

"Well first, may I order us lunch?" Following Tim's affirmative nod, this new acquaintance, who would become a true friend, waved a waiter over and ordered, "Two cucumber soups, a lemonade for my friend, and a gin and tonic for me."

Tim thought, "Gin! Of course. Why not. Gin hangovers

probably weather tropical climates better than ones brought on by scotch or bourbon."

Tim and Jakub were deep in conversation about post-peace Vietnam when their lunch arrived, along with Jakub's second gin and tonic.

"Whoa, that's a surprise," said Tim, as he tasted the soup. "I wasn't expecting cold soup. The only cold soup I've ever had was cold broccoli soup, usually when my mother was tricking my sister into eating vegetables. This is really good."

"Yes," added Jakub. "Remember that old saying, 'Cool as a cucumber?' Seems to be true, for this soup really is cool and refreshing on a hot Saigon day. It's almost as cool and refreshing as my gin and tonic. The chef here usually makes some every Wednesday. The soup I mean, not the G&T's. Those the bartender makes every day."

After a long, satisfying, almost lip-smacking sip of his gin and tonic, Jakub tried the soup. "Chilled cucumbers are always cool on a hot day. But it's the expert blending of mint and lemon juice with the chilled yogurt and sour cream that really refreshes. Although I must admit, I'm only a fan if the house still has enough mint and lemon juice left over to keep my drinks coming."

The two new friends, one of whom would ultimately betray the other, not for silver but for love, continued to talk while enjoying the cucumber soup. Jakub was surprised to learn of Tim's experiences with the 1st Cav and the MACV Vietnamization program.

"One doesn't expect so much experience from a junior lieutenant," murmured Jakub, as he waved over another gin and tonic. Jakub then looked Tim up and down for a minute and said, "Here take this card. It's my tailor. He will make you some tropical leisure suits. Get three: one blue, one tan, and one white. Then you'll have one for every occasion. As a DAO member, in most cases when out and about, you have a choice to wear your uniform or civilian clothes. Let people guess your rank. After talking with you, they will figure you for a senior Captain or a Sergeant First Class. Believe me, you'll get more done either way.

Not that you'll be here very long or get very much done. Not your fault. It's just the way it is."

"Why won't I be here very long?" asked Tim, somewhat concerned. "I'm thinking about a tour of two, maybe three years."

Jakub laughed. "Sorry, Tim. Perhaps you'll get a year or so at most. It's more likely just another six months. Then this latest experiment in futility will be over. South Vietnam's freedom was doomed the day Kissinger signed the Paris Treaty."

"What!" said Tim, sticking his chin out a bit. "I don't believe that. I've been part of the Vietnamization effort. I know it works. It was the South Vietnam Army that stopped the enemy's Easter Offensive two years ago in 1972. That's why we felt we could withdraw all combat troops last year."

Jakub smiled and shook his head. "Ah, it's great to be young. In young men there is little cynicism and much hope. You are right, the South Vietnam Army fought bravely in the Easter Offensive of '72, and they did stop that North Vietnamese invasion. However, it was your B-52 bombers that really broke the back of that invasion. Without those B-52's, I fear the outcome would have been very different. Against the next North Vietnamese invasion, and there will be one, the South won't have any B-52's."

"But Jakub, MACV didn't really disband, it just moved its operations to Thailand. It is there keeping tabs on the North Vietnamese and will help stop any future invasion by bombing enemy supply lines from the north."

Another big sigh from Jakub. Then he lifted four fingers to the waiter. Tim hoped that meant he was just ordering his fourth gin and tonic, not four more gin and tonics.

"Tim, I would like to agree with you, but I can't. The U.S. government will do nothing meaningful to stop the coming invasion. Just politically speaking, because of Watergate, Nixon will do nothing. But that's only part of it. Like I said before, the whole peace thing was doomed from the start. Did you know that as part of the Paris Treaty all North Vietnamese forces deployed in South Vietnam on the day of the signing were allowed to remain in-country? That's right. Although the treaty required all American forces to leave, it allowed all North Vietnam Army units to remain in place. Depending on whose numbers you use, that's between 200,000 and 400,000 enemy soldiers left inside the borders of South Vietnam. Right now these units are resupplying, reequipping, and remanning themselves. The next invasion of South Vietnam will be launched from inside South Vietnam. It will be quick, it will be lethal, and it will be final. There will be no supply lines for your displaced MACV to bomb."

Jakub then looked at his watch and with a look of surprise said, "Well, jigger my gin. It's a little after three. This lunch has turned into a pleasant afternoon of talk and drink. But let me take you by my tailor right now. If I ask him, he'll have your three suits ready for pickup tomorrow."

"Sounds good to me," replied Tim. "But first, tell me, why are you still here? Most of the journalists have left. What's keeping you here?"

Jakub thought for a moment, then in a low, straight-forward tone, "Let me tell you a short story. I was born in Czechoslovakia. I remember in September 1938, when I was 13, my father was reading a newspaper about the English Prime Minister, Neville Chamberlain, signing The Munich Agreement with Adolf Hitler. That agreement conceded the Sudetenland region of Czechoslovakia to Germany. The newspaper headlined Chamberlain's famous statement, "Peace in our time." The very next day my father started selling all our belongings. In less than six months we were in the United States. Almost a year to the date of The Munich Agreement, Hitler attacked Poland and was at war with Britain. World War II had started. My father proved more prescient than the leading statesmen of Europe and America."

"Later, in 1948, I was a 23-year-old student at Harvard, majoring in Journalism and minoring in History. One of my courses focused on solving the issue of Korea. In 1948, the UN, the US, the USSR, and other countries signed an Agreement to accept the division of post-WWII Korea along the thirty-eighth parallel. North of the 38th would be ruled by the communists, supported by Communist China. South of the 38th would be ruled by non-communists, supported by The United States. But that agreement also called for the withdrawal of all US troops from the south by 1949. Sound familiar? My professors extolled those peace negotiations as an example of the only way to solve international crises in the atomic age. I discussed this with my father. He laughed and said the North Koreans would attack to unify the country under Communist rule within a year after the Americans withdrew. As if on cue, North Korea, supported by Communist China and the Soviet Union, attacked in June 1950, a year after US troops had left. Again my father proved more astute, or probably more honest, than America's and the world's leading statesmen. However, in 1950, America was led by Harry Truman. He went back in and kicked ass. I was soon on the ground in Korea reporting on that war. Being on the ground reporting on a war is much different than being in a classroom talking about a war. I have been on the ground reporting on wars ever since."

"I was also on the ground in Hungary in 1956 when Soviet tanks invaded. I no longer needed my father to tell me how things would turn out in negotiations between Communist countries, or any dictatorships for that matter, and those countries or peoples who wanted to be free. Power, not ideas, would win the day."

"I was not in my own Czechoslovakia when Soviet tanks invaded in 1968. I was here reporting on the Communist' Tet Offensive. I came to Vietnam in 1957, after reading about the famous demarcation line agreed to by the North and South Vietnamese in Geneva. I was stunned by the reported one million North Vietnamese who moved south to avoid Communism, as compared to the only 50,000 South Vietnamese who moved north in support of the Communists. I could hear my father whispering in my ear, 'There, son, is the next Communist invasion,' and of course, that's how it turned out. A contest of power against ideas."

"Why am I still here, you ask? Because I want to be here at the end. When the Communists finally get what they want here. Again through force, through another invasion, this time the final one. I will tell the world the sad story, much as I just told it to you. But I'm afraid that, unlike you, no one will listen."

GETTING READY

True to his word, Jakub's tailor had Tim's new suits ready by 1000 hours the next day. Tim liked these suits. They were made of a light cotton-polyester blend and had a loose fit. The jacket looked like a safari jacket from the old Tarzan movies. The jacket was worn outside the pants, had three buttons down the front, two breast pockets, an additional two lower front pockets, and short sleeves. Usually it was worn over just a T-shirt. An additional plus was the easy, loose fit for carrying a pistol in the back waistband of the pants. This "civilian uniform," so called because almost every foreigner wore one, certainly felt more comfortable than his more tailored Army tropical tan uniforms. Tropical tans, not combat fatigues, was the military uniform of the DAO.

Wearing his new blue leisure suit, Tim headed for the DAO motor pool. Yesterday he had ordered a car for today. For today, he would go to Quan.

He walked through the open gates of the chain link fence surrounding the motor pool and headed for the small, cinderblock building that served as the motor pool's management office. As he walked into the office, someone yelled ATTEN-HUT!!! Everyone in the room jumped to attention in a confused jumble. Tim was confused as well. First, he had on his civvies, so how could they know he was an officer. Second, no one called a motor pool office, or any office for that matter, to attention for a 2nd Lieutenant. Tim looked around to see what was going on. What he saw were smiling faces, all of which he recognized. Standing behind the service counter was the biggest smile on a face he knew very well, Sergeant Major Shaffer's. Shaffer, the Sergeant Major from Tim's old 1st Cav unit, reached his hand across the counter saying, "Welcome back, Tim, or should I say, 'Lieutenant' DePalma?"

There were handshakes and back slapping all around. In addition to Shaffer there were four other Sergeants whom Tim knew from his last tour. However, as he soon learned, they were no longer Army Sergeants. Now they all were civilian contractors working for the DAO.

After about 10 minutes of catching up, the group started to disperse, and Shaffer presented a set of keys to Tim. "Here you go, Lieutenant. The car doesn't look like much, but it's the best running vehicle in the motor pool, and there's a little extra steel protection in the doors."

After Tim signed all the paperwork for the car, Shaffer said, "OK, let's go out and inspect it before you take off. It has a few extras I think you will like." The former Sergeant Major showed the new 2nd Lieutenant this and that about the car as they walked around the vehicle. When they got to the trunk, Shaffer opened it.

Tim's mouth let out an, "Are you kidding me? I don't believe it!"

As Tim reached into the trunk, Shaffer stopped him. "Not here. Check it out later, where there are fewer eyes. Are you sure you want it? It's not authorized. There's still no paperwork on it. You're an officer now, not a Sergeant. There'll be more trouble for you, if you're caught bending the rules."

Tim thought for about a millisecond, "Damn right I want it. I'll always have some of the Sergeant in me, thanks to you. This is just great. Thanks, Sergeant Major. Oops, I guess I should call you Mr. Shaffer now."

The former Sergeant Major took Tim's hand, looked at him as a father would, a little proud, and said, "Just call me Cliff. That will do nicely. Remember, anytime you want anything from this motor pool, or anything else in Saigon, you come see me."

Tim shook Cliff's hand and before closing the trunk, he looked one more time at what was in that trunk: his old M-3 submachine gun, what everyone called "the grease gun," along with two full 30-round magazines, and a metal ammo box full to the top with .45 caliber rounds. With a smile, he slammed the trunk closed.

GOING TO QUAN

Leaving the motor pool, Tim felt a little dapper in his new suit and driving an American sedan. He was glad he felt that way because he was on his way to see Quan. He planned to surprise her. However, as the fates would have it, he would be the one surprised, ...unpleasantly so.

Soon he was out of the city and in the countryside. It felt funny to again be driving along this road which he had travelled so many times before. As he turned the last curve and saw the school atop the hill, he thought of the first time he had seen that compound. It was the first time he had seen Quan. She had been standing in the courtyard, resolute against that coming storm. It seemed like so long ago. It seemed like only yesterday. What would it seem like today?

As Tim aimed for the gate, his smile turned into a frown. "What the hell? What's this all about? Has this something to do with that bastard Truc?"

Tim hadn't thought much about Truc in the past year. When he had, it was only to hope that the slimy little weasel had somehow met his maker. But now, the presence of a guard post and a guard at the entrance to Quan's school screamed "Truc!"

Tim stopped at the gate, showed his credentials, and was passed through. Like he had done so many times before, he drove up to the front of the main house, parked his vehicle, and walked up the steps. But unlike so many times before, there were no children playing, no old lady Thu to greet him, and worst of all, no feeling of Quan's presence.

Instead of kids and playing, there were soldiers and marching. Instead of laughter and singing, there were orders and precision. This was no longer a school; it was now a military post. "What the hell had happened?"

Upon entering, he turned to his right, into Quan's office. It was now occupied by a Sergeant at a desk immediately in front of him and by a Captain and a Major reading newspapers at desks in the back. Only the Sergeant looked up, followed by remarkably good English, "May I help you, Sir?"

Tim showed his credentials and asked to speak with the Major. The Sergeant asked Tim to wait outside as the Major was busy at the moment. Tim remembered Jakub's comments of the day before as to what kind of cooperation a 2nd Lieutenant gets. Without a word, he walked past the Sergeant and up to the Major's desk, "Excuse me, Sir, I would like to speak with you."

After checking Tim's credentials, the Major said, "Wait outside, Lieutenant. I see you in short time."

Tim locked eyes with the Major for a second, as his mind raced for a plan. He then said in Vietnamese, "Major, although I am a Lieutenant, I am here representing the United States Defense Attaché to acquire information. I know your time is important, as is mine. This will only take a few minutes. You may call your commander if you wish, but my time is short. Neither your bosses nor mine want my project slowed down."

The Major remained seated and silent. Then he said in Vietnamese, "Captain, give your chair to the Lieutenant. We will only be a few minutes."

On the way back to Saigon, Tim tried to make sense of what he had learned. Under the guise of leading a DAO project to increase supplies to Vietnamese posts around Saigon, Tim had asked questions about the post's former and present uses. Among other information, the Major stated he knew nothing about a former school being there, only an orphanage. He knew nothing more about the orphanage: not what happened to it, not where the kids went, not who the people were who ran it. However, he did suggest that if the Lieutenant needed more information, he should contact a Major Truc at Army Headquarters, because he had something to do with the establishment of this new post and the relocation of the orphanage. Besides, Major Truc was a close friend of the orphanage's headmistress.

Tim was enraged and his driving showed it. He finally stopped his car, got out, and walked around. He'd be damned if he'd go ask Major Truc for information about Quan. He knew he wouldn't get any. Besides, with all US military forces gone, his

personal power relationship with Truc had been severely weak-
ened. In the past, he had the influence of a MACV general to
counter Truc's every move. How would he handle Truc now?

However, his major concern right now was not Truc. It was
finding Quan. He needed a plan. As he walked, he settled down.
As he settled down, he thought better. As he thought better, he
planned better. As he planned better, a plan emerged. He
jumped back into the car and headed for Saigon.

SEARCHING FOR QUAN

It was now late afternoon in Saigon, and Tim was sitting in
the shade of a tree on the patio of the Songbird restaurant. As
the caged birds merrily sang in the trees, he thought about his
first time there. It was the first time he had been with Quan, really been with her, in the biblical sense. He smiled.

His plan to find Quan would start there, at the Songbird. The
plan was simple, yet it had two variations. Version A would be to
start there at the restaurant, walk down the main street, and stop
in every dress shop till he found the one owned by Quan's sister.
Version B would be to wait at the restaurant till all the shops
closed, then walk down the side street to Quan's sister's apartment. Although he had never met Quan's sister, he knew she
would tell him what he needed to know. What he needed to
know was simply where to find Quan. Then he would do the rest.

Tim hadn't eaten since breakfast. While deciding which version of the plan to follow, he ordered a plate of Pho Xao, a traditional Vietnamese dish known to the rest of the world as Pad Thai.
According to his instructors in Monterey, it was the Vietnamese
who had introduced this dish to the Thais. He wondered, "Would
the Thais agree?"

The plate in front of him had the expected stir-fried noodles
and the ever present "aroma" of Nuoc Mam. However, this time
the "aroma" was almost pleasant, softened by a strong and covering presence of garlic. The whole presentation of noodles, rice,
shallots, and eggs was topped with a half dozen steamed shrimp

and a thin layer of chopped roasted peanuts. This would be a tasty 30 minutes of planning.

As he ate, Tim went over the plan's pro's and con's. The main pro for Version A, the search for Quan's sister's shop, was that he could do it right now, no waiting. He would probably find Quan sooner. The main con was that everyone on the street would end up taking about the American looking for Quan and her sister. Quan would not be happy with that amount or kind of notoriety. The pro's and con's for Version B, wait and go to Quan's sister's apartment later, were just the opposite. The main pro was that no one other than Quan's sister would know he was looking for her. The main con was that finding Quan would probably take longer. There was no telling when her sister would return to her apartment, if in fact she still lived there. Tim finally decided to go with Version B, not because he favored it, but because he knew Quan would favor it.

So Tim, in his new leisure suit, leisurely sat in the Songbird, eating his Pho Xao, sipping his sugar cane juice, and thoroughly enjoying the waning hours of a pleasant spring afternoon in Saigon. ...Although he didn't know it at the time, what he was enjoying were the waning hours of a day in the waning months of Saigon's very existence. Tim thought to himself that there now seemed to be more activity on the streets of Saigon than when he was here just a year ago. ...Although he didn't know it at the time, this activity resulted from more and more people moving into the city from the countryside, as the enemy slowly tightened its noose around the capitol. With his meal finished, he focused totally on Quan and fantasized about where and how their reunion would happen. ...Although he didn't know it at the time, his fantasy was about to become reality, just not exactly as he had planned.

He was looking across the boulevard at the side street down which building number 88 and apartment number 20 awaited. There was his past. Around the corner came his future.

At first Tim wasn't sure. He squinted his eyes, shading them with his left hand. His right hand steadied himself against his chair as he had stopped in mid-rise. There, turning the corner of the side street, a young woman. This young woman looked like Quan, but he wasn't sure. Then she smiled. His eyes might still not be sure, but his heart was. It did a back flip with happiness.

Then he realized she was not smiling at him. She was smiling at the Vietnamese man next to her, the one with whom she was walking arm-in-arm. Tim's heart went cold. He fell back into his chair.

He watched her/them, as she/they approached. She was still across the boulevard and about a block away. She had not seen him. She was not looking for him. She was looking at, talking with, and smiling for another man.

Tim looked at her. She had changed. She was not in her traditional *ao dai*. She wore western style, white dress slacks and a pale yellow, short-sleeved blouse. Her hair was different, shorter than before, although still falling past her shoulders, but now lightly styled. She looked as beautiful as ever.

What should he do? Should he go to her? Should he let her pass by? Should he wait for another time? He didn't know what to do. With all his planning, he had not planned for this.

Tim's heart raced as he thought, "Why hadn't I expected this? She is a beautiful woman. I left her. She had no idea I would return. Other men would want her, pursue her, love her." He could not take his eyes from her.

As he watched her walking arm-in-arm with someone else, he slumped still further in his chair. His strength seemed to seep from him. His heart sighed. His soul moaned.

Quan lightly patted her partner's arm and laughed at something he said. As she approached the boulevard, she looked up, preparing to cross. As always, when she came to this spot, she let her eyes travel to the Songbird and let her heart remember.

"What! This could not be!" she thought. She shook her head, as if that would clear her vision. It did not. It was still Tim sitting at that table.

Releasing her arm, she broke into a smile and dashed into the busy street. Screeches, horns, and yells did not slow her. She ran to him.

As Tim was watching her, he saw the moment she looked up and recognized him. He jumped up with fear, as she dashed into the traffic. He had taken but one step toward her, when she burst upon his chest, flinging her arms about his neck, and hugging him until his breath was crushed from him into her. Then she kissed him, -a long, hard kiss that she would not stop.

Finally, she stepped back, tears running down her face, a flurry of hands slapping at his chest, "Why did you not tell me you are back? Why are you back? What are you doing back? I am so glad you are back." Then she again wrapped her arms around his neck and pressed her sobbing face into his chest. She would not let go of him.

Tim held her tightly. He would not let go of her, not again.

Then Tim tensed. Quan's companion was approaching. He was a big man for a Vietnamese, about 5'10" and 160 pounds, in his late 20's or early 30's. He looked concerned and unhappy. Tim prepared for trouble.

Quan felt Tim tensing. She leaned back and looked up. In response to the hardness of his face, she looked back over her shoulder. She stepped back, taking a half turn, and stood between the two men, a restraining hand on Tim's chest and a hand reaching out to the other man.

"It is alright, Bao. This is Tim. I have told you of him."

As far as Tim could tell, the man didn't look any less concerned or any less unhappy. But he did stop advancing. He said nothing. He just looked at Tim.

Quan, now a little more composed and, as she shyly looked around the restaurant, seemingly a little embarrassed by her very public display of affection, continued softly in Vietnamese, "Tim, this is my brother, Bao, from Can Tho. He has been staying at my sister's while doing some work in Saigon."

Although Tim's face remained passive, his heart, his soul, his everything inside was bursting with happiness. They all kept repeating over and over, "Her brother! Her brother! Her brother!"

Tim, still hard-faced on the outside, slightly nodded to Bao and offered his hand, along with a traditional Vietnamese greeting. Bao returned the nod and somewhat reluctantly took Tim's hand. Everyone then sat down.

After a few minutes of polite, yet strained conversation, Bao stood and said his goodbyes. He would be returning to Can Tho immediately. He and Quan hugged. In whispered Vietnamese, he told her to be careful, that getting involved again with this American would not be a good thing. Tim acted as if he could not hear nor understand what was said. But he could hear, and he clearly understood.

Tim was glad Bao had left and didn't hide it. To Tim's gratification, Quan seemed equally glad and also didn't hide it. They talked in a hurried jumble of questions and answers, moved along by a subtext of glances and touches. They were quickly moving toward a renewed closeness. Could they overcome their year of separation? Could they again be what they once were?

After 30 minutes, they were still in close conversation; heads but inches apart, voices low, her hand softly on his, his knee lightly touching hers. Finally, the gaiety of a child's laughter intruded. They looked toward the laughter to see a child clapping her hands after winning a game of Tic Tac Toe.

"Tim, do you remember my school children laughing as you taught them how to play Tic Tac Toe? They had such happy times with you."

"Yes, I remember. Perhaps we should try a new game, one that might again provide happy times." Tim took a pen from his pocket and started writing on a napkin. When done, he pushed the napkin toward Quan, gave her the pen and said, "Here, it's a math game. I started it. You must be the one to finish it."

On the napkin he had written: "88+20 = ___." Quan smiled, looked shyly at him from the corner of her eye, and began writing her answer, covering it with her left hand so he could not see. She folded the napkin and passed it back to him.

Somewhat hesitantly, he opened the napkin. She had cleverly completed the question as: "88+20 = #1." He smiled, laughed, and took her hand. They walked off, hand-in-hand, to 88-20.

In Vietnamese, the term "Number One" meant "The best!"

A COUPLE AGAIN

That night ended the tragedy of their year apart. That night began the happiness of their coming year together. That night was but a year from the coming tragedy that would end that happiness ...forever.

From that night forward they were again a couple. Yet, culture and convention made it difficult to live as a couple.

Since leaving her school, Quan had been living at her parents' home. Tim could not be with her there. She would not go to him in his room at the Rex. He soon rented a small apartment in a middleclass section of Saigon. They made it their own and loved everything about it. They loved everything about being there. They loved everything about being there together. They loved everything about their every moment there. When not there, circumstances and Vietnamese culture forced them to lead their individual lives separately.

In updating Tim on what had happened to her over the past year, Quan told him that when her school was forced to close in favor of the new military post, Major Truc had helped her place her children in three different orphanages, according to the children's ages. Truc then helped her secure a job at the orphanage that had taken in the youngest of her students. She worked there as the headmistress on weekends. During the week she worked at a major bank in downtown Saigon. Again Major Truc had helped her secure that position through his contacts. She acknowledged that she owed much to Truc. Her fluency in French and English, as well as her administrative skills, had made her a perfect fit at the bank. Although she loved her children and her weekend role as their headmistress, she also loved her new duties at the bank. She was caught between two worlds. Now Tim's return added a third.

Tim was not happy with any of this news about Major Truc. He tried to convince her that Truc was responsible for establishing that new military post, forcing the closing of her school, and causing the relocating of her children. Tim saw all Truc's help subsequent to the closing of the school as a not so subtle attempt to ingratiate himself with Quan, to get close to her, to make her dependent on him.

In turn, Quan again tried to softly explain to Tim the intricacies of her relationship with Truc. Their families were close. Their parents had arranged a marriage between them. Quan had refused, but in doing so had tried to be caring and concerned about his feelings. Although Truc might still love her, he now accepted their limited but still strong bonds of friendship. What he did not want to accept was her relationship with a foreigner, with Tim. He often told her how he did not understand how she could do such a thing. Yes, Truc might dislike Tim, even try to hurt him, but Truc would never do anything to hurt her or her children.

Tim and Quan had several conversations, almost arguments, about Truc's intentions. Yes, Quan explained, over the past year she and Truc had many planning meetings together, even some lunches and dinners, but only to discuss options for her and her children. Yes, it was clear that Truc would still like to be more than a friend, that some idea of that arranged marriage still lingered in the back of his mind. However, Quan believed she had made it clear, as she had always done throughout her life, that they could not be more than friends. Tim accepted Quan's beliefs, but he thought them naive as to Truc's actions and intentions. After their initial discussions, he did not bring it up again. Not again, that is, until Truc intruded into their lives.

OF MICE AND MEN, ... and TRUC

Over the next year, Tim and Quan became a true couple. More and more they ventured out into the city together. Tim had always wanted this, but Quan had been reluctant, still fearing censure, not so much against herself, but against her family, against her school.

During their year apart, Quan had changed. In trying to navigate the turmoil in her personal life following Tim's departure and in her professional life following the closure of her school, she had become even more independent, more demonstrative, and in Tim's eyes, more irresistible.

Although Tim tried to spend as much time with Quan as possible, he still had a job to do. He was a liaison officer between the United States Defense Attaché Office (DAO) and selected Vietnamese military units within a 50-mile radius of Saigon. His responsibilities took him to the Cambodian border in the west and the shores of the South China Sea in the east; to the jungles north of the city and to the Delta's waters in the south. His responsibilities often required him to be away from Saigon for days and weeks at a time.

The DAO in Saigon was unlike any other in the world. Whereas most American DAOs numbered less than a 100 personnel, the DAO in the Republic of Vietnam numbered 50 military personnel, over 1,000 U.S. government civilians, and somewhere between 8,000 and 10,000 civilian contractors dispersed throughout the capitol region and 10 subordinate regional offices. This DAO organization had been established after the Paris Peace Accords were signed. It replaced the previous war-running Military Assistance Command, Vietnam (MACV), which was disestablished as a result of the Peace Accords. It even occupied MACV's former massive headquarters building in Saigon, known as Pentagon East. The DAO's major role was to continue technical support to the Vietnamese military. It was not to provide any operational support, including no assistance or advice on the planning or conduct of any combat operations. Tim's orders were to report on the operability status of Vietnamese military equipment from jeeps to helicopters. What he found was not at all heartening. In some units over 75% of the equipment was nonoperational. His findings and those of other liaison officers throughout the country did not bode well for the future survivability of the Republic.

Tim often took Jakub along for company on his liaison trips. They were a good team. Tim still knew some of the local leaders as a result of his previous tour with the old MACV Vietnamization Office. Jakub however, as a result of his 17 years in-country, knew a lot about almost everything and everybody. He often proved an immense help in facilitating Tim's work with local military units. Tim wasn't sure if traveling with a civilian reporter would be approved by his bosses, so he never asked. He had learned while a young sergeant the wisdom of the old adage that it was sometimes better to ask for forgiveness than it was to ask for permission.

For the first 6 months, from April to September, these liaison trips went fairly well. After that, Tim began running into trouble. It first started In the countryside. There he began meeting more and more resistance from local villagers and military commanders. After a while, several villagers who knew him from his previous tour took him aside and informed him that word had come from Saigon suggesting Lieutenant DePalma was submitting unfavorable reports on local military and civilian leaders. Thus, these leaders were now reluctant to work with him. About the same time frame, trouble also started in Saigon, with police constantly stopping and ticketing his vehicles for what he considered non-violations. This police harassment interfered with many of his support missions. Without any evidence to substantiate his suspicions, Tim began to suspect the source of all his problems was that slimy little weasel named Truc.

Saigon police worked closely with the Vietnamese military commanders in Saigon. The Americans had always referred to the Saigon police as the "White Mice," because they wore white shirts, were small in stature, and seemed always to be scurrying around everywhere. Even though the term "White Mice" might seem derogatory, anyone who had been in Saigon in Tet '68 had the greatest respect for how these men could fight when they had to. However, when they weren't carrying out their duties, many were often conspiring as to how to gain more political influence, power, and graft. Tim had no doubts that the White Mice would find working with Major Truc to harass an American officer to be more than an acceptable form of entertainment.

This police harassment reached its most egregious in early November, on November 10th to be precise, on the Marine Corps' birthday. No matter where in the world U. S. Marines might be deployed, they always celebrate the Corps' birthday with a special ceremony and a cake. As Tim was leaving the restaurant where he had just attended the Marines' Saigon celebration, he saw his jeep and supply truck being towed away. While he was yelling at the disappearing vehicles, four White Mice descended upon him. A shouting match in Vietnamese ensued. Tim demanded to know why his vehicles were taken and wanting paperwork stating that reason. One of the *mice* took out his handcuffs. Tim thought the harassment was about to reach a new level, or perhaps the cuffs were just a warning, an indicator of what might be coming later. After the brandishing of the cuffs, the *mice* nested in a little group and talked amongst themselves for a moment, after which they smiled at Tim, waved goodbye, and drove off. Tim got no answers, but he did get a license plate number and a car number.

Tim went back into the restaurant, called the DAO motor pool, and explained to Shaffer what had just happened, providing him the police plate and car numbers. In response to Shaffer's questions as to why the Saigon police had taken the vehicles, Tim told him about Major Truc and the belief that Truc was behind this whole series of troubles.

Shaffer ended the conversation with, "Geeez, young guys fighting over a woman; the world never changes. Lieutenant, go back into the restaurant and keep those jarheads under control before they overdose on cake. All my vehicles are out right now, but I'll have a car there to pick you up in about 2 hours. In the meantime, somebody's going to feel my boot up his ass."

About two and a half hours later, Tim was riding through the open gates of the DAO motor pool. He couldn't believe what he was seeing. There, parked in front of the cinder block office, were his jeep and truck. "Hmm," he said under his breath, "I'm glad it wasn't my butt that size 12 boot went up!"

Tim checked the bed of his truck and found all the replacement parts he had planned to take to the field still there. Then, with a little more apprehension, he went to his jeep and felt underneath the dashboard. He exhaled a sigh of relief. His grease gun was still there. Shaffer had soldered metal clips under the dashboards of both the car and jeep that Tim usually used. These clips firmly held his submachine gun hidden out of sight, while still allowing for its quick release should Tim need it in a hurry.

As Tim entered the cinderblock building, Shaffer boomed out, "Welcome back, Lieutenant. As I'm sure you already realize from what's outside, that while you were partying with the GI'rines, I was covering your butt. You can thank me later with a couple of beers."

"Cliff, I'll buy you a case of beer every day for a month," responded Tim, with a smile as wide as his face. "How did you pull that off?"

"Well, there are a lot of retired Sergeants Major in Saigon controlling almost all aspects of supply distribution to the Vietnamese military and the police. We made it clear to the White Mice that not a truck load of U.S. supplies would be delivered to any facility in or around Saigon unless my trucks were back in front of my motor pool within the hour."

Tim laughed, "Whether active duty or retired, a Sergeant Major always knows how to get the job done."

"You got that right, Lieutenant. And one more thing. I don't think you'll have to worry about that Major Truc again. I located his unit and personally made it clear to his commander that if the major caused you any more problems, his facility would never see another truckload of supplies. I'm pretty confident that they'll keep him on a short leash from now on."

In the short term, the former Sergeant Major was right. But in the long term, the little weasel would eventually slip the leash and turn into a wolf, a rabid wolf.

QUESTION ASKED
QUESTION ANSWERED
QUESTIONS REMAINED

It was Christmas Eve, and Tim and Quan were again seated in downtown Saigon's best French restaurant, The Guillaume Tell. It was almost exactly two years since they had last sat in this restaurant, at this exact table. That night Quan had given Tim the gift of the golden songbird. Tonight it would be Tim's turn to give Quan a gift; one he hoped she would accept.

Tim asked Quan to select their meals because she knew French food better than he did, and she could also order for them, as she could pronounce the names of the French dishes. It was his unstated way of saying that he accepted her as an equal partner, even in a culture where a woman would normally never order food in a restaurant for a man.

"But Tim, the waiter will think badly of you," she whispered in protest.

Tim smiled, "Why would I care what the waiter thinks of me? I only care what you think of me. Do you think me less of a man because I ask you to be my partner rather than my ward?"

She looked at him. She said nothing for a moment, but her eyes spoke volumes. As she looked down at the menu, those eyes reflected the glow of an inner smile. "Let's see what we will have tonight."

As she focused on the menu, he focused on her. She was thinking of what she was about to order for them. He was thinking of what he was about to ask of them.

She looked up, "I love vichyssoise. I will order it for both of us. Is OK, GI?" She laughed as she used the street vernacular for selling something to an American soldier.

Tim also smiled at the phrase, then answered, "I don't know what vichywhatever is, but If you like it, I'll give it a try."

She continued, "I think I will have Cognac Shrimp in Beurre Sauce. However, so waiter not worry too much about you, I think I should order you a steak. An American man is supposed to have steak, yes? How about this one, Steak Au Poivre?"

"Well sure, I like steak. But something called Steak ahh Puff doesn't sound too manly to me. Do you think our waiter will approve?"

"Not Steak ahh Puff," she said, smiling a long sigh over towards him. "I said, Steak Au Poivre. It is a steak with peppercorns and a French mushroom crème sauce. Although French were here long time, Vietnamese do not cook with French sauces. But these sauces are nice when we go to special restaurants like tonight. I think you will like this steak."

Quan ordered the food. At the last minute, probably to save some face with the waiter, Tim ordered the wine. The waiter seemed to approve.

After the wine was poured, the vichyssoise was served. Tim first toasted their night together, then sipped his wine. After that, he sipped his soup. Again he was surprised.

"What is it with Saigon and cold soup? First, as soon as I arrive in country, Jakub orders me cold cucumber soup, and now to celebrate Christmas you order me cold potato soup. This tastes like day-old New England clam chowder straight from the fridge."

Quan looked both a little confused and a little amused. "I'm not sure what this 'new English chowder' is, but it must be good if it tastes like this."

Tim smiled to Quan on the outside and laughed to himself on the inside. Life with her was going to be so much fun. By the time he was scraping the bottom of his bowl, he too was a fan of the smooth, creamy, cool vichywhatever

They became lost in their lovers' holiday dinner. It was almost two hours later when the waiter finally cleared the table. They both decided they were too full for dessert, but they did order hot green tea.

As the tea was being prepared, Tim decided now was the time. He took a deep breath, reached into his pocket, and began.

"Quan, when we were last here, you gave me a Christmas gift. Tonight I want to give you a gift." Tim was not a man of many words, so with those few, he presented her with a small box wrapped in a silk bow.

Quan slowly and delicately unwrapped the box, spread aside the small amount of tissue paper, and took out the gift. It was the same gold songbird she had given him. She was perplexed. "Tim, why are you returning my gift? I am confused."

Tim, his face now reddening from his own confusion, said, "I'm sorry. I should have explained it better. When you gave me this golden songbird and every day since, I have thought of it as a silent witness to our first time together, a silent witness to all our times together. But it is silent no longer. Now it sings a song I hope you will like. Look at it closer."

As Quan picked up the golden songbird, she noticed a small roll of paper held in its beak. As she looked at Tim, she removed the paper from the songbird's beak and unrolled it. There, written between musical note symbols, were the words "Quan, will you marry me?"

With tears in her eyes, but a smile on her face, she simply said, "Yes."

Tim reached across the table, gently took her hand, slipped a heart-shaped diamond ring onto her slender finger, and said, "Quan, with this I promise I will love you forever with all my heart."

Yes, Tim would love her forever. Just not in the way he had imagined that night.

REMAINING QUESTIONS

Their engagement night brought a new kind of happiness to the couple. Before that night, their happiness came from within themselves and was focused on themselves. Now they began thinking about other things and people outside themselves, especially the bringing of their families into their happiness.

Quan wanted to keep their engagement a secret until Tet. Tet was a time of family celebration, good cheer, and good luck. She would tell her family then, hoping the happiness of the holidays would make it easier for her family to accept her decision and welcome Tim into the family.

Although Tet was only six weeks away, Tim was unhappy with keeping their engagement a secret. He wanted the whole world to know and to know right now. However, upon reflecting on it, he realized that now Quan was his whole world, so he acquiesced.

She then reminded him that her parents were very traditional, so Tim would probably have to undergo a traditional Vietnamese engagement ceremony. Such a ceremony requires the young man, dressed in a traditional male *ao dai*, to go to the girl's home bringing engagement gifts for her and all her family; that's when he would formally offer her the ring. Once the father, the girl, and the girl's family members accept the gifts, symbolizing their acceptance of him, the young man then takes his new fiancée and her entire family to a feast at a beautiful location, usually a countryside estate or a very fine restaurant.

Normally, a Vietnamese engagement might last a year or two between the engagement ceremony and the wedding. However, things were changing in traditional Vietnam. Although Quan wanted to honor her parents and her culture with the traditional ceremonies, she would not accept their traditional timelines. She decided on a much shorter timeline. First, she would inform her parents in February, the Tet Holidays, of her intent to marry. The engagement ceremony would be in May. The wedding would be in June. Tim smiled and agreed. Unknowingly, he was already learning to be a husband.

Then Tim and Quan started talking about post-wedding plans. On this subject there were many questions. The most important were the long-term ones, especially: Where and how would they live their lives and raise their children? In what religion would they raise their children? Would Quan be willing to move to America? Would Tim be willing to stay in Vietnam?

Quan told Tim that during their year apart, she had constantly relived her decision to not go with him to America. She knew now that her life must be decided by her own decisions, not those of her family. She now thought moving to America would be an exciting adventure. Yes, she would live with him in America.

Tim then told Quan that during that year apart, he too had many times relived his leaving Vietnam without her. At that time he did not have a choice. However, now he would have a choice. His present tour in Vietnam was scheduled to end in two years. At that time he could leave the military if he so desired. Over the past year he had come to realize that he had already spent more than 20% of his life focused on Vietnam. Even more startling, he realized that he had spent 100% of his adult life, from age 17 to age 22, preparing for, learning about, or being in Vietnam. He thought living in Vietnam with her would be an exciting adventure. Yes, they could make a great life together in Vietnam.

After listening to each other, they laughed over how far their individual ways of thinking had joined together into a couple's way of thinking. Like all young couples in love, this was a joyous, happy time.

The Tet announcement of their engagement went well. Quan had been right. The general feeling of euphoria during Tet had probably made their news more palatable to her family. Her father was certainly not overjoyed by the news, but he did seem accepting of it. Her mother was happy that her daughter was happy. Tim even got a hearty, motherly hug from her. Quan's brothers, like their father, were not visibly overjoyed, but they did seem accepting. As the 3-day Tet celebration wore on, they seemed to warm to Tim. Quan's sister, Lan, was the most excited. She gave both Quan and Tim a big hug and kiss immediately after the announcement, openly showing support for her sister and daring the rest of the family to do anything less. Tim immediately liked Lan.

As the Tet holiday drew to a close, Tim felt comfortable with Quan's family. He came to realize that he was comfortable with his present life. He was also becoming more comfortable with an idea that was growing inside him. He knew he would enjoy the rest of his life with Quan and was beginning to understand that he would enjoy that life no matter where that life was lived.

Yes, Tim probably would have, had he been given the chance.

Vichyssoise

A French classic, Tim was first introduced to vichyssoise by Quan at the Guillaume Tell in Saigon. Although a festive meal at Christmastime, the simplicity and subtle flavors were a pleasant surprise for Tim. Returning to America Tim used the basic recipe but continues to include the Ginger as a tribute to times past.

Ingredients:(Four Servings)

2 – 3	Leeks
1	Onion, sliced and diced
1 Tbsp	Crushed Garlic
2 Tbsp	Butter
3 – 4	Potatoes, peeled and sliced
2 Cups	Chicken Broth
¾ Cup	Sour Cream
¼ Cup	Heavy Cream
Dash	Marjoram
¼ Tsp	Cumin
1	Bayleaf
To Taste	Salt and White Pepper

Directions:

1. Cut off leek tops and slice and dice.
2. Slice and dice one onion.
3. Add butter and garlic to a large saucepan – sauté, but do not burn.
4. Add leeks and onion and stir until tender.
5. Add sliced potatoes, bayleaf, herbs, and chicken broth - bring to a boil and reduce heat; add salt and white pepper to taste.

6. Simmer for 20 – 30 minutes until potatoes are tender.

7. Place mixture in blender until smooth.

8. Stir in sour cream and heavy cream; heat on low until well blended.

9. Chill thoroughly. When ready to serve taste to determine if more herbs and spices are needed. Additional sour cream can be added for rich taste.

Tips:

1. Various recipes substitute cream, crème fraiche, and/or milk as base liquid.

2. Can be made without any cream, using water and broth.

3. Some prefer a "whiter" soup – hence no parsley, dill, etc.

4. Easy to make ahead and store.

Steak Au Poivre with Mushroom and Sherry Sauce

Famous the world 'round, Tim finds this classy dish a little fussy, with a lot of shifting meat and mushroom to and from pans. Tim decided to simplify by making the sauce ahead and concentrating on the steak while entertaining guests. The sauce can easily be used with almost any cut of beef.

Sauce Ingredients:(Four Servings)

2 Tbsp	Olive Oil
2 Tbsp	Butter
½ Cup	Onion, sliced thin
2 Tsp	Minced Garlic
2 Cup	Sliced Mushrooms
3 – 4 Tbsp	Sherry or White Wine
1 Tbsp	Balsamic Vinegar
½ Cup	Heavy Cream

Steak Ingredients:

4 Filets	About 1" to 1-1/2" thick
Steak Rub	Your favorite
Salt/Pepper	To Taste
2 Tbsp	Olive Oil
2 Tbsp	Butter

Sauce Directions:

1. Melt butter and olive oil in saucepan; when bubbling, turn heat to medium and add onion slices and sauté until tender and golden (3 – 4 minutes). Add minced garlic and sauté an additional minute.

2. Add sliced mushrooms and sauté with the onions and garlic, mixing the flavors for about three minutes.

3. Season lightly with salt and pepper, add sherry and balsamic vinegar and heat for about 1 minute. Reduce heat and add cream, stirring for about ½ minute. Remove from heat and store in a glass bowl.

4. When steaks are ready to serve heat sauce in the microwave in 30 second intervals, stirring frequently until hot. Spoon over steaks, distributing mushrooms and onions evenly.

Steak Directions:

1. Rub steaks lightly with olive oil, sprinkle/coat with pepper or your favorite rub.

2 Using a non-stick surfaced pan, heat olive oil and butter until hot but not smoking. Add steaks and quickly sear both sides. Once seared, pan fry the filet for about 3 – 4 minutes per side depending upon thickness, cooking preferences, etc.

3. Remove steaks to plate, heat sauce in microwave, spoon over steaks and serve.

Tips:

1. You can substitute white wine or bourbon for the sherry – depending upon your tastes.

2. Any good cut of beef can be used.

3. Tim prefers to slice the onion thin, vice chopping. It keeps the sauce from being lumpy and, with the thin sliced mushrooms, looks great on the steak.

4. The sauce is normally a soft brown color from the balsamic vinegar, although Tim has occasionally deglazed the steak pan with red wine and added that to the sauce.

5. Another possibility is to ignore the microwave and after the steaks have been plated add the prepared sauce back to the cleaned pan and heat.

6. Pairs nicely with a Pinot Noir.

Chapter 13: FLASHBACK: END TIMES

Day Four: Thursday, 1200 hours, in the Train, Heidelberg to Paris

Again, Tim was now awake and aware on a train between Heidelberg and Paris. His mind and his memories were no longer in Vietnam with Quan. In one rousing moment, his mind had awakened him from his past, made him aware of his present, and alerted him to his future. His mind had stopped rolling its film of the past at the end of Tet, 1974. It had stopped there, for there was the end of the happy times. The only thing that could follow would be the reel of the End Times.

Why had his mind thrown him from his past back into his present? Tim knew why. He knew that his mind didn't want to travel past the Tet celebrations and into the End Times. His mind knew what waited for him there. His mind was in collusion with his heart. Neither one of them wanted to take him where only painful memories lived.

But Tim knew he had to go there. There, in what he called the End Times, existed the causes of his present journey. Facing them anew would strengthen his resolve, renew his purpose, harden his focus, and fortify his will to do what must be done.

He once again looked at and tried to pass through the train's glass-window portal from the his present to his past. At first his mind and heart refused to listen. Finally his mind, but not his heart, gave way to his will and took him back to the End Times.

Tim and Quan's world of calm, happiness, and planning, which began with their Christmas Eve engagement and grew with their Tet celebration, was soon shattered. Within a month after

Tet, South Vietnam began descending into chaos. The descent was quick and violent, the chaos complete. Their lives descended into violence and chaos as well; the chaos would be tumultuous, the violence would be terrible, and the end would be unbearable.

The first sign of trouble came about two weeks after Tet. When Tim returned to their apartment after a long day in the field supporting government troops fighting north of Saigon, Quan was waiting with bad news.

"Tim, I no longer have a job at the bank," she said slowly and softly as she sat on the couch looking at the floor.

"What happened?" as he moved to her.

"I was told that the bank is closing some of its offices in Vietnam. They said the country is becoming too unstable. Thus, some people will not have jobs anymore. I am one of those people because I'm am a newer person at bank."

Tim was thoughtful for a moment, then somewhat suspiciously asked, "Was anyone else let go?"

"Not that I know of," was her almost whispered answer.

Tim's face hardened and his jaw involuntarily clenched. "This is Truc's doing," he exploded. "He found out about our engagement, and now he is going to punish you. I've been expecting something. Yet, I thought he would come after me in some way, not you. Getting you fired is even more vindictive than I thought he would be. I'm going to find that SOB first thing tomorrow."

"No, Tim. It was not Truc. Everything bad that happens to me is not Truc's fault. Truc called me after it happened. He had heard from his friends in the bank that I will no longer work there. He said he was sorry and that if I wished, he would try to find me another job."

Tim stood up and started to pace and to rant, "Not only is he an SOB, he is a clever SOB. I'm telling you, Quan, he is behind this. It is an act of vengeance. Stay away from this guy."

During the night, Quan calmed Tim. She made him promise not to seek out Truc. She also told him she would immediately start looking for another job. Although she had added, "I still have my little ones at the orphanage, and there is also much to do for our wedding. I could use the extra time." The idea and talk of their wedding calmed them both.

He took her to their bed. His intention was to hold her and comfort her; to let her know he was there for her. Her intention was to hold him and be there for him, to calm him. But they were young. The holding turned to touching. The touching turned to kissing. The kissing turned to the release of their tensions in a frenzied act of passion. Their act of passion had been the best way to calm their passions. They were both soon asleep.

The second thunderbolt struck about two weeks after the first. Again, Tim learned of it when he came back to their apartment after several days in the field. As Tim entered, he saw Quan on the couch crying.

"What's wrong, Quan? What's happened?"

"Tim, I no longer work at the orphanage. They told me these are very dangerous times. Many believe North Vietnamese are about to come. They think Americans are again going to leave. Many people say it is now dangerous to be known to work with Americans. They said that my relationship with an American soldier is bad for the orphanage. But most hurtful was they said my personal relationship with an American soldier was a very bad example for the children. Tim, what will I do without my children?"

Tim went to her. As he had done before, he again tried to comfort her. However, to do so, he had to control the rage that was rising inside him. It was hard to control. He knew, just knew, that Truc was behind this, behind all of this; that Truc was punishing Quan for choosing Tim over him.

At first, Tim said nothing to Quan. He did not want to upset her further. Finally, he could no longer control himself.

"Quan, this is Truc again. I know it is. I.."

She cut him off. "Tim, stop it. Please. This is not Truc's fault. This our fault. This my fault. I know what we do is a bad example for my children. I love you, Tim. But I know in my heart that what we do is bad example for my children."

"Quan, we will be married soon. Maybe then they will make you the headmaster again. We will get through this."

"Tim, maybe you are right. I had not thought of that. Perhaps later, after we are married, I can again be headmaster. Perhaps Truc can again help since he knows these people. He got me the job before. It may be possible."

Tim wanted to scream. He wanted to shake her. He wanted to make her understand that Truc was not the nice, helpful person she thought he was. But Tim did not do any of those things. He knew this was not the time to argue with her. He wrapped his arms around her, held her, said the one thing that meant most to him and most to her, "Quan, I love you."

He told himself that he would settle this with Truc. Not tomorrow, for he had something else to do tomorrow, but he would settle this, and soon.

Again, the night began with comforting hugs, but ended in an act of passionate love. Through the years to come, Tim would relive that night in his mind for what seemed a million times. That night would be the last time he would ever see, hear, touch, hold, smell, taste, caress Quan, -the woman he loved, the center of his world.

END TIMES CONTINUED

Just before dawn, following what unknowingly would be their last night together, Tim gently kissed Quan and quietly slipped out of their apartment. He had to pick up Jakub, go to the motor pool for a five truck supply convoy, and then deliver those trucks to a Vietnamese unit which was moving north to the central highlands.

It was mid-March 1975, and there was much movement among North Vietnam units in the jungles of the central highlands. U.S. intelligence expected some trouble, but estimated that the South Vietnam Army would be able to withstand enemy attacks for at least another year or so. That time would allow the US Congress to reinstate its promised, but reneged on, financial and military support to the South Vietnamese government. However, again as the fates would have it, the North Vietnamese Army would be too fast and the U.S. Congress would be too slow.

It was mid-afternoon in a very long day. Tim and Jakub had earlier dropped off the 5 supply trucks with the deploying Vietnamese unit. Now they were heading further north to coordinate support with Vietnamese irregular units that had been in recent contact with Viet Cong. As Tim whizzed by a crossroad, a local police car pulled out and started chasing him.

"I don't believe this. Look back there, Jakub. We're in a warzone, and some local cop wants to stop me for speeding."

Jakub laughed, "Stop. Give him a little money for his trouble, and we'll be on our way again in no time. They do this all the time out here."

Tim pulled over. However, he immediately felt that there was something wrong about this stop. Looking in his review mirror, instead of the usual one cop in the vehicle, Tim saw four uniformed men getting out of the car.

The Vietnamese policeman approached his car yelling, "You, driver, get out of car now. You get out of car now."

Tim opened his door, started to get out, but stopped midway. There, standing behind the cop, was Major Truc. They locked eyes, mutual hate being as a chain stretched taut between them.

Finally, Tim continued his exit and stood next to his car. He ignored the policeman who was yelling at him to put his hands over his head. He was still locked on Truc.

"What's this all about, Truc? What do you want? I have government business to do. You do not want to slow me down!"

Truc waved to the policeman to shut up and moved to within a few feet of Tim, but still kept out of Tim's reach.

Truc put out his hand and, looking at the .45 Cal pistol Tim was wearing on a web belt around his waist, said in Vietnamese "Give me your weapon."

Responding in Vietnamese, Tim simply said, "No!"

"Now, or I will have my men forcibly take it from you."

"What the hell is this all about?" yelled Tim. "You have no authority to stop me, to take my weapon, or do anything else. I am on government business. Now get out of my way."

Tim started to get back into his car. As he did so, the two soldiers with Major Truc clicked off the safeties on their M-16s, now pointed at Tim's midsection. He froze.

"Your weapon, Lieutenant. Now! You can pick it up at the police station in Saigon." Then Truc ominously added, "Should you get back there."

Tim stepped to within a foot of Truc's face. "Don't you threaten me. This is all about Quan, isn't it? You can't accept the fact that she and I are getting married. Well, you better accept it. She does not love you. She loves me. Stop acting like a fool."

Truc did not say a word. He didn't have to. His reddening face said it all. Then he took a step closer to Tim, "This is the last time I will ask. Give me your weapon."

Tim was about to knock Truc on his ass when Jakub intervened. "Tim, give him your weapon. Nothing good can come from further confrontation. We can straighten all this out later."

Truc now looked over to the journalist and said in English, "Good advice Mr. Goblesck. Yes, I know who you are. You think you will write about this? I don't think you will. Lieutenant, take advice from your friend. Give me weapon."

Tim looked at both men, then reluctantly unbuckled his pistol. He handed it to the policeman.

Truc grabbed Tim's weapon and tossed it to one of the soldiers. He took one long look at Tim and then, without warning, delivered a right uppercut to the underside of Tim's jaw that was so unexpected and so powerful that as Tim's head snapped back his knees began to cave, but thankfully held. Truc followed the right uppercut with an immediate left-handed, mid-knuckled karate punch to Tim's exposed throat. Had not Tim dodged about an inch to his left at the last moment, the blow would have paralyzed his windpipe. As it was, the blow left Tim clutching at his neck and gagging. Truc then finished with a hard right fist to Tim's stomach. Tim fell back against his car, trying to suck air back into his lungs through a windpipe that barely worked.

Truc leaned in close and said lowly in English so that the other Vietnamese could not hear, "Remember that day when you come to my office and threaten me? Do you still feel so tough? You are weak. I don't understand why Quan pick you. But now you listen to my threat. I am going to kill you. You will never have Quan. You are no good for her. She is Vietnamese like me. She and I will be together. I love her. I love her family. I am better for her and them. I will have her. If I cannot have her, no one will have her."

With those words blackening Tim's mind as his lungs began to suck in needed air, Truc turned and walked back to the police car. He got in, giving Tim one last glance, a smirk of disgust. The police car wheeled around and headed back to Saigon.

Jakub came around the car to help Tim. Tim waved him away. He was still trying to get his breath and there was blood flowing from his lower lip.

Still gasping, Tim asked, "Jakub, are you armed? I don't think this is over." Tim fumbled-out a 9-mm automatic pistol from his rear waistband holster.

Jakub shook his head, "No, I didn't bring a gun."

As Tim got behind the wheel, he passed his 9-mm over to Jakub. "Here, take this. Since I'm driving, you will have to be the firepower if we end up in trouble."

As Tim started the engine, he looked up, "Oh crap!"

Moving out of the jungle to block the road about 200 yards in front of them was an old pickup truck along with three armed men in black pajamas. "Classic Charlies," Tim muttered. He looked to his rear and saw four more Viet Cong with an ox pulling a cart to block the road about 150 yards behind him.

Tim reached under his dash and pulled out the grease gun. He quickly armed the weapon and said, "Jakub, if we don't get out of this, it's been great to know you. If you get out and I don't, tell Quan I love her."

With that, he gunned the car toward the truck and men in front of him. Just as the VC opened fire, he spun the car around in a 180 degree turn and, with wheels spinning and gravel flying, headed full speed for what had been the VC's rear blocking position, but which was now a little more than 200 yards to his front. Those VC had left their cover behind the cart when it had been to

Tim's rear and had raced forward to join in the killing of the Americans. Now, however, they were caught in the open, with the Americans racing towards them. As the four VC turned to run back to their cover behind the cart, machine gun fire burst from the front windshield of the car bearing down on them. They tried to again turn back toward the car to return fire, but as they did so, both the machine gun's bullets and the car's front grill slammed into them. Simultaneously, their bullets slammed into the car.

Tim heard and saw the shattering of glass all around him. He sensed thudding bullets being absorbed by the front, sides, and rear of the car protecting him. He felt his tires running over bodies beneath him. As he accelerated toward the blockade, he dropped the grease gun and grabbed the wheel with both hands to firmly control the car. He swerved toward and then powered his three thousand pound beast through the front end of the hapless ox. In a moment he was free of the ambush and speeding toward Saigon with only one thought in mind, killing Truc.

About 500 yards down the road and around a curve, he slowed the car enough to look at Jakub, "You OK?"

Jakub was still wide-eyed and stunned. "I've seen some action before, but I've never been that close to death before." He took a deep breath, "It's quite exhilarating isn't it?"

"Yeah," laughed Tim. "Something like that!"

Tim raced towards Saigon, the wind rushing at them through the used-to-be windshield. His mind now again focused on one thing, beating Truc to within an inch of his life, and maybe even a little farther.

After a half hour of driving as fast as the roads would bear, Tim wasn't sure he was going to make it to Saigon. Both a dashboard gauge and steam rushing from beneath the car's hood told him that the engine was overheating. The radiator no doubt had been damaged, either by bullets or when crashing through that ox.

However, Tim did make it to Saigon, and once in the city, he dropped Jakub at the journalist's apartment building and headed directly for the motor pool to trade cars and then find Truc.

After being dropped off in what could best be described as a rolling stop, Jakub ran into his apartment and immediately called the DAO motor pool. He quickly told Shaffer everything that happened. Jakub concluded with, "The kid has bloodlust in his eyes. He is going to kill this Major Truc. Get him out of town for his own good. Otherwise by tomorrow morning he will be either dead or sitting in a Saigon prison."

Jakub hoped he had gotten to Shaffer in time. He shakily poured himself a straight gin, then another.

NO GOODBYE

"I count 21 bullet holes," whistled Shaffer. "Good thing we had a little extra steel in those doors. The front, back, and driver's side windows are gone. The radiator is beyond repair. The left front fender is barely hanging on, covered in ox blood and gristle. The car's a mess. Are you sure you're OK?"

"I'm fine. I need another car, right now. Can you fix me up?"

"Yeah, sure. But you have to do a report on what happened. While you're doing that, I'll get another car ready."

"I don't have time for that," Tim said a little heatedly. "I need the car now. I'll come by tomorrow and do your damn paperwork."

Shaffer stopped and turned to Tim. With the cold eyes of a former Sergeant Major, he looked straight into Tim, "Slow down there, Lieutenant. You know the drill. Go in the office, take the yellow pad there on the counter, and just start writing. While you're doing that, I'll get you another car."

Impatiently, Tim went in, grabbed the pad, and started scribbling. "I don't have time for this," he thought as his hands independently wrote. "I've got to find that bastard now; before he realizes I'm still alive; while I still have the element of surprise. Why is Shaffer taking so long? There I'm done. That'll have to do. Where the hell is Shaffer?"

Just then John Quigley, a Marine Captain whom Tim knew slightly from the DAO guard platoon, walked in. He was followed by a Marine Staff Sergeant.

"Lieutenant DePalma, glad I found you. Come with me. Colonel Dimond wants to see you ASAP. I've got a car outside."

"What? Me? See the colonel? Now? Why? But I can't. I have things to do."

Quigley, raising his eyebrows in surprise, said, "Really? Well, I'm sure the colonel will be interested to know that, and I'm equally sure he can answer all your questions. Me? I can't answer any of them. All he told me was that he wanted to see you ASAP. Let's go."

"But, I can't. I..."

"No more talk, Lieutenant. Let's go. Now."

Tim, a little bewildered, a lot disheartened, and certainly peeved got into the car with the Marines. As the car drove off, Shaffer watched from the door of the maintenance shed and thought, "I hope I did the right thing."

Within 10 minutes, Tim was seated in front of the colonel's desk. Colonel Dimond was Tim's boss, two levels up. Tim knew him fairly well, in an official sense, but he did not have a more personal relationship with him.

Without the normal pleasantries, Colonel Dimond started right in, "I heard you saw some action today. What happened?"

While Tim was retelling his story, leaving out the Major Truc subplot, part of his mind was talking to himself, "How did the colonel find out what happened so soon? I know our intelligence shop isn't that good. What's this all about?"

Then the colonel's following words brought Tim back to full attention about what was going on now, in this office, to him. "Tim, I'm sending you to Da Nang. Things are really getting hot up there. They need more help, and I need a set of eyes that will tell me what's going on without being filtered through a local agenda. Your plane is hot on the runway, ready to go. I want you up there for about two weeks."

"Sir, that's impossible," Tim blurted out before he realized the unprofessional thing he had just said and done, but then he continued anyway. "I need a few days to take care of some ongoing tasks I have here."

Colonel Dimond gave him a long, hard look, then, "Lieutenant DePalma, I'm going to choose to forget you just said that. Let me make myself a little more explicit. I have a new mission for you, a new order. You are going to Da Nang, right now. Help them with their tech support mission. Send me a mission assessment as soon as possible. You will be met at the Da Nang airport by one of our contractors up there. He will have all the mission supplies and personal necessities you will need. Good luck, Tim."

Colonel Dimond then stood up. All discussion was over. As he walked Tim through the office doorway, he said to the Marine Captain in the outer office, "Captain Quigley, please take Lieutenant DePalma directly to Major Holliman over at Hanger 3. No stops along the way. We need to get Tim up to Da Nang immediately. Understand?"

"Yes, Sir. Will do." Captain Quigley, his Staff Sergeant, and Tim headed for Hanger 3.

Colonel Dimond went back into his office, sat down behind his desk, packed and lit his pipe, then let his thoughts follow the pipe's smoke to the ceiling. "That was tough, but I had to do it. Tim's too good of a kid and a soldier to let him screw up his life over some girl. When he gets up there, Wojonski will set his head straight."

END TIMES FOR THE HIGHLANDS

Before getting into the sedan, Tim pulled Quigley aside, "John, I have to get back to my apartment in Saigon. I have to tell my fiancée where I'm going and how long I'll be away. Please, you have to take me there. Then I'll go right to the airfield with you."

Quigley let the sergeant get into the car and behind the wheel, then answered in a whisper, "Tim, you heard the colonel.

Right to Major Holliman at Hanger 3. No stops. Your place would take more than an hour to get there and back. Look, the colonel's not dumb. Even if I wanted to do it, he gave us the order in front of my sergeant. We can't be disregarding the colonel's orders in front of the men. Let's go."

For the entire three-hour flight to Da Nang, Tim kept going over the day's happenings. The circle of questions remained the same for the whole three hours; worse, the answers never got better: "I should never have stopped for that cop. Why was I not more on guard with Truc? How could I let that little piss ant get the drop on me? Why didn't I ask Quigley to take a note to Quan explaining where I was and how long I would be gone? Why did I let my emotions muddy my thinking about all those things? How the hell did Colonel Dimond find out about the ambush? What am I going to do now? I have to get word to Quan as soon as I land."

It was dark when the plane touched down in Da Dang. As Tim jumped down from the passenger's door, a pair of headlights moved across the tarmac toward him. A man stuck his head out the window of a mud-covered Land Rover attached to those head-lights, "Lieutenant DePalma?" Following Tim's affirmatively shaking head, the Land Rover's head yelled in return, "Get in, Lieutenant. I'm your ride."

As soon as Tim got in the old Aussie Land Rover, --he always thought they looked like a bulked-up old Woodie station wagon without the wood, ---he told the driver, "Hey, look, I need to get to a telephone and make a call to Saigon. Get me to a phone that connects to civilian lines in Saigon. I need to get there now."

"Well, hello to you too, Lieutenant. Likewise, it's good to meet you. I'm Gerry Nelson from MobilTek, the main DAO civilian contractor company in Da Nang."

Tim looked confused, then understood. "I'm sorry. Hi, I'm Tim DePalma. Glad to meet you. Thanks for picking me up. But look, I really need to make a call to Saigon."

"Lieutenant, see those three 5-ton trucks over there. They are loaded with ammo that is desperately needed by troops trying to halt an enemy offensive. We have been held up here at the airfield for two hours waiting for you to get here. We cannot waste any more time. You can make your call tomorrow. Put on that flak jacket in the back seat. That M-16 and .45 pistol are also for you. You may not have yelled 'shotgun' when you got in, but now that's your job, riding shotgun, for real."

For the next hour Tim and the driver rode in almost total silence. As they moved higher and deeper into the mountains surrounding Da Nang, they both focused harder on looking for trouble on the road to their front and in the jungle to their sides. The further they got away from the city, the closer they got to the sounds of battle. Soon Tim could see flares fired over distant mountains, bringing near-daylight to night fights, and a myriad of zigzag trails of tracer rounds fired between distant ridge lines.

"Jesus," said Tim. "There's a real battle going on up there. I had no idea things were this bad. How long has this been going on?"

"About three days now. Started with light skirmishes, but now it looks like an all-out North Vietnamese offensive. We are not sure the South Vietnamese can hold. Large numbers of villagers have been fleeing the mountains into Da Nang. The city can't handle many more."

Just then what looked like a squad of South Vietnamese soldiers came walking down the road towards them.

"Damn it," the driver swore in both exasperation and fear. "These guys may be deserters. If they look like they are about to try and take this vehicle, shoot them!" The driver then squawked his radio's hand mike and passed the same message to the trucks behind him.

The Vietnamese passed without incident. They did not even look at the passengers in the Rover. Tim didn't know if that was a good thing or bad.

About an hour later, the convoy passed through a makeshift guard post blocking the mountain road they had just traveled. They were now in a rather large South Vietnamese Army temporary encampment and supply area. The driver pointed to a tent about 50 yards to their front, "That's the headquarters for the MobilTek command group supporting this Vietnamese regiment. Report there. They'll know what to do with you. Good luck."

Tim trudged the 50 yards through the darkness to the tent, went in, and looked around for someone to report to. As soon as his eyes adjusted to the lights, he knew whom that someone would be.

As Tim stood there squinting in the lights, he saw the familiar face widen in a smile and move toward him. "Well, I'll be. It's Lieutenant DePalma. Finally. We've been expecting you. What took you so long? Good to see you, Tim." With that, Platon Wojonski extended a welcoming hand.

While still shaking Tim's hand, Plat led him the few steps to a field table and two metal chairs in a corner of the tent. Plat started, "So, you got yourself into a little trouble over a gal, and you had to get out of Dodge City, heh?"

"What?" responded Tim. "Who told you that? I'm here to support you and provide situational reports back to Colonel Dimond."

Plat cut in on him, "Well, let's get a few things straight right away. First, you don't support me. I'm not Major Wojonski anymore. Now I'm Mr. Wojonski. I'm a private contractor supporting the DAO and Colonel Dimond. At the moment, right here and now, I work for you, Lieutenant. I'm the one who reports to you."

"Second, what I heard from Saigon was that you were about to kill some Vietnamese Major over some girl, so Colonel Dimond got you out of town to keep you out of jail. I heard he also coordinated with his Vietnamese counterpart to get the Vietnamese Major out of town for the same reason. I think they were sending him down south to the Delta, while you were sent up north to Da Nang. You two couldn't be farther apart and still be in the same country. They'll keep you like that until your blood cools. Me? I would have just hosed you young studs down with some cold water. However, believe me when I say that no matter the reason, I'm glad you're here. I need everyone I can get who has some combat experience and sense. We're in big trouble here."

Tim jumped in, more than a little upset with this rendition of why he was up in Da Nang. "Look, Plat, I already got hosed down, and it wasn't with water. It was with AK-47 fire. Here's what really went down." Tim then provided Wojonski the whole long story, from his first meeting with Truc to his last, highlighting both ambushes: the first that was probably just meant to be a warning, and the last, which was probably meant to be fatal.

Wojonski whistled. "Well, it's probably a good thing that the Colonel did send you up here. But I agree with you Tim, this Truc guy needs to be dealt with. But think long and hard about what you're going to do. I understand that a man's got to do what a man's got to do and all that macho stuff. It's like I always say, life is a series of choices. But remember, every choice has its consequences."

Wojonski looked hard at Tim, as if he was considering saying something else, then he changed the subject, going on to explain the present tactical and strategic situation in the highlands. As Plat and Tim poured over the combat and logistics maps, Tim forgot about Truc, about the revelation that he was sent north to stop him from killing Truc, and he even forgot about Quan. For the moment, he was no longer a lover; he was again a warrior.

For the next week, he led supply convoys deep into and through the jungles to units in contact. Although he wasn't supposed to engage in actual combat support, he did help several ARVN units (Army of the Republic of Vietnam) set up strong defensive positions along ridgelines and mountain tops. On two separate occasions, he actually fought alongside those troops. What else could he do? He couldn't just drop off guns and ammo and let the mostly green ARVN troops fend for themselves.

Soon after the first time he found himself pulling a trigger in support of these young ARVN soldiers, he was alone eating a breakfast of C-Rations in his Land Rover alongside a jungle road. "What the hell am I doing? I'm not supposed to be fighting the North Vietnamese. The Treaty's clear on that. Just logistics and technical support. That's supposed to be my only job." Then he smiled to himself, "Well, well, look at me. Little old Timmy

DePalma thumbing my nose at the great Dr. Kissinger and all those weak-kneed Congressmen. Man, it's quite a life you're leading for yourself, Timmy me'boy. Besides, if old Henry was here, he'd probably be right alongside me shooting the Commie bastards. My guess is he's really a tough old bird."

Then Tim looked at his C-Ration can of ham and lima beans. "What a difference just a couple of days make. Last week I was eating great meals in Saigon restaurants. This week I'm either eating Pho Ga from some ARVN soldier's camp kettle, or I'm chowing down C-Rations. Today, it's the absolute worst of all C's, Ham and Lima Beans. Well, at least today they're hot!"

Like so many soldiers before him, Tim had placed his C-Ration cans in a metal mesh bag and tied the bag to his vehicle's engine block. When he was ready to stop for chow, his C's were hot.

After a week of combat and combat rations, he found himself back in the ARVN's main forward resupply area where he had last met with Wojonski. He was again sitting in the MobilTek Headquarters tent with Plat.

"Well, what do you think, Lieutenant? What's your assessment of the situation?

"Bad. Really bad," Tim responded. "Everywhere I go, we're on the defense. I look at ARVN maps and your maps, and I don't see any ARVN units on the offense anywhere. The North Vietnamese, on the other hand, are moving forward everywhere. I don't know how we can hold much longer."

"Good assessment, Lieutenant. The answer is, we cannot hold much longer, and I'm sorry to say, we will not hold much longer. My assessment is two more days at most. Then the ARVN will be in total retreat or worse, they'll break and run. It will be chaos. The North Vietnamese will be in control of Da Nang within the week. The bastards will be running my harbor."

"What are we going to do, Plat?"

"First, I suggest that tomorrow you take the rest of my contractors back to Da Dang. There they will board a MobilTek ship in the harbor and will head south to Saigon. It will take them a couple of days to get there, as they will make several stops along the coastline to pick up other company personnel. If you want, you can go on the ship. Or if you want to get back to Saigon sooner, perhaps you can talk yourself onto a plane at the airfield."

"Second, I got some info for you on your situation in Saigon. One of my people tried to personally contact your lady friend, but no luck. Saigon too is starting to fray at the edges. I think we can hold there, but who the hell knows. However, my friend did leave a note at your apartment and another with your girl's father at his hospital. So I think she's well aware of where you are and what you're doing."

"Finally, some really interesting news on your Major Truc. Seems he never got to the Delta. Although all the info on this guy is still a little murky, it seems your buddy was a double agent of some kind. Although he was a Major in the South Vietnamese Army, he was also some kind of informant for the VC and the North Vietnamese Army. He might even have been an NVA officer all the time he was working for the ARVN. Now here are two more bits of info you are not to ever tell anyone. Truc was also an informant for our intelligence guys. And finally, it turns out that he might have siphoned off millions of dollars' worth of supplies to the black market and funneled that money to personal bank accounts in Hong Kong. A busy little bugger wasn't he? Right now everyone seems to be looking for him. No one seems to know where he is or where his true loyalties are. A good case can be made that he has no loyalties to anyone and just wants to avoid being hung by everyone. If he does have money stashed in Hong Kong, he may just disappear and never be found."

Tim was stunned by all he had just heard. He was glad and relieved to hear about Quan. Amazed by what he had heard about Truc. However, he was mostly focused on Plat's dire assessment that the South Vietnamese were about to lose control of the highlands, the port of Da Nang, and maybe eventually, even Saigon.

"Plat, thanks for getting word to Quan. That's a load off my mind. And this stuff on Truc, truly amazing. How did you get all this information?"

"Look, Tim. All this stuff on Truc is just between you and me. Let's just say my company has lots of resources. But I'm telling you, I'd bet money that it's mostly right on."

"Plat, you told me that you wanted me and your men to leave tomorrow, but what about you? What are you going to do? Why aren't you taking the rest of the contractors to the ship?"

"Tim, I can't go. I just can't. I've known many of these ARVN commanders and local villagers for years. If I left them now, I would feel like I'm betraying them. My country may have betrayed them, but I cannot."

"Geeez, Plat, betrayed is a big word. You've spent almost ten years of your life helping these people. America has spent ten years of treasure and blood helping Vietnam. Almost 60,000 American soldiers have died fighting to preserve South Vietnam's freedom. We have spent much money and effort on the Vietnamization program. If the Vietnamese can't defend their country on their own, what more can we be expected to do?"

"I know, Tim. That argument make a lot of sense. But don't forget, we had our own motives for helping the Vietnamese. This is a proxy war. Yes, on a tactical level, it is fought on Vietnamese soil. However, on a strategic level, it's a fight between Washington and Moscow. We chose to be here primarily for that reason."

"And yes, Tim, you're right. We have spent a lot of money and lost a lot of lives. But as we stood alongside these people in their fight, they have also stood alongside us in our fight. ARVN losses have been four times our number. That's right, four times our number, and I fear they are about to suffer a lot more. They have done their best."

"The truth is, Tim, the South Vietnamese did not readily agree with the conditions of the Paris Treaty, but what choice did they have other than to submit to our political pressure. In the end, they went along based on our promises of continued monetary and technical support. However, as soon as our troops were home, our Congress began drastically cutting that promised support, until we are here in the present situation: great Vietnamese need, no American support. I'm often ashamed to tell these commanders that I can no longer provide them the equipment and support my country promised. I can only give them my continued personal support by fighting at their side."

"No, Tim. I cannot leave tomorrow. I cannot betray my fellow soldiers. I will stay and fight with the South Vietnamese and protect these people till I'm driven into the sea."

Tim listened. Then there was a moment of stillness. His spirit was disheartened by what seemed like the callous disregard of politicians. As a soldier, he could not believe the almost cavalier attitude of politicians in not honoring their country's promises, especially when that disregard would result in the loss of the lives and freedoms of allies. At the same time, his spirit was buoyed by the true warrior who sat in front of him, committed to honor his words with life-risking actions.

"I'm staying with you," announced Tim.

Plat smiled. "Thanks, Tim, but no, you're not. Tomorrow, Lieutenant, you have two important missions to accomplish. The first, take your DAO contractor personnel to safety. The second, provide a clear, truthful report on our situation here in the highlands to Colonel Dimond in Saigon."

Eventually, Tim reluctantly agreed. As he was about to leave the tent, he turned to Wojonski, "Plat, one more question. Do you still have your BOQ in Da Nang? Do you still have your philosophy paintings there?"

"No, Tim. I turned over the port to the ARVNs. I now have a hotel room in Da Nang. As for my 'Philosophy Paintings' as you call them, I still have my philosophy, but I no longer have my paintings. Some I sent back to the States. Others I gave to people who I thought would appreciate them. Now, I wish I would have saved one for you, maybe one of the Jonathan Livingston Seagull paintings. I've always thought of you as a young 'Jonathan,' looking for adventure and trying to be all you can be."

"Thanks, Plat. I appreciate that. Perhaps when this is all over, you'll have some time to paint me one. I'd like that."

Tim then headed to his tent for some much needed sleep. Although tired, sleep did not come quickly, as he thought about all the actions necessary to accomplish the next day's two missions.

Unfortunately, Tim would accomplish neither of those missions.

TOMORROW NEVER CAME

Tim was thrown from his cot by the first explosion. He was further pressed into the muddy ground of his tent by the powerful overpressures of the following explosions. He then struggled to his feet. He was already fully dressed, as that's how a soldier sleeps in combat. He grabbed his helmet, M-16 and .45 pistol from beneath his cot and headed out of the tent. "Damn," he thought as he ran, "where's my flak jacket? Crap! I left it in the Land Rover. No time to get it now. Damn!"

Outside the tent, chaos reigned. Everyone was running everywhere. Tim raced the several hundred yards to the northern defensive wire, for that is where he believed the main enemy ground assault would come. By the time he reached the loosely strewn circles of barbed wire that the ARVN had spread round the camp, the enemy was already breaking through them. He quickly fired two full M-16 magazines of ammo into the dark forms stumbling through the wire. He saw several fall. Just then a flare lit up the sky above him, illuminating a football-size piece of the battlefield and the hundreds of enemy soldiers running to and through the wire.

Tim and the ARVN soldiers around him turned and broke for their secondary line of defensive positions to their rear. Tim never made it. The force of an exploding rocket picked him up and flung him into a tree. He felt his back and head slam into the rough bark and his body make a bloody, agonizing slide to the ground. After that, nothing.

THE ROAD BACK TO QUAN

Tim heard voices around him, but saw nothing but darkness. He felt wetness, his wetness, a clammy wetness. He could not move. He seemed to try, but nothing. The voices became clearer, but they seemed distant. They were Vietnamese voices. Still the darkness. He tried to say something, but heard only a moan, his moan. He tried harder, the moan became louder. The Vietnamese voices quieted. He did not want them to stop. He moaned louder still. An opaque brightness appeared where his vision should be. Then shadows. Then a blurred movement. Then a face. A beautiful face. He forced out the question, "Quan?"

A soft hand was cool on his brow, and a soft Vietnamese voice with soothing Vietnamese words was warm on his ear, "You are all right. You are safe. You are with friends." More faces appeared above him. More voices, all asking questions. "Shush," the soothing voice said. "He is just waking up. Leave him alone. I will tend him until he can talk."

Tim was soon talking, walking, and finding out what had happened. It turned out that he had been either unconscious or delirious for four days. The ARVN encampment had been overrun. Three escaping ARVN soldiers had carried Tim with them. As those soldiers were passing through this village, they told the villagers that they could no longer carry the wounded American and asked the villagers to hide him and care for him. As his volunteer nurse told him, they said, "This American is a brave one. He did not leave us. We could not leave him."

Tim knew his presence in the village placed all the villagers in great danger. He must leave as soon as possible. His back was severely bruised and still mighty sore. There were shrapnel wounds and cuts over the rest of his body. Yet, within three days he felt strong enough to leave. He informed the village leaders he would depart the next morning before dawn.

As dawn started to break, Tim exited the house in which he had been hidden and cared for. There stood the village leaders. They returned his web belt with its .45cal pistol, full ammo pouches, and bayonet. They also provided him with five days rations of rice, nuts, and vegetables, along with a guide who would take him to the outskirts of Da Nang. Tim thanked them and, along with his guide, slipped away into the pre-dawn dimness of a new world, a world where he was now a fugitive trying to evade capture on a 400-mile journey, mostly behind enemy lines.

His guide led him on what turned out to be a 24-hour trek to a hilltop overlooking Da Nang. The trek was harrowing. Chaos truly reigned everywhere. Roads were clogged with people trying to escape from the countryside to Da Nang, and people trying to escape from Da Nang to the countryside, all mingled with NVA soldiers who sometimes tried to bring order to the mass of people on the roads, while at other times just ran them over if they did not move out of the way of a fast moving convoy.

From his perch above Da Nang, Tim looked down upon the city. There was much destruction between him and it. His watch showed the date to be 5 April, seven days since his camp had been overrun.

In those seven days, the NVA had established complete control of Da Nang, of its airfield, and of its port. A sad thought pushed its way to the forefront of his mind, "It was no longer Wojonski's port." For a moment, Tim's mind again wondered as to what had happened to Plat. "Was he still alive? Was he a prisoner? Did he escape to the port before it was captured?"

Tim had many questions, but no answers. However, he knew one thing: Da Nang no longer offered him a way back to Saigon, a way back to Quan.

He turned away from the fallen city and headed south. At the time, he did not know that by 5 April almost half of South Vietnam had already fallen to the enemy. The first 200 miles of his 400 mile journey would be through enemy territory. The last 200 miles would be through what could only be described as contested territory.

Tim's odyssey, for it truly was a journey of epic challenges worthy of a Greek hero, would take 14 days. Training and experience would be his main weapons on this journey. After three years in Nam, he knew his enemy. After Ranger School, he knew how to survive alone. Every day reminded him of his lessons from Miss Khiem given over a bowl of Pho Ga in Monterey in what seemed like a lifetime ago. She had encouraged him to work with and to learn from Vietnam's peasants. Since his first day in Nam, he had done as she had advised. On this journey her words proved more prophetic than ever: "You must also listen and work with peasants. That is how you will win. That is how you will stay alive."

With almost every step along the way, he reminded himself, "I may not have won, but I will stay alive!"

For 14 days, really mostly nights, he sought help from the Vietnamese people. They provided him directions, they gave him food, they provided transportation. Everything they did for him was a danger for themselves. For years he had risked his life for them; now they risked their lives for him.

On the night of 20 April, dirty, tired, and almost in rags, he jumped off the back of a small jitney bus and stood in front of his Saigon apartment building. He looked up at his windows. There were no lights welcoming him home.

Tim, with his last dregs and drags of energy, climbed the stairs two at a time, keyed the lock, staggered into their apartment, and turned on the light. Quan was not there. As he looked around, he saw no indication that she had been there for some time. It was just over a month since that morning when he had last gently kissed her goodbye and quietly left.

"Where is she?" he sighed, with the weariness of Odysseus, recognizing that there was yet one more challenge to overcome. "I must find her. I must find her now." He flopped on the bed to think for just a moment but stayed to sleep for almost a day.

QUAN

A combination of sunlight, noonday heat, and noisy traffic awakened Tim. He looked at his watch, "Damn, it's 1130 hours. Quan! Where are you? I must find you."

He came to life under the bathroom's faucet shower. Put on a clean tan leisure suit. Stowed his 9mm in his back waistband holster and his .45 in his front waistband without a holster. "Very uncomfortable," he thought, "and very dangerous!"

"Now, to find Quan." He picked up the phone, "Ah, it works."

First, he called Quan's home. No answer. Next, he called Quan's sister's apartment. No answer. The third call was to Jakub. Again, no answer. "What the hell is going on," he complained to her absence. "Has everyone already evacuated the city?" His fourth call was to Cliff Shaffer.

"Damn, Tim, it's great to hear from you. No one knew what the hell happened to you in Da Nang. We all feared the worst. Get your ass over here now, and I can still get you evacuated on one of our planes or ships. There's not much time left. Did you hear President's Thieu's resignation speech today? The bastard is going to cut and run, and he blames it all on us. We've already evacuated over 40,000 Vietnamese. There's another 2 million expecting us to somehow save them from the Commies. We'll be lucky if we get another 10,000 out. Get over here now!"

All this information overwhelmed Tim. He had no idea things were so bad. "Cliff, I've got to find Quan. I cannot leave without her. Can you give me a car?"

"Not many left, but yeah, I can give you one. However, my cars get mobbed wherever they go. Everyone wants the drivers to evacuate them. If I were you, I'd bribe some moped driver to take you where you want to go. If you have some dollars hidden around, they still mean something, but not much. Gold watches, rings, jewels, guns, ammo are the currency of the day. Find your lady and bring her here. I can still get you two out. But Tim, if she wants to bring her family members, I'm not sure I can do that."

Tim was on the street flagging down a moped driver within minutes. People surrounded him everywhere the moped stopped. All wanted him, begged him, to help them. After a while the moped driver refused to stop for lights, traffic, anything.

First destination was Quan's house. No one was home. Next stop, the hospital where Quan's father worked. He was not there.

He was working at a field hospital north of the city, helping wounded soldiers who were still manning defensive positions.

It took Tim five hours to find the right hospital, and that time cost him his .45 cal pistol. The moped driver had spotted the gun in Tim's waistband and would accept no other payment for the dangers associated with finding the field hospital. Tim was reluctant but nevertheless paid up.

Dusk was setting on what had been a long day as Tim walked into the field hospital. After asking a few questions and following a few directions, he soon found Quan's father. When her father first saw Tim, he seemed both surprised and apprehensive at the same time. 'Happy' wasn't anywhere in that facial expression.

"Where's Quan?" Tim blurted out.

Her father stood there for a moment. Then he excused himself from the other doctors with a promise to return the next day. He took Tim's arm and led him out of the hospital and to his car. He gave no answer to Tim's continued question, "Where's Quan?"

Once in the car, her father said, "Tim, I will take you to Quan. But you must not ask me any more questions. Tell me, where have you been and what have you been doing for the last month."

Tim did not understand what was going on, but played along. Nothing mattered to him but getting to Quan.

The ride to the city through the mobs of displaced persons took an hour. As Tim was finishing his story, he noticed they were driving past the family's house.

"Enough is enough," he said in exasperation. "Just tell me where I can find Quan. Please. Where is she? Tell me!"

The car turned a corner and parked near a large, walled garden area. In a low voice, riding a slowly exhaled sigh, her father said, "Quan is here." He then got out of the car and walked to the garden. Tim, confused, got out of the car and followed him.

Tim stopped. His arms chilled. His lungs gasped. His legs refused to move. His mind refused to comprehend. Then the blazing horror of realization, the realization that this was not a garden. This was a cemetery.

"No! No! This can't be," Tim growled. "No, Quan can't be here. This is a cemetery. She is life. My life."

Tim staggered forward to where her father stood. A father looking down, grieving at the grave of his daughter. Tim stood with him, looked down with him, grieved with him. Then in a moment of probable insanity, he grabbed the old man and shook him, yelling "NO! NO! NO! How did this happen? Tell me, damn you. Tell me! No! No! No!" He then slid down to his knees and fell across her stone, arms spread wide as if to embrace her. He sobbed, at first uncontrollably, then more softly, then acceptingly.

After a few minutes, her father helped him up and led him a few steps to a small cement bench. They sat. They spoke no words. Sadness was now the language between them.

Soon a coldness came over Tim. Not over his body, but over his soul. With eyes no longer moist, he looked at her father, "When? How? Tell me everything. Leave out nothing."

In a whisper, "Tim, you were right. I was wrong. Truc is a bad man." With those words of confession, the father began the sad story of his daughter's death. The words tumbled out, rapid, scattered, and sometimes incoherent. The trouble started soon after Tim had left for Da Nang. Truc was in some kind of trouble with the Army. He wanted Quan to leave the country with him. He said the North was about to invade, and the South was about to fall. He said she was no longer safe; the whole family was no longer safe. Her family would especially suffer because her mother was a close relative of President Thieu. Truc offered to take Quan and the whole family to Thailand. He said he knew how to get through enemy lines to safety. He told Quan that once again her American lover had left her. That her American would not return for her. That her American would not save her. Truc told her this day after day, trying to persuade her to go with him. She did not believe him. She would not listen. He told her that he could save her and her family; that he loved her; that she would come to love him; that they could make a life together. He became more and more forceful, as he was becoming more and more frantic, believing the Army and the government were trying

296

to arrest him. Two weeks ago as Quan's mother was returning to their house, she saw Truc running from the house, looking panicked and frightened. She rushed in to find Quan lying on the floor, blood pooling round her head. Quan was dead! The police believed there had been a struggle, as chairs, a table, and dishes were strewn across the room. The doctors at the hospital said Quan had died from a blow to the head, caused when she fell against the iron rim of a table. The police were still trying to find and arrest Truc, but he had vanished.

Quan's father ended with, "Tim, I am sorry. Be at peace, knowing she loved you."

Tim sat in silence, staring at her grave. Finally, he rasped, "Thank you. Now, please leave me."

When her father tried to protest, Tim raised a hand, "No. Stop. Thank you. But please, leave me now. I want to be alone with Quan." Her father left. Her lover stayed

Tim went to her. He laid himself across her stone, again embracing it, trying to embrace her. "Quan, how could this happen? How could you leave me? I need you. Why didn't I stay with you? Why didn't I protect you?" For hours he carved those questions into her stone ...with his tears.

REVENGE

Paris en vingt minutes!
Paris in zwanzig minuten!
Paris in twenty minutes!

The train conductor's words bellowed down the aisle of the bullet train to Paris and ripped Tim back from his garden of sorrow, from his own Gethsemane. However, unlike Jesus, Tim could not forgive. He was but a man. A flawed man. A man consumed with both love and hate. Now it was hate that drove him, compelled him. A hate that could only be quenched with revenge.

Would Paris, the city of light and love, also be the city of revenge?

C-Rations

Tim had a love-hate relationship with C-Rations that began in boot camp. He loved the idea of C-rations, i.e., meals a soldier could carry with him and which were always ready to eat anywhere, anytime, under any conditions. However, sometimes he loathed the reality of the C-rations. C-rations were OK if you only had to eat them once a day, with the other two meals being hot meals in a mess hall or choppered out to the field. C-rats came in cans, so a three-day load took up backpack space, had to be placed inside socks so they wouldn't make noise, and added extra weight, a problem a foot soldier never likes. Most annoying was the taste, running from barely tolerable to just tolerable. Eaten cold the main items were pieces of congealed meat and fat. Eaten hot they were just tolerable, except for Ham and Lima Beans, which was the worst of all the meals and never tolerable. In the jungle they were better than nothing, but not by much.

Basics of C-Rations:(One Serving)

C-Ration meals came in 12 types, listed here in order of Tim's favorites:

#1 Spaghetti and Meatballs   #2 Meatballs and Beans

#11 Beef Steak,   #11 Ham and Eggs
#11 Ham Slices   #11 Turkey Loaf
#11 Beans and Wienies   #11 Boned Chicken
#11 Chicken and Noodles   #11 Meat Loaf
#11-Spiced Beef   #12 Ham and Lima Beans

Each meal came in a small box containing three small olive drab cans: one can containing one of the above meats, one can of a fruit, and one can of a bread, cracker, cheese, or dessert item. Additionally, there was a small paper package containing such things as a spoon, gum, salt, pepper, sheets of toilet paper, cigarettes, and matches. Even though Tim didn't smoke, he kept the cigarettes and matches for use in burning off leeches

Each meal contained about 1,200 calories; a day's rations totaled 3,600 calories. Field soldiers expended more calories than that, so even when having periodic access to mess halls, field soldiers usually left Vietnam 20 or more pounds lighter than when they arrived.

A key ingredient for any C-rats meal was the famous P-38 folding can opener. The P-38 (also referred to as the John Wayne key) is only 1 1/2 inches long and consists of a single metal strip that serves as a handle and a small, hinged metal blade that folds out and is used to pierce the can along its edge. By twisting the handle up and down, the blade cuts out the can's lid, much like a conventional can opener. Tim, like almost every soldier, carried a P-38 on his dog tag chain while in Vietnam and still to this day carries one on his key chain (it also serves as a handy little screwdriver).

Directions:

1. Pick the boxes containing the meals you like best. This is a problem if the top Sergeant spreads the boxes upside down so you aren't able to see the names, now relying on luck vice quickness.
2. Heat the meals however and whenever possible. If you have access to a jeep or other vehicle, place the cans on the engine block, usually in some kind of metal container if possible, and let the engine do the rest. Another way is to make a bonfire stack of the small cardboard boxes and the toilet tissues, using

the matches to light the bonfire. Throw the cans into the fire, unopened. Alternatively, use an old can as a small "stove "employing a heat tablet and place the opened meal can on top of this "stove."

3. Take off your dog tag chain and use the P-38 to open all the cans.

4. Dig in; usually served with water or bug juice.

Tips:

1. If you are lucky enough, get a bottle of *TABASCO Pepper Sauce* and a copy of *"The Charlie Ration Cookbook."* Enough *TABASCO* sauce hides the flavor and adds zest to any C-Ration. The McIlhenny Company of Louisiana (producers of *TABASCO*) printed the Cookbook, which was illustrated in comic book style by Fred Rhoads and contained about 20 recipes. During the Vietnam War, the McIlhenny Company sold a small water-resistant metal tube, about the size of a cigar cylinder, containing the COOKBOOK wrapped around a 2-ounce bottle of *TABASCO* sauce. For a couple of bucks, Tim's Zia Mary sent him the answer to "tasty" C-ration meals.

Tim's Favorite C-Ration Recipe from The Charlie Ration Cookbook

"BREAST OF CHICKEN UNDER BULLETS"

One can	Boned Chicken
One can	Cheese Spread
To Taste	Salt and Pepper

One bottle   *TABASCO* Pepper Sauce

One can   Crackers or White Bread

Directions:

1. Heat the can of boned chicken. Season with salt, pepper, and *TABASCO* to taste.
2. Cut the small white bread in half or use two crackers.
3. Heat the can of cheese spread.
4. Place a mound of chicken over each half of the bread or on each cracker.
5. Cover each with the hot melted cheese sauce and enjoy.

CHAPTER 14: A PLACE OF LIGHT, LOVE AND REVENGE.

DAY FOUR: Thursday, 1330 hours, in Paris

Tim was taking in his first sights of Paris. They weren't pretty. Not at all like Hollywood had led him to expect. From where he stood, there was no Eiffel Tower looming on the horizon. There was no gentle River Seine flowing by. There were no artists bent over easels, capturing the beauties of Paris to be hung on walls around the world. There wasn't even a mime working the street, a la Marcel Marceau. Besides all that, it was raining. So much for springtime in Paris.

To be fair, Tim realized train stations were not usually listed as tourist attractions. He had just exited Paris' Gare de L'Est, the East Station, one of six train stations that ringed the city. The East Station was the usual terminus for trains arriving from Germany. Now to find Madame Bouvier and then Truc.

He stood under an overhang, protecting himself from a light drizzle. Hopefully, the rain, like his train, had finally run its course. Tim was glad to be walking again. As he looked out from under the overhang, he saw a city like many others, lots of traffic, lots of people, lots of stores, and lots of honking horns.

Tim let an ironic laugh escape through an ironic smile. He always enjoyed the irony of life. To Tim, what stretched before him was truly ironic. What stretched before him was a regiment's worth of German tanks, right here in Paris. Well, they weren't exactly German tanks, they were German cars, almost everyone a

Mercedes Benz. Black, gray, and white Parisian taxis, all Mercedes, were lined up along the street and into the parking lot. More were crawling through traffic in every direction. German tanks may have once failed to control the streets of Paris, but now German Mercedes Benz taxis seemed to be doing the job credibly.

Tim waved a taxi over, threw his suitcase on to the back seat, then followed it in. It was a little after 1300 hours (1 PM). Only four hours until many of the stores closed. Tim would need to create another identity to meet with Madame Bouvier. Time was short. He would have to move quickly.

"Do you speak English?" were his first words to the driver. Only then did he realize that he should have asked that question before getting in.

"But of course, monsieur. Where to go?"

With many hand gestures and by speaking louder than normal, as if that would help, Tim tried to explain that he wanted to go to a high-end department store where he could get an expensive men's suit and get it tailored overnight. He also tried to transfer the idea that the faster he got there the bigger the tip.

"Okey, dokey. No problemo. Suit store. On double." The driver immediately pulled into the line of traffic, waving his left arm out the window as if it were strong enough to hold back the flow of cars. Somehow it worked, and the taxi was on its way.

"Monsieur, would you like me to drive by the Eiffel Tower or around the Arch?"

'No, thanks. Look, I don't mean to offend, but I need to get to a department store now."

"Okey, dokey. No problemo. Of course, of course, monsieur, we go fast. But a trip to Paris without seeing the Eiffel Tower is like a trip to New York without seeing your Rockettes. You can do it, yes? But what's the fun?" The driver laughed uproariously, then headed for the tower.

So on the way to the department store, the driver took a run by the Eiffel Tower. Tim reluctantly listened and learned that the Tower was built in 1889 for the Paris World Fair and to commemorate the centennial of the 1789 French Revolution. The Tower was over 1,000 feet high and was the tallest manmade structure in the world, until the Americans copied the Tower's steel beaming and constructed their Empire State Building in the 1930's, at least that was the driver's opinion. As a young man in 1989, the driver picnicked on the lawn below the Tower and watched the fireworks celebration of the Tower's 100th anniversary.

Eventually, certainly not as fast as Tim wanted, they arrived at the department store. Tim paid the driver and headed directly for the men's department. Within 10 minutes he tried on and bought a pair of black leather ankle-high dress boots with one-inch heels. Fifteen minutes later, he tried on and bought a black suit with thin, beige pinstripes in a continental cut, and a multi-pocketed garment bag to carry it in. Ten minutes after that, he owned a high-collared, dark purple dress shirt. Five minutes after that, he was standing on a corner two blocks away from the department store and hailing another taxi.

Tim followed this procedure through five more taxi rides. He took a different taxi to each destination. He always hailed the next taxi at least two blocks away from the previous destination. Before hailing that next taxi, he placed his latest purchases either in his suitcase or in the pockets of his new garment bag and discarded the previous store's logo bags.

This process was time consuming, but it would make any future police effort to backtrack his movements in Paris very difficult. After the department store, his destinations were a wig shop, an optical boutique, a theatrical supplies warehouse, a jewelry outlet, and a sidewalk cosmetics stall. By 1800 hours (6 PM), he had gathered everything necessary to birth Angelo Napolitano, San Francisco art and antiques dealer.

During those five additional taxi rides, Tim also learned that the Louvre has over 6,000 paintings, including the Mona Lisa; that French is the language of love; that Paris is called the City of Light because it is where the Age of Enlightenment began; that there are more single women in France than married ones; that Napoleon commissioned the Arch of Triumph in 1806, and it is the grave of France's Unknown Soldier; that within the Paris city limits there are 35 bridges across the River Seine; that Notre Dame Cathedral took over 170 years to build; and that a Da Vinci Code Tour of Paris could be had for just 100 euros, or about $140. By the time he was done, Tim could not decide whether he loathed or loved Parisian taxi drivers.

THURSDAY EVENING

Following his hectic race around Paris in the afternoon, Tim took a short jog and then stopped for a quick meal at a small restaurant near his hotel. He had a lot to do that night, so the jog and the meal, things he usually liked to take time with, both had to be quick. This restaurant looked like a place where he could get a quick but good meal. Once seated, a look at the menu proved him right. First, the menu was in French and English. Second, the meals were mostly of the meat, potatoes, and vegetable variety, sometimes hard to find in Paris. Finally, there was a special tonight, Crab and Shrimp Bouillabaisse. A "soup special" meant that the soup was already in a pot simmering on a stove somewhere, waiting to be rushed to a hungry, or impatient, customer. At least that is what this hungry and impatient customer hoped.

Tim wasn't in his chair more than two minutes, when the waiter came to take his order. The waiter didn't speak English, or didn't want to speak English. "Was it the jogging clothes?" Tim wondered. Eventually he pointed to the "Special" listed on the menu, and then he also pointed to a pasta salad on another table. After the waiter departed, Tim started reviewing his battle plan for tomorrow. He didn't get far, as the waiter soon returned and placed both the bowl of bouillabaisse and the plate of pasta in front of Tim, along with a perfunctory *"Bon Appetit,"* and then left.

Tim called the waiter back and asked for a bottle of water. The waiter took on a confused look and responded in French, which Tim assumed meant "I'm sorry, I do not understand. What do you want?" Tim tried again. The waiter looked confused again. Tim began thinking he was being played. People must ask for water in this restaurant 50 times a day, and more than a few must do it in English. He decided that it was now his turn to play.

Tim then asked for a bottle of water in Vietnamese. This time he was rewarded with a real confused look. Then he asked in Russian. Then he asked in Italian. Then he asked in German.

"Oh," responded the waiter in heavily accented English. "You would like a bottle of water. But of course, Monsieur." The waiter left and returned within seconds with the bottle of water. "*Bon Appetit, Monsieur.*"

In a voice just a tad louder than necessary, Tim said to himself, "Interesting. He only responded to me when I spoke German." Geeezz, thought Tim, "Am I being an ugly American? I need to lighten up a bit."

The Crab and Shrimp Bouillabaisse was quite tasty. To Tim's delight, it had way more crab than shrimp. As he ate, Tim's mind went back to Federal Hill and the first time he used the word "bouillabaisse." He was all of 15 and eating a bowl of Frutti de Mare, a tomato-based fish stew poured over angel hair pasta, at his Uncle Carmine's restaurant. Tim made the mistake of saying something like, "This is really good, Uncle Carmine. It's a lot like the bowl of French bouillabaisse I had the other day." Probably the only reason Tim mentioned it was that he liked the sound of the word, bouillabaisse, as it rolled off his tongue.

Tim could still remember in great detail what happened next. Uncle Carmine rose from his seat, simultaneously slammed both his fists, knuckles-down, onto the table, and with a reddening face exclaimed, "What? My'a Frutti de Mare is'a nothing like'a Frenchy's bouillabaisse. My'a Frutti de Mare has only the finest of'a mussels, and'a best'a shrimp, and'a best'a scallops, and'a best'a calamari, and'a best'a clams, and'a when you'a come, Tim, I also add'a little lobster. No, I add'a lot'a lobster. Never say that'a the Froga's bouillabaisse is like'a my Frutti de Mare. Bouillabaisse is'a the Frog'a word'a for'a garbage! Any fish they can no sell'a for five days, they put in a pot of water and call it'a bouillabaisse. Just'a fancy Frog'a word'a for no good'a fish. Never ever eat'a any bouillabaisse. Now you are'a forgiven for what'a you just said. Now, eat'a the rest of your dinner." Then Uncle Carmine sat down, as if nothing had happened, and poured himself and Tim a glass of Chianti.

Sometimes Uncle Carmine could be a little dramatic. Even now in his late 80's, he could still put on quite a show at family gatherings. Even though over the years Tim had come to like a lot of "Frog'a" food, he never mentioned it whenever in Carmine's presence.

This bouillabaisse tonight, loaded with crab, also reminded Tim of dinners with another of his relatives, this time on his Irish side, his cousin Maureen Quinn. Although he had enjoyed plenty of steamed crabs, crab salad rolls, and even some crab soup in Rhode Island, he never had a truly creamy crab soup until he tasted Maureen's great "She Crab Soup."

Maureen was the only other of his relatives who had moved out of Rhode Island. Maureen now lived in an old fishing village, St. Michaels, on Maryland's Chesapeake Bay. Since St. Michaels was only a little more than an hour from D.C., Tim visited her about once a year, starting in 1993 following his return from a 2-year duty assignment in Belgium. Maureen had told him that if he was going to visit her only once a year, he should always come in the spring.

"Why in the spring?" he asked.

"Because I know you like different kinds of dishes, Tim. So I want to make my two favorite dishes for you. The first is 'She Crab Soup', and the crabs are best in the springtime. The second is a great ice cream pie dessert."

During his first visit to her home, while they were standing on her pier looking out at the Bay and talking about dinner, he asked her, "Why do they call it She Crab Soup. Why not just Crab Soup?"

Maureen, putting her hand over her eyes to block out the sun, looked at him now through smiling, rather than squinting, eyes, and turned the question back on him, "Why do YOU think they call it SHE Crab Soup?"

"I don't know. Probably because only women are supposed to cook it?"

She laughed and slapped his arm. "You are still such a chauvinist. No wonder no one will marry you. No. They call it 'SHE' Crab Soup because it is best when made with female crabs. While female crabs always taste better than male crabs, female crabs are especially good in the spring, because they are loaded with eggs. This mini-caviar adds a special sweetness to the soup."

Tim thought about what she said, then asked, "Isn't it hard to tell the difference between male and female crabs? I mean, when I see them crawling around the beach, to me they all look alike."

Again she laughed. That's why she liked Tim so much. He constantly made her laugh, whether he meant to or not. "You are such a city boy! Haven't you ever cracked a bushel of crabs? Come with me."

Maureen took Tim down to the docks and bought a bushel of live crabs off a boat that had just come in off the Bay. Maureen showed Tim how to ensure the crabs were lively or "feisty" as she called it. She poked her fingers at a crab. If it reared up and brandished its claws at her, then it was a keeper. She warned him never to buy dead or listless crabs. Then she showed Tim how to turn the crabs over and determine which were males and which were females. Tim immediately realized that telling the difference between male and female crabs was not a difficult task. The male crab had a man tool about half the size of its body.

When they returned home, Maureen boiled the crabs in a large 10-gallon pot, adding a bottle of white wine along with salt and other seasonings. She then dumped them on her, for the moment, brown-paper-covered kitchen table. The whole family then sat down to a "Crab Cracking" party. The meat from the females ended up in his cousin's soup pot, while the meat from the males ended up in a crab salad.

After they had feasted on the crab soup and salad, Maureen delivered to the table an ice cream pie for dessert. Almost unbelievable to Maureen, Tim admitted that he had never had an ice cream pie before. However, he knew after he finished just one piece that he would certainly be having more. Maureen had made a two-layer ice cream pie, one layer chocolate ice cream and the other layer a coconut gelato. The ice cream and gelato layers were separated by a layer of crushed cookie and pretzel crumbs. The top was covered with whipped cream and a delicious drizzled chocolate sauce. This ice cream pie soon became his "go to" dessert during the hot summer months in D.C.

As Tim, now sitting in a Paris restaurant, thought back on his visits to Maureen's, he found himself scraping the bottom of his bowl of bouillabaisse and wishing that it would be followed by a slice of Maureen's ice cream pie. Sorry to say, that night the bouillabaisse would not be followed by ice cream pie. However, it would be followed by a great pasta dish. He had ordered the pasta because he wanted a quick load of carbs. However, the colors and the aroma caused him to linger on this dish for a few moments longer than he intended. The penne was mixed with equal amounts of cherry tomato halves and spinach. All were tossed in olive oil with a great smelling and great tasting blend of herbs and spices. Yet there was one taste that took Tim a while to discern. "Pine nuts? Yes, pine nuts!" This pasta-vegetable mix was prepared with pine nuts. Tim loved pine nuts. They provided a subtle but tasty flavor.

Even though Tim, while sitting in this little restaurant in Paris, had traveled back to Federal Hill and then to Maryland's Chesapeake Bay, this whole travelogue, -highlighted by bouillabaisse, Frutti de Mare, She Crab Soup, Ice Cream Pie, Pasta, and pine nuts- had taken less than 30 minutes. This brief dinner had been an unexpected pleasure. However, now it was time for work. Time for planning. Time for preparation. Tim left euros on the table and headed back to his hotel.

At 2000 hours (8 PM), Tim was sitting on his hotel bed with all his day's purchases displayed before him. After returning to his room, he had taken a quick shower to wash away the stress of the day and prepare for the stress of tomorrow. Hectic and quick were now done. Deliberate and purposeful were now taking their place.

He looked at each individual purchase closely, while at the same time seeing the whole of a new persona, i.e., Angelo Napolitano, art and antiques dealer from San Francisco, known to his friends as Angel. Angel would appear to be about 6' 3" to Tim's 6', to weigh about 170 lbs to Tim's 185 lbs, to be one of the new metro-sexuals compared to Tim being one of the old usual-sexuals; and to be a sharp dresser compared to Tim's more casual preferences. Additionally, Angel would also appear to be younger than Tim. Angel Napolitano, San Francisco art and antiques dealer, would be a much harder persona to create than was John Stiglatti, the rich and boorish Bronx restaurateur.

In Heidelberg, Tim had created two personas: John Stiglatti and Giuseppe Gero. Giuseppe had been a go-between persona, a device designed to impede possible future investigators from uncovering any direct connections between Tim, the tourist, and Stiglatti, the man trying to get information about Truc. Tim had made that extra effort because Heidelberg was a comparatively small city, especially the Old Town's hotel, restaurant, and gallery district. In Heidelberg, someone might have remembered seeing Tim and Stiglatti at the same place about the same time. Tim did not see that possibility as a real threat in a city as big as Paris. This time there would be no go-between.

With the Stiglatti persona, Tim had taken the easier path of creating someone heavier and older than himself. This meant the easier devices of whitening his hair; darkening under his eyes; padding the arm, waist and butt areas of his clothes; and using cotton balls to puff out his cheeks. In creating disguises, it was usually easier to add things than it was to remove things.

Thus the difficulty of the task at hand, creating Angel Napolitano, a thinner, taller, younger version of Tim. Again, all this was being done to thwart any future investigators from backtracking Tim's path after he had terminated Truc. If done correctly, there should be no similarities between Stiglatti, the person looking for information on Truc in Heidelberg, and Napolitano, the person looking for information on Truc in Paris. Certainly, there should be no connections between either one of these two persons and

Tim. Even though Tim had been in both those cities when their activities were going on, there should be nothing to connect him to either of them.

However, even if some bright detective or Interpol agent uncovered the fact that Tim had been in both those cities at the same time as the persons searching for the recently deceased Truc, and then somehow this detective or agent achieved the improbable feat of uncovering a 30-year-old relationship between Tim and Truc, such information would be circumstantial at best. No, Tim was confident he could pull this off without getting caught, avenge the murder of Quan, and live with that fact and himself without any remorse for hopefully many years to come.

Now, he must prepare to bring Angel Napolitano to life. Tim began to look at all the items spread across the bed one by one. First he examined the suit. The black color would have a slimming effect on his appearance. The vertical beige stripes would add to that slimming effect and additionally would make him appear taller. The suit's continental-cut tapered the jacket at the waist, making the waist look smaller. Padding each shoulder with a face cloth would add to that effect, kind of like the shoulder pads women used in their suits back in the 1940s and '50s for the same effect, a thinner-looking waist. To further enhance the impressions of height and thinness, Tim bought the pants an inch longer than his usual length. He could do this because he also bought leather dress boots that had one-inch heels, which of course would actually add an inch to his height. He also purchased a pair of Dr.-Scholl-like shoe inserts, if he felt he needed even more height. Before moving to the next item, Tim removed all labels from the suit, making it more difficult to trace back to the store where he purchased it and to him.

Next he examined the black dress boots with the 1-inch heels. Very stylish he thought. Maybe he might even buy himself a similar pair when he returned to Washington. What guy doesn't want to be an inch taller? Or for that matter, an inch longer.

He fingered the cloth of the dark purple shirt. Very dramatic he thought -the color, the almost sheer fabric, and the movie-star-

311

style high collar. It should draw the observer's eye away from Angel's face. True, the color was dramatic, but not garish. It would blend well with his black pinstripe suit, giving the impression of a man who knew how to dress. "Damn," Tim said as he pulled his hand down along the sleeve. "Why didn't I think of this?" The shirt had French cuffs, but Tim had not bought cufflinks. "No sweat. I'll do that tomorrow on the way to the gallery."

He picked up the cosmetic contact lenses. The lenses he used in Heidelberg had been blue, because he wanted his face to have a softer, wider look. These lenses that he would use in Paris were a very dark brown because he wanted Angel's eyes to look like dots in hollow sockets, giving the sense of a narrow, thin face.

The next item, Tim had never used before, but he thought that Angel might be the kind of guy who would have one. In his hand he held a small ponytail made of hair extenders attached to a comb-like clip. Tim's own hair on the back of his head was about one and a half inches long, cut in a slight shag, thick, and squared off along his neck. The wigmaker had crafted a small four-inch ponytail that could be attached to Tim's hair, with the clip being almost undetectable except to the touch. The ponytail added length to the distance from the tip of the nose to the back of the head, making the head appear narrower from both the side and front views. This perception of narrowness would be further accentuated by Angel greasing down the hair along the sides of his head and flat-combing it towards the back. In a nice sartorial touch, the wigmaker had tied the ponytail with a rich purple ribbon that matched Angel's shirt.

Jewelry was the next addition to the disguise. Tim never wore much jewelry, only his Timex watch and Brileen's wedding ring. Most of Tim's disguises included jewelry. Jewelry drew the onlooker's eyes away from his face. Usually gaudy jewelry worked best, like the gold watch and big rings worn by John Stiglatti in Heidelberg. However, for Angel, Tim bought an expensive looking silver watch for his left wrist, a somewhat ornate looking silver bracelet for his right wrist, and a long, thick, silver chain for his neck. On the chain was an inch and a half long silver pendant of an artist's easel. The long necklace with the long pendant would further draw the onlooker's eye away from Angel's face, down his neck, and into his opened-collared shirt. It would further add to the impression of height and thinness that Tim was trying to achieve.

The next two items would be used to change the look of Tim's facial features. First was makeup. Tim would use contour makeup down the bridge of his nose, under his cheekbones, and along his jawbone to give the impression of a little hollowness in the cheeks, further adding to the look of a narrow face and overall thinness. He would also use an eyebrow pencil to arch his eyebrows just a little, again to add to the impression of a more narrow face. Although the application of this makeup would be subtle, it would be apparent to a close observer. Tim didn't think that a big problem, since Angel was apparently a new age metrosexual not afraid to use a little makeup to enhance his looks under the city lights.

The other essential face altering device was a pair of silver rimmed glasses containing non-prescription lenses. Tim picked this particular pair because it had a very wide bar going across the top of the lenses. In addition to looking very artsy and dramatically changing Tim's facial appearance, the wide top bar would obscure some of the top part of Tim's nose and the space between his eyebrows. This would be important in trying to evade any facial recognition program that the gallery might be using. Tim figured that most galleries would have surveillance cameras. However, it was also very likely that high-end galleries in big cities like New York, London, and Paris might now be using facial recognition programs as a part of their surveillance setup. Art galleries were notorious for being security conscious, sometimes to the point of paranoia.

In the beginning of their development, facial recognition programs were crude and could be easily defeated. However, like almost everything else in the information-tech world, over time they had become very dependable and hard to defeat. Although all systems were different, many started with focusing on the facial dimensions around the triangle formed by the bridge of the nose and the eyebrows.

Until recently, such facial recognition systems were only hooked into police and Interpol criminal files. So if you were not a criminal whose photo was already in police files, these automated recognition systems wouldn't come up with a match. However, over the years these systems have been connected to many government and corporate data bases, so if you've had a badge picture taken, you might be able to be matched. In recent years, these systems have become even more formidable. Now many of these systems are hooked into open social networking sites. So if you have pictures on the net from your last birthday party, you may well be susceptible to being matched by a facial recognition program. Neither Tim nor Angel wanted that to happen. Angel would use these glasses and some evasive movement techniques while in the gallery. Hopefully, successfully.

The last element of the disguise would be a scar. Tim had bought the necessary ingredients at a theatrical supply store. The planned scar would be located on his chest, be about four inches long, begin just below the silver easel pendant, travel downward, and end somewhere beneath the unbuttoned, almost sheer, purple shirt. Additionally, the scar would be an ugly one. The scar's purpose was twofold. First, it would be another device to draw the observer's eyes down and away from Angelo's face. Second, it would be a very memorable feature. In any possible future police questioning of people who had met Angelo, they all would undoubtedly remember and mention Angelo's scar. However, if the police should ever try to prove that Angelo and Tim were the same person, Tim's lack of such a prominent chest scar would be one more difference that would make such a charge hard to prove

Tim took the suit and shirt which were on hangers and placed them in the garment bag. He then set aside the ingredients needed to create the scar. All other items he put in the various pockets of the garment bag and then placed the bag in the closet.

Now for the scar. The whole process would take about three, maybe four hours: one hour to make the scar and about two or three hours to let it set, just like a recipe for a nice stew. Tim started with about three ounces of silicon rubber and then slowly and alternately mixed in small amounts of alcohol, adhesive, color pigmentation, and a few other additives till he achieved the consistency and color of human skin. He formed the mixture into a four-inch tube and placed it on his chest. He then used a small, stiff bristled brush to patiently feather the edges onto his skin. Using a toothpick, he made a small channel along the top of the "scar" from one end to the other. He then placed into the channel some reddish-gray color pigmentation mix, which when dry would have the look of an old, healed gash. As a final step, he brushed on a clear, flexible, polyurethane coating. Now he had to let the scar set. To do this properly, he would have to sit upright in a chair, not moving his chest or arms for several hours.

Tim used those hours to plan how Angel would walk, would talk, would charm or bribe the needed information from the art dealer, Madame Bouvier. He reviewed in his mind all the information he had accumulated about Spanish Surrealism and the artist, Detero. He gamed how he would stroll through the gallery, first trying to locate its surveillance cameras and then trying to evade them. Somewhere in the middle of trying to figure out how he would detect not only the ceiling cameras but also any front-on cameras that might be located at face level, Tim fell asleep.

Just before nodding off, he slowly turned his left wrist to see his watch. He was four days from the last time he had tasted Zia Mary's meata'balls. How many days to go until he tasted some revenge?

FRIDAY MORNING

Day Five: Friday, 0700 hours, in Paris

Tim awoke about 7 AM. He was still sitting in the chair. He bent his stiff neck to look down at the scar. From this angle, and through his hazy-just-woke-up vision, it looked pretty good. He touched it, running his fingers all along the edge. It felt solid. No breaks in the seal between scar and skin. He slowly lifted himself from the chair. It took three steps before his body could stand completely upright. Four more steps and he was peering into the bathroom mirror. He moved his shoulders to the left, then to the right, then he bent forward, closely watching the scar as he moved, and as it moved with him. It moved well. It looked great. "Perfecto," he said with a flourish to an audience of one.

After a quick continental breakfast in the hotel's dining room, Tim was back in his own room changing into running gear. He was not actually going to go running because he didn't want to take chances with his scar. However, the running clothes would provide him with good cover for his next stop, the place where he would meet Angel Napolitano for the first time. He did not yet know that it would also be the place where, later that day, he would meet Angel Napolitano for the last time.

Tim grabbed his garment bag, checked its contents one more time, and headed for the street. After exiting the hotel, he turned to the right and walked three blocks. He turned right again and walked for another two blocks. Thanks to the directions of one of the hotel workers the previous evening, he was standing in front of a small neighborhood fitness center and gym. It looked just like the kind of place he wanted.

Tim looked at his watch. It was 0830 hours. In military terms, he had two time hacks to make this morning. The first was this one at 0830 (Zero Eight Thirty) hours. He hoped this gym would be relatively empty at this hour. Most of the people who would exercise here before going to their jobs should be gone by now. Most of the others, who had to see their spouses and children off before they could come to the gym, would not be here yet. This should be the perfect time for Tim to become Angel.

The second time hack of the morning would be at 1000 (Ten Hundred Hours), the time Madame Bouvier's gallery opened. An anonymous phone call he made the day before had confirmed the gallery's opening time and that Madame Bouvier was scheduled to be there. He wanted to check out the gallery and casually meet with her before she might become entangled in other business. He was right on track to meet both his planned time hacks.

Tim entered the gym. He was pleased. It was almost empty. He paid for a week's "tourist" membership and headed for the locker room. It was empty. He stripped down to his skivvies, threw his clothes into a locker, and started putting on Angelo.

After a few minutes, Angelo stood before the mirror. He felt good in his new boots, pants, and shirt. Even the dark brown cosmetic lenses felt good. He had just put on his silver watch and ornate silver bracelet and was now hooking up his silver chain with easel pendant, when another guy entered the locker room. The new guy looked Angelo over, maybe a second too long, his eyes slowly following the north-south lines of the handsome face, the necklace, pendant, open shirt, then lingering on the scar. He said something to Angelo in French, probably about the day or the weather, because Angelo only understood the word "Bonjour." Angelo nodded and smiled. The guy smiled back, and then spoke some more French. This time Angelo responded in Italian, explaining in melodic tones and swirling hand gestures that he did not speak French and needed to hurry. The guy smiled, nodded, then headed for the showers.

Angelo greased back the hair on the sides of his head, then gelled the top a bit, pulling some of the hair there straight up, adding yet another touch to the illusion of even more height. It only took another minute to attach the ponytail and its purple bow. He turned left, then right, then left again to get good sideway views. He even moved to the end of the wash counter, where mirrors joined in a corner, in order to get a reflected straight-on view of the back. He liked what he saw. The ponytail was a nice touch.

Then came the application of contour makeup under the cheek bones and along the bridge of the nose and jaw line. Angel broke out the eyebrow pencil and used it to arch and lengthen the brows.

He locked the locker, put on his suit coat, and as the final touch, slipped on the silver eyeglasses. Oops, he almost forgot. He pulled off Brileen's ring, wrapped it in a paper towel, and carefully slipped it into his left side pocket. Angelo stood again in front of the mirror. He looked taller, thinner, younger, and even essentially different than his creator. Angelo admired the finished product that was himself. He was joined in this admiration by the guy returning from the showers, who showered Angelo with another smile and yet another lingering glance.

After exiting the gym, Angelo turned right and, adding a subtle lightness to his gait, walked two blocks before hailing one of those new German tanks. He instructed the driver to take him to the Eiffel Tower. Along the way, Angelo did a detailed review of his plan for the gallery and for his conversation with Madame Bouvier. Upon arrival, Angelo exited the tank, paid the driver, and then walked around the base of the Tower for about five minutes.

Angelo decided it was time to hail another taxi. This time he asked to be taken to an address about two blocks from the gallery. Again, during this ride, as during the previous one, he tuned-out the driver and did a detailed review of his plan. However, he did have the driver make a brief stop in order to purchase a pair of cufflinks. As the taxi approached its final destination, it passed by the Paris Galerie d'Art et Centre Restauration, stopping two blocks further down the street. After paying the driver, Angelo began walking in a direction that took him away from the gallery. However, as soon as the taxi was out of sight, he immediately turned around and headed back toward the gallery, and, unbeknownst to Angelo or Tim, to an unexpected happening that would change all Tim's plans, ...and perhaps his entire life.

Eastern Shore Cream of She Crab Soup

Tim first tried this soup when visiting Maryland's Eastern Shore in 1993. He was visiting his cousin, Maureen Quinn, who lived in the seaside village of St. Michaels. Maureen wanted to share her favorite dishes with her favorite cousin, especially her "She Crab Soup." She showed him how to buy the best crabs at dockside, the best way to cook them, and how to crack and shell them. Although Maureen preferred to buy, boil, crack, and shell the beasts herself, when she wanted She Crab Soup "all made easy", she followed the below recipe, which highlighted the use of the best canned crab meat available. The only place Tim had ever had a crab soup that even came close to Maureen's was at the now defunct Market Inn in Washington DC where Cream of Crab soup was a mainstay.

Ingredients:(Four to Six Servings)

¾ Cup	Butter
¾ Cup	Flour
2 Qts	Half and Half
1 Lb	Backfin Crabmeat
2	Chicken Bouillon Cubes or packages
1 Tbsp	*Old Bay Seasoning*
Dash	White Pepper
Dash	Salt

Directions:

1. Rinse crabmeat and remove any shell/cartilage.
2. Melt butter in a Dutch Oven.
3. Blend in flour, *Old Bay Seasoning*, and white pepper; stir the roux over low heat for two to three minutes.
4. Add Half-and-Half and crushed/powdered bullion.
5. Simmer and stir until bullion is absorbed and mixture thickens.

6. Add crabmeat and continue to heat crab and mixture; do not boil.

Tips:

1. Can be refrigerated and served later – be careful not to boil.
2. Other grades of crabmeats or combinations can be used --- Jumbo, Lump, or White.
3. If *Old Bay Seasoning* is not available try another seafood seasoning or make your own favorite.
4. Garnish with a few croutons and add a slug of sherry to the soup as an option.

French Ice Cream Pie

Maureen, Tim's cousin, introduced him to this taste delight in 1993, and since then it has vied with Tiramisu as his favorite dessert. Maureen first tasted this ice cream marvel in a small French restaurant on the famous Saint Catherine's Street in Montreal during a "Fête du Canada" celebration, a Canadian national celebration similar to our 4th of July. Maureen was already familiar with Canada's famous Nanaimo Ice Cream Bars, a no-bake, three layered bar with a crumb base, ice cream filling, and a chocolate topping. However, the restaurant rendition on Saint Catherine's Street was the first time she had seen a pie variation of this treat. Over the years Maureen developed several recipes, her favorite being the version with macaroons and gelato. At a party, some ten years later, Tim was explaining the difficulty he had in trying to make this dessert to Yvette, a friend's wife who made the world's best cream puffs (as far as Tim was concerned). Yvette suggested that he just go back to the basics, use easy ingredients, and, of course, her ganache as the topping. This no-cook recipe can easily be made ahead of time.

Ingredients:(Six Servings)

1 Prepared	Chocolate Cookie Crumb Pie Crust
2 Pints	Favorite Ice Cream(s)
4 - 6	Pretzel Rods (crumbled)
6 - 8 Oz	Chocolate Ganache.

Directions:

1. Remove plastic cover from pie crust and set aside.

2. Slightly defrost your favorite ice cream.

3. Warm the ganache and drizzle a little over the crust. Sprinkle half the crumbled pretzel rods on top.

4. Spread one pint of ice cream over the crust using a warm spoon; sprinkle the remaining crumbled pretzel over the ice cream; refreeze.

5. Spread second pint of ice cream on top and refreeze for about one hour.

6. Spread warmed ganache atop ice cream, cover (with the original plastic pie shell cover, now inverted) and put back in freezer.

7. Five minutes before serving remove from freezer. Cut and remove from foil plate. Top with whipped cream and enjoy.

Tips:

1. If ice cream becomes too soft, just put into freezer until solid.

2. Tim's two favorite mixtures are a combination of coconut gelato for the bottom and dark chocolate gelato for the top layer, or just salted caramel butter pecan ice cream for both layers.

3. Tim has made this from scratch crushing cookies and/or graham crackers, but for a quick and easy solution for dessert, use the ready-made shells and fill with a premium ice cream.

4. True decadence includes topping with flavored whipped cream.

Chocolate Ganache

A favorite and versatile frosting, ganache is equally at home as a topping for éclairs, cream puffs, cakes, and even ice cream. It is a required staple of any pastry maker. Yvette introduced Tim to a proper ganache at the same time she and her husband, Frans, were teaching him how to make proper cream puffs. From that night on, for Tim there was no such thing as a great cream puff that didn't have a great ganache topping. This is a time-proven recipe; just start with a ratio of one and a half parts of chocolate to one part cream and enjoy.

Ingredients:(As Needed and Used)

1 Cup	Heavy Cream
2 Tbsp	Unsalted Butter
2 Tbsp	Granulated Sugar
12 Oz	Semi-sweet Chocolate

Directions:

1. Break semi-sweet blocks into small pieces
2. Heat the heavy cream, butter, and sugar in a sauce-pan over medium high heat.
3. When hot, stir in the sugar and bring mixture just to a low boil.
4. Place chocolate in a heatproof bowl; pour the boiling cream over the chocolate and allow to stand for five minutes.
5. Stir until smooth and allow to cool before using.

Tips:

1. Another use of ganache is as a filling for truffles. Allow it to refrigerate and harden, roll into balls, and cover with nuts, powdered cocoa, or sugar and nuts.
2. You can easily add a flavoring or liqueur.

Cherry Tomato and Spinach Summer Pasta

A summer staple in Italy, Tim first enjoyed this in Sorrento in the 1990s after seeing this being presented to another diner--- the colors and aroma captured him. Over the years Tim replaced the arugula (Italian staple) with spinach for a less peppery taste and refined the sauce. Paired with prosecco, a dry Italian sparkling wine, or a light rose, this is an absolute must in the summer. Serve it alone and save room for the gelato or tiramisu.

Ingredients:(Four to Six Servings)

¼ Cup	Olive Oil
1 Lemon	Juice and Zest
½ Tsp	Sea Salt and Pepper(each).
Dash	Red Pepper Flakes
1 Tbsp	Minced Garlic
1-2 Pints	Cherry/Grape Tomatoes
¼ Cup	Butter
2-3 Cups	Baby Spinach
1 Lb	Penna or Shell Pasta
1 – 1 1/2Cup	Parmesan Cheese – Grated
¼ Cup	Toasted Pine Nuts
1-2 Tbsp	Capers

Directions:

1. Cut tomatoes in half/quarters depending upon size.
2. Combine olive oil, lemon juice and lemon zest, salt, pepper, red pepper flakes, and minced garlic. Pour mixture over cut tomatoes, toss, cover, and set aside at room temperature for 3 – 4 hours.
3. Rinse spinach and remove long stems.
4. Cook pasta at a boil for about 10 minutes – al dente.
5. Drain pasta, leave in sieve, and return pan to heat.

6. Melt butter until golden brown; add pasta, spinach, and capers; stir to mix and allow spinach to wilt.
7. Add tomato/olive oil mixture and toasted pine nuts – stir.
8. Add 1 cup parmesan cheese – stir.
9. Add hot water as necessary to create sauce.
10. Taste and add salt, pepper, and additional parmesan as necessary.
11. Transfer to large bowl and garnish with additional parmesan and parsley and/or basil.

Tips:

1. Roast pine nuts ahead – roasting adds that nutty flavor.
2. Careful with the salt – capers bring their own salty taste – so add sparingly at end.
3. You can add mushrooms when you are browning the butter.
4. Using angel hair or string type pasta makes this dish very difficult to stir and eat.

CHAPTER 15: MADAME BOUVIER

Day Five: Friday, 1000 hours, in Paris

As Angelo approached the gallery, he checked his watch. No military time on this baby. It read 2 minutes past 10. The plan was unfolding right on schedule. However, neither Angel nor Tim yet knew that all their planning would be for naught.

As Angelo entered the gallery, he noted that it appeared empty of customers. Only one attendant was in view and he apparently was busy on a computer. The attendant looked up briefly and said something in French. Angelo could not hear what was said because of the distance, but interpreted it to mean that the young man would be with him in a moment. Angelo nodded and began to stroll the gallery.

He moved from the main showroom to the smaller, side showrooms and showareas, casting a surreptitious glance here, then there, then almost everywhere, detecting surveillance cameras in almost every corner of every ceiling in every room. He did not note any head-on cameras, but with today's miniaturization technology, his failure to detect any did not mean that there weren't any.

After about ten minutes, the attendant came up to Angelo and in French, apparently introduced himself and asked if he could assist in any way. Angelo responded in English. saying that he did not speak French. The attendant smiled and in English asked Angelo if there was anything in particular he was looking for.

In order to heighten the illusion of thinness of the face, Angelo constantly kept his cheeks pressed inward against his teeth, which also resulted in a slight pursing of his lips. When he spoke, this tight-cheeked, pursed-lips delivery resulted in a low volume, slightly affected speech pattern. However, most importantly, it was a highly memorable speech pattern and one entirely different from Tim's.

Angelo Napolitano introduced himself as an arts and antiques dealer from San Francisco and added that his friends called him Angel. He then asked the young man also to please call him Angel. The young man seemed to blush as he looked up at Angel, but soon his eyes appeared fixated on Angel's scar which was little more than a foot in front of the attendant's face.

After about five minutes of general art talk, Angel stated that he was very interested in Spanish Surrealism, especially Dali and his melting clocks, as well as some of Dali's students and imitators. The young man led Angel to an area that contained about 10 paintings and fine prints, all from the early 20th Century era of Spanish Surrealism.

Completely of his own volition, the young man began telling Angel of the gallery's recent brokering of a painting by Detero, an artist who emulated but expanded on Dali's techniques. When pushed for further details, he said that the sale had been handled personally by Madame Bouvier, the gallery's owner. He added that Madame Bouvier was in the gallery at that moment and would be happy to discuss that sale and any other questions Angel might have on the availability of works from the Spanish Surrealism era.

Angel was pleased with this turn of events. The attendant's openness about the Detero sale might make his task a little easier. Angel responded that he would really like to speak with the gallery's owner, but did not have a lot of time left in Paris. "Would it be possible to speak with her right now?"

"But of course. Let me take you to her."

As they walked back toward the main showroom, Angel pretended to listen to what the attendant was saying, but he was mentally reviewing once again the conversation that he would be having with Madame Bouvier.

As he was about to enter the main showroom, Angelo stopped abruptly. For just a moment Angel was replaced by Tim. Angel's cheeks unclenched, his lips loosened, his body posture strengthened, but it was Tim's heart that seemingly stopped.

On the other side of the showroom, a women was standing with a man in front of a painting. This woman was obviously explaining something about the painting. Mostly her back was turned to Tim, with just a slight profile of her face. Tim would know this woman anywhere, even if only but an inch of her body was open to his gaze.

Tim stopped. Time stopped. Everything stopped.

Tim remained rooted in place. After a moment, but a moment that seemed like an eternity, his heart thankfully started beating again. As the heart beats returned, so did Angel. Angel reached out with his right hand and held back his young friend. As Angel's cheeks retightened and his lips repursed, he asked in a whisper, "Who is that woman over there?"

The young man looked, then answered, "That is Madame Bouvier. Let me introduce you."

The young man began to move. For a second time, Angel held him back.

Again, Angel didn't seem to know what to do. He again seemed to fade. He started to say something then stopped. Just a moment ago, his heart had all but stopped. Now his heart was beating at a pace to explode.

Angel began to regain control. He looked again at the woman. Then at the young man. Then at his watch. "I just remembered. I have to be at another meeting right now. I'm late. Madame Bouvier looks quite busy right now with that other customer. I'll come back later and talk with her. Thanks for your help. I must go now."`

The young man protested, but Angel repeated, "No, I'm sorry, but I can't stay. Thanks again for your help. I'll be back, but now I must go." He took one more quick look at the woman, then headed for and then out the door.

The young man was left looking at Angel's ponytail with its

purple ribbon bobbing in his wake.

After leaving the gallery, Angelo quickly walked down the block, around the corner, and into a sidewalk bistro. Once inside, Tim took a small table in the corner near the front window and ordered a glass of Beaujolais. He needed something to drink and time to think.

Tim's mind kept repeating the same questions over and over, not quite believing what it was hearing from itself, and not providing itself with any answers: "Colette? Colette is Madame Bouvier? How could this be? How could Colette come back into my life now? Especially in this role? This changes everything!" ... "Colette? Colette is Madame Bouvier? How could ...? ... etc., etc., etc."

After about 30 minutes and three Beaujolais, Tim had come to terms with what had just happened in the gallery. In slow, deliberate, precise language, he clarified the situation to himself, "OK. Madame Bouvier was my only hope of finding Truc. Madame Bouvier and Colette Javier are one and the same person. So now, Colette Javier is my only hope of finding Truc. None, absolutely none, of the disguise, the cover story, and the persuasive techniques I prepared for Madame Bouvier will work with Colette Javier. I must change everything. With Colette, I must approach her directly and tell her the truth. Well, not necessarily the whole truth. Some holding back will be necessary, both for my protection and for hers. Colette knows me. Colette will want to help me. Colette once loved me."

COLETTE JAVIER

Having formulated a new plan, Tim looked around for a way to implement it.

One table over, a young man sat working on some type of electronic notepad. Next to the notepad was the kid's phone. Tim leaned over and asked, "Excuse me, do you speak English?"

"Oui, monsieur," the kid answered somewhat paradoxically. He said nothing more.

Tim said, "Great. I would like to make a local call. May I use your phone. I'll give you five euros for troubling you."

The kid said nothing, just raised his eyebrows.

After 5 to 10 seconds of silence, Tim said, "OK, make it 10 euros."

The kid picked up his phone and in English, "Make it 20, and it is a deal."

Tim gave him the 20 euros and thought, "There's nothing socialist about this Frog. There is still hope for France."

Tim took out Herr Buckner's card with Madame Bouvier's telephone number scribbled on the back and dialed.

"Bonjour. Paris Galerie d'Art et Centre Restauration. Andre. Que puis-je faire pour vous?" answered a young man, asking how he may help. This "Andre" was probably the little guy with whom Angelo had just talked earlier in the gallery.

Speaking in his own voice now, Tim said, "I'm sorry but unfortunately I do not speak French. However, I would like to speak with Madame Bouvier please."

"Who may I say is calling?"

Tim hesitated for a moment, and then said, "Just say an old friend."

There was a long minute of silence, during which Tim thought of hanging up and thinking this new plan through a little more thoroughly. Then he heard the noise of the phone being picked up, and then a voice he knew so well saying...

"Hello. This is Madame Bouvier, how may I help you?"

Tim was again frozen for another moment and then said in almost a whisper, "Colette?"

There was a moment of silence, and perhaps a small escape of breath on the other end. Then a soft, questioning voice, "Timothy?" ...and then again, slowly but a little more forcefully, "Timothy, is that you?"

In all the world, no one else called him Timothy, but her.

Tim had control of himself again and responded in a slightly louder, yet still quiet voice, "Yes, Colette, it's me. How are you?"

Colette sidestepped the pleasantry and asked cautiously, yet with a rising sense of expectation, "Timothy, you sound close. Are you in Paris?"

"Yes."

Then another moment of silence.

"Oh, now I remember. You are a man of few words. You are in Paris! When am I going to see you?"

Just like Colette, he thought. She did not ask, "Am I going to see you?" But rather, "When am I going to see you?" He smiled. "How about tonight? Are you free?"

"Well, I am not free, but I am good," she laughed. "Hmmmm, perhaps I am busy tonight. Are you disappointed?" letting a short pause linger for just a moment. Then she continued, "However, I will cancel everything, so you can see me. Would you like to have dinner at my apartment?"

"No," Tim said, perhaps too quickly and emphatically. He wanted to meet her alone, not with her husband and possibly kids around the table.

Trying to recover, he said more smoothly, "Let me take you to your favorite French restaurant. We can catch up over wine and candlelight." As soon as those words left his lips, Tim was sorry he had spoken them. That was an OK way to talk to an old flame, but not to one who was now another man's wife.

Colette laughed. "Well, in this city, all my favorite restaurants are French. Do you already forget you are in Paris?" Tim's face reddened on his side of the connection.

She continued, "I have things to finish here in my gallery, then I must go home and make myself pretty for you. Let's meet at Le Petit Chatelet, number 39, on the Rue de la Bucherie." She spelled the name and the street for him, and Tim wrote them down. Then she asked, "How does eightish sound?" using the English slang suffix, "ish", she had recently learned.

"Eightish sounds fine. I'm looking forward to seeing you again. See you at eight," he responded, a little inelegantly. His heart was beating like a schoolboy's, and he thought he probably sounded like one too.

"Good then," said Colette. "I will make the arrangements."

Then in a softer, lower voice she added, "Timothy, I also am looking forward to being again with you," slightly emphasizing the last two words. "See you at eight," she brightly added, with an almost audible smile, then hung up.

Tim thumbed off the phone, gave it back to the kid with a "Merci," sat back in his chair, and thought about what just happened. After about 10 minutes, he got up, left euros on the table, exited the bistro, and hailed a taxi. He now had a good feeling about this latest turn of events.

Just over an hour later Tim was unlocking the door to his hotel room. He had taken two taxis to get himself back to the gym. Once there, he quickly shed the skin of Angelo Napolitano, rapidly stuffing him into the inner chambers of what would now be Angelo's garment bag sarcophagus. It was doubtful that Angelo would be resurrected.

As Tim entered his room, he tossed his key on the dresser, Angelo's coffin over a chair, took one step, and launched himself into a half pirouette onto the bed, landing on his back with his hands already locked behind his head, his feet crossed, and his eyes staring at the ceiling. "Colette! How could Colette come back into my life now, in the middle of all this, especially in the middle of all this?"

Tim had had three great loves in his life. His first had been Quan, a love that was taken from him before it had a chance to fully mature. A wartime love was often quick and passionate, but also deep and meaningful. But to become fully mature, to fully accommodate the two personalities with all their strengths and weaknesses, to be lasting, it of course needed to survive the war. Unfortunately, theirs, in a heart-wrenching way, had not. His second love was Brileen. Their love was everything a man could hope for: passionate, deep, passionate, meaningful, passionate, exciting, passionate, challenging, passionate, sharing, passionate, fun, and of course, passionate. Unfortunately, in perhaps an even more heart-wrenching way, Brileen and their love also had been taken from him. Colette had been his third great love. Their love had been different from the others. Oh, it had been passionate, no doubt about that. It had also been meaningful, deep, challenging, and certainly fun. However, there had always been a holding back on both their parts, a seeming unwillingness to totally give one's self to the other. In the end, that holding back, that unwillingness to totally sacrifice one's self for the other, had led to their going their separate ways.

Lying there in the solitude of his room, Tim's memory had apparently independently launched a search of its archives and now began playing the movie of when he and Colette first met. After serving in the first Gulf War, Tim had been assigned to NATO (North Atlantic Treaty Organization) Headquarters in Mons, Belgium. He had been serving there for about three months when he met Colette. It was early December and time for the annual Christmas Ball. All American staff officers were expected to attend, including newly promoted Colonel DePalma. Tim had never been big on military balls and such, but they were part of the military tradition, so he usually attended, made the obligatory rounds, had drinks with good friends, enjoyed a flirt here and there, then often left before midnight. However, that night in Mons would last a little longer, about two years longer.

As Tim walked into the ballroom, he straightened his ridiculous bowtie one more time, appraised the glassy shine on his dress shoes one last time, and then began to check out the room for the shortest route to the bar that had the fewest required stops to exchange pleasantries. Then he saw her.

His vision immediately tunneled right to her on the dance floor. All else around that path between him and her dissolved into a colorful haze and a distant, muffled sound. She was moving in side silhouette to him, wearing an emerald green gown of a muted satin sheen cloth, a high collar, and a hem that barely touched the top of her gold braided shoes. The gown was cut straight to emphasize her slender body. Undoubtedly, it was for a woman like her that the French had invented the words "petite" and "magnifique." Her hair was long and raven black, pulled rearward over her ears and flowing down her back. She turned slightly, revealing that flow being channeled between two tightly twisted French braids, one holding in each side of her raven river. Her face in profile was like that of a porcelain figurine by Lladro. As her dancing partner unknowingly turned her full to Tim's vision, her face captivated him, her smile enchanted him, her eyes drew him.

Tim was half way to her before he even realized he had stepped onto the dance floor. Without taking his eyes from hers, he tapped her partner on the shoulder and said, not asked, "I would like to cut in."

"But of course, Colonel DePalma," her partner said, stepping back and presenting the lady. "Colette, this is Colonel Tim DePalma of the American contingent. Colonel DePalma, this is Colette, my daughter."

His daughter? For the first time, Tim looked at the man. It was Jacques Javier, the French Ambassador to NATO. Tim stammered a "Thank you, Sir." Then he took this beautiful young woman into his arms and began, literally, to waltz his way into her life.

After a minute or so of silent dance, she asked with a smile, "Do you talk, Colonel?"

"Yes," he answered, continuing to credibly, if less than expertly, move her across the floor.

After another minute of silence, she stated, again with a smile, "Oh, I see. You are a Gary Cooper American."

This time Tim answered with his body, tilting his head to the side, slightly squinting his right eye, and raising his left eyebrow in a questioning arch.

She smiled and observed, "Oh, yes. I can see you are a Gary Cooper American. The strong, silent type. A man of few words." Now she tilted her head to the side mimicking him, and then added with a widening smile, "But that is OK. I like Gary Cooper."

Tim would probably have preferred to be thought of as Sylvester Stallone, the Italian Stallion, but Gary Cooper would have to do. When the music stopped, Tim, realizing that many young officers were probably waiting to dance with the fair Colette, whisked her out a side door onto the patio. There, he quickly removed his blue dress uniform jacket and placed it around her shoulders. While doing so, he thought as to how the jacket's many medals were outshone by the brightness of her smile and the hot glow of her eyes. Eventually moving back inside to the club's library and its warming fire, Gary Cooper and his fan talked for hours.

Over the next two weeks, they saw each other every day. By Christmas, they had become a couple, spending that holiday in the romantic mountain village of Zermatt, Switzerland, where no cars were allowed, …just new fallen snow, Byron-like nights of "cloudless climes and starry skies," and people either falling in love or already there.

That first night in Zermatt, Colette had done something that made Tim feel he could really fall in love with this woman. They had spent the afternoon skiing an Alpine slope, then by a warm fireside had supped on cheese fondue and hot gluhwein, and finally, with what must have been their last reserves of energy, had shared themselves with each other. While cuddling in the crook of his right arm, Colette had reached up and softly clasped his left hand, which was lying across his chest, letting her fingers close around the gold band on his little finger. In a drowsy voice she whispered, "She must have been a wonderful woman. Her leaving must hurt you deeply."

Tim had been both stilled and moved by her words. Colette had never mentioned his ring before. He had never mentioned Brileen. He then said in a soft voice, "Yes, she was a wonderful woman. Yes, her leaving still hurts me deeply." He turned to tell her more about Brileen, but found Colette deep in sleep. Colette had not been asking him questions about the ring. Rather, she had just been letting him know that somehow she intuitively understood, and accepted, its meaning and its importance to him.

For the next two years, they were almost inseparable. Although they didn't see much of each other during the day, she working in the French Ambassador's Office and he working in the United States' Political-Military Office, most of their nights were spent at her cottage in a nearby Belgium village.

All their vacations were spent together in Italy. There they visited places where she had studied art; or they visited places where his relatives lived and he could practice his Italian; or they visited new places, there making new memories exclusive only to them as a couple. It had been a wonderful time.

For Tim, two concerns always lingered in the background of their relationship. One was the difference in their ages. When they met, Tim was 39 and Colette was 27. The 12 year difference didn't seem to bother Colette. It certainly didn't bother Tim. At least not at that time. However, would it in the future? If there was to be a future?

The other concern was their love for, and focus on, their professions. Tim had gone far in the military, from private to colonel. He had fought his wars. He had trained and led his soldiers. He had taught in his Army's war colleges. He had served his nation with distinction. However, he knew more challenges awaited him. He felt he still had much to contribute. Colette, of course, was still striving to reach the heights of her profession. She had extended her planned time in Belgium in order to be with Tim. However, one day she would want to return to Paris to finish her PhD art studies at the Sorbonne. She had worked in art galleries since she was 15 and wanted one of her own someday, maybe more than one. She also had thoughts of one day serving France as a member of its National Arts Council or perhaps even as its director. For the most part, these concerns had lain dormant in the distant shadows of their relationship. There they had remained dormant, that is until the day Tim received orders for a new assignment to Washington.

That night Tim asked Colette to return with him to Washington. She said she would think about it. The next night Colette asked Tim to return with her to Paris. He said he would think about it. And think about it he did. He had already completed 22 years in the Army, so he could retire with a modest pension. But what would he do in Paris? Love Colette of course, but would that be enough? He imagined that she was having the same thoughts, evaluating the same unknowns, fighting the same fears

336

of losing the other, or of losing one's self.

As Tim's departure day approached, they became more and more aware of both the strengths and also the limitations of their feelings for each other. They talked and planned for ways to keep these feelings alive, ways to fight through the problems of distance and time apart. During their last night together, they held each other closely through the sleepless hours. The next morning they said a long, lingering goodbye, both knowing that it might well be their last moment together. It had been. Until today.

Tim, now lying in his Paris hotel room, shook himself awake from these memories, looked at his watch, and cursed himself for wallowing so long in the nostalgia of unrealized love. He was just wasting time, for he had long ago concluded that their parting had been for the best.

Tim took a shower, dressed casually in a jacket and black knit shirt, and then called for a taxi. Tim had no plan for what would happen tonight. He would play it by the proverbial ear. However, he knew one thing. Colette was his only lead to Truc. He better not screw this up.

FRIDAY EVENING

Tim stepped out of the taxi, leaned in, paid the driver, then looked up and was stunned. There, on the other side of the road and across the Seine, not 300 yards away, was Notre Dame Cathedral. The cathedral was bathed in flood lights, accenting its gothic magnificence against the darkening night sky. "I'll be damned. Notre Dame. Right there in front of this kid from Federal Hill. So close I feel I can reach out and touch it." He stood there for a long moment, taking it all in.

The thoughts of Federal Hill made him look at his watch and sigh. He was five days from when he had that last serving of Zia Mary's meata'balls, and still no idea as to how many more days to a satisfying serving of revenge. He hoped this night would bring him closer to that day.

Tim raised his eyes to once more take in the majesty that was

Notre Dame, then did an "about face," and walked down a curving staircase of four wide, low steps to the La Petit Chatelet. Upon seeing it, he came to a halt, stood still, and smiled. This place was so Colette.

The restaurant looked like an old Cape Cod cottage, beaten by many years of wind and sand, sandwiched between two much taller urban business buildings. Its major colors were dark chocolate brown and dark red wine. What better colors for a French restaurant? The first floor's entire front was small-pane, brown, wooden windows and doors. Above the glass-paned front, a single brown- and wine-colored awning spanned the entire width of the restaurant. The second floor had a cottage's sloping roof, broken by two large dormers, which also had small-pane wooden windows that were covered by red awnings. Flowers hung from lighted boxes beneath the dormers. Other plants were scattered amongst sidewalk tables in front of the cottage-restaurant. All this was bathed in a soft, welcoming glow provided by several light posts, styled as Eighteenth century gas lamps. Colette's favorite restaurant could not have been more charming or inviting.

As Tim walked into the small entryway, he was met by the sounds of happy diners and the aromas of fine food. An open brazier on the other side of the room was filled with spits of roasting meats ordered by the patrons. The restaurant was small and intimate, ...just like Colette.

"May I help you sir," asked a waiter in English.

"Hmm," thought Tim, "he recognizes right off that I am an American and yet doesn't embarrass me with French. I like this place already."

"Yes, thank you. I'm here to meet with Madame Bouvier."

"Oh, but of course, Monsieur. Please follow me. We have reserved Madame Bouvier's regular table upstairs."

The waiter led Tim upstairs to an even smaller and more intimate room and sat him at a table in front of one of the dormer windows. In addition to everything else, this table had a view of the light-bathed Notre Dame.

The waiter continued, "When Madame Bouvier graces us, she

always sits at this table, but always alone, except for a book. You must be a very special friend, no?"

"Just a very old friend," said Tim.

After a few more words, the waiter responded to a request from Tim with a raised and questioning eyebrow, disappeared, then quickly reappeared with a smile and a glass of Bonal Gentiane Quina. While placing the drink before Tim, he said, "I was not sure we had any Quina in the restaurant, Monsieur. But I found one bottle, unopened. This is a new flow just for you."

As the waiter walked away, Tim looked at the Quina. He raised the glass and made slow circles with his wrist, watching the thick aperitif wine and the ice flow one over the other. Colette had introduced him to Quina. She said the French call it "ouvre lappet" --the key to the appetite. He remembered that it was made from French grapes, selected herbs, and the bark of the South American Quina tree, the same source for the medicine quinine. Tim had often joked that instead of drinking himself sick; with Quina, he could drink himself healthy. When she saw him tonight, would she also go back to those memories?

Tim drew the Quina's aroma up into his nostrils and let it's tingle settle there. After a moment, he took a small taste and just let it linger on his lips and the tip of his tongue. Then he took a sip, letting the nectar slowly flow over his tongue, savoring it, then in the next moment feeling its warmth spread throughout his chest. He remembered Colette's voice from so long ago guiding him through these steps. To her, drinking an aperitif was not to quench a thirst, but rather to awaken the senses of the nose and the mouth in preparation for the meal that was to follow.

Now, Tim began to remember more. Colette ate a meal the same way she made love. With her, it had been all about sensing, ...and savoring, ...and ultimately, ...devouring. It had been extraordinary.

Yes, it had been extraordinary. Yet, it also had been more than 10 years since he had last spoken with Colette. It also had been more than 10 years since he had last tasted a Quina. Why had he stopped? Well, he knew why he had stopped drinking the

Quina. It was damn hard to get in the States, and when a restaurant would have it, it was damn expensive. He guessed that he also knew why he had stopped calling Colette. Their lives had converged together for two wonderful years in Belgium, but then their journeys diverged down two separate paths. Or at least they had allowed themselves to go down different paths, each too stubborn, or too selfish, to sacrifice for the other. Si-i-i-i-igh. It was such a long time ago. Then there had been the news from some friends that she might have married. After that? Well, after that, there had been nothing.

Tim heard footsteps coming up the stairs. He turned to see Colette in the doorway. He rose, let his hands fall to his sides, and began to say hello. She danced past his formality, put her arms around his neck, and placed a maybe-a-moment-too-long kiss on his cheek. Then stepped back.

He looked at her. Her hair was shorter than when last he'd seen her; now cut just above the shoulders and swept back slightly; still a rich, dark brown with just the subtlest shades of auburn. She wore a trimly cut black evening dress, flared slightly at the waist, and stopping just above the knee, enticing the eye further downward to a slender, well-toned calf. Protecting the delicate smoothness of her shoulders was a light shawl, a forest green in color. All that she wore gracefully accentuated her large, chocolate brown eyes. She was still so beautiful to him.

They sat and talked about easy things. The view of Notre Dame. The Paris traffic. How and when he had arrived. The waiter peeked in, but immediately knew not to interrupt. The nothing conversation continued.

Then Colette reached across the table and picked up Tim's drink. "May I?" she asked.

"Of course."

"Ah, just as I thought, a Quina. You remembered."

"I remember everything about us, Colette. Our time together was very special to me."

She looked at him mischievously for a moment. Then she asked, with a smile, "Timothy, what should I have for dinner tonight?"

Tim, slightly surprised by the question, shrugged his shoulders, "I don't know, Colette. This is your favorite restaurant. I was going to ask you the same question."

She looked at him, her lips and eyes turning down in a make-believe frown. "Ah, Timothy, I think perhaps you have not remembered everything. When I ask you what should I have for dinner tonight, I mean you should advise me, like when we were as one. Guide me, Timothy. Should I have a hearty red wine and red meat dinner? Or, should I have a light fish dinner with a light white wine, perhaps a Chenin Blanc?"

Tim's face reddened. How could she still make him blush? Her words had jarred his memory. He now remembered that her asking him, "Timothy, what should I have for dinner tonight" was her code for asking, "Timothy, are we having sex tonight?"

When they had been "as one," if she knew a night of intimacy awaited them, then she would eat a light meal, usually a river fish or a salad, complemented with a glass of Chenin Blanc. Chenin Blanc loosened her inhibitions just enough, without in turn inhibiting any of her senses. She called Chenin Blanc her love wine.

However, if it was to be a night at the theater, or at an official party, or at another couple's house, all of which were usually followed by coming home and falling into bed tired and almost asleep, then her dinner would usually consist of some hearty beef, complemented by a strong burgundy wine.

Now it was Tim's turn to look into her eyes, and they were beautiful eyes. He leaned closer, and said, perhaps too intensely, "Colette, I would like to say that you, Colette, should have a light meal tonight, complemented by a glass of Chenin Blanc. However, I am hesitant to say the same to Madame Bouvier."

She looked puzzled for a moment, then smiled, her eyes now quite amused. "Oh, I see. Ever the chivalrous American officer. Ever the highly moral Gary Cooper. You would eagerly bed Colette, an old lover, ...but not Madame Bouvier, a married woman."

She paused and then continued, still amused, "I am sorry. I did not realize that you did not know. Monsieur Bouvier and I were divorced over five years ago. I keep his name mostly for business purposes. All my business relationships know me as Madame Bouvier. I thought it would be too inconvenient to change."

She again placed her hand on Tim's and coyly whispered, "Now, let me ask you again, Timothy. What should I have for dinner tonight?"

Tim cupped her hand in both of his, and replied, "Whatever you have, I think it should be something light."

She smiled.

Then Tim added, "Colette, before you order, I want to tell you why I am here in Paris. What I say may affect the rest of our night, ...and maybe, what you will want to order."

She drew back slightly, "Mais oui. But of course. Talk to me."

He took a deep breath and started, "I came to Paris looking for a certain man. I do not know his name or where he lives. But I think you do. I need ..."

Colette, frowning, interrupted, "Just ask me. If I know, I will tell you."

"Please, let me finish," he said softly. "You recently brokered a sale of a Detero painting for this person. He ..."

Colette's hand involuntarily flew to her mouth, covering the slight dropping of her jaw and the escaping gasp of surprise, "Oooh! That was you in my gallery today. Wasn't it, Timothy? You were the American there to look at our Spanish surrealist paintings. That was you, Timothy! Wasn't it?""

Tim's normal reflex was to lie and evade in order to maintain the cover story. But not to Colette. What purpose would evasion serve now. "Yes, that was me. How did you know?"

"Well, I did not know. Not till just now. Remember when you called me today? After your call, my assistant, Andre, commented that I had two mysterious American men in my life today. He said one American wanted to talk to me on the phone, but did not want to give his name. Then the other American did give his name in the gallery, but then suddenly did not want to talk to me. After Andre told me of the second American, the one from San

Francisco, I went to my office and reviewed my surveillance tape. I could not get a clear view of the man's face. He was always keeping his head, I think you say, tilted down. I did not recognize him by his walk, or by his dress, or by his mannerisms. I most certainly did not think of them as yours, Timothy."

Tim smiled, pleased that she had not recognized him on the tapes. He must congratulate Angelo for his fine work, should he ever see him again. Tim was about to speak, when Colette's eyes and voice began reflecting another idea arising in her mind.

"Timothy, are you on some kind of a government mission? Is that what this is all about? Is that what all this silly mystery is about? Is that why you are trying to find Mr. Van?"

Tim locked on the name "Van." Again, his reflex was to lie and evade in order to enhance the chance of cornering his prey. Why not tell her it was a government mission? She would certainly be willing to cooperate then. Yet, he heard and felt an internal sigh. No, he could not lie to Colette about this. He must be honest with her, well honest up to a point anyway. The honesty had to be leavened with caution. He must still protect her from any possible blowback after Truc's death.

"Colette (he loved the sound of her name again on his lips, almost lyrical), yes I am on a mission. But it isn't a government mission. It's a personal mission. You said "Mr. Van." Is that his name? Van? Is he the man who sold the Detero? Can you tell me more about him? Where he lives?"

She ignored his questions and focused on his admission. "Timothy, what do you mean that it is a personal mission? What kind of personal mission? I want to help. But please, you must tell me more."

He again leaned in and took her hands in his. "Colette, I can't tell you more. I don't mean to sound mysterious or melodramatic. I'm only interested in your safety. I can only tell you that there must be no connection between you and what I am doing."

She again interrupted. "You are concerned about me? Yet, you come to me. To me, in Paris. To help you. You come here, willing to involve me in whatever it is you are doing. Yet you will not tell me what it is. Timothy, honestly, I want to help. But I need to know what it is that you are doing, ...and what I am getting into."

Tim thought for a moment. Why not cave to her persistence? After all, it was based on her caring for him. At least he felt that she still cared for him. It had been a long time since they had been partners in life. People change. Yet, he felt he could still trust her. Then his sense of responsibility began to take sway. This was not about trusting her. This was all about protecting her.

"Colette, I did not come to Paris to involve you. I came to Paris to meet Madame Bouvier. To persuade her to help me find this man. Believe me, I had no idea that you were Madame Bouvier. Nevertheless, here we are. Believe me when I say it is better for you that you do not know what I am doing. Also believe me when I say you are my only link to this man. Without you, I cannot find him. I am asking for your help, because I must ask for your help. I am not telling you more, because I cannot tell you more. I cannot tell you more and still protect you. Will you tell me this Mr. Van's full name? Will you tell me where I can find him? Will you tell me everything you know about him? Will you help me? Colette, I am not just asking for your help. I need your help. I need you."

Colette did not answer. She did not move. She seemed not to breathe. Her face remained motionless. Only her eyes seemed alive. They were locked onto Tim's. No, they had passed through Tim's and were now searching his heart, his soul. These seconds of silence seemed endless.

As the waiter walked in, she looked up. Tim actually felt her gaze being pulled from within him, back through him, back into her.

"Henri, we are ready to order." As the waiter approached, she put her hand on Tim's. The warmth of her touch was rivaled by the warmth of her smile, and both were now overwhelmed by the heat of her eyes. Tim felt like he was melting.

Colette talked to Henri, but continued to look at Tim. "Henri, I think we want to eat light tonight. We will start with a sharing of

344

foie gras. Please toast the bread in the open brazier. My ....partner...will have the plate of Goat Cheese and Herb Tart. I will have the plate of Shrimp and Avocado Salad. Oh yes, please bring us a bottle of your best Chenin Blanc."

Avocado and Shrimp Salad

Since Tim's first exposure to this dish in Paris, he perfected a quick, easy, and multi-use recipe for this light meal. Borrowing from his Italian heritage he settled on a variation of the simple vinaigrette and prefers the use of baby spinach leaves for the base.

Ingredients:(Four Servings)

3 – 4 Tbsp	Fresh Lemon Juice
3 – 4 Tbsp	Extra Virgin Olive Oil
1 – 2 Tbsp	Capers (mulled)
1 – 2 Pkgs	Sugar Substitute
Salt/Pepper	To Taste
8 Cups (bag)	Baby Spinach leaves, long stems removed
1 Lb Shrimp	Cooked, cleaned, and deveined.
½ Tomato	Chopped into cubes
1 Avocado	Sliced thin
¼ Cup	Walnuts

Directions:

1. Whisk together the lemon juice, olive oil, crushed capers, and sweetener. Taste and add salt and pepper as desired.
2. Combine spinach, shrimp, avocados, and tomatoes; pour dressing over salad, toss, and serve.

Tips:

1. To avoid mashing the avocado, cut in half, remove pit, and using a thin-bladed knife, go along the inside edge of the skin to free it up and pull off.
2. Sugar or honey could be substituted for the lighter sweetener.

3. Pairs nicely with a light white wine.
4. Strawberries and Roquefort cheese can replace the avocado and shrimp, making a wonderful summer salad.
5. If you add the above, remove the tomatoes and replace with walnuts.

Goat Cheese and Herb Quiche

A favorite for Tim and Colette, this has become a standard quick meal. The first time Tim prepared it he labored over the "from scratch" crust. Over the years Tim switched to the prepared (box) crust and hasn't looked back. One concession he does make is to both lightly dust the quiche pan with dried dill before the crust is put in and also to paint the top of the uncooked crust with melted butter, sprinkled with dried dill and a little sea salt.

Ingredients:(Six Servings)

1 Sheet	Prepared Dough (usually ½ of the box)
3 – 4	Eggs
4 Oz	Goat Cheese (crumbled)
4 Oz	Jarlsberg Cheese (shredded)
1 ¼ Cups	Heavy Cream
½ Tsp	Lemon Zest
2 Tbsp	Fresh Chives (chopped)
2 Tbsp	Parsley (chopped)
1 Tbsp	Dried Minced Onions
Salt/Pepper	To Taste

Directions:

1. Preheat oven to 375F with rack in center.
2. Unroll prepared dough and place in 9 – 10 inch pie pan or tart pan; see above for crust preparation.
3. Bake pie crust for 15 to 20 minutes until lightly browned.
4. In a mixing bowl, beat cream, eggs, salt and pepper, and herbs into custard; set aside.
5. Place crumbled goat cheese evenly on the pie crust; sprinkle half the grated Jarlsberg/Swiss evenly over

the crust and pour the custard atop. Sprinkle the remaining Jarlsberg/Swiss atop.

6. Bake at 375F for 30 to 40 minutes or until firm and golden brown.
7. Remove and let cool for at least 10 minutes before slicing and serving.

Tips:

1. Easily adapts to added vegetables, crab, etc.
2. Broil for the last few minutes to brown the top.
3. Great micro-waved the next day for breakfast.

CHAPTER 16: A DASH OF HOPE

Day Six: Saturday, 0730 hours, in Paris

Tim awoke to a persistent sun as it pushed its way through Colette's curtains and into his eyes. As his eyes slowly opened, he pressed the glow button on his watch, even though he didn't need it, moving his left wrist to and fro till the numbers came into focus. 0730. The sun he had brushed from his eyes apparently settled on Colette, covering her with a soft patina glow. Asleep, she looked almost like a child.

However, the memories of last night that now started pushing into his mind were not of a child, but of a woman. A woman he had once known so well. A woman it felt so well to know once again. She felt new, yet comfortable. He rolled back onto his pillow. He hadn't felt this happy, this contented in a long time. Had there been a mirror on the ceiling, he would not have been surprised to see the growing grin on his face.

As the thoughts of her flooded his mind, his body relaxed, almost flowing into her bedding. He was reliving last night. In the beginning she ravaged him. Her fierceness and hunger surprised him. As his own passion mounted, her fierceness receded, replaced by a strong, independent submission. She responded to him, yet at the same time guided him. They traveled back in time to a younger them. Then they came back to the heat of a reunited them. First it was her, with a turn of her head, an arch of her back, a light gasp from her throat. Then it was him, stronger, more forceful, just as complete. He rolled to his side. She rolled to him. He had begun to say something. She put a small finger to his lips. He felt the lightness of her hair across his chest. She felt the warmth of his breath upon her cheek. They had become lost in each other, exhausted in each other, found in each other. All as if it was the first time. It was the first time, at least in a very long time. They drifted and were gone. Tim now followed them and was soon again asleep.

Tim drifted back, slowly, reluctantly. Again, the sun was prying at his eyelids. This time the sun brought along an accomplice. The accomplice invaded through his nostrils, stimulating the receptors in his brain. The dual assaults continued on his eyes and nose till he stirred himself awake. Again, the wrist moved to and fro. No need now for the glow button. The numbers again came into focus. O935!

He had slept another two hours. He began to again remember the previous night. He again turned toward Colette. She was no longer there. He touched her imprint. It was no longer warm. He covered his eyes from the sun's continued assault. That worked. However, the assault on his sense of smell grew stronger. The aromas were all around him. His hearing now came awake, providing him light sounds of dishes, utensils, and movement. A grin again began to spread across his face.

Memories of last night and Colette once again flooded his senses. But this time, his mind was more awake. It took control. Slowly, reluctantly, Tim's grin morphed into a frown and then into a grimace. Parts of last night's dinner conversation were now vying with the evening's happier moments for his attention. Soon his mind shifted from remembering to analyzing.

Colette told him that she met Van only once, in Heidelberg, after she acquiesced to his demand that she join him there to personally broker the final aspect of the sale of his Detero. When they met, Van berated her for his having to be there to personally seal the deal. On the way out of the castle in which the auction was held, he told her she was incompetent for allowing newspaper men and photographers to be present at his private sale. He called her again two days later, still irate, again berating her and demanding her commission back, or he would blacklist her. She gave him back her commission, less the travel expenses to Heidelberg, just to be rid of him, but feared that he might yet try to hurt the reputation of her gallery. She did not like this man.

Tim listened, and as he did, his bloodlust for Truc only grew and intensified. He was unable to accept that she did not know more. He refused to accept it. He could not let the trail run cold. He refused to allow it to do so.

Then the slightest sliver of hope had presented itself. In trying to convince Tim that there was no more to tell, Colette told him that Van had been referred to her by an art dealer in Italy who had been too busy to broker the sale himself. Tim locked onto that comment, almost scaring Colette with what must have seemed to her like an interrogation: Who? What art Dealer? What's his name? Where in Italy? Did this art dealer know more about Van? I want to meet him! Now! Tomorrow!

Colette had taken his arm, squeezed it tightly, asked him to calm down. Only then had she begun to fully realize how important this was to him. She wanted to help. She would help. She promised that on the morrow she would contact the art dealer and find out what he knew. Tim could not ask for more. The trail had not gone cold, well, not stone cold anyway. He realized that he needed to take a deep breath, maybe three. Then he changed the dinner's table talk back to them. Back to their past. Back to their present. No words had been said about their future.

FRITTATAS

Having now remembered that conversation from the night before, Tim jumped out of bed and did the one-footed hop into his pants, which had been lying on the floor. Slightly annoyed that he could not find his shirt, -where had he dropped that?- he followed a strong trail of aromas to the kitchen. There he found his shirt, not lying on the floor, but wrapped around and holding in the warmth that was Colette. Smiling he said, "I'm cold. I want my shirt back. I want it back right now!"

She looked up towards him, her lips smiling and her eyes sparking, "I bet you do." Then she turned her back to him, stuck out her tush just a bit, and peeked into the oven, "I just started a frittata baking. That will warm you up."

"Yeah. Well, I can think of several things that could warm me up. What kind of frittata is it?" he asked, as he closed in on his shirt and her.

"Your favorite. Tomato, basil, asparagus, and fontina," she giggled, as she backed away from him.

"Hmmmm. If I remember correctly, that should take about 15 minutes to finish. Just enough time to take my shirt back." He swooped her up and headed for the bedroom, with her laughing hysterically into his neck.

It had been a frittata that had started one of the most intimate parts of their long ago affair. A frittata had also been there at the end.

Within several weeks of the start of their relationship, Tim had been spending more time at Colette's than at his own place. She was happy to find that he also enjoyed fine food and was willing to try many different dishes. She was slightly disappointed that, like most American men, he did not know how to cook. She would try to change that, and ultimately she did.

She delighted in his stories of "plates and planes" taking him around the world and across time from Federal Hill to her. He delighted in her story about her star, ...and her, as a star.

Early on, Colette drew him into her star, and she started with a frittata. For Colette, she had the starring role in her own life. She thought that everyone should be the star in the play that is his or her own life. She believed that in addition to being the star in that play, each of us should also be the director and the lead writer.

She would also explain that like the symbolic drawing of a star, her life was carefully constructed around five points. One of those points was food. The others were her profession that she loved; her philosophy that sustained her; her body that she cared for and which cared for her; and of course the point that held it all together, love. For Colette, a person must have love for her profession, love for her philosophy, love for her body, love for her food, and most of all she must completely love at least one some-one other than herself, and that someone must love her back, and love her back completely. Colette had found the last point of her star the hardest to fulfill.

As she explained to Tim, for a star to survive it must live in the heavens amongst other stars, illuminating them as they illu-minated it; feeding on and growing from each other's energy. A star could not survive living among rocks. It was the same for her.

For Colette, Tim was another star.

As they shared their lives for those two years, growing closer and closer, Colette revealed more and more of herself, of her star. She could spend hours talking in depth about each facet of her star. Food, as one of those facets, became an important part of their shared life. Colette showed Tim that there was more to the love for food than just the eating of it. To her food was the very physical sustenance of life. Without food there was no life. Thus one should enjoy all facets of food: the growing of it, the prepar-ing of it, and of course, the consuming of it.

Colette grew many of her vegetables in a small garden along-side her rented Belgian cottage. In back, she also had a potted herb garden. Although Tim wasn't big on working the vegetable garden, he liked cultivating the herb garden. He enjoyed picking the herbs for use in their meals, especially the mint and basil. As he knelt to pick them, they would send off scented flares that would burst all around him, bathing him in a natural cologne that would last for hours.

A frittata of tomato, basil, asparagus, and fontina cheese was the first meal that Tim made entirely on his own for Colette. Most of the ingredients came from her gardens. Although he had cer-tainly cooked many other meals before meeting Colette, this was the first meal he cooked in the style of what he came to call "The Colette School of Culinary Arts."

That frittata was the first meal he ever prepared with the body's full array of senses in mind. The eye would be stimulated by the greens of the basil and asparagus mixed with the red of the tomatoes and the white of the cheese, all against the yellow background of the eggs. The texture would please both the eye and the mouth. The aroma would tantalize the nose. Most important of all, the taste would be savory, exploding joy across the taste buds of the tongue, sending messages of pleasure to the brain. Throughout the meal, the ear should be entertained by music with which to sway and dance one's way around the kitchen and around one's cooking partner. Unexplainably, among Colette's favorite cooking music was early Billy Joel, especially lyrics like, "A bottle of white, a bottle of red, perhaps a bottle of rosé instead." That was cooking "a la Colette."

Two years later, on the morning of the day their lives parted along separate paths, Tim made another, their last, basil and fontina frittata. They ate it slowly, not wanting it to be finished. Then he left for the airport to return to the States and to a life without frittatas and without Colette.

Now, here in Paris, a frittata was once again center stage in their lives, and at this moment with an insistent, annoying announcement of its arrival, in the form of an oven bell.

"Timothy," she gasped and laughed, "the frittata is ready."

"Well, I'm not."

As Tim continued, so did the bell.

"Timothy!" she laughed again, "The frittata!"

He looked at her. He smiled through his heavy breathing, "The frittata? Now? Really?"

She rolled from him, leaving a smile in the air, and followed the call of the bell back to the kitchen. He followed her. She still in his shirt. He still in his annoyance.

A DASH OF HOPE

About halfway through the frittata and café au lait, she ended the lovers' talk and began in a more level voice, "Timothy, I have good news and bad news. Which would you like first?"

Tim knew immediately that this was about Truc. "Give me the good news first, then we will deal with the bad."

Colette hesitated for a moment, as she internalized his spoken "we." Did that mean Timothy was thinking of them as a couple again? As her heart pondered that question, she said, "This morning, while you were sleeping, I called the art dealer in Florence. He said that he had the information you wanted about Van. I did not mention you of course. I told him I wanted to contact Mr. Van about further confidential details concerning the sale of the Detero. I ..."

"That is good news," Tim excitedly interjected, not allowing her to finish. "Where is this Mr. Van?"

"Ah, now for the bad news," she sighed. "My associate dealer said that Mr. Van was an extremely private person and would not be happy if he found out that his confidential information was being passed around. He further stated that he could not give me the information over the phone, nor put it in writing in an email. He would only agree to give me the information, if I asked him for it in person."

"What? In person? In Florence?" said Tim, slightly confused. "I understand this guy's respect for his client's confidentiality and not wanting an audio or paper trail of his breaking that confidentiality, but asking you to fly to Florence is nuts."

This time she interrupted him. "I know. I tried to reason with him. But these are his conditions. I have..."

Tim again cut in. "You said this guy was a friend. Friends don't make you jump through hoops like this. Give me this guy's name and address. I'll go talk to him myself."

As he was speaking those words, Tim saw a flicker of concern, and something else he could not identify, pass over her face, for just a moment, but it was there. He immediately knew there was something else going on here.

"Who is this art dealer? How well do you know him?"

Colette drew in a small breath. She hesitated for a moment. She seemed reluctant to answer. But she did. "I know him very well. His name is Gerard Bouvier. He is my ex-husband."

"What? Your ex-husband? This art dealer is your ex-husband? Why didn't you tell me this before? He's your ex-husband and he makes you do this? He makes you come personally to beg him. I don't like this. I won't let you go. I'm going. I'll get the information I need. Believe me, if there is any begging going on, he'll be begging me. He'll be begging me to take the information and leave him be. That's the only begging that will be going on. I'll..."

Colette got up from her chair. Went to him. Straddled his lap, causing his shirt to rise up onto her hips. Clasped his face in her hands. Looked into his eyes. Smiled the smile that had always calmed him down.

"Timothy, shush! Yes, Gerard is an A-hole with a capitol A. But I know how to handle him. When I am done with him, he will feel like the beggar, not me. I'm going. I know you need this information. I don't know exactly why, but I know you do. If I can help, I must. So I have already booked a flight. I leave in three hours."

She put a finger to his lips. Her tone softened, as did her eyes and her lips. She whispered, "Timothy, can you think of a proper way to relax me before such a long flight?"

Simple Frittata

Italian pride has it that the French omelet is just a cheap cousin of the frittata. As long as eggs are available and there is a small garden patch, the frittata is a staple of an Italian household, especially during Lent. Zia Mary and Aunt Rose would both prepare this for Tim and as he grew up Tim learned his first lesson in diplomacy when he inadvertently told Zia Mary that Aunt Rose's was a "little better". After a flood of less than appropriate native Italian, Tim was forced to assist his Zia Mary in preparation of the dish so she could find out exactly what it was that her sister did to make it better. In the end Tim never was able to tell the difference.

Years later Tim learned that the time the frittata cooks in the oven can be very rewarding.

Ingredients:(Four Servings)

1 Onion	Medium, thinly sliced
½ Lb	Fresh spinach - stems removed and just wilted
8 Eggs	Large
2 Tbsp	Milk
1/3 to ½ Cup	Grated Parmesan/Fontina Cheese
Fresh Herbs	Chopped (basil, parsley, chives, oregano, etc)
1 -2 Tbsp	Olive Oil
1/3 Cup	Ricotta Cheese
Salt/Pepper	To Taste

Directions:

1. Preheat oven to 400F.
2. Cook spinach in a little water until wilted - about 2 to 3 minutes; drain and set aside.
3. In a large mixing bowl, whisk eggs, milk, herbs, and

Parmesan Cheese.

4. In a large ovenproof skillet, sauté onions until soft and translucent (about 4 - 5 minutes).
5. Add wilted spinach and mix with onions.
6. Evenly distribute mixture in the skillet and pour egg mixture over spinach, ensuring that egg mixture gets underneath the spinach.
7. Cook until set, probably about 3 minutes; remove from heat and add dollops of ricotta to the top.
8. Place in oven and bake about 15 minutes or until firm and golden.
9. Let set for two minutes and cut in pan and serve to plates.

Tips:
1. Prepare and have ready all ingredients.
2. A fluffier mixture can be accomplished by using a blender or blending stick.
3. This can be cooked on the stove top alone with a cover using medium to low heat.
4. You can add a strip of diced red pepper or a little cut-up tomato to provide more color.
5. To stretch the baking time to 30 minutes, adjust the oven to about 300F.
6. The skillet handle will be hot - careful!

Kitchen Herb Garden

No matter what your tastes or favorites, you probably cook with herbs. You also have discovered that freshly picked herbs really add a punch to your meals and garnish complements (pun intended). You can run to the market and purchase what you need; plant a large garden in back corner of your yard; or you can plant containers on your patio and snip away when needed. If you have time and funds, your herb garden can be as formal as a Potager (French kitchen garden), mixing herbs, fruits, flowers, and a few vegetables in a small space (the Smithsonian has its version at the American History Museum). On the other hand, a less formal Italian Orto (vegetable garden) would include a lot more vegetables and multiple tomato varieties. As a gardener, Tim has planted many herbs over the years and learned/relearned a basic lesson – keep it simple. Tim settled on containers filled with herbs right on the patio – ten feet from the door. These not only complement other plants but also add a pleasant aroma – especially after you cut some. Tim tried different combinations but recommends that each of the basic herbs have their own container – don't mix. Depending upon the varieties you plant, none will obtain the same height nor have the same growing rates; eventually the strongest and tallest (usually the basil) will overshadow and limit growth of the other, smaller herbs (such as parsley, oregano, etc). As your plants grow and begin to flower – pinch off/snip off the flowers. This encourages leaf and sprig growth beneath the flower. In the fall and before the first frost Tim harvests the remaining herbs, cleans, packages, and freezes them both as individual herbs and as a mixture (Herbs du Provence).

Suggested Herbs:

Basil:

The most popular and versatile, basil blends easily with most Italian tomato dishes. "Sweet Basil" is probably the easiest to grow; most varieties do not winter over.

Chives:

As basil is to Italian cooking, so are chives to French cuisine when added to soups, fish, and potatoes. Chives are great for decoration (baking potatoes), yet mild in flavor. Almost perennial in nature, if chives are protected in winter they will come back year after year.

Cilantro:

As a leaf, this is the Mexican parsley-like version that is prevalent in salsa and as a garnish, it can be used interchangeably with parsley for many dishes. Cilantro is also referred to as Chinese Parsley.

Dill:

Like chives, dill has a tendency to winter over. Native to Europe, it is popular from Scandinavia to the Mid-East. Dill accents fish well, maybe added to mustard, served with cucumbers and yogurt, and for pickling vegetables. . Probably Tim's favorite herb.

Oregano:

A Mediterranean favorite, probably first known for its use on pizza. Sweet, pungent, and invasive, oregano is a member of the mint family. Mid-Eastern use would include flavoring for meat and lamb dishes.

Parsley:

Your first experience with this herb was probably as a garnish atop of potatoes, soups, or rice. It adds color and flavor to whatever you pair it with – an excellent addition to melted butter for toasted Italian bread. "Italian parsley'" is probably the easiest to grow.

Rosemary:

Great aroma - used primarily with lamb and meat. Used with marinades, especially kebabs. A perennial, rosemary has a 50% survival rate over winter. Trimmed and potted, mature rosemary plants are often seen around Christmas as a fragrant indoor Christmas plant.

CHAPTER 17: HER DINNER

Day Six: Saturday, 1330 hours, in Paris

Tim stood about 100 yards from the front of the massive Pantheon, one of France's great national monuments. As he looked at the monument, his thoughts were still of Colette.

It had been an hour since Colette left for the airport. They decided she would call him that night at her apartment at 7 PM. If sometime in the future her phone records were checked as part of an investigation of Truc's death, they would only reveal that her home phone received a call from Florence and a short message had been left on her answering machine. Tonight, in a simple code, the message would say whether or not she had the information Tim needed, and when she would return. Then Tim would erase the message. There would be no phone record of a direct connection between her and him. All this was done for her protection. Colette agreed with his precautions. Little did Tim know that Colette had other, very different plans for that 7 PM call.

After Colette's departure, Tim decided to spend the afternoon doing a little sightseeing. He needed to get his mind off Truc for awhile. More to the point, he also needed to get his mind off wanting to go to Florence and teach Monsieur Bouvier how to treat a lady.

With only about four hours before he was to be back in Colette's apartment for the 7 PM call, Tim would not be able to see much of Paris. Like most people who have never been to Paris before, he could have chosen to see the Eiffel Tower, or visit Notre Dame, or walk under the Arc de Triomphe, or gaze on the

Mona Lisa at the Louvre. However, Colonel Tim DePalma was not like most people. That's why he was standing 100 yards from the front of the Pantheon.

Le Pantheon is a massive building, originally constructed to be a Catholic Cathedral. However, it now serves as a monument and mausoleum to great French men and women. It is almost 30 stories high with its old cathedral base designed as a cross. The east-west axis of the cross is almost a football field in length, while the north-south axis is well over the length of a football field.

As Tim stood studying the structure, its six massive Roman columns in the front reminded him of the American Supreme Court, which in his mind was a temple to justice. The Pantheon's massive dome reminded him of the U.S. Capitol and its dome, which Jefferson had once called "the first temple dedicated to the sovereignty of the people."

Le Pantheon too was a temple dedicated to the people; not to their sovereignty, but to their talents. As Tim learned from his guide book, the building was originally commissioned by King Louis XV as a cathedral in 1744. However, the building was not completed until 1790, a year after the French Revolution. That fact did not bode well for a new cathedral. The French had not only revolted against their aristocracy, they had also revolted against their clergy. Thus, the leaders of the revolution redesignated the just-finished, meant-to-be cathedral as Le Pantheon, in the Greek tradition of a temple to the gods. However, they dedicated it not to the remembrance of the Christ-God and his saints but to the remembrance of heroes of France, past and future. Among the first to be honored with entombment within the walls of the Pantheon were Voltaire and Jean Jacques Rousseau, France's giants of the Age of Enlightenment and Reason. These were the Frenchmen whose ideas on the rights of man, along with the example of the recently successful American Revolution, had led to the French Revolution of 1789. Tim was here today to visit with Monsieurs Voltaire and Rousseau.

Over the years, the Army afforded Tim many opportunities he would probably never have had otherwise. One was higher education. Tim held a college degree in Political Science as well as a Masters degree in Foreign Affairs. The Army had provided the money. Tim had provided the work. Both had benefited from the effort.

While Tim had majored in Political Science, he minored in Philosophy. Big ideas had always fascinated him. Unanswerable questions intrigued him. The men and women who generated both had always earned his admiration. Although these men and women were almost always flawed in their personal lives, their ideas transcended these flaws and often changed the course of history in both good ways and bad. Tim was also a flawed man; all the better to admire their achievements.

As Tim walked between the great columns into the Pantheon's spacious rotunda, he did not feel as he had expected to feel. The large space beneath the vaulted dome felt cold and empty. It felt like what it was, a house of God, without God. He slowly walked through thousands of square feet of almost empty space, except for a few colorless statues which were supposed to represent man's political freedom. Although they shouldn't have, they looked very small and insignificant in such a setting. He eventually came to a downward flight of stairs beneath a sign which read "Crypts."

As he descended the stairs, he began to feel the presence of the over 70 heroes of France buried there, the country's most revered writers, poets, scientists, and philosophers. Among them were Victor Hugo, author of such social commentaries as Les Miserables and The Hunchback of Notre Dame; Emile Zola, fighter against anti-Semitism; Alexander Dumas, author of adventures such as The Three Musketeers and The Count of Monte Cristo; Louis Braille, the inventor of the system of reading and writing for the blind; Marie Curie, the first woman to win a Nobel Prize; and of course the philosophers of politics and reason, Voltaire and Rousseau.

The first crypts to meet the visitor were those of Rousseau and Voltaire. When Tim finally stood before Rousseau's large wooden sepulcher, he had to laugh. There, not 50 feet away, was the sepulcher and a statue of Voltaire. These two great minds could not untangle themselves from each other in life, and here they remained, faced-off against each other in death.

Voltaire and Rousseau were contemporaries, but rivals. In fact, they reportedly hated each other. Voltaire came from wealth and enjoyed living in luxury. Rousseau came from poverty and remained in it most of his life. Tim believed that in private, they probably appreciated each other's work, but in public, they disparaged each other at every opportunity. However, they had complementary beliefs in that they both opposed The State and The Church, earning themselves periods of prosecution, imprisonment, and exile. They both proposed primarily similar, yet somewhat differing, theories on the political rights of the individual and the supremacy of reason over ignorance and superstition. Tim would never forget the feeling he had when he first read the opening sentence of Rousseau's great work, The Social Contract, which presented a new political order based on the rights of the citizens. That sentence stated, "Man is born free, but everywhere he is in chains."

Over the years Tim forgot the exact classroom distinctions between the philosophies of Voltaire and Rousseau. However, he did remember that these Frenchmen; along with the Englishmen John Locke and Isaac Newton; and the Americans Franklin, Jefferson, and Madison; and many others as well, brought the world the Age of Enlightenment and Reason. Flowing from their minds and their pens were words and ideas that led to the great democracies and republics of the modern Western World where citizens deposed their kings and ruled themselves. The downstream results from these French, English, and American philosophers and scientists would be very different in many ways, but their headwaters were the same: beliefs in the political, economic, and moral rights of the individual. Tim had chosen a life that protected these ideas of the pen with the strength of the sword, ...or perhaps, that life had chosen him.

Every now and then over the years, Tim would become depressed, believing that many of his fellow citizens had no idea where their freedoms came from or how easily they could be lost. Citizens' faith in their political leaders was often misplaced, sometimes with devastating consequences. America's warriors, as a class, continued to raise their hands to God and their own honor, swearing to defend these freedoms, as formulated in the Constitution, from enemies both foreign and domestic. Defend if necessary, with their lives. In the hearts of these warriors lived the ideals of Voltaire, Rousseau, Locke, Jefferson, Franklin, and Madison, and there also resided the promise and the will to protect those ideas and ideals. That was why Tim was visiting with Voltaire and Rousseau today, to review their ideas in his mind and refresh their ideals in his heart.

As Tim walked back out through the Pantheon's majestic columns into the waning daylight, he felt renewed. Spending this afternoon amongst these great ideas and ideals had buoyed his spirits. It was a feeling similar to those he had when he often spent an afternoon walking the National Mall in Washington, D.C. There he would circle the Washington Monument, visit with long ago comrades in the foxhole that is the Vietnam Memorial, sit on the bench with the grandfatherly Einstein, gaze for endless minutes on the wise visage of Lincoln, stand next to the crossed-arm determination of King, then end in the temple to Jefferson, there sitting on a bench rereading Jefferson's words along the temple's walls for what seemed like the thousandth time, dwelling on all that those words had wrought for his country, for its citizens, and for himself. If only every American could have that same experience. The wonder of it all was that they could. The opportunity was always there.

Outside, on the top step of the Pantheon, Tim stood quietly for a moment before descending down into the constant motion that was Paris. Paris was truly a great city. The men and women entombed here had helped make it so. As Tim was about to leave the company of France's heroes, a grumble rumbled from his stomach. He was getting hungry. Before he headed back to Colette's apartment, he turned around once more to look again at the Pantheon. But this time he laughed as a new thought struck him as funny. All these great Frenchmen honored here, and not one of them a chef!

SATURDAY EVENING

It was 7 PM. Tim was sitting by the phone in Colette's apartment. Waiting.

7:02, ...7:04 ...still waiting, but getting a little nervous. Or was it perturbed?

It was now 7:05. Tim began to get up from the couch, then the phone rang. He slid back into the cushions, waiting for the call to go to the answering machine. Hopefully the message would say, "I accomplished everything today that I wanted to accomplish. I'll arrive at..." That was the message they had agreed upon if she had gotten the needed information on her "Mr. Van" and had booked a flight home that night. He did not want to hear any of the other variations they had discussed, which would only be used if she failed to get all that was needed. He would not accept failure. He could not. Tim would then erase the message and head out to eat.

He heard her voice begin, "Timothy, please pick up the phone. Do not let this call go to the answering machine. Timothy, are you there?"

Tim jerked up, alert. A "Damn!" escaped his lips. This change in the plan could not be a good thing. He reached for the phone, "Colette, what's wrong?"

"Oh, Timothy. I'm glad you picked up." Her voice did not sound scared, or frightened, or even strained. Why was she deviating from the plan?

She continued in an almost sprightly voice, "You know that good news - bad news thing you Americans like to do?"

"Y---e---s," Tim said slowly. What the hell was she doing? Tim decided he better play along, but he was not liking this, not one bit.

"Well, I have bad news, good news, some more bad news, and then finally some more good news. You want to hear it?"

Tim was becoming a little annoyed, but he said, "Yeah, let it roll."

She started, "Well, first the bad news. I did NOT get everything accomplished today."

"Damn!" thought Tim. That meant she was unable to get any useful information on Truc, especially where he was located. That was bad news.

She continued, "Now for some good news. I am pretty sure that tomorrow morning I will be able to accomplish everything."

Tim's shoulders eased back onto the couch. This was good news. He interpreted her words to mean that she felt confident about getting the needed info on "Mr. Van" to include his whereabouts. "That's great," he almost shouted into the phone.

"Now again, some bad news," she said.

The sound of a pout and a frown came through his handpiece and reformulated itself into a picture of her in his mind, a picture of her toying with him the way she did when she was in a playful mood. 'What the hell was she up to?' he asked himself with a silent exasperated sigh, then to her in a more moderate tone, "OK, give me this new bad news. I'm ready."

"OK, here it comes," her voice continuing to feed the picture in his mind of her pouting lips and feigned frown toying with him. "I am depressed that I will not be home to spend this night with you, as I had planned. I wanted to cook you a "light" meal, then play with you till the light of tomorrow ended what I feared might have been our last night together."

His breath stopped for a moment. Her directness often startled him. Yet he was also often softened by the way she delivered it, from behind the dual masks of coyness and shyness in order to protect her vulnerability to his response. Again he remembered why he had once so adored this woman.

"I understand Colette. I too am depressed. I wish you were with me right now," he answered softly, ... and truthfully.

Her next words changed the mood dramatically. A new picture of a light-hearted Colette immediately began to form in his mind. She, now with a smile in her voice, said, "Then here is the next good news. If we cannot spend the night together, we can at least share a romantic dinner together."

Now it was Tim's turn to frown, but his frown was real. He was confused. What the heck was she talking about?

"Timothy, answer the knock on the door, and the dance of our dinner will begin."

Tim slightly confused and a little perturbed started to answer, "But there is no knock, what are you…" Then there was a knock.

Tim's immediate response was to scan first for a weapon, then for an escape route. He immediately realized such thoughts were foolish, but reflexes are reflexes. He moved cautiously toward the door, peered through the eyehole, and asked "Who's there?"

"Front desk," came the reply.

'What is this?' Tim thought. 'A grade B movie?'

Then a distorted face moved into the vision of the peephole, and Tim recognized the building's concierge. The distorted face announced, "It's Pierre, the concierge. Madame Bouvier has sent us."

Tim let out an exasperated sigh and opened the door. His security, his precautions, her plausible deniability, all were now shot to hell.

As Tim pulled the door back a parade began. First through the door came Pierre, the concierge, who purposefully strode to the middle of the living room. He was followed by what seemed like four more little Pierres. The first one carried a small dinner table and placed it in front of Pierre the Concierge. He then pulled a white table cloth from under his arm and spread it over the table. From his left coat pocket came a small, crystal candle holder, while from his right pocket came a small white candle. He slapped the two together and placed the holder with candle in the left center of the table. Pierre the Concierge clapped, and little Pierre Number One bowed to Tim and left.

Pierre Number Two approached and placed a dinner plate and a bread plate on the table. From his left jacket pocket came utensils wrapped in a linen napkin, while from his right pocket came a bottle of wine. Pierre the Concierge clapped, and little Pierre Number Two bowed to Tim and left.

Pierre Number Three rolled a cart up to the table. From it he took a wine glass and placed it on the table about two inches above the top of the plate. Then with a flourish, he pulled away the cloth that covered the cart, revealing five silver domed plates and releasing aromas from what promised to be a tasty dinner. Pierre the Concierge clapped, and little Pierre Number Three bowed to Tim and left.

Pierre Number Four now approached. He was carrying, of all things, a laptop computer. He placed the computer on the table across from the plates; opened it; pressed a few buttons; and then smiled at his success. Pierre the Concierge clapped, and little Pierre Number Four, the computer magician, bowed to Tim and left.

Tim was surprised and smiling. There, sitting at the table across from him was Colette.

"Good evening, Timothy. Do you forgive me for changing our plans a bit?" she purred from the computer screen.

Pierre the Concierge had quickly moved a chair from the kitchen to a position in front of the plates and, with a theatrical sweep of his arm, offered the seat to Tim.

As Tim sat down, he replied to Colette in a make-believe stern voice, "No, I do not forgive you." Then more softly, "But I will so enjoy sharing this meal with you."

While Tim was talking, Pierre lit the candle, uncorked the wine, then turned to the computerized Colette, "Madame Bouvier, will that be all?

"Oui, Pierre. Merci beaucoup."

Pierre the Concierge bowed to Colette, turned and bowed to Tim saying, "Bon appetit, Monsieur" then left, closing the door behind him.

Colette spoke first, "Timothy, don't be angry with me. I think this is better than your silly spy precautions. Assuredly, Pierre and possibly others who work in my apartment building already knew you spent last night with me. This, my open act of affection for a close friend, is a good, what do you call it, cover story too, yes?"

"Yes, Colette. This is more than a good cover story, this is a wonderful cover story." Tim, surprising himself, meant every word of what he just said.

"Timothy, have you noticed the plates in front of you?"

Tim looked down and for the first time noticed the plates before him had an image of a plane on them. She had remembered his stories of "plates and planes" taking him to numerous spots around the globe on adventures both culinary and life affirming. Their two years together had been one of the most life affirming of those adventures. For the fleetest of moments his eyes fixed on Brileen's ring, with thoughts of its inscription. Yes, Brileen would approve of Colette.

Tim raised his eyes to the screen, "Very nice, Colette. Those conversations were so long ago, but you remembered. Then this! Thank you."

"Yes, I remembered. I remember a lot of our time together. But now, I just want to think about tonight. Well, OK," she smiled, somewhat coquettishly, "maybe I also want to think a little bit about last night, ...and maybe also about this morning."

Colette then talked, smiled, and laughed Tim through the removing of the silver domes that kept the dinner hot and fresh and then moving their contents to the plates on the table. As he "assembled" the dinner in front of him, she did the same. Colette had arranged that she and Tim would be eating the same dinner, laid out in the same manner, and complemented by the same wine, even though they were at tables more than 500 miles apart.

The dinner was Italian in tastes and origin. The appetizer was a Caprese Salad, named after the Island of Capri, where the salad's light and airy tastes originated. The main dish was Veal Piccata Bellagio, named so for the Bellagio Lake Region of Northern Italy, where veal is prepared in light sauces, oils, and white wines. The dessert was Dolce Crostata Napoli, a pear tart named, in this case by Colette long ago, for Tim's grandfather's place of birth, Naples, and also for the fact that his grandfather liked to add a little limoncello liqueur to his wife's recipe. There were two iced dishes of intermezzos, one with lime sherbet and the other with raspberry sherbet, to cleanse the palate between courses. The only part of the dinner not Italian was the bottle of Sancerre, a white wine from the Loire River Valley in France. Tim didn't immediately catch "The-What-Doesn't-Belong" significance of that wine, but Colette would soon remind him.

"Colette, this is so wonderfully imaginative. So thoughtful. It really is like sharing this meal with you," he said with real awe in his voice.

She was both pleased and wondering. She was pleased that he understood the effort it required to accomplish this evening. She was wondering, did he also understand the love that was involved?

"Timothy, do you remember when last we had almost this exact meal?"

Tim took on a deer-in-the-headlights look.

She laughed. "Timothy, look at this room." She picked up her computer and rotated it so he could see most of her surroundings. "Anything, Timothy?"

"Nice place. It must have set you back quite a few euros," he quipped.

"Honestly! Men!" an exasperated, yet amused Colette bug-eyed her face through the screen. "This is the Saint Regis."

No response from Tim.

She coaxed, "This is the Saint Regis Hotel on Piazza Ogniasante, near one of your favorite spots in Florence, the Ponte Vecchio."

Still no response from Tim the deer.

"Timothy, this is the same room we had when we last visited Italy together. This is the same meal we had in the hotel's restaurant on that last night in Florence."

Still the deer in the headlights.

In one final attempt to help him remember, she said, "Well, it's the same meal we had then, except for the wine. This is French wine, not Italian wine."

The deer was about to dart from the road to safety.

"Ah, yes, now I remember," Tim nodded. "As you said, it was our last trip together to Italy, about a month before I had to leave my NATO assignment in Belgium and return to the States."

He had almost said that the Florence trip was just a month before the last time he would ever see her, because she refused to leave with him. Luckily, his brain had restrained his mouth and prevented him from saying something that surely would have introduced a sour note into this wonderful evening.

"And yes," said Tim, "I remember what you told me about the differences between how a man should drink French and Italian wines. Even now, I remember that discussion every time I bring a glass of wine to my lips."

She was pleased. "Tell me. Let me see how good a teacher I was."

"Oh, you were a good teacher. I remember you said something like American men do not know how to drink wine. That we drink wine to quench our thirsts, while we should be drinking wine to nourish our souls. Then you got a little raunchy, comparing how French and Italian men drink their wines to the way they take their women."

"Raunchy?" she said quizzically. "What does this 'raunchy' mean?"

"Well, in your case, it means you're sometimes naughty, in a cute kind of way. That night in Florence you didn't like the way I was drinking my Italian wine. You thought I was gulping it down. Then you said Italian wines were like Italian women: full bodied, flashy colors, throaty tastes, and sweaty aromas. Then you added that Italian men, meaning me I suppose, drank those wines the same way they took those women: too fast, too lustily, and ending with too much headache and too little woman the next day."

"I said that?! I guess that was a little naughty of me, wasn't it?"

"Yes," said Tim, mockingly shaking his finger at her feigned wide-eyed innocence on the screen. "And also a little politically incorrect by today's standards."

"Now, my sweet little innocent Colette, pour yourself a bit

374

more of this Sancerre, and I'll remind you of what you said about French wine and French women."

The computer screen caught them almost simultaneously lifting their bottles and pouring more wine into their glasses, as if their movements were part of a choreographed couple's dance. Were they already acting as a comfortable, well-tuned couple again?

Tim moved aside his dishes and placed his newly poured glass of wine center table in front of him and in front of the screen. "What you said that night went something along these lines: a French wine and a French woman are alike in that a man should enjoy both slowly, savoring them completely, with all his senses, for the man would be much rewarded for doing so."

"First, the sense of hearing, coming into play as the wine is poured into the glass. Does it sound bubbly? Is there a hiss of effervescence? What kind of music plays in the man's mind as the wine lands on the inside of the glass and swirls itself into a full bodied presence before his eyes? Is this music light and sprightly for the whites? Firm and strong for the reds?"

"You also said that, just like with the wine, when a man first meets a woman, he should first listen closely to what she says, but even more closely to the way she says it. Only if he likes what he hears should he go further. Then you added that unfortunately men are not made that way."

"The sense of sight almost simultaneously comes into play. The wine should be poured into a crystal dress that shapes its form. The crystal glassware should enhance the wine's appearance, while at the same time allowing the wine's inner beauty and colors to come through to the beholder. Depending on the wine, its colors may be light and clear, dark and opaque, or many shades and hues between, but all beautiful to the eye."

"As for the sense of touch, the crystal dress should then be taken lightly in hand at the narrow waist of the stem, just like a woman on a dance floor. The man should then slowly guide the body of the wine through sunlight by day or through candlelight at night, in order to peer more deeply into and through its colors, learning more about its myriad shades within, anticipating more about the tastes these hues yet withhold."

"Next the sense of smell should draw in the wine's aromas, holding them in the nasal passage until types of fruits can be determined, like peach or plum; or types of grapes can be discerned, like pinot or merlot; or types of herbs can be detected. The scents of all these components should then be rushed to the brain, causing it to swoon or dizzy with pleasure."

"Finally, as you said, the sense of taste brings the fullness of meaning and pleasure from the wine. To accomplish this, the wine must first be brought gently to the mouth, so that just the smallest of tastes will alight on the lips and the tip of the tongue. Its presence there provides the first hints of the wine's sweetness or tartness, its flavors, its strengths, its warmth, its liveliness. A second, fuller sip should then be taken and held on the front part of the tongue and against the roof of the mouth. Here the wine tastes different than it did on the lips. All the hints of its potential that were given to the lips now become fuller and more apparent. The wine's full essence is released, now known and hopefully appreciated. Finally, the wine is then drawn more deeply through the back of the mouth, where again it tastes different than before, leaving a less lively but a still full, lingering taste that urges one to drink more."

"When taken slowly, fully, and sensually like this, the French wine, or the French woman, fulfills the man's spirit and excites his mind, leaving him contented and happy."

"Yes," continued Tim, "I learned and still remember that this slow, sensual process unveiled for me many facets of the varied scents, tastes, and secrets of French wines, ...and also of one particular French woman."

Tim, now holding his glass of wine gently by the stem, passed the Sancerre in front of the candlelight and took in its glow. He raised it to his nose and drew in its bouquet, letting it slowly drift upwards and inwards, discerning its scents along the way. After a moment he took a small taste, holding it momentarily on his lips and the tip of his tongue. Then he drew a second, larger sip and let it slowly flow onto the center of his tongue, there swirling it gently, savoring all its flavors. Finally, he let the wine glide over the back of the tongue, down into the warmth around his heart. All the while, he stared intently into Colette's eyes.

Colette moved closer in the screen. In a throaty whisper that came from somewhere deep within her, she said, "Timothy, I want you right now."

"And I you," he said with a passion, whose strength he found surprising.

After a moment, their eyes and souls unlocked, and a lighter mood began to grow as they talked of the food, of Italy, of their past trips there, and finally of Tim's grandfather and just how much limoncello he actually slipped into grandma's crostata recipe.

After much laughter, many smiles, and a few confident statements about tomorrow's expected success, they ended their dinner, and reluctantly darkened their screens.

Tim sat back in his chair. What was he feeling? Usually, when alone in his apartment, he felt solitude. Here, alone in Colette's apartment, he felt loneliness. Solitude was often good. Loneliness was almost always bad. Perhaps he needed to address this issue of loneliness more fully, especially now after having reunited with Colette.

Then his mind slapped him back into reality. "Stop acting like a love-sick teenager! The issue you need to address now is not loneliness. The issue you need to address is revenge. No, that's not right either. The issue is not revenge. The issue is justice."

Traditional Caprese Salad

Everyone's favorite, Tim was served this by all of his father's relatives. The recipe is simple and a staple of the Italian community, the difference being the ingredients. Not served until early July when the homegrowns are ripe, this is best when served with Italian Buffa Mozzarella. Tim uses Extra Virgin Olive Oil, a reduced balsamic vinegar, and adorns with chopped fresh herbs. Zia Mary once told Tim that if none of the relatives had fresh tomatoes, he could rely on the Greek families from Pawtucket because they really knew how to grow tomatoes (but don't tell her sisters she said that!).

Ingredients:(Four Servings)

1 to 3	Ripe, Homegrown Tomatoes
½ to 1 Lb	Mozzarella(Buffa/Water-buffalo-milk based)
4 Tbsp	Balsamic Vinegar
4 Tbsp	Extra Virgin Olive Oil
Salt/Pepper	To taste
1/8th Cup	Mixed fresh herbs

Directions:

1. Cut tomatoes into ¼ inch slices.
2. Cut mozzarella cheese into ¼ inch slices.
3. Arrange alternate layers of tomatoes and Mozzarella.
4. Salt and pepper, then drizzle with oil and vinegar.
5. Top with chopped fresh herbs.

Tips:

1. Don't skimp on the quality of the ingredients!

Veal Piccata Bellagio

A wonderful dish that is surprisingly easy to prepare – especially with a glass of white wine.

On a holiday to Italy with Colette, they traveled to the Lombardy region of Italy where he first sampled a true veal picatta – not the heavy Wiener Schnitzel that he had so much of in Germany. Many recipes and experiments later Tim was ready to serve this beyond the immediate family. One of the guests (who brought the Riesling) was with Tim in the kitchen and suggested the capers – they have been a part of this recipe ever since!

Ingredients:(Four Servings)

½ Cup	All Purpose Flour
2 Tsp	Salt
1 Egg	Whisked
½ Tsp	Lemon Pepper to Taste
4 - 6	Veal Scallops (3/4 to 1 Lb) Pounded thin
2 Tbsp	Olive Oil (Vegetable Oil OK)
6 Plus Tbsp	Butter
1 Cup	Dry White Wine (Riesling/Sancerre/etc)
¾ Cup	Chicken Stock
1 Clove Garlic	Crushed
1 – 2	Lemons for Lemon Juice
2 Tbsp	Capers
1 – 2 Tbsp	Chopped Herbs to Taste

Directions:

1. Combine flour, salt, and pepper; transfer to plate; dredge veal in egg then pat into flour (both sides); set aside.

2. Heat oil in large skillet until hot; add in 1 – 2Tbsp butter.
3. Sauté the veal quickly until just golden brown --- but not completely --- about one minute each side.
4. Transfer veal to a plate – you will cook this again.
5. With wine and chicken stock deglaze the skillet (reduce total to one-half the original).
6. Add the garlic, lemon juice, and capers. Cook for five minutes or until the sauce thickens.
7. Add remaining butter, salt, lemon pepper, and herbs; when the butter is melted add the veal back into the skillet.
8. Cook for about a minute or two; this completes the veal and allows the sauce to thicken.
9. Sample sauce and add herbs, salt, pepper, and lemon to taste.

Tips:
1. For a lighter coating – eliminate the egg and just dredge in flour.
2. For a heavier coating – add bread crumbs and/or parmesan cheese to flour.
3. For a more complex sauce add onions, mushrooms, and thin lemon slices.
4. Do not overcook initially, veal will toughen.
5. Canned or powdered chicken stock works well.
6. Pairs nicely with asparagus or green beans and scalloped potatoes.

Pear Tart (Dolche Crostata Napoli)

A simple yet elegant finish to a wonderful meal, the below recipe combines the convenience of the prepared crust with the availability of the thinly sliced pears. Paired with fresh whipped cream or vanilla ice cream, the only thing missing is the expresso.

Ingredients:(Six to Eight Servings)

Pie Crust	Prepared box type
1 Can	Sliced pears, drained and patted dry, and sliced thin
1 Pkg	Cream Cheese (8 ounce)
1 Tbsp	Vanilla Extract
1 Egg	Beaten
1 Tbsp	Almond Extract
1/3 Cup	Chopped Walnuts or Almonds
2 Oz	Calvados (pear brandy) or rum
2/3 Cup	Sugar
1 Tbsp	Ground Cinnamon

Directions:

1. Line a 9" tart dish with prepared pie crust, bake 15 – 20 minutes or until crust is golden brown.
2. Mix cream cheese, 1/3 cup sugar, vanilla and almond extract, chopped   nuts, and egg.   Drizzle Calvados or rum into mixture until blended mixture is smooth and spreadable.
3. Spread mixture over crust; arrange pears in circles on top.
4. Combine 1/3rd cup sugar and cinnamon; sprinkle over pears and cream cheese .
5. Cover edge of crust with aluminum foil collar to pre-

vent excessive browning. Bake at 375F for about 30 minutes or until filling is set.

6. Cool for one hour and refrigerate for at least two hours; slice and enjoy.

Tips:

1. Tart cooks will recognize a mixture of two recipes – one originally with almond paste and the primary one with cream cheese.

2 Purists may desire to substitute a homemade dough for the package mix.

3. Likewise, if fresh pears are available, they can be used instead of canned variations. Tim prefers a European brand of canned pears; popular US brands of pears are more often suited for canned fruit cocktail than a tart.

4. You can remove the baked shell and cook the final version without the tart dish; but Tim prefers to use a spring form pan or a "loose base" tart pan.

5. Tim's grandfather would routinely add a little bit of limoncello to the mix for some contrasting flavor.

CHAPTER 18: HIS DINNER

Day Seven: Sunday, 1015 hours, in Paris

Tim stood atop the Arch of Triumph. He was fifteen stories above the ground. He looked out over the twelve streets that radiated from the Arch out across Paris. He was at the symbolic center of French military history.

As a soldier, Tim thought of all the soldiers who had marched through this Arch, around this Arch, or were remembered on this Arch. He shared with these soldiers, with all warriors, their joy of victory, their sorrow of defeat, their loss of innocence. He knew about war. He had lived war. It was not all triumph.

The Arch is a massive edifice. Commissioned by Napoleon in 1806, it was not completed till 1836. It is over 15 stories high, half a football field in width, and more than 70 feet in depth. Napoleon, its inspiration, passed through it only once. The great warrior did not pass through it in triumph after battle as planned, but in a funeral procession, as his remains were returned to Paris in 1840, twenty years after his death in exile on Britain's island of Saint Helena.

After arriving at the Arch that morning, Tim had stood in a moment of contemplation at its Tomb of the Unknown Soldier, feeling just a tad disrespectful standing there in jogging clothes. The top of the Unknown's tomb was a large black stone slab, level with the pavement, outlined by copper bricks, and surrounded by a foot-high black chain barrier. At the head of the tomb was a copper-encased eternal flame. At the foot of the tomb was a copper sculpture of a military shield and a military sword. The shield symbolized the people's will to defend against tyranny. The sword symbolized the soldier's will to go to war in defense of the people. The eternal flame expressed the people's promise never to forget the soldier's sacrifice. Tim thought of the Tomb of the Unknown in Arlington. He thought of all the other tombs of the unknowns at which he had paid homage, stretching from Ottawa, to London, to Warsaw, to Tokyo. He prayed that all had ultimately found peace.

As he withdrew from the solemnity of the tomb, he slowly walked around the base of the Arch. He stopped at each of the four large sculptured scenes attached to its façade: one depicting Resistance, not wanting to go to war; another, Esprit in the March to Battle; the next, Victory; and the fourth, Peace. As he walked from one scene to the next, it was as if he were viewing sculptures of his own life's journey. However, left off the walls were the other sculptures, but not their ghosts; the ghosts of sorrow, of horror, of death. Civilians did not see those ghosts, but soldiers did.

As Tim ascended the almost 300 steps to the top of this Arch memorializing battles and wars, memories of his own ascent from a private in Vietnam to a senior officer in the Pentagon rolled through his mind. There was the defeat that was Vietnam and his loss of Quan. The victory that was Grenada and his loss of Brileen. The victory that was the first Gulf War which had unfolded like a Desert Storm. The victory-turned-into-defeat that was the second Gulf War, which had ultimately unfolded like a nightmare. So many places along the way. So many faces to go with those places. In many cases names had been forgotten, but never the faces.

As Tim now stood atop the Arch of Triumph, he felt personally triumphant, yet at the same time still unfulfilled. As he looked out across Paris, his mind looked far past the city's limits to places he had been, to people he had known, to things he had done. His life, like most people's, was filled with both joys and sorrows. Yet there was no doubt that he loved the life he lived, and lived the life he loved. He believed he lived the life he had been born to live.

Like most people in the quiet moments, and this was a quiet

moment, he asked himself the ancient question, "What does it all mean?" Getting no answer, he ruefully smiled to the heavens, took one last long look around the panorama before him that was Paris, then turned away, and headed back down to the reality of his present, the reality of an old soldier seeking revenge.

As he walked back down those 300 steps, the reality of the present was illuminated by a fantasy from the past. For some reason, at first totally incomprehensible to Tim, his mind presented him an image of Ingrid Bergman. "Now there's a beautiful woman," he thought. "No, not beautiful," he corrected himself, "she was more than just beautiful. She was alluring, totally alluring. But why her? Why here? Why now?"

His mind's picture started becoming clearer. Ingrid was in a scene from a post-World War II black-and-white film titled, "Arch of Triumph." "Ah, so that's why Ingrid has come to visit me. The mind does work in strange ways." As the scene with Ingrid became clearer, so did his memory of the film's plot. The male lead, whom Tim could not remember at the moment, had also been on a mission of revenge; revenge against a personal enemy, a Nazi officer; a revenge that also had its roots in war. This character had tracked the Nazi, had cornered him, had killed him, and then had successfully disposed of the body. Unlike most Hollywood films up to that time, the censors had allowed this killer, this avenger, to go unpunished.

Tim stopped his descent down the Arch for just a moment and asked himself, "Will the gods who censor men's acts also allow me to go unpunished?" When he received no answer, he answered himself, "We'll see!" Tim then continued his descent into the reality drama that would soon unfold, and end, in just a few days.

SUNDAY AFTERNOON

With the Arch of Triumph now at his back, Tim was beginning a slow jog eastward down the Avenue des Champs-Elysees, arguably the most famous and the most beautiful street in the world.

At least that's what the French were always ready to argue.

As for Tim, since he was unable even to pronounce the street's name correctly, it was doubtful he would ever enter into any arguments about the street's merits. However, on a clear, crisp, sun-shiny day like today, he had to admit that the street was indeed beautiful.

Tim intended to take a slow, one mile jog along the north side of the avenue, take a turn around the Obelisk of Luxor at the avenue's east end, then slowly jog back the mile along the avenue's south side. He could then say that he jogged what was arguably the most famous and the most beautiful street in the world.

It didn't escape Tim's sense of history that he was jogging along the avenue that had witnessed some of the most famous military parades of the past 200 years. He was following, or more correctly jogging, in the footsteps of soldiers who had marched in parades of French victories led by Napoleon; in parades of French defeats led by the German Generals of Bismarck in 1871 and Hitler in 1940; and again in parades of French victories following the end of WWI in 1919 and again in the 1944 liberation of France from Nazi occupation.

As sobering as these thoughts of war were, Tim also knew this avenue had seen many light and happy moments. One of those lighter moments came to mind as Tim saw the glint of sunlight reflect off the golden point of the 75-foot high Luxor Obelisk at the other end of the avenue. Egypt presented this 3,500-year old obelisk as a gift to France almost 200 years ago. Back in 1993, when Tim was stationed at NATO Headquarters in Belgium, gay activists in Paris conducted a night operation against the obelisk and covered all 75 feet of it in a bright pink condom. The message was "Prevent AIDS, Use a Condom." Needless to say, everyone at NATO had a good time at the expense of the French. That was until the French started posting pictures of the pink condom-covered obelisk with the caption, "Only 25 meters? So they must have used a Frenchman's "small size" condom!"

Just as Tim had jogged about a third of the way down the avenue, he saw a young woman doing something that made him slow down, then stop. She was turning a corner onto the Champs-Elysees eating one of the biggest cream puffs he had ever seen, and she seemed to be enjoying herself immensely. Tim circled back towards the girl, then looked past her, down the street from which she came.

There on the second storefront window, in large white letters, was the word "Boulangerie," the French word for bakery. Tim always acknowledged that he had many weaknesses. Since being a kid, one of those weaknesses was cream puffs. He approached the window and looked in. A slight gasp escaped his lips. There, displayed in cooling cases, were what seemed to be a hundred different kinds of crème puffs and éclairs. With so many choices, Tim had no choice. He went in.

Tim had a sweet tooth, and nothing satisfied it like a cream puff, except maybe two cream puffs. Back in his Washington office, Tim had an officemate, Franz, who fancied himself quite a chef. Franz would often bring in homemade cream puffs, knowing Tim would do almost anything to have one. Franz would always joke that his French maid, Yvette, had made them. Franz of course was referring to his lovely wife, Yvette. Who knows? Maybe Franz wore a chef's hat and apron, while Yvette wore a French maid's outfit, and they chased each other around the kitchen, as the puffs were baking in the oven. Tim didn't care. He just loved the cream puffs and éclairs that came from that oven.

One day Tim decided to bring in a half dozen éclairs from his local bakery to surprise Franz. Franz took one look in the box and said "Nein! Nein!. These are not éclairs. These are those Long John things!"

"What's the difference?"

"What's the difference?" exclaimed Franz in disbelief. "These -'things'- are made out of donut dough, yuk; filled with pudding, yuk; and then slathered with chocolate cake frosting, double yuk. What I bring to this office, my Yvette's éclairs, are made from light pastry clouds, baked till crisp and hollow inside, then filled with cream or custard, and finally drizzled with a chocolate ganache. And when I do it, I drizzle the ganache with panache!"

That weekend Franz invited Tim over for dinner. The evening's entertainment was having Tim make a batch of cream puffs and éclairs from scratch. In honor of Tim's half Irish heritage, Franz decided he needed to spice things up a bit "in the Irish way." So he added rum to the custard and Baileys to the ganache. Tim remembered the ganache recipe: take heated cream, pour it over chopped semi-sweet chocolate, stir or blend till smooth, then add Baileys to taste. Franz even taught him how to drizzle the ganache with panache! It had something to do with dripping the ganache onto the pastry from a height of no less than 12 inches, and only with the left hand. Hey, who knows? It seemed to work!

Tim was now sitting on a bench, along what was arguably the most beautiful street in the world, located in arguably the most magnificent city in the world, eating what unarguably must be the most delicious cream puff in the universe.

At that moment, life was good.

SUNDAY EVENING

After completing his interrupted jog around the Avenue des Champs-Elysees, Tim returned to his room, showered, dressed, and headed for Colette's. She was expected back from Florence about 5:30 PM.

Tim looked at his watch. It was 1530 hours. It was also 7 days from when last he had Zia Mary's meata'balls, and still no idea as to how many more days till he settled the score with Truc. However, he hoped that the information that Colette was bringing with her tonight would bring that day closer, much closer. He had a feeling, deep down, that it would.

On the way to Colette's, Tim stopped at a small international food market and purchased the things necessary for the night's dinner. Tim had decided to make a Greek salad. It was one of Colette's favorite dinners after a hectic day. Tim was pretty confident that she had had a hectic day.

Although they both liked Greek salad, they liked it made in

slightly different ways. "At least that used to be true. I wonder if it still is? There are so many things I don't know about her now," Tim said to himself, as he opened the cupboards looking for bowls, pans, plates, and glasses. He threw on a Billy Joel CD and started making the salad.

Real Greek salad doesn't usually have lettuce. However, both he and Colette liked it better with lettuce. The problem was she liked Romaine, but he liked Iceberg. He took the head of Iceberg, ripped off pieces, washed them, and into the bowl they went. Colette might remind him later that Romaine had more nutrients. He'd agree, but wouldn't care. Iceberg tasted better.

Next came the tomatoes. She liked Roma, but he liked Plum. She liked her tomatoes seeded, he didn't. He took the four Plum tomatoes he had bought, washed them, and cut them into wedges. Into the bowl they went, seeds and all. "I wonder if she'll remember?"

The tomatoes were followed by a cucumber. She liked them peeled and seeded, he didn't. Tim washed the cucumber, sliced it, halved the slices, and into the bowl they went; skin and seeds adding their flavors. "I wonder if she'll notice?"

Then came the bell peppers; washed, chopped, diced, and then mixed in with the rest. The peppers were followed by red onions, which were sliced, their rings and strings separated, then all dropped into the bowl. "If I remember correctly, we at least agreed on the peppers and the onions."

Two items remained: feta cheese and olives. Tim sighed, "Right, we certainly didn't agree on these. How did we stay together for those two years?"

First, he took the feta cheese. They both agreed that the feta had to be made the Greek way, from sheep's milk. However, Colette preferred Valbreso brand primarily Tim assumed, because it was made in southern France. "What a chauvinist she is," he muttered, as he unwrapped Dodoni feta, the brand he preferred. Dodoni was made in Greece, and there was no better feta as far as Tim was concerned. He started crumbling it into the bowl. "She should know and notice the difference, but she probably won't," he chuckled.

Now, for the olives. True, they both preferred black olives. However, that's where the agreement ended. Colette preferred the French Nicoise black olives grown only along the French Riviera. The Nicoise are rather small in size but have an enticingly mellow, nutty flavor. "God, she is such a chauvinist. What's the point of having a Greek salad, if everything you put in it is French!" He smiled, as he imagined the hands-on-hips pose she would take if he actually said that to her.

Tim preferred the Greek Kalamata black olives. Tim once picked these olives when visiting the city of Kalamata in southern Greece. While on the tree, the olives are a deep purple. It is truly a beautiful sight when a whole grove of these shimmering, glimmering, tasty, purple-black jewels are ripening in the sun. Now, every time he ate one, fond memories of his time in Kalamata were enjoyed along with the olive's incredible fruity taste. Tim pitted and chopped a cup full and spread them across the top of the bowl's other delights. Then he dropped in another half dozen or so whole olives, uncut and unpitted. He knew that Colette would daintily pick these out, nibble off the meat, slowly suck the flavors from the stone, then lick the remaining juices from her fingers. He knew she did this in an attempt to arouse him. He smiled at the picture and the memories of her usual success.

Tim had bought a bottle of light Greek salad dressing. Both he and Colette preferred to make their own dressing and surprise, surprise, they usually agreed on all the ingredients. However, tonight he did not have the several hours it took for all the ingredients to properly blend. Thus, the bottled stuff. He poured the dressing over the salad, stirred, tossed, covered it with plastic wrap, then placed it in the fridge. Hopefully, it would not be in there long, since Colette was due home shortly.

Next to the salad bowl was a box of stuffed Greek Grape Leaves which Tim had also purchased at the market. The grape leaves were wrapped around small amounts of seasoned rice and meat, and sealed with a mixture of olive oil, wine vinegar, and herbs. Stuffed Grape Leaves added a little heft to the salad. He would place four on each of their plates. One at each compass point.

Tim reached over and replaced the first Billy Joel CD with another. After a few minutes, he turned up the volume, grabbed a cucumber as a microphone, and began singing along with the Piano Man in a voice it was good only Tim could hear:

> "A bottle of white, a bottle of red
> Perhaps a bottle of rose' instead
> We'll get a ...da da la la da,
> La da la da da
> (Tim could never remember all the words,
> even when the Piano Man was helping him)
> "A bottle of red, a bottle of white
> It all depends on her appetite."

Well, Tim knew what her appetite would be tonight. It would be for a bottle of white and a night of him. Or at least he hoped so. However, it would not be her favorite love wine, a French Chenin Blanc, that would be on tonight's table.

"She's such a chauvinist," he repeated, smiling at the thought of her. "Nope, tonight there will be no French wine with this Greek salad."

He then uncorked a Greek Assyrtiko wine from the isle of Santorini in the Greek Archipelago. On the same trip in which he visited Kalamata, he also visited the beautiful island of Santorini. As he had picked olives in Kalamata, he had likewise picked Assyrtiko grapes on Santorini. Ever since that day, he loved the wines made from those grapes. The pleasure of those two days in the groves and vineyards picking olives and grapes, as well as the rest of that trip to Greece, was still a strong pleasure in his memory. He placed the bottle of Assyrtiko in Colette's wine chiller and placed the chiller on the table. He set their places. All was ready. All that was needed was Colette.

As Tim sat on her sofa waiting, memories of their earlier "salad days" played in his head, and in his heart. He could see her, smell her, taste her. He loved how those meals went. All smiles, and laughter, and smoldering eyes, and seduction. She would eat most of her salad with her hands. The salad's scents, its flavors, its oils would all transfer to her fingers. Her fingers would transfer them to her lips, and to her cheeks, and eventually into her hair, as she stroked her hands through it. Later, she would transfer those scents, those flavors to his lips, to him.

First there was the key in the door. Then there was Colette in the doorway.

He stood up. She let go of the handle of her overnight bag. They moved toward each other, embraced each other, held tightly to each other. Tim was surprised at his level of emotion. He knew he missed her. He hadn't known how much. He knew he wanted her. He hadn't known how much. Did she know how much? Well, he was holding her so tightly against him, it should not be too hard for her to guess.

Tim started to move back. Colette held him tighter. She whispered into his ear, "Do you want it now, or later?"

Tim stepped back. His face reddened. He started to stammer, "Well, ...errr, ..ahh...I thought maybe dinner, ..well, sure..." and took her hand to lead her to the bedroom.

She held back. "Not that, you silly. Men! Really! Is that all you ever think about?"

He was confused.

Colette explained, "You sent me on a mission, remember? I have brought back information. Do you want it right now or later?"

He reddened further. Sometimes he felt like such an ass.

But then he quickly reconsidered. Sure, sometimes he was an ass. However, this time he quickly realized she was toying with him again. She knew what she had said and more importantly, she knew exactly how she had said it.

Tim figured he'd call her bluff. "No, I don't want that now. I want you now." He again started dragging her off to the bedroom.

She laughed. She pulled him slowly back into her embrace. "I see you have set the table. Let's eat first. I'm assuming you have prepared us a light meal, with some Chenin Blanc?"

He kissed her again, slowly, less physically, but still as passionately. "A light meal, yes. Chenin Blanc, no."

"Hmm," Colette softly purred in a disappointed tone, "I'll be right back. Perhaps you'll have changed the wine by then?"

As Colette freshened up, Tim fixed the plates, poured the wine --the Assyrtiko, lit a candle, and turned on the music. This time it was Sinatra, a CD of his old 1957 vinyl, "Where Are You?" Tim loved Sinatra. In his boyhood Italian home, Sinatra was the music of his youth.

When Colette came back into the room, her eyes roamed in quick sequence from the table, to the salad, to the wine, to the candle, to Timothy. She smiled. Then her eyes moved to the CD player. "Timothy, could we change the music, please?"

"Of course. I just thought Frank would be good company for our evening," he said, as he moved to the player. "Sinatra has always been one of my favorites. I..."

Colette came to him, touched his arm, "I know you like Sinatra. I have come to like him too. I bought that CD after ...after we ...after we parted. At first, I played it every night. Later, I played it now and then. I still know every word to "Maybe You'll Be There" and "I Think of You." That album was to bring you close to me, when you were far from me. But tonight you are close to me, so I don't need Frank. I have you."

Tim was moved. Now, he really did want to forget about dinner. At that moment, he wanted to sweep her up into his arms and take her to where he could take her.

Colette continued, "That album is for lonely nights. Tonight is not a lonely night. Since I see that you still have that Greek wine on the table and those big ugly Greek olives in our salads, here - put in Yanni. He will keep the entire meal Greek."

Tim said nothing, but thought, "Wow, she had taken in all that while walking across the room. You just had to appreciate a woman like this!"

They walked back to the table, she holding his arm with her

cheek on his shoulder, and he with his heart on his sleeve.

After they sat down and toasted with the wine, a Greek wine she again reminded him, she leaned toward him and slipped two pieces of paper across the table.

"Timothy, let's get this out of the way now. I understand you're just trying to be thoughtful in not rushing me, but I know you want this information. I can only guess how much it means to you. Here, on the top piece of paper, is Van's name, his address in Spain, and his telephone number. You will see that 'Van' is not his real name. The second paper contains the name, address, and number of a friend of mine in Seville. If you need anything, and I say again 'anything,' my friend will help you; like you say in your movies, --no questions asked."

Tim froze for a second. There it was. Not six inches from his hand. All the information he needed. Spain? He wanted to grab the papers. Run from her apartment. Take the earliest train or plane to Spain. He wanted to do it all that very moment. But he didn't do it. Yes, he wanted to run after Truc. However, he did not want to run away from Colette.

"Colette, thank you for doing this for me. You are right, it does mean a lot to me. I have no words adequate to express just how much. I hope it wasn't too hard for you, dealing with your ex-husband. Was it?"

Colette looked at Timothy for a moment, wondering what was behind his question. Was Timothy really concerned about her? Or was he trying to find out if she still had feelings for Gerard? Was Timothy perhaps a little jealous that she had just spent the last 24 hours in romantic Florence with her former hus-band? Was she hoping that he was jealous, at least just a little?

Maybe a little of all of that was true. She then pushed all that aside and responded, "Surprisingly, no. In fact, Gerard was very nice. It seems he never trusted Van. Never believed Van was who he said he was, nor lived where he said he lived. Gerard was al-ways suspicious of him. At best, he thought Van was a criminal who could get Gerard in trouble if he wasn't careful. At worst, he thought Van might be an Interpol agent who was trying to entrap him. Often, art dealers work in the netherworld. What you call an underworld. While in that world, most of us try to be just short-term visitors, not long-term denizens."

She then tapped the second piece of paper in front of Tim. "This man here is of that netherworld, but you can trust him."

"Here's something interesting," Colette added, changing the subject before Tim could ask her any questions about Mr. Netherworld and how she had come to know him. "Remember those photographers in Heidelberg whom you were concerned about? Well, that was all Gerard's handiwork. When he heard that Van was coming to Heidelberg to close the deal, he called all the Heidelberg papers and told them a large, important art sale would occur and that they should cover it with writers and photographers."

"Then Gerard also sent a private photographer. Gerard wanted a good picture of Van. First, he wanted to send it to several other art dealers in order to know what information they might be able to provide on Van. Second, Gerard wanted to give some good pictures of Van to a private investigator whom he had hired to track Van when he left Heidelberg. It was that investigator who followed Van to this location in Spain and stayed there for a week to ensure it was Van's final destination. When the investigator was sure, he sent this information to Gerard."

"I hope that this is Van's permanent location," Tim said in a concerned tone, and with emphasis on the word, "permanent." For Tim, the word had two meanings. "And I can only hope he's still there."

"Oh, that is one more thing," Colette interrupted. "When I was in Gerard's office, he made a call to Spain. I do not know with whom he spoke. But he asked if Van was still there. When Gerard hung up, he confirmed that Van was still at this address in Spain. At least he was there as of 10 AM this morning."

Colette then looked down at the papers, then up at Tim and said, "Timothy, I'm really, truly surprised. I actually expected that after I gave you these papers, you would grab them, run from my apartment, and take the first night train to Spain."

Tim tried to feign a hurt expression. He wondered if he had pulled it off. He also wondered how this woman could still know him so well!

"Colette, I'm hurt. I thought you knew me better than that. Yes, this information is very important to me. However, you ...we, are more important." Tim surprised himself. After saying those words, he realized that he actually meant them. He was even more surprised that he actually continued to leave those papers, that holy grail of information, untouched on the table.

Tim started to back up his words with actions. He ignored the holy grail and concentrated on the dinner, their dinner. He talked about his tourist walks around Paris the last two days, his jog down the Avenues des Champs-Elysees (she laughed at his pronunciation), and, of course, the most wonderful cream puff ever. He thanked her again for her wonderful TV dinner the night before. She again laughed, this time in response to the term "TV Dinner." She made him laugh too. It felt good to laugh. It felt good to laugh with her.

Then she started. Colette put down her fork and started eating her salad with her fingers. There was her nibbling of the olives and her sucking of the juice from the stones. The onion strings were slurped slowly from her fingers through her lips into her mouth. Her fingers were wiped down along her neck and up across her cheeks. Bites of this and that were interrupted by long sips of wine which first stopped for tasting and glistening on her lips, then were drawn deeper for swirling across her tongue, and finally were freed to slip away down her throat with an "ahh.". Sometimes the wine glass never made it to her lips; rather, her fingers strolled around its rim, now and then dipping down into the wine, with the fingertips bringing back drips and dabs of the nectar to her lips where it was slowly licked into her mouth. She constantly wiped her hands through her hair, leaving aromas and scents hidden there while she went back for more. All of this was accompanied by frequent half glances, and coy glances, and smoldering glances.

Tim had had enough. A guy could only take so much. He got

up, grabbed her wrist, and said, "Enough! Enough, already. Come with me."

She got up smiling, but slightly pulled back against his pull forward. "But wait. We haven't had dessert yet!" she pleaded, with little conviction.

"You are the dessert. I'm in the mood for another French pastry," he answered, as he continued to gently pull her behind him.

She laughed, stopped pulling back, and started pushing him toward the bed. "Will you enjoy me as much as that cream puff?"

"We'll see," was his muffled response, as he began to lick her neck.

She laughed both lustily and lustfully with her throat, with her eyes, with her hands, with all of her.

They became the night's dessert.

SUNDAY NIGHT / MONDAY MORNING: THE WEE HOURS

Tim was awake. Colette was beside him, asleep. His mind was racing. Racing to Truc. To Truc in Spain. To Truc's termination.

His mind had fixated on a rewording of the "My Fair Lady" song, "The Rain in Spain." Tim's version went, "The train to Spain ends mainly in Truc's pain, ...in Truc's pain. Where will he be in pain? ...in Spain! ..in Spain!" Stupid little ditty, he realized. Nevertheless, there it was in his head, apparently forever. Tonight, sleep was not to be his. However, perhaps tomorrow, or the day after, revenge would be.

Greek Island Salad

While stationed in Belgium Tim was assigned to a NATO inspection team that traveled to Athens to investigate the possibility of stationing a US Navy Squadron of ships at the Piraeus Naval Base. Arriving on a Friday, Tim had the weekend to explore Athens. Not waiting for the rest of the party, Tim left the hotel, kept the Parthenon ahead of him, and started walking up! What a wonderful experience. On the way back to Constitution Square and his hotel, 'The George', Tim cut through the market area and with the sun setting over the Acropolis, found an arbored outdoor restaurant, surveyed the menu and other diners, and selected a simple Greek Salad. Tim was not only amazed with the simplicity of the meal but also with the wonderful taste of Greek tomatoes and olives. During the remainder of his trip to Athens, Tim always ordered a small salad and regretted that upon return to Belgium he could never find the same there. It was a few years later that Tim realized that all the "pseudo" Greek Salads were made with lettuce! Although Tim and Colette both like Greek Salad with some lettuce, when they want to be really native, they serve the below recipe.

Dressing Ingredients (Vinaigrette):(Four Servings)

3 Tbsp	Red Wine Vinegar
6 Tbsp	Olive Oil
1 Garlic	Minced
Salt/Pepper	To taste
2 Tsp	Fresh Oregano, chopped
2 Tsp	Fresh Dill, chopped
1 Lemon	Juiced

Salad Ingredients:

3 Tomatoes	Ripe and cut into chucks
½ Red Onion	Sliced thin
1 Medium	European Cucumber, sliced and cubed
1 Red Pepper	Sliced thin

1 Green PepperSliced thin
1 Cup   Greek Kalamata Olives
¼ Cup   Fresh Herbs, cut and diced
1 Tsp   Oregano
2 Pieces   Feta Cheese (about 6 Oz)

Directions:

1. Mix vinaigrette in a large bowl, add cucumbers, and set aside.
2. Combine remaining vegetables, olives, and herbs.
3. Pour the vinaigrette over the salad and let stand for 20 minutes.
4. Spread salad on plates and place a slice of feta on each.

Tips:

1. Feta can be served as slices, large chunks, or crumbled and mixed into the salad.
2. Often served with warm pita bread used to sop up the vinaigrette.
3. Tim uses whatever herbs are available in addition to oregano and dill.

Yvette's Cream Puffs

Tim's office mate would always bring these in for pot luck meals and no other dessert was ever asked for – everyone would sign him up for his wife's cream puffs! Tim finally convinced Yvette to share the recipes. Tim has been able to almost replicate the taste but he is sure she left something out – but it is still the best; a family favorite.

Pastry Ingredients:(Eight to Twelve Servings)

1 Cup	Water
½ Cup	Butter
4 Eggs	Whipped
1 Cup	All Purpose Flour

Pastry Directions:

1. Heat oven to 400F.
2. Bring water and butter to boil; add flour. Stir/whisk over lowered heat until mixture starts to ball – about 1 minute.
3. Remove pan from heat – add eggs and beat (electric mixer) until smooth.
4. Drop large tablespoons of pastry dough onto an ungreased cookie/baking sheet.
5. Space about 4 – 6 inches apart depending upon por-tion. Bake 35 to 40 minutes or until golden brown and puffed up.
6. Remove and allow to cool – see assembly directions below.

Filling Ingredients (traditional Crème Patisserie)

1 ¼ Cup	Whole Milk
3 Eggs	Yolk only
¼ Cup	Granulated Sugar

1/8 Cup	All Purpose Flour
2 – 3 Tbsp	Cornstarch
1 – 2 Tsp	Vanilla Extract

Filling Directions (Traditional Crème Patisserie):

1. Whisk together egg yolks, sugar, flour, and cornstarch until smooth – put aside. In a non-stick saucepan, warm the milk until it begins to steam.
2. Add half of warm milk to egg mixture – whisking constantly; add this mixture back into the remaining warm milk – stirring constantly (take your time on this step – you don't want to curdle the eggs).
3. Continue to heat for 1 – 2 minutes until very thick; remove from heat.
4. Stir in vanilla extract and chill until ready to assemble.

Filling Ingredients (The easy way):

1 Pkg	French Vanilla Instant Pudding Cream Filling
1 Cup	Cold Whole Milk
2 Cups	Chilled Heavy Whipping Cream

Filling Directions (The easy way):

1. Mix milk and pudding together at low speed.
2. Add chilled cream and beat about two minutes until mixture is stiff and forms peaks – refrigerate.

Assembly:

1. Cut off tops of baked puffs; using your fingers pull out soft interior dough of puff – eat or discard.

2. Spoon filling into puff; replace top; and drizzle with chocolate ganache.
3. Makes 8 to 12 cream puffs.

Tips:
1. Allow puffs to cool in a draft free space so they will not collapse.
2. Entire recipe can be made ahead of time. Leftovers keep well in the refrigerator.
3. This is one dessert that cannot be replicated from a box; spend time with the pastry – it pays dividends in taste!
4. French Vanilla Instant Pudding is a good choice for filling.

Chocolate Ganache

A favorite and versatile frosting, ganache is equally at home as a topping for éclairs, cream puffs, cakes, and even ice cream. It is a required staple of any pastry or confection maker. Yvette introduced Tim to a proper ganache when they first met and when the ganache met Yvette's Cream Puff, there was no separating them. This is a time-proven recipe; just start with a ratio of one and a half parts of chocolate to one part cream and enjoy.

Ingredients:(As Desired and Needed)

1 Cup	Heavy Cream
2 Tbsp	Unsalted Butter
2 Tbsp	Granulated Sugar
12 Oz	Semi-sweet Chocolate

Directions:

1. Break semi-sweet blocks into small pieces
2. Heat the heavy cream, butter, and sugar in a saucepan over medium high heat.
3. When hot, stir in the sugar and bring mixture just to a low boil.
4. Place chocolate in a heatproof bowl; pour the boiling cream over the chocolate and allow to stand for five minutes.
5. Stir until smooth and allow to cool before using.

Tips:

1. Another use of ganache is as a filling for truffles. Allow it to refrigerate and harden, roll into balls, and cover with nuts, powdered cocoa, or sugar and nuts.
2. You can easily add a flavoring or liqueur.
3. Use for topping of ice cream pie also in this book.

CHAPTER 19: ANOTHER TRAIN OF THOUGHT

Day Eight: Monday, 2000 hours, in a Train from Paris to Seville

The previous night at this time, Tim was having a great Greek Salad for supper with an even better French pastry for dessert. However, this night he was in the dining car of a train. He was not expecting such a great meal, but he was hoping for at least a good meal.

Tim looked at the stack of handwritten notes on the table in front of him. Colette's note with Truc's address was on top. Ronda, Spain. When he first looked at the note the previous night after Colette had given it to him, he had no idea where Ronda, Spain was. However, he knew where Spain was. He knew Truc was in Spain. That was enough.

So now he was again on a train; this time on a train to Spain. He reflected on how fate or his choices were bringing him to Ronda. He also reflected on what fate or his choices would have him do once in Ronda. "So, Truc, we will finally meet again, for the last time, in a place called Ronda, ...half way round'a da world from where it all started." He laughed, his phrasing of "round'a da world" making him think of the way Zia Mary always pronounced, "Meata'ball." Tim was feeling good. He was ready.

The thought of food brought him back to his present surroundings. He was sitting in the dining car of an Elipsos Trainhotel waiting for the dinner he had ordered, Basque Cod with fresh vegetables. Elipsos was, as Tim had learned during the day, a joint French-Spanish effort begun in 2001 to improve train travel between France and Spain. As far as Tim was concerned, Elipsos was a success. He had purchased a Grand Class ticket which provided a private cabin with a real bed and his own bathroom with shower. This "Trainhotel" also boasted a gourmet dining car which purportedly served chef-prepared meals with fresh ingredients provided daily. After a long day, he was about to test that boast.

While waiting for his dinner, Tim reviewed his day. After he had left Colette's apartment that morning, he had returned to his hotel and extended his stay there for another week, prepaying with his credit card. The credit card prepay was a modest attempt to add to the cover story of his still being in Paris should the need for a cover story arise. He then packed the things he thought he would need in Spain in his suitcase, walked two blocks from his hotel, and there hailed a taxi, telling the driver to take him to the Paris train station that had the best travel connections to Spain. Within 20 minutes, Tim was at Gare d'Austerlitz checking train schedules. He was disappointed to learn that a train did not go all the way to Ronda and that it would take him over 17 hours just to reach Seville, in southwestern Spain. From there it would take another two hours by car to reach the remote, mountaintop city of Ronda.

Tim seriously thought about flying to Seville. Again, it was a tossup between speed in getting to Truc and security for his cover story should the "termination" go awry. However, he soon realized that even if he flew out on the first flight available that day, he wouldn't reach Seville till late in the afternoon, would have to overnight there in a hotel, and then reach Ronda by car the next day around noon. The biggest drawback to that course of action was the need to provide identification to purchase the airline ticket and board the aircraft. Thus there would be an official record of his travel to Seville, something he did not want.

The choice to go by train would provide him better security, as he could buy his ticket with cash at the station without an official record of his identity. Of course there were always those damnable security cameras everywhere, but he would just have to be on constant guard and employ evasive measures as best he could. The big drawback of going by train was that it would take more time. By taking an overnight Elipsos Trainhotel, which was the only way to get there, he would not reach Seville until 3 PM the next day and not be in Ronda until 7 PM that evening. The result? Opting for better security by taking a train would cost him seven hours, the difference between arriving in Ronda the next day at 7 PM if he went by train, instead of noon if he went by air. In those seven hours would Truc leave Ronda? Tim thought that risk was low. He opted for security. He bought a train ticket for the Elipsos Trainhotel to Seville.

The next issue was that the train to Spain did not leave Paris till 6:30 PM. It was only 9:30 AM when Tim bought his ticket. What would he do for the next nine hours? For him there were only two choices. One, go back to Colette's and spend the day with her; a pleasant possibility. Or two, find an English library or bookstore and try to learn as much as possible about Ronda, his new battleground.

Going back to Colette's would be difficult, for it had been difficult to leave her that morning. As he had bent down to gently kiss her goodbye, she had opened her sleep-shrouded eyes, looked into his, and whispered, "Timothy, don't leave." She then rose onto her right forearm to be closer to him, and confessed, "I am afraid. I am afraid that perhaps what you have to do now is very dangerous, and you will not be able to come back to me. Or perhaps what you do now will finally set you free from whatever is torturing you, and then you will not want to come back to me." With that, her left hand drew back her bedcovers. Her heat rose to warm his face. Her scent rose to dizzy his head. Her beauty rose to excite his heart. "Timothy, stay here with me."

He sat down on the bed next to her, drifting his fingers across the sleepy softness of her face, "Colette, I can't stay. I want to, but I cannot. I must go. I must do this." He finished the gentle kiss he had started and moved away.

She looked up at him for a long moment and with what he hoped was one of her make-believe pouts grumbled, "I hate you." With that, she pulled the covers up over her head.

No, Tim decided that going back to Colette's was not the thing to do. After inquiring at the train station's information booth as to the best English bookstore or library in Paris, he stowed his suitcase in a locker, walked down the street about a quarter mile from the station's entrance, and flagged a taxi to take him to *Shakespeare and Company,* #37 Rue de la Bucherie. When he arrived, he was surprised to find that this bookstore was right next to the *La Petit Chatelet,* Colette's favorite restaurant where she and he had rekindled their relationship only three days before.

"Was it just three days ago?" he thought. "It seems longer. A lot has happened since then. What a coincidence to be here again." However, Tim didn't really believe in coincidence, but he was beginning to believe in fate.

Before entering the bookstore, he gazed a moment longer at the restaurant. He sighed to himself, "That was a wonderful meal. That was a wonderful night. She is a wonderful woman." He then opened the green, wooden, glass-paneled door to the bookstore and went in to see what The Bard and his company had to offer.

It did not take Tim long to realize the great find he had made in this bookstore. *Shakespeare and Company* had been opened by an expatriate GI after World War II. The GI had named his store after a bookstore and meeting place that had served the needs of expatriate writers in Paris during the 1920s and '30s; writers such as Hemingway, Fitzgerald, and Joyce. The Nazis had closed that bookstore while occupying Paris in the '40s. In the 1950s and '60s, this new *Shakespeare and Company* served a similar purpose to the previous one, but for a new generation of writers; writers like Ginsberg, Burroughs, and Baldwin. Tim also learned, while talking with the staff, that Woody Allen even included *Shakespeare and Company* in his 2011 movie, *Midnight in Paris.*

Now the bookstore was serving the needs of one Tim DePalma, and it served him well. He found several travel and photography books on Spain that contained information on and pictures of Ronda. No wonder Truc had chosen this city as his refuge. It was reportedly birthed as a Roman bastion outpost on the edge of then civilization. Now in Spain's southern autonomous region of Andalusia, it is perched atop high mountainous bluffs protected on three sides by 400-foot rock cliffs. Weatherwise, the area is one of the warmest in Europe, a characteristic that would appeal to a fugitive Vietnamese. Tim spent almost four hours researching, taking notes, and drawing maps. When he left, he felt confident in his battlefield analysis.

As he now reviewed these notes in the train's dining car, the waiter arrived and placed his dinner before him, "Monsieur, your Basque Cod. Bon appétit!"

Being a New Englander, Tim loved a good cod dinner. As he cut his first piece of the fish before him, he knew it would be good, as the cod was white, firm, and flakey. His first bite confirmed his expectations. The cod had been cooked in white wine; the wine's subtle taste still lingering. In addition to tantalizing his taste, the dinner's presentation excited his eye, with the golden baked cod encircled by colorful red cherry tomatoes, green and yellow peppers, and white onions. Furthermore, there was a slight aroma of basil to please yet another of his senses. Although Tim would have preferred a cold Bud with this meal, the chef had complemented his creation with a small bottle of Spanish Rioja White from the Rioja Valley wine region near Basque, an area along Spain's northern coast and the origin of this particular cod recipe.

After this surprisingly enjoyable meal, Tim collected his notes on Ronda and headed back to his cabin. Once there he stretched out on his bed. He was ready for whatever tomorrow would bring.

It seemed that while travelling on trains over the past week, whenever his body was confined within those trains, his mind had often wandered to regions and times far beyond the tracks. However, this time his mind focused primarily on what would happen when he came to the end of those tracks.

Tim began reviewing his plans. A warrior, whose wars had begun in jungles forty years ago, now prepared for one more battle, perhaps his last battle.

Just as he had been taught to do so many years ago as a young Lieutenant, he began reviewing the five "W's" of the mission planning process: the What? Who? When? Where? and Why?

The What. The "what" would be a "termination." "Stop with the foolish euphemisms," Tim told himself. "Call it what it really is; it's a kill. No, Tim, you're still not being honest with yourself. Remember Sun Tzu. 'Know yourself, know your enemy. A hundred battles, a hundred victories.' So be honest with yourself. Is what you're going to do a kill? No. No, it isn't a kill. What I'm going to do is a murder."

Tim's being honest with himself called forth a memory from long ago. He was in a jungle, in a tent, in confession. After his first firefights in Nam, he had been troubled. He sought out his chaplain and asked, "God's Commandment says, 'Thou shalt not kill.' Yet my country, my Church, my generals, and even you, Chaplain, send me into battle to kill. Is God OK with what I'm doing?"

The chaplain was silent for a very long moment. Then from behind the olive-drab towel that hung as a confessional cloak between them, "Soldier, I believe God is OK with what we are doing here. It was God who sent David against Goliath, Joshua against Jericho. Go in peace knowing that you are doing the work of the righteous."

"But father," countered Tim. "David and Joshua were warriors of the Old Testament. Did not Christ bring a new message of peace and love in the New Testament?"

Again the chaplain was silent for a long moment. Then, "You ask a hard question that all we Christian soldiers must grapple with. From my studies for the priesthood, it is clear to me that the authors of the original gospel texts, all written in Greek, attributed to Christ the phrasing of the commandment as being 'Thou shalt not murder.' There is great difference between lawful killing and murder, which is unlawful killing. I have become confident that Christ supports the soldier's lawful defense of the weak, the soldier's lawful protection of the defenseless. As a soldier like you, I also take comfort in the words of Saint Paul in the Bible. When speaking to the Romans, he said that the righteous government does 'not have a sword in vain;' that the righteous government uses that sword as 'an avenger to execute wrath upon him that does evil.' Soldier, you and I are that sword."

Those words had fortified Tim through many battles across many years. But this next battle, this next kill, would not be one done in the service of a righteous government. However, this did not bother Tim. He knew in his soul that this coming kill, although perhaps an unlawful one, would still be a righteous one.

The next "W" was the Who. The "who" for the soldier-planner was both the "who" of the friendlies and the "who" of the enemy. The soldier-planner must gather all the information he can obtain on both of them and their capabilities. He must come to "know" them both in the sense that Sun Tzu meant. Tim of course knew who he was and his own capabilities. He also knew who Truc was, but he did not know Truc's present capabilities.

Yes, Tim knew "who" Truc was. Truc was a traitor to his country. Truc was the man who tried to murder Tim. Truc was the man who did murder Quan. Tim thought back to the night with Quan's father in the garden that was his family's cemetery. That night Quan's father had retold the story of his daughter's death almost as if it had been an accident. Tim had never believed there was anything accidental about it. He knew from his own experience that Truc was a coldblooded killer. In his mind that night in the garden, in his mind a thousand times since that night, and in his mind right now tonight, Tim saw Truc brutally killing Quan because she would not believe his lies, would not go with him, would not love him. Tim clearly remembered the last time he had seen Truc on that ambush road so long ago. He clearly remembered the last brutal words he had heard Truc threaten, "If I cannot have her, no one will have her." Oh yes, Tim knew "who" Truc was. Truc was a killer; a killer who was about to be killed.

However, although Tim certainly knew "who" his enemy was, he did not yet know all of his enemy's capabilities. Would Truc have weapons to defend himself? Would he have guards? Both Peter Buckner, the gallery owner in Heidelberg, and Colette had said that Truc had a personal bodyguard while in Heidelberg. Would he still have that guard? Other guards? Only the final reconnaissance in Ronda would tell. In truth Tim didn't care how many enemy there would be in Ronda. He would be the avenging sword that would deliver righteous wrath upon this traitor, this murderer, as well as upon all those who would try to protect him.

The next two "W's," the "When" and "Where" of Tim's plan were still a little murky. The "where" of course would be in Ronda. But specifically where in Ronda would depend on Tim's final reconnaissance of Truc's home and his movements. But for the moment, just knowing that Truc was in Ronda was enough to move forward. The "When" would start tomorrow with Tim's arrival on the battlefield. It would end with Truc's death. Tim planned for an operation of three days, starting with his arrival and ending with Truc's departure.

The fifth "W," the "Why" of the battle plan was always the hardest. Not only did the "Why" call for a detailed understanding of the causes of the battle or the war, it also called for a detailed understanding of the desired outcome for that battle: "Why" did one go to war? This "essential why" is the desired end state, the goal the warrior wants to achieve. Is it just the death of the enemy? The destruction of his army? The occupation of his country? The total annihilation of his culture? For Tim, for this battle, he now knew the final goal was not revenge. The final goal was justice for Quan and peace for his own soul. Tim believed Truc's death would achieve both.

In a soldier's planning process, the information gathered in answering the five W's is used to answer one last question, "How?" How will the soldier use his assembled information on the time, place, and means available to achieve the ends he desired? For the coming battle the general time and place were known and would soon be refined to a specific time and place. The desired ends were also known: death for Truc, justice for Quan, peace for Tim. The means? Tim slipped his hand into his suitcase and withdrew the Spanish dagger. When he purchased this dagger in Mannheim along with the more practical switch-blade, he hadn't really known why he had selected this weapon. He had just liked its look and feel. Now this dagger, really a mini-sword, seemed the perfect means to avenge the death of an innocent young woman from so long ago, at last providing her justice.

The "How," the exact detailed battle plan of how Tim would kill Truc would have to await his final reconnaissance. Then he would decide the final time, place, and actions of the kill.

Tim placed the dagger on top his suitcase, then reached up and switched off the light above his bed. He closed his eyes, exhaled a long sigh, and slept the sleep of the righteous.

Basque Cod with Fresh Vegetables

This popular dish, found along the Atlantic or Mediterranean coast, is a simple but classic recipe - a standard both around family tables and in restaurants. This recipe is from the Basque autonomous region along the northern Spanish coast. There are similar recipes from many other countries, especially France, Portugal, and Italy; all featuring a flakey white fish and colorful salad vegetables. These recipes have changed little over the decades and feature the local catch prepared simply with local vegetables. Tim had first tasted a version of this recipe at a friend's house in the Portuguese ethnic enclave in Bristol, Rhode Island. Since then he has tasted many variations, the one on his train to Seville being one of the best.

Ingredients:(Two to Four Servings)

1 – 2 Lbs	Flakey White Fish Fillets (Cod or other)
1	Large Onion
1 Lb	Cherry Tomatoes, cleaned and cut
1 – 2	Colorful Bell Peppers, thinly sliced and chopped, with pith and seeds removed
¼ Cup	Capers
1/3 Cup	Extra Virgin Olive Oil
½ Cup	White Wine
½ Cup	Mixed Fresh Herbs, chopped
Salt/Pepper	To Taste

Directions:

1. Preheat oven to 400F.
2. Cut onions, peppers, and cherry tomatoes - toss and combine with olive oil, herbs, and capers.
3. Pat dry fish filets and season both sides, place in a large oven dish, cover with sliced/chopped vegetables, and add white wine. If desired, add salt and

pepper.

4. Bake in oven for 30 minutes, or more, depending upon the thickness of the fillet.
5. Remove from oven when fish is white and flakey.
6. Plate either as a complete dish or with rice.

Tips:

1. Can be prepared using either a whole cleaned fish or fillets; thick filets provide more consistency.
2. Tim uses a mixture of green, red, and orange bell peppers – a colorful addition.
3. The Italian version includes sliced mushrooms and a chunky tomato sauce vice sliced cherry tomatoes.
4. Serve with a crisp, cold white wine and crusty bread.

CHAPTER 20:   REVENGE. AVENGE. JUSTICE.

Day Nine: Tuesday, 1700 hours, in Seville

Tim sat in an outer office in a large warehouse building located alongside Seville's main train yard. There were two other individuals in the room with him, a beautiful young Spanish woman who spoke very little English and an ugly older Spanish man who hadn't spoken anything at all. The young woman had taken Tim's note from Colette, the note listing Colette's "netherworld" contact in Seville. She took the note to someone behind the door separating the outer office, where Tim sat, from what he assumed was the inner office where the Netherworld Man sat. Now Tim was alone with the ugly silent Spaniard standing with his back against the far wall, just watching Tim. He probably didn't like what he saw.

Tim had changed since arriving in Seville. Immediately after getting off the train he had placed his suitcase, along with his identification documents and Brileen's ring, in a station locker, and then corralled a taxi, telling the driver in equal parts English, Italian, and hand language to take him to a secondhand clothing store. Once in the store, Tim purchased two old shirts, a pair of baggy pants, a set of old clip-on suspenders, some hard-worn work boots, and a small, tattered suitcase just a little bigger than a briefcase. Upon exiting the clothing store, he entered a restaurant across the street and headed for its rest room. There he took off and discarded his traveling clothes and put on his newly-bought old clothes. He placed the extra shirt and socks in the tattered case. As he walked to a taxi stand about a block away, he scooped up a handful of dirt from a storefront flower pot and rubbed it deep into his hands and forearms, pushing as much as he could up under his fingernails. The little that was left he wiped on his pants and shirt. By the time he reached the taxi stand, he was a poor, itinerate Italian worker, Niccolo Poverelli.

Niccolo now sat in the outer office of the train yard warehouse staring at his work boots. The old Spaniard stood staring at Niccolo. The secretary was listening to the phone that had just buzzed on her desk, then said, looking at Niccolo, "OK, entra." The clock on the wall chimed five times. It was 5 PM. Tim was already behind schedule.

As Niccolo rose to enter the inner office, the old Spaniard moved into his path, barring him from entering. He motioned to Niccolo to raise his hands over his head. The Spaniard then roughly frisked him.

As Niccolo entered the office, the man behind the desk appeared to be preparing to come forward and shake hands. Apparently after seeing Niccolo, the man thought better of it. He stayed behind his desk and said, "*Hola, Senor Poverelli. Mucho gusto.*"

Seeing the dull look in Senor Poverelli's eyes, the man behind the desk added, "*Hablas espanol, Senor Poverelli?*"

Following Niccolo's negative shaking of his head, the man tried once again, "*Parlez-vous Francais?*"

"*Je ne parle Francais,*" answered Niccolo. "*Je parle italien et anglais.*"

"Well then," said the man behind the desk, "since you speak both Italian and English, and I do not speak Italian very well, let's speak in English. My name is Francisco Delgado. Please sit. What can I do for you?"

Niccolo did not attempt to move forward and shake hands. Rather he responded as directed and meekly sat down in front of the large desk. As Niccolo did so, Tim made a quick appraisal of Senor Delgado. He was tall, dark, handsome and ...a snake. What were Colette's ties to him? Tim hoped they had not been close, personal ones.

Niccolo spoke up, "Sir, I do not speak good English, so please speak slow with me. I just come from Paris today. I want to stay and work in Spain. I need'a car. Madame Bouvier give me one thousands euros. She say maybe you will'a help me. Will you?"

Senor Delgado raised his eyebrows when hearing that Madame Bouvier had given this sad-looking Italian a thousand euros, obviously to run away from somebody, probably the law, and hide in Spain. Delgado, slowly turning over Colette's note in his hands, asked, "Why did Colette give you one thousand euors, and why did she say I could help you?"

Tim judged that Delgado's use of Colette's first name was an attempt to see just how familiar, or maybe even intimate, this Italian was with Madame Bouvier. Niccolo answered, "Sir, Madame Bouvier always kind to me. I work as gardener for'a her and Monsieur Bouvier when they had'a house outside of Paris. Before they divorce. I do not know why she say you will help me. She just say maybe you will."

Tim thought it interesting that Delgado made no outward sign of being surprised that Colette was divorced. "Hmm. Has he known her since her divorce?"

Delgado asked Niccolo more questions, mostly about what kind of trouble he was in, what he would be using the car for, and where he would be going in it. However, a few other questions were but lightly veiled attempts to find out more information on Colette and her relationship with this Mr. Poverelli. Niccolo answered all Delgado's questions. He answered them all with lies. Hopefully, believable lies, for Delgado was obviously not a man to be trifled with.

Francisco Delgado sat in his chair looking at this Niccolo. Undoubtedly something wasn't right about this immigrant. Under other circumstances he would have him roughed up a bit till the truth came tumbling out. However, this ostensibly itinerant Italian laborer, speaking in a fake broken-English accent, came with a note from Colette requesting help, written in her hand, and on her stationary. He could not refuse Colette.

Delgado picked up the phone, punched in a number, and directed the person on the other end in Spanish, "I'm sending you a Mr. Niccolo Poverelli. He will give you one thousand euros. You will give him the old tan Fiat we have in building number three. ...Yes, I know it has no air-conditioning. Make sure it has passable plates and papers. Also include a six month temporary driver's license, but one without a picture. Explain to him what to do with the car when he no longer has a use for it. Of course, clearly explain to him the parameters and consequences of our special relationship should he ever wish to reveal it."

Delgado again looked at Senor Poverelli, "Niccolo, is there anything else I can do for you?"

Tim thought about asking for a gun, but then quickly thought better of it. Way too many complications. "No, Senor Delgado. You help me very much. Thank you."

As Tim was walking out of the office, Delgado asked, "Niccolo, where did you learn your English? You speak it very well."

Niccolo stopped, turned, and said, "I study it in school when I'a little boy in Napoli. I not use much. Again, thank you senor Delgado. Arrivederci." With that Niccolo left.

Francisco Delgado sat down behind his desk. He wondered, "Why is Colette involved with this Niccolo? Almost everything he just told me was a lie. He is obviously an American trying to pass himself off as a poor Italian laborer, and he's not doing a very good job of it? I must call her tomorrow. No matter the story, it will again be a pleasure to talk with Colette."

THE ROAD TO RONDA

Day Ten: Wednesday, 0900 hours, on the road to Ronda

It was 0900 hours (9 AM) the next morning after his meeting with Delgado, and Tim was finally on the road to Ronda. He was already 14 hours behind schedule in his battle plan. This was not a good way to start what might be his final battle.

Every soldier knows that the battle plan rarely survives the battle. Once a battle starts, the plan usually undergoes some revisions due to unexpected changes in enemy behavior, weather conditions, or terrain impediments. More often than not, the plan undergoes many such changes as the battle unfolds. However, Tim's plan started to fall apart even before he got to his battlefield.

The problems started the previous afternoon. First, the train had arrived in Seville more than an hour late. Apparently trains from France to Spain did not operate as efficiently as trains from Germany to France. Surprise! Surprise! A second problem arose when Tim decided to change the disguise he was going to use when meeting with Colette's contact, Francisco Delgado. Initially he had planned to use the suit, shirt, and shoes he had purchased to create Angel Napolitano for Paris. However, for Seville he was going to use those clothes for a new character, one who was a pleasant, outgoing, Italian businessman from Florence. At the last minute Tim thought better of that approach, because it would take too much time to develop the backstory, and besides he decided he didn't really want to engage Delgado any longer than he absolutely had to. He just wanted to get in, get a car, and get out. This last minute change in disguise resulted in extra time needed to find a secondhand clothing store. Finally, although the meeting with Delgado was fairly brief, the wait to get in to see him had been longer than expected, as was the drill Tim had to go through to finally get the car. Although he had planned on being in Ronda by 1800 hours (6 PM) last night, he didn't even drive the car out of the Seville warehouse area until 2000 hours (8 PM).

Because of those problems, Tim decided against driving the long, desolate road to Ronda at night, probably arriving about 2300 hours (11 PM) with no place to stay once he got there. So he remained in Seville, a city certainly big enough for him to remain comfortably anonymous. His research at *Shakespeare and Company* in Paris told him that Seville had a population of about 700,000, making it the fourth largest city in Spain. It was also the capitol of one of the poorest regions of Spain, the autonomous region of Andalusia. Tim thought the city itself, what little he had a chance to see, was nice in an old-world-charm kind of way, especially the city's Old Town section. However, he chose to spend the night in a seedier part of the city where rundown hotels didn't ask for identification, just for euros.

Last night it was already after 9 PM when Tim paid just 30 euros (about $40) for his room, indicating the quality of the hotel he ended up in. Even though it wasn't quite a 4-Star Hilton, it asked no questions and required no credit cards. Further on the plus side, it did provide some much needed advice on close-by places to eat. Tim hadn't eaten since lunch and that was just a sandwich on the train. To say he was famished, pretty much captured the truth. According to the hotel's night clerk, there was a passable restaurant about a block from the hotel, but it closed at 10 PM.

Within a few minutes Tim was seated in this small eatery which had about 10 wooden, 4-person tables, all with naked tops except for each having a pair of plastic white and black bull-shaped salt and pepper shakers. There was only one other person there, an apparently dual-purpose waiter and cook about 40 years old who, by the look of him, had already put in a long day.

The waiter-cook spoke only Spanish. After a few moments of fruitless Spanish-English babble, Tim decided to hold up his end of the conversation in Italian, a not too distant sister Romance language. However, apparently the sisters weren't getting along very well that night because the ordering was going nowhere. Finally after hearing the waiter shout the words "La especial de hoy" several times, Tim guessed the guy was trying to tell him to have "The special of the day." Tim smiled and said, "Si, si. La especial de hoy!" The cook smiled in return and disappeared into the kitchen.

Tim wondered, "What the heck am I going to end up with? Doesn't matter. I'm hungry enough to eat one of these here plastic bulls, and I just might, if the cook doesn't hurry." As Tim sat there, he started reviewing his day and planning for his tomorrow.

Tim was surprised, as the cook returned in less than five minutes with his dinner. The good thing about having a restaurant's "La Especial de Hoy" was that often a good amount of it was already prepared and waiting in the kitchen. Then Tim was doubly surprised when he looked at the plate: two grilled lamb chops with a side order of grilled vegetables! Had Tim been able to read the menu, this meal before him probably would have been the one he would have ordered. Then Tim was triply surprised after he took his first bite. The lamb was juicy, tender, and tasty. The only problem Tim had was that the chops were small, with only two or maybe three bites per chop. Tonight he needed more. Speaking this time only in universal hand language, he ordered two more chops and a glass of red wine. He smiled, thinking "I'm going to remember this dinner tonight as *Triple Surprise Spanish Lamb Chops.*" It was already a good memory.

In his younger days Tim had closed many a bar after great nights of drinking and partying. As he walked back to his hotel, he sighed, "Instead of closing a bar at 2 AM after a long night of great partying, I'm now closing restaurants at 10 PM after a short night of good eating. My definition of a good time has sure changed over the years."

The next morning, after a good eight hours of sound sleep, Tim needed a little exercise. Running would have drawn too much attention, and besides he had no running gear. So he just walked the streets for about an hour.

A sidewalk cart, which sported a large sign that read *"Empanadas"* and was surrounded by irresistible aromas, became his breakfast spot. Tim soon found out that empanadas were small fried pies in half-moon shapes, usually containing meats and vegetables. To Tim they looked a lot like the small piroski meat pies that he had first tasted as a boy in the Polish neighborhoods close to Federal Hill and had later grown to love in cold winter visits to Moscow. His first bite however told him that the Spanish version of this pastry pocket was a little different. These empanadas tasted a little livelier, moistened by the inclusion of onions, olives, raisins, and spices. Tim ordered three more to take with him on his ride to Ronda.

As Tim was driving out of Seville, he decided he liked this city. Before his day spent at the *Shakespeare and Company* bookstore, Tim had only known two things about Seville, and he had learned them both from his Uncle Carmine. First, Tim knew that Seville claimed as one of its famous sons some crazy barber named Figaro. Uncle Carmine was a big opera fan, and his favorite comic opera was *The Barber of Seville*. Carmine would add to it his own brand of comedy whenever Tim's grandfather, Ernie, who was a real barber, would enter a room. Carmine would jump up and sing the opera's aria, Figaro-Figaro-Figaro, while dancing in circles around Grandpa Ernie. Carmine always thought this was hilarious, except for the last time he sang for Grandpa Ernie. The last time he sang Figaro for Grandpa Ernie, "The Barber of Providence," was at Ernie's funeral. There wasn't a dry eye in the church.

The other thing Tim knew about Seville, again from Uncle Carmine, was that Christopher Columbus was buried there. He had also learned that this was not a good thing. Uncle Carmine was a major force behind the annual Columbus Day Parade in Providence. Since more than half the city was Italian, this was a big celebration. Carmine had a pet project he always made part of the city's Columbus Day festivities: a petition to move Columbus' tomb from Seville, Spain to Genoa, Italy, Columbus' birthplace. If Genoa didn't want to participate, then the petition called for Columbus' tomb to be relocated to Providence, preferably to somewhere on Federal Hill. Every year at the parade, Tim would help his Uncle Carmine gather signatures. These petitions never achieved anything, but Carmine always had a good time. Carmine became known around Providence as the "Italian Soldier of The Unmoved Tomb."

"Too bad I don't have time to visit Columbus' tomb now," thought Tim as he sped away from the city that entombed that tomb. "A picture of me with old Chris would make a great memento for Carmine. Perhaps another day."

Then a much needed thought pushed its way to the forefront of his consciousness, "Geez, Tim. You're not here on a tourist visa. Get your head back in the game!"

Tim spent the next two hours getting his head back in the game. However, what was about to happen was not a game. It was literally a life and death situation, -Tim's life and Truc's death.

RONDA

The road had been long, in many places harrowing, in some areas lonely, but everywhere beautiful, ...and hot, especially in a car without air-conditioning. Now at the end of that road, appearing before him like a granite fist exploding up through the valley floor, was the giant rock outcropping on whose top, protected on three sides by 400-foot cliff walls, was Ronda. As Tim's Fiat climbed the ascending road to the ancient fortress, he was truly struck by its sheer brutal majesty. As he entered through its ancient gates he was equally struck by man's added beauty of an entire city of white stucco buildings with red tile roofs, hardly any building being more than three or four-stories high, creating one of the great White Villages (Pueblo Blanco) of southern Spain. As he began to weave through the winding, hilly, cobblestoned streets, he soon passed by the city's ancient bull ring, purportedly the first bull ring in all of Spain. Did that ancient battleground know a new matador had just entered town?

In accordance with his plan, he slowly drove through the oldest parts of the city, studying traffic patterns, noting bottlenecks, and testing several alternate routes from the city's gates through its congested heart. He wanted to become as familiar with the city as possible in the shortest time possible. There may come a moment in the next few days when he might have to make a quick, unplanned retreat from the city or quickly find an effective hiding place within its more crowed neighborhoods. When the hour he had allotted for this general city reconnaissance passed, he took a quick look at one of his hand-drawn maps, then headed for the spot where he hoped he would do his final reconnaissance. After that, he would be ready to complete his mission.

Tim was beginning to sweat. He could feel the driblets finding their ways down his sides. The day's heat was a partial cause. The day's mission was the primary cause. Tim could feel the tension build. He didn't mind. It would keep him alert, aware, alive.

He was finally on "the" street. It housed individual, one-story, white stucco homes on small plots, the even-numbered ones being on Tim's left and backed up to the very edge of a high rock cliff. That location provided both stunning views and excellent security. He counted down the house numbers on his left as the Fiat rolled along, the sweat now rolling down his sides in seeming rivers. There it was, #32, the last house on the street.

Tim continued on around a curve and behind a hill. He parked there on the other side of the hill and climbed the backside to its top, which was covered by a small forest, and moved through the forest to the other side of the hill. There he squatted, several yards back from the edge of the tree line and behind a small stand of bushes. Down the hill and about 300 yards to his front was Truc's house.

TRUC

All was quiet on the distant street below. It was now 1300 hours (1 PM). Tim had not eaten since breakfast. He opened the small tattered suitcase which he had carried with him from the car to the hill top. Along with his extra clothes, the case held a couple of the wrapped empanadas he had bought from the food cart that morning before leaving Seville, a small pair of tourist binoculars which he had bought from another street vender, and the dagger. The switchblade was in his pocket. He was still dressed as Niccolo, but his every thought, his every move was all Tim. Without moving his eyes from Truc's house, he took an empanada from the case, unwrapped it, and took a few bites. Then he made a trade with the suitcase, the half-eaten empanada for the binoculars.

The binoculars were certainly not the greatest, but they did provide Tim a better view of the house. The house appeared modest by American standards, but was probably substantial by Ronda standards, a crowded city where space was probably always at a premium. Tim guessed the house's area at about 1200 to 1500 square feet. It probably had three bedrooms, a sitting room, a kitchen, a bathroom, maybe a bath and a half. There was also a chimney, suggesting a fireplace or wood burning stove for the short winter. It was one of the few houses on the street that had an attached garage. There were probably three entrances/exits, although Tim could only observe one, the door located in the front which was bracketed on each side by a small tree, a large potted plant, and several low-cut bushes. No place for Tim to hide there. Good security. He assumed another door led from the garage into the house. A third door was probably located at the back of the house. From his observation post atop the hill, Tim could only see part of the backyard, the part near the cliff, but not the back of the house. However, he could see about half of a satellite dish sticking out from under the back roofline, suggesting either TV or computer service, or most probably both. Surrounding the house was a 4-foot high stucco wall with two breaches, one for the front gate and one for the gated driveway. The wall was high enough to deter unwanted animals, kids, and even adults, but would not deny someone intent on approaching the house. The two gates were presently open and appeared to be made of wood and manually operated.

This was not the home of a paranoid security freak as Truc had appeared to be in Heidelberg. "Is this actually Truc's house?" Tim asked himself. "Am I at the right place? And if I am at the right place, is he still here? There's no sign of anyone in that house."

Tim did a quick review of his recent operations timeline. "Let's see, today is Wednesday. This past Sunday, Colette's ex-husband said his private detective had trailed Truc from Heidelberg to Ronda. According to Colette, her Ex had confirmed Truc's presence at this address Sunday morning by telephone with someone here in Ronda. Colette relayed that information to me on Sunday night during our Greek Salad dinner. ---Hmmm, that was a great dinner, and the way she acted at the table, ...and afterwards. A tasty French pastry indeed! Geez, Tim, what are you doing! Get your mind off that stuff. Let's concentrate on what's going on here.--- On Monday, I spent most of the day in the bookstore planning for my trip to Ronda. Monday night I took the overnight Trainhotel to Seville, arriving Tuesday afternoon. After acquiring the car from Delgado, I spent Tuesday night in that No-Tell-Hotel in Seville. This morning, Wednesday, I drove here to Ronda, and now, Wednesday afternoon, I'm sitting on a hilltop looking down at what I think, hope is Truc's house. From Sunday morning to this moment is almost three and a half days, or more exactly, about 77 hours. During that time, I traveled halfway across Europe. What the hell did Truc do during those same three and a half days? By now he could be anywhere. Did I take too long getting here?"

At that moment, there was movement below. The garage door opened mechanically. A small, black Mercedes began backing out. Tim almost fell forward in his excitement. "Get yourself under control, Timmy me'boy," he ordered, as he brought the binoculars to his eyes. "This isn't your first time doing this."

As the car moved out of the garage and backed through the gate, Tim could not tell who was driving or how many people were in the car. Except for the front windshield, the car's windows were tinted. Tim could see almost nothing inside the car. As the car exited the driveway and turned to Tim's left towards downtown, the garage door closed. No one else appeared.

Tim grabbed his things and walked slowly back down the other side of the hill. He wanted to run; but someone might be watching. Once in his car, he wheeled the Fiat around and started after the Mercedes. Again, he wanted to race, but he did not want to draw attention. So his heart raced, but the Fiat crawled. After he circled back around the hill and onto Truc's street, he could no longer see the Mercedes. This was not good.

Once off Truc's street, Tim increased speed. Not knowing where the Mercedes was, he decided to just follow this main road into the center of town and hope to again pick up the Mercedes. Tim drove in this search mode for about 10 minutes. Just as he reached the downtown area and was about to give up, he spotted the Mercedes. It was trying to park along the curb about 100 yards up the street and holding up a line of traffic, and Tim, as it did so.

The Mercedes finished its clumsy parking and traffic began to move. As Tim moved forward, he kept one eye on the car in front of him and one eye on the Mercedes. As Tim came up beside the Mercedes, which was on his right, it took all his operational disciple to turn his head to the left so that the Mercedes' driver would not see him. However, the only problem with not letting the Mercedes' driver get a look at him was that he in turn could not get a look at the Mercedes' driver. After Tim passed and was slowly moving forward, he looked in his review mirror. His eyes widened, his fists clenched, his skin crawled. The man getting out of the Mercedes was Truc. Just as Tim had immediately recognized him in the Providence paper ten days ago, he immediately recognized him in the review mirror ten milliseconds ago. He had finally found Quan's killer.

Tim wanted to pull over immediately, get out, and trail Truc. But he couldn't take that chance. He could not take the chance of Truc spotting him. This public square could not be the place where their final meeting would occur. Tim had too many things to say, too many things to do, and would have too many things to cover-up. The Fiat continued down the street. At the next stop sign, Tim made a left turn, circled the block, was soon back on the main street, but was then going in the opposite direction. Within a minute he pulled along the curb and parked. He was about 30 yards from Truc's car and on the opposite side of the street, a perfect observation point.

As Tim watched, Truc came out of what appeared to be a post office. No doubt about it, this was Truc. Older. Stockier. Slower. But it was Truc. The newly-found Truc walked to a sidewalk café two shops from the post office and sat at an outdoor table. A waiter immediately brought him a newspaper and a cup of something. The waiter and Truc talked for several minutes. It appeared they knew each other quite well. Truc then began to read his paper and sip his drink. He did so for the next half hour, refreshing his cup only once.

Tim could hardly restrain himself. Every measure of his warrior's discipline learned over 40 years was needed. He had to keep pushing away memories of Quan, Quan's grave, the ambushes. He had to focus on the here and now. He had to observe, assess, plan. For the whole half hour, he never took his eyes or mind off Truc. He never stopped thinking about how he was going to kill him.

Then the target began to move. Truc stood, dropped some euros on the table, talked with the waiter for a moment, then headed for his car. Just as he opened the door to the Mercedes, he took a quick look around, as if to check to see if anyone was watching. Tim jerked his head away from his window. No eye contact had been made. Tim was sure Truc had not seen him, and even if he had, it was very unlikely he would have recognized the man in the Fiat as his old nemesis from so long ago. No, Tim was sure Truc hadn't seen him, certainly hadn't recognized him. Sure? Certain? Well, …at least he hoped so.

The Mercedes pulled away from the curb and headed in the opposite direction from where Tim's Fiat was pointed. Tim decided not to pull out and do a U-turn in order to tail Truc. It would be too obvious, too easily spotted. Besides, he knew all he needed to know for now. He knew Truc was here and where he lived. Tim headed back to Truc's house.

When back in Truc's neighborhood, Tim did not again drive past Truc's house to reach his hilltop perch. He took a side street that curled around to the back of the hill from a different direction. This time he parked his car in a little more secluded spot and walked up the back of the hill and then to his observation post.

Within 10 minutes, Tim observed the Mercedes with Truc behind the wheel moving down the street below. The garage door opened. The Mercedes turned left onto the driveway and into the garage. The door rolled down. Then nothing.

It was another hour before lights appeared in the windows at the front of the house. Tim was now munching on his last empanada. He wondered, "Had Truc been at the back of the house all that time? Had he been in the front of the house and just now had the need to turn on the lights? Did that even matter? No!

What really matters is whether he is in there alone or with a body guard, does he have any weapons, and how long can I depend on him staying there."

At about 2200 hours (10 PM), all the lights in the house went out. Tim waited another hour. Nothing. He decided to head back to the heart of town. As he drove, he had but one question on his mind, "Would tomorrow be the day?"

PREPARING

Day Eleven: Thursday, 0930 hours, Atop a Hill in Ronda

It was a little after 0930 hours (9:30 AM) the next morning when Tim again finally settled into his observation post overlooking Truc's house. He would have liked to have been there earlier, but he had something he had to do before leaving downtown Ronda. As soon as the shops had opened, he went into an arts supplies shop and purchased a small artist's easel, a small canvas, some paints, and some brushes. He also special-ordered something to be ready the next day when the shop opened at 9 AM. He then took the art supplies and headed for Truc's.

After he walked up the back side of the hill across from Truc's home, he placed the easel just inside that side of the hill's tree line and quickly painted a modernistic representation of the valley below. In other words he just quickly slapped on some paint strokes here and there on the canvas. He left the easel set up just inside that tree line and then walked through the woods to his observation post on the other side. The easel and canvas would act as a cover story for any nosey neighbor who might climb the hill to inquire as to what Niccolo was doing. He was painting landscapes of course.

Tim now focused on the house below. All was quiet. No sign of life. He hoped that by arriving late, he hadn't missed an early departure by Truc. There was no way of telling. He would just have to wait and watch.

Time moved slowly. The hours passed. Around 1400 hours (2

PM), Tim started getting worried. The entire day had been spent noting nothing. Had Truc recognized him in town the day before and escaped during the night? Tim didn't want to think about that possibility. If it were true, Tim might never find him again.

Even though he tried hard to concentrate on the target in front of him, as the day went on his mind kept drifting back to Nam where all this had started. He kept thinking about the day of the ambush. If only he could have gotten to Truc then, things would have been much different. Quan would still be alive.

Tim had never been able to forgive Jakub and Shaffer for their betrayal that day of the ambush. Yes, he came to understand that they were just trying to protect him, to save his life. But in doing so, they had cost Quan hers. Had Tim not been sent to Da Nang, he would have been in Saigon to protect her, to evacuate her, to save her. He understood their good intentions, and even though he knew better, he could never get past thinking of their actions as a betrayal. He could never forgive or forget the terrible conse- quences. He never again saw either of the former friends.

His mind continued to drift, this time to another friend from Nam whom he would like to have seen again, but never did: Platon Wojonski. In the years after Nam, Tim had tried to locate Plat several times. Once he even hired a private detective. All efforts always led to Army discharge papers dated April, 1973, the month the Paris Peace Accords called for all U.S. troops to be out of Vietnam. Although Tim knew Plat had stayed on as a private contractor with MobilTek in Da Nang, he could never find any offi- cial records of such service. Then in 1996, information. Infor- mation that brought him more sorrow.

In 1996, Tim attended an Anti-Terrorism Conference at the National Defense University in D.C. At an evening gathering in a local bar, conference attendees from several of the nation's major intelligence agencies were drinking and swapping stories. Tim joined in the telling of war stories, something he didn't usually do. That night, for some unknown reason, all his stories seemed to be about Wojonski, from "Wojonski Orders," to his wall of philoso- phy paintings, to his beer butt chicken roasts, to his sunset salutes, to his refusal to abandon his Vietnamese allies, to Tim's own inability to locate Wojonski after losing him in Nam's final death throes.

Several days after that night of war stories, Tim arrived at his Pentagon office to find an envelope on his desk with just one word written on it: "Wojo." With questioning fingers Tim ripped the envelope open. It contained a single sheet of paper with a handwritten cryptic note containing the letters "ANC" and three numbers. Tim went cold. He knew what the note meant.

He abruptly left his office, sorrowfully walked the Pentagon's long halls and staircases to its own shopping center on the first floor, and from there exited through the guarded access to the Metro subway. He hopped onto an escalator that made a steep, 100-yard drop to the subway tracks running deep beneath the Pentagon. A five minute Metro ride brought him to his destination, Arlington National Cemetery.

As Tim walked through the cemetery's gate, he again looked at the cryptic note. ANC was Arlington National Cemetery, and he knew the three numbers would be the Section, Row, and Grave where he would find his old friend. After a 15 minute walk among the nation's honored warriors, he stood reading Plat's marker: Platon Wojonski, MAJ, US Army, 1938-1985, Philosopher-Warrior.

"1985?" Tim silently asked his friend. "What were you doing between the last time I saw you in Da Nang in April, 1975 and 1985? I couldn't find you or any record of you. I suppose I'll never know. Although I think I can make a pretty good guess."

Tim smiled at the epithet engraved at the bottom of the marker: Philosopher-Warrior. "Yes, my friend, that is how I remember you from our first discussion of your philosophy paintings to our last discussion of your warrior ethics. On that last night, as I was leaving your tent, you said you might one day paint me my own copy of your personal philosophy as depicted through Jonathan Livingston Seagull's searches for perfection and adventure. Don't worry, old friend. You left such a painting in my soul. I wonder, did you ever finish your painting of Aquinas, your canvas treatise on religion? You could never quite get it right, as you struggled to understand the Almighty. Well, now you know the answers. Are they as you expected? Rest here in peace, Plat. You are among those who understand you best. But also know that wherever I go, you always go with me."

As Tim now sat on this hillside in Spain, Plat was still with him; for Plat, probably more than any other person, set Tim on the path to the man he became. Although Tim forgot where he had heard or read it, thinking of Plat brought a quote to mind, "Each of us is the result of many unknown causes, and each of us is the cause of many unknown results." Major Wojonski was a cause; Colonel DePalma was the result.

While Tim was still thinking about Wojonski, Truc's garage door opened and the Mercedes backed out and moved off toward the town center. As Tim watched, the garage door closed. Again, no one else appeared.

"Well," thought Tim, as he hurriedly moved through the stand of trees to swoop up his art supplies and get to his car, "I may be the result of many unknown causes, but soon I am going to be the cause of at least one known result: the dispatch of one known murderer and traitor."

Once in the Fiat, Tim circled round the back of the hill and onto the main street leading to the town center. Soon he could see Truc's Mercedes about 300 yards in front of him. There were no other cars between Truc and him. Tim pulled over to the curb and stopped. He needed cars between them. He could not take the chance that Truc would spot the Fiat following him. Tim waited for other cars to come. None came.

After waiting about five minutes, Tim pulled away from the curb and again headed toward the town center. Had he lost Truc? "Damn!" thought Tim. "This could be disastrous. Suppose Truc detected me watching his house or just sensed something was wrong and decided to leave Ronda? I can't lose him now. I have two choices. One, check out the restaurant where he stopped yesterday. The other, immediately head for the road out of town to see if I can spot him or catch up to him before he gets too far away."

Without knowing why, Tim headed for the restaurant where Truc had stopped yesterday. Soon gut feeling was rewarded. Truc was there at the same table, reading a paper. Tim parked in a different location than the day before, but still in a spot from which he could observe Truc. The next half hour went pretty much the same as the previous day's visit, a cup of probable coffee, a paper, and a few words with the waiter. As also happened the day before, Truc drove away in one direction, and Tim drove away in the other. Tim was heading back to his hilltop. He hoped Truc was heading back to his house.

The remainder of the afternoon and evening went by pretty much as had the previous day's. Tim was back on the hilltop in time to see Truc drive down the street, turn left onto his driveway and into his garage. After that, nothing until the lights went out at about 2200 hours (10 PM). After remaining another hour in the darkness atop the hill, Tim finally headed back to town.

As he drove, he thought "Truc's in a rut. He's become too comfortable in this mountain refuge. He has let himself be ruled by routine. He has become an easy target. I've finally got him."

Then after a moment's reflection, "Whoa there, Timmy me'boy. Slow down. Let's not get overly confident here. Truc could have detected your presence and be lulling you into a trap. Be cautious. Be thorough. Be ready."

After yet another moment's reflection, "No. I'm not being overconfident. I'm ready. There are still a few unknowns, like what's the interior layout of the house? Has he fortified the damn place? Will the SOB have a gun? All those are unknowns that I will just have to deal with once I get inside. In any case, there is no benefit in waiting any longer. Tomorrow, one of us will die."

Grilled Lamb Chops

Since the first caveman grilled meat over a fire, millions of recipes have surfaced discussing the best way to do it – some intricate and some basic. This falls into the latter. Tim perfected this in his backyard near the Pentagon while assigned to the National Security Council. Tim's version involves being selective at the meat counter of the grocery store/member warehouse, finding the right balsamic/red wine vinegar reduction, and stoking a grill. The secret is that Tim always buys "Frenched" rack of lamb with eight to ten chops (two inches of bone exposed at the end of each chop with excess fat/cartilage/tendons removed); cuts it in half; and is not afraid of searing/charcoaling the exterior of the mini-racks. After grilling Tim lets it sit before carving into individual chops (a nice measure is three to four chops per serving).

Ingredients:(See Below)

Rack of Lamb	Frenched, usually 8 Chops, 2 pounds (1 rack for two guests)
Olive Oil	To brush Grill and Lamb
2 - 3Tbsp	Balsamic Vinegar/Red Wine reduction
Salt/Pepper	To Taste
Herbs	Rosemary/Thyme/Herbs of Choice

Directions:

1. Remove full lamb rack from plastic wrappings, cut in half (four ribs each piece).

2. Wrap exposed bones (the "Frenched" area) with aluminum foil to reduce/prevent burning.

3. Rub with olive oil, salt and pepper, herbs, and balsamic vinegar/red wine reduction.

4. Fire-up grill and, when hot, lower flame and place mini-racks over flames; sear the lamb for one minute on each side and then grill with fat side down over

low to moderate flame for 6 – 8 minutes. **Caution, lamb will flare up as fat drips into fire**. Turnover and repeat on second side for same length, adjusting flame as necessary.

5. Check temperature and remove when internal meat temperature reaches 130F (medium rare). Exterior will be crusty and burnt and "Frenched" rib bones may have also incinerated. Remove from grill and let stand 5 – 10 minutes before cutting into individual chops.

6. Arrange on plate and add a little balsamic/red wine reduction.

Tips:

1. Can be done in oven, but lamb chops release fat and smoke.

2. If no balsamic/red wine reduction is available, you can use balsamic vinegar and red wine separately for coating the racks of lamb before grilling.

3. Pairs well with a light red wine and Tim usually serves with a potato/onion side.

4. As the individual chops are small, do not be surprised if you see your guests picking up the chop to remove the final bits of meat.

5. A balsamic and red wine reduction is easily made, but best made outside as the aroma of heated vinegar diffuses throughout the kitchen and beyond.

Empanadas

Tim was reintroduced to this universal food while in Spain and was thrust back to his childhood in Rhode Island. Empanadas, brought to Southern Europe in the 15ᵗʰ Century by the Moors, spread first through the Latin community in Europe, then to South and Central America, and were enjoyed by Portuguese seaman and immigrants wherever they landed, including Bristol, Rhode Island. Universally prepared under different names (empanada, empada, patty, pasties, pierogi, stromboli, and finally, Hot Pockets) they are enjoyed as a breakfast, main course, and even dessert. A great way to use leftovers, this versatile dough pocket continues to grow in popularity. Tim's favorite way to prepare is to use a prepared pizza dough as the vessel and sausage and onions as the core, throwing in whatever is left over, including rice and barbeque. The below recipe is for baked empanadas, although more than half the world, especially street vendors, prefer to deep fry.

Ingredients:(Four to Six Servings)

1 Package	Prepared Pizza Dough (room temperature)
1 Onion	Sliced and diced
2 – 3 Links	Savory Sausage (Chorizo, Hot Italian, Andouille, etc)
1 Red Pepper	Smoked, skinned, and cut into chunks (canned works well)
Handful	Each of Green and Black Olives, sliced
¼ Lb	Pancetta, cut into strips (Bacon is a good substitute)
1 Can	Diced or Spicy Diced Tomatoes
Salt/Pepper	To Taste
2 – 3 Tbsp	Olive Oil
1 Egg	Medium, for wash

Directions:

1. Fry pancetta/bacon in large skillet for 5 – 6 minutes to allow fat to release.
2. Add crumpled sausage after removing from casings – fry for another 5 – 6 minutes.
3. Add onions, peppers, and olives; cook until softened.
4. Drain diced tomatoes and squeeze liquid from fruit.
5. Add tomatoes and cook for another 5 - 10 minutes until flavors are mixed.
6. Take off heat, cover, and put aside.
7. Roll out pizza dough until thin (1/4 inch or less).
8. Cut out desired shapes – Tim uses bowls
9. Lay out shapes on Teflon baking sheet or oiled parchment paper.
10. Spray dough lightly with butter/olive oil and place about a ¼ cup of filling in the center of one side.
11. Moisten edges with water and fold one side over the other. Crimp edges and brush top with egg.
12. Place into a 350F oven for 25 – 30 minutes; cover with foil if browning too quickly.
13. Serve hot or at room temperature.

Tips:

1. Tim has used pork, beef, fish, and almost anything as filling.
2. Can be prepared ahead of time and frozen, un-cooked. Likewise you can fry empanada. Use leftover filling as a starter for chili, meatloaf, etc.

CHAPTER 21: JUDGMENT DAY

Day Twelve: Friday, 0930 hours, Atop a Hill in Ronda

For the third day in a row, Tim was back at his hilltop observation post. It was 0930 hours (9:30 AM). Again, as yesterday, he would have liked to have been there earlier. But again, like yesterday, he stopped at the art shop; this time for the items he had ordered the day before. Those items were now in the backseat of the Fiat, parked at the bottom of the backside of the hill.

This day of watching and waiting unfolded pretty much like the two previous days. A car or two moving on the street, but none coming to the end of the street where Truc's house was located. The same with two walkers and a bicyclist.

"That's probably one reason Truc picked this place," thought Tim, "very little traffic on the last street at the end of town, and even less traffic by the last house on the end of that last street. Oddly enough, this isolation now serves my purposes as well as his."

As the morning wore into the afternoon, Tim decided it was time to act. He went over his battle assessment and plan one last time. In his assessment, Tim finally decided Truc was alone in the house. Tim had not seen a single sign of a bodyguard. He decided Truc's bodyguard in Heidelberg had been a onetime thing. Tim now believed Truc went to Heidelberg to sell his painting because he needed cash. The stash he had looted from Vietnam had probably dwindled to almost nothing over time. Why else would he take such a chance at such a public appearance after all those years? Tim assumed that Truc had paid cash for this house, so that there would be no need to disclose his financials or anything else about himself. He also assumed that Truc had transformed some of his cash into valuables such as paintings and jewels. Selling a painting for 100,000 euros would provide him enough cash to last a long time in Ronda. No, Tim didn't believe Truc was using what money he had left for a fulltime bodyguard.

As for the best time to attack, Tim believed, based on his reconnaissance, that Truc, like a lot of Spaniards, took a siesta every afternoon. However, he probably got up earlier than most to go into town on errands at a time when there would be the fewest people in the shops. Tim decided the best time to attack would be 1500 hours (3 PM). He figured that was about the time Truc was getting up each day from his siesta. He would still be a little groggy, not as alert as he should be, especially not as alert as he should be this day.

Finally, Tim's plan of attack was a simple one, one seen in many Class B movies and detective books. He would approach the door as a flower deliveryman who was lost. He had memorized the necessary Spanish words; they were few and simple. He would hold the bouquet of flowers in front of his face seemingly in both his hands as he stood at the door, but in fact would be holding the bouquet in his left hand and the dagger in his right.

As soon as Truc opened the door, Tim would lunge forward with his right hand and plant the dagger in Truc's left thigh, immediately immobilizing him. With his left hand, Tim would simultaneously push the flowers, containing a hidden iron rod, into Truc's face, while at the same time scanning Truc's right hand for a weapon. Lastly, the third part of his assault would have two variations. First, if he saw a weapon in Truc's right hand, it would have to be dealt with immediately by dropping the flowers and sweeping for the gun or knife with his left hand, while simultaneously twisting the dagger with his right hand deeper into Truc's left thigh, the excruciating pain hopefully causing Truc to drop the weapon or at least momentarily incapacitating his ability to react. If there was no weapon, the third part of his assault move would be to simply use his left foot to kick the door closed behind him to prevent some passerby from observing what was happening. Tim had practiced this 3-part assault in both variations at least a hundred times over the past two days. His body now knew its every facet thoroughly and had burned it into its muscle memory as a single, fluid, lightning-fast movement. Once Truc was immobilized and, if necessary, disarmed, then the rest would be just Tim living out a scene he had imagined for what seemed like a million times.

But what if Truc refused to open the door for the flower deliveryman? What then? Tim had prepared two alternate backup plans. Neither of them very good in his estimation, but both workable. Backup Plan #1 was to just turn around and leave, going to the next house and there playing the role of the lost delivery man, hopefully protecting his cover story and not alerting Truc. Backup Plan #2 was to pick up the potted planters on each side of the front door, hurl them through the large living room window, and then immediately climb through the smashed pane. The main problem with this plan was giving Truc enough time to react, especially if he had quick access to a weapon. Even given that danger, Tim was inclined to go with this Backup Plan #2 because it provided him immediate access to Truc. He believed the elements of surprise and violence would render Truc sufficiently stunned and confused, allowing Tim to successfully subdue him.

However, Tim believed he wouldn't need to resort to either of the backup plans. He felt confident that Truc's security alertness was pretty low and that he would open his front door to a deliveryman. In any case, no need to worry about it further, because Tim would know in a just few minutes.

The decision to attack now having been made, Tim headed for his car, picking up his artist's cover story along the way. Once at the car, he threw the cover story on the back floor. From the backseat, he picked up three specially-ordered signs that said "FLORISTA" in big red letters on a white background and placed one in each of the back side-windows and one in the back rear-window. They were held in place by rubber adhesive pads located on their corners. If neighbors were later asked by the police to describe any cars that might have been in the area at the time of the murder, Tim hoped they would not say "tan Fiat," but rather "just a car that had 'FLORISTA' signs in all its windows."

Tim then checked the flower bouquet and the iron rod he had

secured in the center of the flowers. He put the bouquet on the front passenger seat. He checked the dagger one last time. It was in its sheath, and the sheath was secured to his belt lengthwise on his right front side and further secured behind two belt loops. The dagger could easily be withdrawn from its sheath with his right hand. All was ready. He got into the car, drove it around the hill, and stopped in front of Truc's house.

Tim picked up the bouquet, exited the car, opened the gate, walked to the door, knocked, and unsheathed the dagger. After a moment, he knocked again. He heard someone coming. His left hand was tightly holding the iron-rod bouquet. His right hand was clasping the dagger. As the door opened, Tim tensed, ready for the lunging stab whose force would be as a thunderbolt, bringing Truc to his knees.

But that did not happen! Instead, it was Tim who was struck, as if by a thunderbolt. He was left dazed. His brain was scrambled by the shock. His mind failed to comprehend what was happening. It was as if his body had been paralyzed by a powerful blow to his gut, leaving him unable to breathe, unable to move. The dagger remained clenched in his hand, but there was no lunging attack. He remained immobilized in the doorway. His knees were going weak, forcing him to lean against the doorframe for support. He could not speak.

RESURRECTION IN TRUTH

At first, she also did not comprehend. What did this flower deliveryman want? Why didn't he speak? Then her eyes widened in recognition. Then seemed to widen even further in disbelief. Just one word escaped her lips in a gasp, "Tim?"

He did not hear her, but one word also escaped his lips in a gasp, "Quan?"

As Tim steadied himself against the doorframe, he looked at the woman in front of him. Through the daze, his heart's voice tried to convince his mind, "It is Quan!" His mind tried to answer, "How can this be? Quan is dead! This woman is alive!"

441

Tim looked at the woman, still not fully comprehending. His shocked mind was both appreciating and questioning. He stared, eyes wide as if in total darkness searching for some light, some means of understanding this apparition in front of him. Her lips were moving, but he was not hearing. He was just staring, still trying to comprehend.

"This is Quan," his recovering senses were trying to convince him. "Thirty-five years later; but this is Quan."

He continued immobile, just staring. "She is still so beautiful. Her face is as it was the first day I saw it, in the rain of the storm on the hill, that of a Madonna whose almond eyes could calm and comfort the world. Small wrinkles now edge out from the corners of her eyes and mouth. Why was I not there to see them grow? Her hair is now black and silver, pulled back into a bun at the nape of her neck, just as it was that first day we had lunch together in her school so long ago. Her body is still slim and delicate; oh, how I remember it against mine, entwined as if one. But this can't be Quan. Quan is dead. This woman before me is alive."

Quan looked at this man before her, still not fully comprehending. Her shocked mind was both appreciating and questioning. She stared, eyes wide as if in total darkness searching for some light, some means of understanding this apparition in front of her. She was just staring, still trying to comprehend.

"This is Tim," her recovering senses were trying to convince her. "Thirty-five years later; but this is Tim."

She continued to stare. "He is still handsome. His face is as it was the first day I saw it, in the rain of the storm on the hill, that of a soldier, a warrior, yet also of an idealistic young man who wanted to save the world. Small wrinkles now edge out from the corners of his eyes and mouth. Who had been there with him to see them grow? His hair is now black and silver, longer than the soldier's of so long ago. His body is still lean and strong; oh, how I remember it against mine, entwined as if one. But this can't be him. This is some florista in baggy pants, suspenders, and work boots. This cannot be Tim!" She then heard her voice ask, "Tim, is it you?"

Tim did not answer, could not answer.

She went to him, guided him to the couch. "Would you like a glass of water?"

He sat there looking at her, not hearing a word she was saying. He was still listening to the competing, cacophonous clamoring of his heart and mind, "This woman in front of you is Quan. Quan is alive! This woman can't be Quan. Quan is dead!"

He finally whispered. "Quan, is it you? Is it really you?"

With tears welling in her eyes, "Yes, Tim, it is me. I can't believe you are here. What are you doing here? How did you find me?"

Then her eyes widened, first in surprise and then in fear. Her eyes had drifted down to the dagger in his hand.

At first he did not understand the fear in her eyes. He followed her gaze. He understood. He sheathed his sword.

In a blaze of comprehension she understood, Tim had not come for her. He had come for Truc!

"No, Tim," She gently whispered. "That is all in the past. Truc is my husband, the father of my children. We have made a life together. All else is in the past."

Tim squinted his eyes, clenched his jaw, tightened his lips, all an effort to suppress the primordial cry of "NO!" that was welling up from somewhere very deep within him. The cry was suppressed.

The hoarse voice of a drained man spoke, "Quan, I thought you were dead. All these years, I thought you were dead. I saw your grave." Then a flash of understanding. The grave had not been for her, it had been for him. It had been meant to stop him from looking for her.

She began her story in a soft voice, "Tim, it was so long ago. It was a time of turmoil, of war, of death. You left me. You were mad at me the night before you left. I did not know where you went. I heard nothing from you. One week went by, then another. Many Americans were leaving. I did not know if you had left. I waited. I wanted to wait forever. My heart told me you would come for me. But my country was dying. The enemy was at the door. My family would suffer greatly. I could save them, save myself. I didn't want to do it, but I did. I felt I had no choice. I left with Truc. He did as he promised; he saved me and my family. It was my fate."

As Tim listened to her words, watched her face, felt her truth, his shock of finding her was overcome by his ever-present love for her and a growing understanding of what had happened and the terrible choice he had left her with.

"Quan I did come back for you. A friend left notes at our apartment and with your father. I travelled four hundred miles on foot through the jungle with only the thought of you providing me the will to keep going. When I reached Saigon, your father took me to your grave. He told me that Truc had killed you. That night I left my soul on your grave."

"I know, Tim. I know now, but I did not know then. After we left Vietnam we never returned. Truc was wanted by the authorities. We could not return. The only member of my family who stayed in Vietnam was my father. Fifteen years later, sick and dying, he left Vietnam and came to us in Malaysia where we were living. On his deathbed, he confessed to me that he had done a terrible thing. He told me how he had received your notes but did not give them to me. He knew you would come for me and never stop looking for me. He felt your doing so would put me and my family in great danger. He created my grave to convince you that our love had ended. Only that night did he really realize the depth of your love for me and that maybe he had made a mistake. But he kept his secret, only telling me on the day he died. By then the world had long spun past our moment. Our worlds had changed. By then we were different people living different lives."

Tim did not know what to say. He wanted to sweep her up in his arms and take here from this mountain fortress to a place ...where? Where was a place for them now? Their only place was in the past.

At that moment Truc walked into the room. He stopped abruptly. At first he did not recognize Tim. But something, maybe the emotional electricity in the room, triggered his awareness of just who this ragged looking man was.

Truc tensed. Tim tensed.

Quan rose, stepped to her husband, and with a gentle hand on his arm, "Truc, it is fine. All is fine. Tim was in Ronda and found out we were here. He has come to say a final goodbye."

Truc eased back, his eyes still fixed on Tim. But the eyes did not blaze the hate they did on that ambush road so long ago. These eyes were tired, looking as if they now knew more and felt less, as if they now appreciated more and hated less.

Still looking at Tim, Truc asked, "It was the picture in the Heidelberg paper, wasn't it? I knew you would come."

Tim said nothing, just nodded.

Truc turned, looking at Quan. She lightly patted his arm and gently smiled. He did not look again at Tim. He smiled at his wife and left.

Quan sat back on the couch with Tim. They talked for many more minutes, not touching on how they had felt over the years but only on what they had done. However, he knew that for him, and he felt that for her also, there was an undercurrent of thoughts and yearnings for what might have been.

Then Quan stood. Tim reluctantly followed her lead.

They said their goodbyes, knowing that they would never see each other again. Knowing also that they would never forget each other and what they once were.

Quan leaned in, lifted up on her toes, and gently kissed his cheek. Oh, how part of him wanted to grab her, forcefully hold her close, not let her go. But as she stepped back, he held her gently for another moment, kissed her cheek, and let her go.

As he moved to the door, he looked back at her. She looked at him and then toward the mantel. Tim's eyes followed hers. There on the mantel was a golden songbird with a heart-shaped diamond implanted in its breast. The songbird forever singing a silent love song.

CHAPTER 22: GAZPACHO AND REVENGE

Day Twelve: Friday, 8 PM, A Restaurant in Seville

Tim was back in Seville after a long, hot ride from Ronda. He sat at a table by the front window of a restaurant, listlessly watching the world go by. As he had entered the heart of the city, the restaurant's name caught his eye, *El Restaurante Caliente y Frio*, The Hot and Cold. He thought it beckoned to him. It had been a long, hot ride, and he needed a long, cold beer.

A half empty bottle of San Miguel now stood on the table before him. He wished it was a Gansett or even a Bud.

"Do we ever really get away from our roots," he wondered. "From a beer to a country, can we ever really accept the new over the old? Or is the old the core of who we are? ...Getting a little philosophical aren't we Timmy me'boy? Why not just ask yourself the fruitless question whether the bottle in front of you is half empty or half full?"

Tim thought about that for a moment. Then he took the bottle and chugged it. "Not a question anymore. The bottle is empty! Like my life."

The two hours on the road had given him time to think. He had needed it. Over the past twelve days, he had almost relived a lifetime, his lifetime. Over the last twelve hours he had questioned a lot of what he had learned in that lifetime.

A belief he had held at his core for almost 40 years turned out to be untrue. He now had to let go of that belief. He had to integrate into his core a new reality. Quan had survived the war. Somehow Tim had failed her. So she had to survive the war with-

446

out him. She, like South Vietnam itself, had risen from the ashes of the war and built herself a new reality.

Now Tim must do the same. That afternoon the live Quan had loosed the grip with which the dead Quan had so long held his heart, his mind, his very soul. Now it was up to him to let her go, not totally, but to let her go to a corner of his heart, to a recess of his memory, there to live forever, in a quiet way.

Today had reinforced two hard-earned lessons in Tim's life. First, a man must know what is worth fighting for, then fight for it, even if sometimes he loses. For the fight makes him a better man and the world he lives in a better place. That was part of what Wojonski had called a man's "Personal Philosophy of Life." Second, love, not hate, is the driving force of life, of his life. Love for his God. Love for his country. Love for his family. Love for himself. And love for the person with whom he could share it all.

Quan had been the first love and Vietnam had been the first quest of his young life. In the paradox that is life, he had won both and he had lost both.

Since that time, he had gone on many quests, losing some but winning most, always the better for the trying.

Love had been more elusive. Both Quan and Brileen had brought him the kind of love for which a man yearns, needs, must have if he is to be happy in this life, at least that was true if Tim was to be happy in his life. Yet, when love like that was taken from him, not once but twice, perhaps he just stopped trying to find it, because the trying hurt too much. However, he was the worse for not trying. Only now did he fully realize that.

"War and peace. Love and hate. Past and present. Now, in this restaurant, hot and cold," thought Tim, "these are the extremes and the paradoxes of life through which we must find our 'way.' In finding that 'way' we must keep our balance, a balance of body, mind, and spirit. I let go of a big part of my past today. Where will my 'way' take me tomorrow?"

Just then the owner of the restaurant brought Tim his supper, the specialty of the house, a bowl of gazpacho.

"Do you mind if I sit with you for a moment, *mi amigo*? I like to practice my English whenever I get a chance," said the aproned man through his white beard. "My name is Alejandro."

"Of course," said Tim. "Please sit, Alijandro. My name is Tim.

"Are you enjoying your time in Seville, Tim?"

Tim hesitated for a moment, then, "I am learning a lot."

Alijandro smiled, "Ah, a man who thinks before he speaks, then answers a question not asked. I like that. Andalusia is a place for such men, men who first brood as they must and then act as they wish. I myself am such a man."

"Aren't all men like that?" posed Tim, as he enjoyed his gazpacho, this time not surprised at a soup served cold.

"No! Absolutely not. At least not here in Spain. We Spaniards are hot-blooded men, letting our loins direct us in both love and war," laughed Alijandro. Then he added with a smile, "Except of course maybe me and those from my village. Yes, we are hot-blooded men, but we moderate our passions. Here are just two examples: gazpacho (as he pointed to Tim's bowl) and revenge (as he pointed to his own heart). My ancient village invented them both for Andalusia and for the world. We moderate the heat of the day with the coolness of the gazpacho. We temper the heat of revenge with the coolness of time. Yes, my friend, both gazpacho and revenge are plates best served cold."

Tim ordered two beers; the new friends talked into the night.

A NEW DAY

Day Thirteen: Saturday, 1 PM, The Seville Airport

Tim now stood in line at the Information Desk in the Seville Airport. He had had a busy morning. First, he had to shake from his head the six bottles of San Miguel from the night before. Then he showered, shaved, and had breakfast with Alijandro and his wife, for that is where he had spent the night. He then went to the train station and reclaimed his suitcase, redressed himself as Tim DePalma, and stored Niccolo in the suitcase. He could not bring himself to discard the clothes that Quan had touched.

After the train station, he drove to Seville's massive cathedral, the largest Gothic cathedral in the world. There was the tomb of Uncle Carmine's good friend, Chris Columbus. Situated just inside the Cathedral's massive entrance doors, the tomb consisted of a carved, 3-foot-high by 10-foot-square marble slab, upon which stood four life-sized gold and silver figures in 16th Century Spanish court attire. Each figure held aloft a corner of Columbus' coffin-shaped sarcophagus, as if carrying it to the altar. The great traveler, adventurer, navigator was on one last journey, this time to meet his maker.

Tim got creative, and maybe a little sacrilegious, as he crafted a makeshift sign which he held while standing in front of the tomb and then asked a tourist to take his picture. The sign read, "OK, boys. On to Federal Hill." Uncle Carmine would love this picture. Family was important.

The last item on Tim's to-do list was to dispose of Delgado's car. As instructed, he parked the Fiat on a side street off a busy shopping plaza. He was also instructed to leave the keys and all paperwork in the trunk. He left the keys in the trunk, but not the paperwork. He didn't know why, probably just because he didn't like Delgado. Tim tore the papers into pieces and scattered them in receptacles throughout the Plaza on his way to the taxi stand.

Now he was in the line at the airport's Information Desk. As he stood there, he checked the Airport's various travel posters and the large Departure Board. Of the many destinations, his mind focused on only two, New York and Paris. New York was the pathway back to the Pentagon and the life he loved. Paris was the pathway back to Colette and a challenging love that had failed once before. Tim was reminded once again: Life is a series of choices. What choice would he make now?

"Next?" said the young man behind the counter. "How may I help you?" He was talking to Tim.

Tim moved closer. He looked again at the posters and the Departure Board, sighed, and said, "I would like to buy a ticket."

THE END

Simple Summer Gazpacho

Now one of Tim's favorites – it incorporates his most useful ingre-dient (can of diced tomatoes) and whatever is in the crisper draw-er of the refrigerator. The tips include various items Tim now adds since his first encounter with this wonderful dish that warm even-ing at El Restaurante Caliente y Frio in Seville, Spain.

Ingredients:(Four Servings)

1 Can	Diced tomatoes (14 – 16 Oz)
2	Cucumbers (peeled, seeded, and diced)
½ Cup	Roasted Red Peppers.
½ Cup	Onions – cut and diced
1 Can	Can Spicy Tomato Juice
1/3 Cup	Red Wine Vinegar
1/3 Cup	Extra Virgin Olive Oil
Salt/Pepper	To Taste
1 – 3 Pieces	Stale bread, croissants, rolls, etc.

Directions:

1. Place the diced tomatoes (with liquid) in a large bowl; add the remaining ingredients.
2. Transfer the mixture to a blender and puree to a semi-coarse consistency (hold back some of the mix-ture for a coarser soup). Divide and chill.
3. Serve chilled with an herb sprig (dill/parsley/cilantro), a few croutons, dollop of sour cream, etc

Tips:

1. Tim routinely adds celery, green peppers, spring on-ions, and various herbs.
2. Amounts are variable and can be adjusted to taste.
3. Best to make ahead and store.
4. Remember, **Gazpacho & Revenge --Best Served Cold!**

EPILOGUE

Six Months Later

Tim was speaking into his phone, "Yes, general. My report is in your in-box. Your aide put it there this morning." ...(after a pause)..."Yes, I'll be flying to Moscow later this month. See you there. Oh, I almost forgot. The classified annex to my report is on your classified computer. I just sent it from my new office at the embassy this morning. See you soon."

Tim ended that call and immediately hit the speed dial. "I'd like to speak with Mr. Robinson please." ...(after a moment)... "He's in a meeting? Tell him it's Tim DePalma. We're old friends. I think he'll take my call." ...(after another pause)..."Hi, John. Yeah, I'm fine. How's an old Airborne trooper like yourself hold-ing up chairborne in a Wall Street skyscraper? You probably have a better view from your high-priced corner office than from a jump door. ...(another pause)..."OK. OK. Yes, you're right. it's been a long time since I've stood in a jump door too. Hey, I don't want to take up a lot of your time. I just wanted to make sure you got my email with all the particulars about the house-buy tomor-row and that you transferred the money to my bank." ...(a longer pause this time)... "OK then, everything is a go for buying the country house. Great! One more thing, John, and I really mean this. I want to thank you for all you've done for me. Opps, the boss is waving me over. I gotta go. Hope to see you again soon. Bye." Tim flip-closed his mobile phone and smiled.

Tim and John were friends from that first day they met so long ago on that Airborne School running track at Fort Benning. Later, John, as the higher-ranking Sergeant, had mentored Tim through his first year in Nam. After that first year, they chose different paths, John to Columbia University, Harvard Business School, and Wall Street; Tim to two extended tours in Nam, one rescue mission in Grenada, and a war in Iraq. Through it all they remained close friends.

As Tim went to put the phone in his jacket pocket, the sun glinted off Brileen's ring. Her freckled face came to the forefront of his mind, smiled at him, and then faded away. She still came to him often, but now in a gentler way.

John had also been Tim's shoulder after Brileen's death. From those days to the present, Tim had the Army send a percentage of his pay every month to John to invest for him. Over the years John had made Tim a wealthy man.

"The acts of choice and fate make life's journey an ironic one in deed," thought Tim. Then that train of thoughts and memories was broken, as he again saw the wave and heard the call. His boss wanted him.

"Timothy, come see what I have for our new home."

She held up a wall hanging consisting of four small paintings, each four inches square, in small ornate frames. The paintings were connected in a column by two, short, fine-linked chains extending from the bottom two corners of the top painting to the top two corners of the painting below it. Each painting showed the same scene in the French countryside but in the different seasons of the year, spring through winter.

Colette smiled, "Do you like it? Do you not think they look like the pasture behind our new country home in Provence? Timothy, look at them and tell me what season of our lives you think we are in."

Tim moved closer to Colette. They were outside of Paris in what Tim could only describe as a Flea Market, a place where people sell what they now see as junk to people who buy what they now see as treasures. Colette was showing him what she hoped he would see as a treasure. Tim looked at the offered flow of life's seasons dangling from her outstretched hand. As he looked at the paintings, he thought about her question. Before making the choice to fly to Paris, he had thought of himself as entering the autumn of his years. Now, since he chose to join his life with hers, he thought of them both in their springtime or at least in their early summer of their life together.

He looked up from what were now depictions of the seasons of their life and said, "I love them. But will you love me when my skin crinkles and has brown spots like these leaves in painting three? Will you love me when my hair turns thin and white like the snow in this winter scene?"

She laughed and with smiling eyes answered, "Perhaps. We will have to take that journey and see. But since you like them, they will be the first thing we place in our new home."

"Great," said Tim, starting to move towards their car. "Let's get back to the city before the traffic starts."

"Timothy, wait. Please. I have one more thing to show you. This moves me in special ways. I just love it. Here, look."

Tim turned back to see what she was holding. He stopped. He stared. He remembered. His barely audible words escaped on a winged breath, "A Jonathan!"

She was holding a painting for him to look at. It was a painting of two white seagulls soaring in dark blue skies over turbulent blue seas. Their wings were slightly touching, not so as to hold each other back but as to guide each other forward. There was an almost indiscernible question mark in the lower right corner.

"Well, Timothy, do you like it? I think it is just wonderful. Please, say something."

"Colette, I love it."

Without another word, he gave the vender a 100 euro note. Both the vender and Colette looked on in astonishment. Tim wrapped his left arm around the painting and his right arm around Colette and again started walking toward their car.

After a minute, Tim stopped. He looked at Colette. He looked into her. In almost a whisper, "Colette, I love you."

ABOUT THE AUTHORS
Dennis Quinn

Dennis is a retired US Army Colonel with 28 years of service as an Infantry and Military Intelligence Officer. He served two tours in Vietnam, three tours in Europe, and multiple tours within the United States, including assignments in the Pentagon and on the faculties of the Army Command and General Staff College and the National Defense University. Dennis has a BA in Political Science and an MA in International Relations. He grew up in Rhode Island as part of a great Irish-Italian family and now lives with his wife, Ellen, in Bug Tussle, Alabama.

Fritz Knecht

Fritz is a retired US Navy Captain with 28 years of service as a Surface Warfare and Intelligence Officer. He served two tours in Europe and fifteen assignments throughout the United States. Born in Bethlehem, Pennsylvania, he spent his public school years in Nazareth. Fritz graduated from Pennsylvania State University with a BA in Political Science and the Wharton School, University of Pennsylvania, pursuing a MGA. Fritz resides outside Washington, DC with his bride, Lynn.

Gazpacho and Revenge

Following their military service, happenstance found Fritz and Dennis in second careers sharing an office in Washington, D.C. where they formed an enduring friendship. When finally in retirement, Fritz took on cooking at home, first as a hobby, then as a passion. Shortly thereafter he decided to write an "adventure cookbook," but couldn't find a co-author for the story. Several years later, happenstance again found the Quinns and Knechts together and after a "few bottles of wine," a deal was struck: Dennis would write the adventure and Fritz would supply the recipes. Nearly two years later the final product was complete. We hope you enjoy both the food and the food for thought.

Made in the USA
Lexington, KY
04 January 2014